The Human Being

Also by Walter Wink

Peace Is the Way: Writings on Nonviolence from the Fellowship of Reconciliation (editor)

Homosexuality and Christian Faith: Questions of Conscience for the Churches (editor)

The Powers That Be: Theology for a New Millennium

When the Powers Fall: Reconciliation in the Healing of Nations

Cracking the Gnostic Code: The Powers in Gnosticism

Proclamation 5: Holy Week, Year B

Engaging the Powers: Discernment and Resistance in a World of Domination

Transforming Bible Study

Violence and Nonviolence in South Africa

Unmasking the Powers: The Invisible Forces That Determine Human Existence

Naming the Powers: The Language of Power in the New Testament

The Bible in Human Transformation

John the Baptist in the Gospel Tradition

The Human Being

Jesus and the Enigma
of the Son of the Man

Walter Wink

FORTRESS PRESS   MINNEAPOLIS

THE HUMAN BEING
Jesus and the Enigma of the Son of the Man

Cover art: Pomona Hallenbeck. © 2001 Pomona Hallenbeck. Used by permission.
Book design: Ann Delgehausen
Author photo: Tricia Bergland

Library of Congress Cataloging-in-Publication Data
Wink, Walter.
  The human being: Jesus and the enigma of the Son of the Man / Walter Wink.
      p. cm.
  Includes bibliographical references (p.) and indexes.
  ISBN: 0-8006-3262-1 (alk. paper)
    1. Man (Christian theology)—Biblical teaching. I. Title.

BS661 .W56 2001
233—dc21   2001040352

The paper used in this publication meets the minimum requirements of American National Standard for Information Sciences—Permanence of Paper for Printed Library Materials, ANSI Z329.48-1984.

Manufactured in the U.S.A.   AF 1-3262
06   05   04   03   02   2   3   4   5   6   7   8   9   10

To Elizabeth Howes,
who cared for my soul
until I could—
or would

Contents

Preface   xi

Abbreviations   xiii

Introduction   1

Part One   The Original Impulse of Jesus   5

1. THE HUMAN BEING IN THE QUEST FOR THE HISTORICAL JESUS   7
   A. The End of Objectivism   7
   B. The Myth of God Incarnate
      versus the Myth of the Human Jesus   9
   C. The Myth of History   12
   D. Jesus' Original Impulse   13

Part Two   The Anthropic Revelation: The Human Being   17

2. THE ENIGMA OF THE SON OF THE MAN   19
   A. The Human Being in Ezekiel   22
   B. Ezekiel's Vision   25

3. FEUERBACH'S CHALLENGE   35
   A. Evaluating Feuerbach   36
   B. On Anthropomorphism   41
   C. We Are the Seer and the Seen   45
   D. From Feuerbach to Berdyayev   47

4. OTHER BIBLICAL AND EXTRABIBLICAL REFERENCES
   TO THE HUMAN BEING UP TO 100 C.E.   50
   A. Psalm 8   50
   B. Psalm 80   50
   C. *1 Enoch* 14   51
   D. Daniel 7   51
   E. Ezekiel the Tragedian   54
   F. The Dead Sea Scrolls   55
   G. The Similitudes of Enoch   55
   H. *4 Ezra*   59
   I. *Odes of Solomon*   59
   J. Conclusion   61

Part Three   The Human Being: Pre-Easter Sayings   63

5. **Jesus and the Human Being**   67
    A. Plucking Grain on the Sabbath   67
    B. The Healing of the Paralytic   74
    C. Foxes Have Dens   80
    D. Blasphemy against the Human Being   83
    E. A Glutton and a Drunkard   86
    F. The Human Being Refuses Signs   90
    G. The Human Being Serves   92
    H. The Human Being Seeks and Saves the Lost   97
    I. The Human Being Must Suffer . . .   98
    J. . . . And Be Killed   104
    K. Conclusion   111

6. **Jesus and the Messianic Hope**   113
    A. Peter's Obsession   116
    B. John's Question to Jesus   118
    C. Exorcising by the Finger of God   119
    D. Rejection at Nazareth   119
    E. Plucking Grain on the Sabbath   120
    F. About David's Son   120
    G. The Rich Fool   121
    H. Jesus' Temptation   122
    I. Jesus before the Sanhedrin   122

7. **Projection and the Messianic Hope**   128
    A. Breaking Messianic Projections   132
    B. Incarnating God   138
    C. Death: Shatterer of Projections   140
    D. Projection and Inflation   145

Part Four   The Human Being: Post-Easter Sayings   149

8. **The Human Being: Catalyst of Human Transformation**   151
    A. Ascension . . .   152
    B. . . . Into an Archetypal Image   154

9. THE HUMAN BEING: APOCALYPTIC VERSUS ESCHATOLOGY   158
   A. Eschatology versus Apocalyptic   158
   B. Was Jesus an Apocalypticist?   161

10. APOCALYPTIC 1: THE HUMAN BEING COMES   166
   A. Mark 14:62 par.   166
   B. Mark 13:24-27 par.   167
   C. Matt. 10:23 and 16:28   171
   D. Luke 17:24 // Matt. 24:27   172
   E. Luke 17:26-30 // Matt. 24:37-41;
      see also Matt. 24:44 // Luke 12.10   172
   F. Luke 18:8   173

11. APOCALYPTIC 2: THE HUMAN BEING JUDGES   177
   A. Acknowledging the Human Being   181
   B. Judging the Twelve Tribes   183
   C. The Human Being Is in the Least of These   183
   D. The Parable of the Wheat and the Weeds   186

12. APOCALYPTIC 3: THE FUTURE OF THE HUMAN BEING   188
   A. The Eclipse of the Human Being   189
   B. The Recovery of the Human Being   191

13. THE HUMAN BEING IN JOHN   198
   A. The Leader Is a Ladder   198
   B. Exaltation through Execution   203

14. THE HUMAN BEING IN LETTERS ASCRIBED TO PAUL   207
   A. The Inner Anthropos   208
   B. The Body of Christ   209
   C. In Christ   210

Part Five The Human Being in Jewish Mysticism and Gnosticism   213

15. THE HUMAN BEING IN JEWISH MYSTICISM   215
   A. God as Human in Jewish Mysticism   216
   B. Enoch/Metatron and the Human Being in Jewish Mysticism   224
   C. Ascended Humans in Jewish Mysticism   225
   D. Conclusion   229

16. THE HUMAN BEING IN GNOSTICISM   **231**
  A. The Human Being in the Nag Hammadi Library   233
  B. The "Orthodox" Theologians' Reports about the Gnostics   241
  C. The Human Being in *Poimandres*   244
  D. Conclusion   245

Part Six   Results and Conclusions   249

  A. Once More, Seeing   249
  B. Will the Real Human Being Please Stand Up?   251
  C. The Human Being   257

Appendix 1: Was There a Primal Man Myth?   261
Appendix 2: Philo on the Archetypes   264
Appendix 3: Ezekiel's Influence on Jesus   267
Glossary   270
Notes   272
Index of Ancient Sources   341
Index of Authors   352

Preface

"The son of the man" is the expression Jesus almost exclusively used to describe himself. In Hebrew the phrase simply means "a human being." The implication seems to be that Jesus intentionally avoided honorific titles, and preferred to be known simply as "the man," or "the human being." Apparently he saw his task as helping people become more truly human.

All of the ancient texts that refer to the "son of the man" come packaged in male language. I have tried to translate that language into gender-inclusive terms, keeping male language to a minimum, and substituting other terms as often as possible, while still identifying the original terms. If I have failed to find the happy medium, please accept my apologies in advance. The gold of ancient wisdom is often hidden in mud such as this, and those who refuse to get dirty may forfeit the treasure.

This study may strike some who have read my earlier works on the biblical "principalities and powers" as a major departure from the concerns that animated that inquiry.[1] While the current book explores new territory, it is by no means discontinuous with that earlier effort. In studying the Powers, I attempted to understand the forces that *prevented* people from becoming more human. In studying "the son of the man" I have attempted to gain some idea of what it *means* to become more human. In a sequel, I will search for clues about *how* to become more human.

Work on the Powers began in 1964. Research on "the son of the man" began in 1971, when I first attended a seminar given by the Guild for Psychological Studies in San Francisco. Those two research themes have been running on parallel tracks ever since. I must acknowledge my profound debt to the Guild, and especially to its founder and presiding genius, Elizabeth Boyden Howes, for insights that not only informed me but in part transformed me, and are transforming me still. I will attempt to acknowledge use of material that came out of almost twenty summers of Guild seminars, but I no longer can be sure where the Guild's insights stop and mine begin. Please regard this book, then, as a community enterprise of which I am a scribe.

I have also benefited greatly from my participation in the Jesus Seminar, where I have found the collegial support and scholarly friendships that I had not been able to find elsewhere. That this book deviates so greatly from the conclusions of the Seminar simply demonstrates that the Seminar is not a monolithic collection of lockstep thinkers. Throughout my research and writing they have encouraged me to proceed despite sometimes great differences of opinion.

I must express my gratitude for those who have read the whole or parts. I am especially indebted to two readers: Amy-Jill Levine, who painstakingly challenged every unreflective statement and every trace of thoughtless anti-Judaism, and Ethné Gray, who drew my attention to resources I would never have discovered on my own, and who helped me navigate through the thought of Carl Jung and others. In addition, Brewster Beach, Elizabeth Becker, Delbert Burkett, Richard Deats, Arthur Dewey, James W. Douglass, Robert T. Fortna, Dwayne Huebner, Daniel Merkur, and Mahlon Smith offered helpful comments. Special thanks go to colleagues at the Guild for Psychological Studies, especially Hal Childs and John Petroni. Once again, Pomona Hallenbeck has provided an exceptional cover. My wife, June Keener Wink, not only helped me work out innumerable problems, but represents for me an authentic human being. The dedication of this study to Elizabeth Boyden Howes is only a token of my deep gratitude for her impact on my life.[2]

Citations from the Bible are generally from the New Revised Standard Version. I have frequently modified them, however, to read "the son of the man" or one of its English paraphrases. Words marked by an asterisk (*) are defined in a glossary that begins on page 270.

Abbreviations

'Abod. Zar.	'Abodah Zarah
ANF	Ante-Nicene Fathers
ANRW	Aufstieg und Niedergang der römischen Welt: Geschichte und Kultur Roms im Spiegel der neueren Forschung. Edited by H. Temporini and W. Haase. 1972–
Apoc. Ab.	Apocalypse of Abraham
APOT	The Apocrypha and Pseudepigrapha of the Old Testament. Edited by R. H. Charles. 2 vols. 1913
ASTI	Annual of the Swedish Theological Institute
ATR	Australasian Theological Review
b.	Babylonian Talmud
BAR	Biblical Archaeology Review
BBR	Bulletin for Biblical Research
Ber.	Berakot
BJRL	Bulletin of the John Rylands University Library of Manchester
BR	Bible Review
CBQ	Catholic Biblical Quarterly
Conf.	Philo, On the Confusion of Tongues
CW	Collected Works of Carl Jung
Deut. Rab.	Deuteronomy Rabbah
Dial.	Justin Martyr, Dialogues
ETL	Ephemerides theologicae lovanienses
FFF	Foundations and Facets Forum
FRLANT	Forschungen zur Religion und Literatur des Alten und Neuen Testaments

GCS	Die griechische christliche Schriftsteller der ersten Jahrhunderte
Gen. Rab.	*Genesis Rabbah*
HR	*History of Religions*
HSM	Harvard Semitic Monographs
HTR	*Harvard Theological Review*
HUCA	*Hebrew Union College Annual*
ICC	International Critical Commentary
JAAR	*Journal of the American Academy of Religion*
JBL	*Journal of Biblical Literature*
JJS	*Journal of Jewish Studies*
JQR	*Jewish Quarterly Review*
JSJ	*Journal for the Study of Judaism in the Persian, Hellenistic, and Roman Periods*
JSNT	*Journal for the Study of the New Testament*
JTS	*Journal of Theological Studies*
Ker.	*Kerithot*
LCL	Loeb Classical Library
LXX	The Septuagint (a Greek translation of the Hebrew Scriptures)
m.	Mishnah (Danby edition)
NHL	*Nag Hammadi Library in English.* Edited by J. M. Robinson. 4th rev. ed. 1996
NHS	Nag Hammadi Studies
Nov. Test.	*Novum Testamentum*
NRSV	New Revised Standard Version of the Bible
NTApoc	*New Testament Apocrypha.* Edited by E. Hennecke and W. Schneemelcher. Translated by R. McL. Wilson. 2 vols. 1963.
NTS	*New Testament Studies*
OLZ	*Orientalistische Literaturzeitung*
OTP	*Old Testament Pseudepigrapha.* Edited by J. H. Charlesworth. 2 vols. 1983
par.	parallels
PGM	*Papyri graecae magicae: Die griechischen Zauberpapyri.* Edited by K. Preisendanz. 1928
P.Oxy.	Oxyrhynchus Papyri
Qidd.	*Qiddušin*

REB	Revised English Bible
RIP	*Revue internationale de philosophie*
RRR	*Review of Religious Research*
RSR	*Recherches de science religieuse*
RSV	Revised Standard Version of the Bible
SBLSP	*SBL Seminar Papers*
Sci. rel.	*Science religieuse*
Shab.	*Shabbat*
SNTSMS	Society for New Testament Studies Monograph Series
SV	Scholars Version of the New Testament (Jesus Seminar)
t.	Tosefta
TDNT	*Theological Dictionary of the New Testament.* Edited by G. Kittel and G. Friedrich. Translated by G. W. Bromiley. 10 vols. 1964–76
TEV	Today's English Version
USQR	*Union Seminary Quarterly Review*
VC	*Vigiliae christianae*
WMANT	Wissenschaftliche Monographien zum Alten und Neuen Testament
y.	Jerusalem Talmud
ZAW	*Zeitschrift für die alttestamentliche Wissenschaft*
ZNW	*Zeitschrift für die neutestamentliche Wissenschaft und die Kunde der älteren Kirche*
ZTK	*Zeitschrift für Theologie und Kirche*

The historical Jesus will be to our time
a stranger and an enigma.

—Albert Schweitzer

Introduction

I am puzzled that a species that has subjected virtually the entire universe to its analytical gaze and that has penetrated to the tiniest constituents of matter still knows next to nothing about how to become human. I am greatly agitated that our society seems to be losing the battle for humanization. Violence, domination, killing, disrespect, terror, environmental degradation, and want have reached intolerable levels. Likewise, I am bewildered, having lived the greater part of my life, that I know so little about becoming human myself. I am shocked that I am still largely an amalgam of conventions and opinions and so little in touch with my real thoughts and feelings. Who am I? What might I become? Why have so many of us sold out to miniaturized versions of ourselves?

These are some of the questions that prompt this study of the biblical expression "the son of the man." The farther I penetrate into the mystery of this term, the more profound and provocative it seems. I have struggled with this puzzle long enough to suspect that the real reward lies not in deciphering the riddle but in wrestling with it. It may be that "the son of the man" is a genuine enigma, an irreducible riddle. But nothing so piques the curiosity of humans as the inexplicable. Perhaps our curiosity is a symptom of a desire to become more human. Like those who have gone before and who will follow, I rise to the bait.

In this book I explore the hypothesis that this opaque figure, the son of the man, is a catalyst for human transformation: unchanging and unchanged, yet changing those who dare to come in contact with it. It seems that within us, deeply buried or just below the surface, is something that knows better than we the contours of our true face, or that "new name that no one knows except the one who receives it," as Rev. 2:17 hints.[1]

1

A word, then, about the spirit in which I conduct this inquiry. This book shares in a growing effort to cast the original truths of Christianity in molds that have more appeal for people in our day. For my part, I have been searching the records of Judaism and Christianity to see if there are other ways to interpret, and to live out, the original impulse of Jesus. I want to reflect both exegetically and theologically on how that impulse, which Jesus inaugurated, can open us to the present possibilities of the past. I do so as one deeply committed to what Jesus revealed. I believe that the churches have to a tragic extent abandoned elements of that revelation. I do not, however, wish to throw the whole enterprise overboard. The Gospels continue to feed me, as does all of Scripture, even the worst parts, and some churches are impressively faithful. But if Scripture is to speak to those who find its words dust, we will have to radically reconstitute our reading.

My supposition is that something terrible has gone wrong in Christian history. The churches have too often failed to continue Jesus' mission. I grant that the church fathers sometimes understood the implications of the gospel better than the earliest Christians, who lacked the perspective of hindsight. But there is a disappointing side as well: anti-Semitism, collaboration with oppressive political regimes, the establishment of hierarchical power arrangements in the churches, the squeezing of women from leadership positions, the abandonment of radical egalitarianism, and the rule of patriarchy in church affairs. Those of us who are to varying degrees disillusioned by the churches feel that it is not only our right but our sacred obligation to delve deeply into the church's records to find answers to these legitimate and urgent questions:

- Before he was worshiped as God incarnate, how did Jesus struggle to incarnate God?
- Before he became identified as the source of all healing, how did he relate to, and how did he teach his disciples to relate to, the healing Source?
- Before forgiveness became a function solely of his cross, how did he understand people to have been forgiven?
- Before the kingdom of God became a compensatory afterlife or a future utopia adorned with all the political trappings that Jesus resolutely rejected, what did he mean by "the kingdom"?
- Before he became identified as Messiah, how did he relate to the profound meaning in the messianic image?
- Before he himself was made the sole mediator between God and humanity, how did Jesus experience and communicate the presence of God?

It is, of course, conceivable that the surviving data do not permit us to distinguish the Jesus of the Gospels from the gospel of Jesus. It is my judgment, however, that there is sufficient evidence to develop an alternative mode of access to Jesus. Specifically, traces in the Gospels provide flashes of authenticity that seem incontrovertibly to go back to Jesus, or to a memory of him equally true. When we finish our quest, however, we will not have the historical Jesus "as he really was," for such a feat is impossible. If we are successful, we will have contributed, through historical reflection and inter- ✓ pretation, to a new myth,* *the myth of the human Jesus.*

Toward that end, I have attempted to construct a Christology from below, using the son-of-the-man sayings as my guide. Our itinerary starts with the use of the expression in the Hebrew Scriptures and in later, non-canonical data. Then I focus on the pre-Easter and post-Easter son-of-the-man sayings ascribed to Jesus. I conclude with the striking parallels in Jewish mysticism and Gnosticism that show that the son of the man was an archetypal* phenomenon touching even non-Christians in the ancient ✓ world. But first I turn to the presuppositions and methods that undergird this book.

Part One

The Original Impulse of Jesus

In the struggle to become human, I find myself returning over and over to ancient texts that, for me, still contain the original impulse of Jesus. That impulse was the spirit that drove Jesus through the villages of Galilee and ultimately to death in Jerusalem. It was the inner fire that impelled him to preach the coming of God's reign, the spirit that caused him to cry out, "I came to cast fire upon the earth, and how I wish it were already kindled!" (Luke 12:49). Even though that impulse may lie buried under the detritus of routinized religion, I am convinced that we can recover priceless rubies among the rubble. For nothing else can provide seekers with the interpretive clues that might enable them to revitalize that tradition.

In reading the texts dealing with the son of the man, then, I will not seek to get *behind* the text (for that implies that some other, superior text lies behind the received text). Rather, I wish to penetrate deeply *into* the text so as to provide an alternative means of access to Jesus. I seek a fresh picture of what Christianity might more truly be in our time. So I invite the reader to join me in the prophetic task of listening for what God might be saying to us today, individually and collectively. I attempt to carry out that task by means of an "extremely verbatim reading," requiring what the great scholar of Jewish mysticism, Gershom Scholem, called "mystical precision."[1] To that end, I employ historical-critical tools wherever they seem appropriate, and any other approaches that can render valid insights. I hew to the biblical tradition with unrelenting determination, on the promise, as another Jewish scholar, Daniel Matt, puts it, that we will find God in the details. If that happens, if the words dissolve into the reality, and language into experience, we will understand what mystics have always known: that the exegete stands, with Israel, at the Sinai of the soul, where God still speaks.[2]

1. The Human Being in the Quest for the Historical Jesus

A. The End of Objectivism

What stands in the way of new/ancient readings of Scripture is the heritage of positivism and objectivism—the belief that we can handle these radioactive texts without ourselves being irradiated. Biblical scholars have been exceedingly slow to grasp the implications of the Heisenberg principle: that the observer is always a part of the field being observed, and disturbs that field by the very act of observation. In terms of the interpretive task, this means that there can be no question of an objective view of Jesus "as he really was." "Objective view" is itself an oxymoron; every view is subjective, from a particular angle of vision. We always encounter the biblical text with interests. We always have a stake in our reading of it. We always have angles of vision, which can be helpful or harmful in interpreting texts. "Historical writing does not treat reality; it treats the interpreter's relation to it," according to Brian Stock.[1] "All history," said the poet Wallace Stevens, "is modern history." All meaning, says Lynn Poland, is present meaning.[2] "All truly creative scholarship in the humanities is autobiographical," says Wendy Doniger O'Flaherty.[3] "Historical criticism is a form of criticism of the present," according to Walter Kasper.[4] All that is true, but only partially. For historical criticism still can help us understand that past that holds out present meaning.

According to Hal Childs of the Guild for Psychological Studies (see preface), the past is not an object we can observe. It is an idea we have in the present about the past. History is constantly being rewritten from within history. Thus there is no absolute perspective available outside of history that could provide a final truth of history.[5] Childs contends that Jesus of Nazareth, as a real person who once lived but who now no longer exists, is unapproachable by historical-critical methods. Obviously it is possible to continue to reinterpret the documents that reveal his onetime presence in history. But this is a reinterpretation of meaning in the present and not a reconstruction of the past. Following Jung, Childs believes that whether we can ever know what happened in the past is, in the final analysis, undecidable. All we can know is the past's effect on us today.

While I agree with much of Childs's critique, I believe he goes too far when he declares that the past is unapproachable by historical methods. Historical criticism still can help us recover an understanding of a past that holds present meaning. The text is a brute fact, not a Rorschach inkblot onto which any conceivable interpretation can be read. The great if limited value of the historical-critical approach is that it debunks arbitrary notions of what the text might mean. From every hypothesis and reconstruction it demands warrants, or reasonable evidence, within the text. Arguments can sometimes be falsified by historical and literary data. Not just anything goes, but only positions that other scholars can examine and debate. In order to discern the past in its present meaning, it is essential that we have as accurate a picture of the past as possible. We do not need "a final truth of history," but only approximate truth, backed up by evidence.

We can find meaning in the present, not *instead of* a reconstruction of the past, but *by means of* a reconstruction of the past. There is not just one horizon—the present—but two—past and present. It is their interplay and dialogue, often tacit and unconscious, that provides meaning. This built-in, self-critical aspect of historical method prevents pure subjectivity. So I want two things at once: to overcome the objectivist illusion that disinterested exegesis is possible; and to affirm the present meaning of the past by means of the most rigorous exegesis possible.

The *present* meaning of the historical Jesus has been the unconscious agenda of the Jesus-quest these past two centuries. Driving that enormous undertaking was an inchoate desire among Christian scholars to recover something numinous* and lost *within themselves,* and within contemporary religion. The means used in this quest, however, were not capable of rejuvenating the springs of faith. In fact, the historical approach became a kind of Midas touch. The very act of projecting that longing for the numinous back into the first century concealed its present motivation. This meant that the Jesus found in the past, however much a projection* of modern religious ideals, could not then be brought forward into the present. To do so would have violated those scientific principles that had been used to recover Jesus in his original setting. Having found him again, in all his compelling modernity, scholars had to abandon him to the past. For no one was aware, until Albert Schweitzer exposed it, that the driving force behind this scholarly exertion was a modern longing to be encountered by the divine. Scholarship pretended to be able to dispense with that longing through its objectivist methodology and detached attitude. Paradoxically, the Jesus they found by scholarly means was located on the far side of an unbridgeable gulf—the past—a gulf created by the very method scholars had chosen to recover Jesus as their contemporary.

No legitimate quest for the historical Jesus is possible as long as the real motives behind the quest are denied. Once the false objectivity of historians has been renounced, however, we can acknowledge that most scholars study the past *in order to change its effect on the present.*[6]

B. The Myth of God Incarnate versus the Myth of the Human Jesus

It is not, however, a choice between the human, nonmythological Jesus versus the divine, mythological Christ. For *both* are archetypal images. The human Jesus of the quest has already entered into the archetype of humanness, and seems to have affected people even during Jesus' active ministry. Indeed, the son of man was already archetypally charged as early as Ezekiel 1 and Daniel 7.[7]

The quest of the historical Jesus, then, functions in service of the myth of the human Jesus. It attempts to recover the humanity of Jesus in order to liberate it from the accretions of dogma that have made Jesus a God-Man. For two centuries, scholars have believed that they were simply going behind the gospel traditions to these traditions' earliest forms. But the scandalous lack of historical consensus reveals the true situation: they were not recovering Jesus as he really was; rather, they were forging the myth of the human Jesus. This statement is as true of "unbelievers" as "believers," as true of liberals as conservatives. Ultimately, we find ourselves reading the myth of the human Jesus in the light of our own personal myths.

No wonder there was no scholarly consensus. Every picture of Jesus that scholars produced was inevitably invested with that scholar's projections onto Jesus, positive or negative. Since these projections were by definition unconscious, and disguised the scholar's personal needs and interests, we scholars often became dogmatic about our exegetical conclusions when only tentative answers were appropriate. We had to be dogmatic, it seemed; the myth of the human Jesus that we were unwittingly helping to fashion offered us a kind of salvation. Since the driving spirit behind the quest was the hope of discovering our own humanness in God, the very meaning of our lives hung in the balance. And because scholars brought their own set of needs to the quest, there could never be unanimity as to the historical-critical results. Our contributions to the quest, then, are not "the truth" about Jesus, but rather personal probes of various value into the humanity of Jesus. Each contribution, however subjective, adds to the wild proliferation of flowers and weeds that make up the riotous garden of Jesus studies.

I in no way deplore these efforts to construct a new, liberating Jesus-myth. I believe it is the most important theological enterprise since the Protestant Reformation, urgently to be pursued. The problem is that many scholars believed they were producing objective historiography rather than creating a necessary new myth. That myth, to be sure, draws on historical methodologies. But it marshals those methodologies in the service of what I hope will become a powerful mythic alternative to the Christ-myth that we have known these past two thousand years. *Historical criticism is essential for Jesus research because the myth of the human Jesus is itself historically constructed.* As Bruce Malina puts it, "While history must be imaginative, it should not be imaginary."[8]

In short, the quest for the *historical* Jesus all along has been the quest for the *human* Jesus. There is no need for consensus or unanimity on what constitutes authentic Jesus tradition. The myth of the human Jesus is a wide field with room for many divergent views. Yet it is a field with boundaries. It is still possible to reject, on historical-critical grounds, constructions that are not supported by the text—though there will be disagreement even over the boundaries. It is not the case, then, that we scholars initiated the quest for the human Jesus. Rather, the archetype of the Human Being initiated the quest as long ago as Ezekiel, and, if some scholars are right, even earlier, in myths of the Primal Man. And the archetype continues to provide the dynamic impetus that has driven that quest. We are not the drivers, but the driven.

The Jesus-quest, however, faces two major limitations: the paucity of the biblical data, and the poverty of our selves. The myth of the human Jesus cannot simply be spun out of the air, because that myth insists on the historicity of the human Jesus. The myth itself demands that we provide warrants for all our assertions and a plausible synthesis of the data. I believe that fallible persons such as ourselves can nevertheless exercise those critical judgments and, in so doing, provide information about the human Jesus. It is precisely that wager that leads exegetes to engross themselves in the "extremely verbatim reading" of which the mystics spoke. We cannot abandon the historical method, because it provides one of the most powerful tools we have for constructing the myth of the human Jesus.

Scholars seek to rectify the limitation on our data by turning over every leaf in search of new information about the ancient world. Newly discovered texts, new ways of reading texts, new disciplines applied to the texts, all provide invaluable aid in understanding Jesus' world and his relation to it. Such research participates in perpetual feedback, in which our interpretation of solitary sayings and deeds of Jesus continually modify our overall picture of him, while our overall picture in turn exercises a powerful influence on the way we read the solitary pieces.

It is by now a truism that information with which to write a biography of Jesus, or even to profile his personality, is inadequate. It is also true that scholarly reconstructions of the *teaching* of Jesus (for which we have considerably more data) do not carry the religious impact of the mythologized Gospels. *That is why we must attempt to recover the archetypal meaning of the "son of the man." Only then can we hope to offer an alternative to the perfect, almost inhuman Christ of dogma that has dominated these two millennia of Christian orthodoxy.* As Richard Rohr, OFM, comments, "without sacred mythology, all we have left is private pathology: my little story disconnected from any group story and surely disconnected from any Great Story."[9]

What I and others similarly inclined are trying to do is to move Christianity in a more humane direction. For that task we seek a Jesus who is not the omnipotent God in a man-suit, but someone like us, who looked for God at the center of his life and called the world to join him. What we do not know how to do, or even whether it can be done, is to position ourselves to experience the Human Being as numinously activating, religiously compelling, and spiritually transformative. If such a thing is possible, then new liturgies, music, meditative practices, disciplines, and commitments will spring up spontaneously.[10]

Even if we are able to recover something of the human Jesus, we might still be subject to the second limitation mentioned above: the poverty of our selves. No matter how vast our knowledge of Jesus' historical period, unless we are also addressing our spiritual inadequacies we will be unable to proceed closer to the mystery of Human Being. We will continue to circle its perimeter, accumulating more information without being changed by the encounter.

No scholar can construct a picture of Jesus beyond the level of spiritual awareness that they have attained. No reconstruction outstrips its reconstructor. We cannot explain truths we have not yet understood. We cannot present insights that we have not yet grasped. Our picture of Jesus reflects not only Jesus, but the person portraying Jesus. If we are spiritual infants or adolescents, whole realms of human reality will simply escape us. As Gerald

O'Collins remarked, writing about Jesus betrays what we have experienced and done as human beings.[11] Or as a very wise black woman in Texas once said to me, "You caint no more give someone something you ain't got than you can come back from somewhere you ain't been."

The Jesus-quest as it manifests itself today entails a high but necessary cost, and that is self-exposure, self-mortification, and personal transformation. Once we step out from behind the screen of historical objectivism into Heisenberg's universe, we become as much the subject of study as Jesus.

After all, "Jesus," "quest," and "Scripture" are not merely artifacts for study or names for an inquiry. They are great religious impulses and archetypal powers, and they are not just "out there" in the texts to be studied, but already "in here," in the self* that is fascinated, repelled, driven, wounded, and possibly healed by these realities.

C. The Myth of History

The historical-critical method cannot deliver Jesus as he really was. But we should never have demanded that it do so. Its real contribution has been to sift through the Jesus traditions in order to establish the elements of a reconstruction. We can create the myth of the human Jesus because, as W. Taylor Stevenson has noted, the historical approach is basically a *mythic* way of perceiving the world. The idea of history *is* our modern myth.

To be sure, the myth of history is falsified when we pass from claiming that reality is historical in nature, to insisting that reality can *only* be discerned by use of historical method.[12] Historical investigation cannot, for example, establish whether one person truly loves another, or is acting from the motives she gives for her behavior. Historical study, while indispensable, is incapable of providing the kind of insights that can make the Bible come alive with the power to facilitate transformation—which is the manifest intention behind its writing and preservation in the first place. Every historical image of Jesus that is created serves the myth of the human Jesus, because today we *are* constituted by the myth of history. As Hal Childs commented to me,

> A significant dimension of our ontology today, our core being, is the myth of history. This is why "history" is so important to us, why it is so important to perceive and portray Jesus historically. We conceive of ourselves as historical be-ings; history is our be-ing. History does not mean "true facts." It is a grand narrative with ontological status, which because of its ontological status,

feels absolutely real at a pre-reflective level within us, as our being. I am trying to make this myth more conscious, but because it is still mostly unconscious, or we are mostly unconscious to it, there is ongoing confusion as we
try to think about it.

However much scholars differ on details, and however much they quib-
ble over interpretations, most agree that Jesus really was a human being, and
that our historical findings can help recover aspects of his humanity. Because traditional Christianity suppressed his humanness in favor of his divinity, the recovery of Jesus' full humanity is felt as a remedial and even, for
some, as a sacred task.

That Jesus really lived is, to be sure, required, not by some putative historical science, but by the Christian myth itself. Faith is not dependent on
historiography. But it can certainly be helped by it. Historical criticism can
fashion alternative images of Jesus that can free us from oppressive pictures
spawned by churches that themselves are too often oppressive. Critical
scholarship can help us recover Jesus' critique of domination. Scholarship
also lets us appreciate Jesus without an overlay of dogma that claims absolute truth and that negates the value of other approaches to understanding
Jesus.

Bruce Chilton's recent *Rabbi Jesus* is an excellent example of the careful use of historiography to paint a plausible picture of Jesus. It is full of speculation, informed guesses, and novelistic narrative. Because Chilton has
performed such exhaustive research, and because he has tethered his imagination to reliable facts from the period and its places, he is able to make a
significant contribution to the quest for the human Jesus. In a society in
which, for many, the great living myths have lost their cogency, what we
once held as beliefs can now be held self-consciously as "true fiction," as
"creative nonfiction," or as "myths" in quotation marks. We no longer have
to defend our meaning-stories, notes mythologist Betty Sue Flowers. We
simply watch them evolve as we tell them and live in the present created by
the future we tell.[13]

D. Jesus' Original Impulse

My goal in studying the Gospels is to recover what Jesus unleashed—the
original impulse that prompted the spread of his message into new contexts
that required new formulations, in his spirit. In this book I have attempted
to develop a perspective on Jesus using the historical-critical method and a

critique of domination. I have developed that critique more fully in chapter 6 of *Engaging the Powers* (= chapter 3 of *The Powers That Be*).[14] To summarize that critique briefly, Jesus condemned all forms of domination:

- patriarchy and the oppression of women and children;
- the economic exploitation and the impoverishment of entire classes of people;
- the family as chief instrument for the socialization of children into oppressive roles and values;
- hierarchical power arrangements that disadvantage the weak while benefiting the strong;
- the subversion of the law by the defenders of privilege;
- rules of purity that keep people separated;
- racial superiority and ethnocentrism;
- the entire sacrificial system with its belief in sacral violence.

Jesus proclaimed the Reign of God (or "God's Domination-Free Order"), not only as coming in the future, but as having already dawned in his healings and exorcisms and his preaching of good news to the poor. He created a new family, based not on bloodlines, but on doing the will of God. He espoused nonviolence as a means for breaking the spiral of violence without creating new forms of violence. He called people to repent of their collusion in the Domination System* and sought to heal them from the various ways the system had dehumanized them.

In my analysis of texts in this book I privilege Jesus' critique of domination over all other viewpoints because, after a lifetime of study, I have found it to be the most radical and comprehensive framework for understanding what he was about. Using a critique of the Domination System as my critical lens enables me to recover emphases lost as the gospel was domesticated in the early church. Although occasionally Jesus' teachings were further radicalized (as in Stephen's speech in Acts 7 or in the opening of the church to include Gentiles), the more pronounced tendency of the tradition was to accommodate the gospel to structures of domination (for example, the treatment of women in later New Testament writings). This critique of domination does not replace the historical criteria worked out with care by New Testament scholars. It does provide the primary criterion for discerning what was revelatory in Jesus' life and message.

I should add that I am using "revelatory" not in a theological but in an epistemological sense.[15] I regard a "revelation" as any new idea that bursts upon the world with sufficient force to bring about positive change in people and history. A revelation begins as a private, subjective *experience* that happens to individuals. But if it has cogency, it becomes a public, historic occasion. What we call a revelation is a positive mutation in the history of thought or being. Buddha was a revealer, as was Lao-Tzu, Zoroaster, Muhammad, St. Francis, Karl Marx, Sigmund Freud, Mohandas Gandhi, Teilhard de Chardin, Carl Jung, and others, some of far less fame and accomplishment. But it was Jesus who exposed the Domination System with such devastating effect and envisioned God as nonviolent and all-inclusive. There were antecedent revelations, of course, but the revelation Jesus brought was so at odds with the world's power arrangements that we have yet to take its measure.

I am concerned not so much with whether Jesus actually said something, but with whether it is true, regardless of who said it. If truth is our goal rather than historicity, then revelation is a far more appropriate category than facticity for weighing the impact of Jesus. If a statement is revelatory, if it provides insights about becoming more fully human, if it exposes the Domination System for what it is, then we may call it "true." But we should not assume that something is true because Jesus said it. Rather, he would have said it because he thought it was true. Some sayings later developed by various churches are no doubt true; it is even conceivable that some things Jesus said are not true, though most of these would have been filtered out in transmitting the tradition. (The church did courageously retain passages that were clearly disconfirmed, such as the second coming, Mark 9:1 par.) The myth of the human Jesus *requires* that Jesus must have made mistakes, have had flaws in his personality, sinned, and otherwise exhibited imperfect (that is, human) behavior. But the issue of historicity, while occasionally crucial, is far less significant than *consistency with the original impulse of Jesus*, whether articulated by him or by his followers later. That impulse was the spirit that drove Jesus to challenge his own religious tradition and those who were its protectors. Working from the vantage point provided by a critique of domination, the criteria of historicity can, when needed, isolate texts that illuminate the human Jesus. To be sure, this involves us in a hermeneutical spiral (*not* a circle), in which the fragments are interpreted by that critique, and that critique is modified by the fragments, and on and on. All historical work proceeds in this manner. Indeed, failure to continue the spiral is to abort the entire enterprise. Consequently, if a critique of domination fails to account for significant elements of the tradition, it would have to be modified or abandoned altogether.

The presence of a particular critical perspective does not spell the end of objectivity; we are still required to provide warrants for our claims. Once one abandons the chimera of disinterestedness, however, objectivity is free to become what it should have been all along: just another name for simple honesty and the willingness, as Schweitzer demonstrated, to be changed by what we discover.

I listen intently to the Book. But I do not acquiesce in it. I rail at it. I make accusations. I censure it for endorsing patriarchalism, violence, anti-Judaism, homophobia, and slavery. It rails back at me, accusing me of greed, presumption, narcissism, and cowardice. We wrestle. We roll on the ground, neither of us capitulating, until it wounds my thigh with "new-ancient" words. And the Holy Spirit* is there the whole time, strengthening us both.

Such wrestling ensures that our pictures of Jesus are not mere repetitions of the prevailing fashion. They can be a groping for plenitude, an attempt to carry on the mission of Jesus, and an effort to transcend the influence of the Domination System. In the end, we may not just be conforming Jesus to ourselves, but in some faint way conforming ourselves to the truth revealed by Jesus.

My deepest interest in encountering Jesus is not to confirm my own prejudices (though I certainly do that), but to be delivered from a stunted soul, a limited mind, and an unjust social order. No doubt a part of me wants to whittle Jesus down to my size so that I can avoid painful, even costly, change. But another part of me is exhilarated by the possibility of becoming more human. So I listen in order to be transformed. Somehow the gospel itself has the power to activate in people that "hunger and thirst for righteousness" of which Matt. 5:6 speaks (whether it is Jesus or someone of the same mind speaking). There are people who want to be involved in inaugurating God's domination-free order, even if it costs their lives. *Respondeo etsi mutabor*: I respond though I must change.[16] And in my better moments, I respond *in order to change*.

Truth is, had Jesus never lived, we could not have invented him.

Part Two

The Anthropic Revelation: The Human Being

There are few expressions in biblical studies as perplexing as the "son of the man." Scarcely any topic in New Testament studies has received more attention, and with less result. Here are the few facts that define the problem. "Son of man" appears 108 times in the Hebrew Scriptures, 93 of these uses in Ezekiel. Curiously, God refuses to call Ezekiel by his given name, but addresses him solely as "son of man" (no definite articles). No one else calls Ezekiel by that name, only God.

The same expression appears in the New Testament some 87 times,[1] all but three cases in the Gospels (Matthew, 31 times; Mark, 14; Luke, 26; John, 13).[2] Counting the parallels only once (25 paralleled, 15 unparalleled), and adding uses of the expression in John, there are a total of 53 different sayings in the Gospels that feature "the son of the man" (*ho huios tou anthrōpou*).[3] This odd Greek idiom is so awkward that virtually all translators omit the second definite article. In this study I will render the expression literally, with both articles, to underscore its oddness and crudity.[4]

2.   The Enigma of the Son of the Man

This, then, is the enigma of the son of the man. In the Synoptic Gospels, Jesus is depicted as avoiding designation as messiah, son of God, or God, though his disciples gave these titles to him after his death and resurrection.[1] But the Gospels repeatedly depict Jesus using the expression "the son of the man," as virtually his only form of self-reference. Not once in the Gospels does he call himself by his own name. Not once does anyone else call him the son of the man. The expression appears only on his lips. (He also calls himself a prophet twice, but each time only by implication.)[2] Yet there is little evidence of the expression's use after his death. Paul never uses it, nor do the later writers of the New Testament (with three exceptions). It appears only a few times in the early church theologians.[3] Insofar as churches later used the expression, they merely amalgamated it with the other christological titles, or treated it as an expression indicating Jesus' human nature.[4] The churches never made "the son of the man" the basis of any church confession or creed or developed it as a christological concept. So far as we know, it was never used in prayer or worship. In time it virtually disappeared from usage.

Furthermore, the expression occurs very seldom in other Jewish sources of the period. The second- and third-century Gnostics alone used the phrase frequently. But it is the uniqueness and intensity of this usage, concentrated on the human Jesus, that demands explanation.

The conclusion of a number of philologists who have been laboring over this question recently is that the expression has no theological meaning, but that it is a way of referring to oneself in the third person. It might, then, be a circumlocution for "I" or "one" or "a person" or "this fellow" or "myself and people like me." Such conclusions ignore the fact that no one but Jesus made this phrase his exclusive self-designation. There are no significant instances in the Hebrew Scriptures in which individuals speak of themselves in the third person, as Jesus does.[5] Nor are the nine rabbinical "son of man" parallels cited by Geza Vermes helpful, since they are scattered among thousands of pages of Jewish texts, dated three to four centuries later than the Gospels.[6] Jesus, by contrast, is depicted as using the expression more than eighty times in only 121 pages (NRSV), and it is *only* Jesus who uses it. It was inevitable that indirect forms of self-address would occasionally crop up in Palestinian Aramaic sources; such forms of address appear in many languages. One need look no farther than the 1996 U.S. presidential election, in which Republican candidate Bob Dole repeatedly spoke of himself in the third person ("Bob Dole won't raise your taxes").[7] Such elliptical forms of self-address have a variety of functions (not wishing to appear to boast, or as a self-deprecating way of speaking about oneself, or just as a manner of speaking of oneself in general terms—"Can't a person [= "I"] have any privacy?").[8] But it is inconceivable that Jesus used these forms with such frequency when no one else did. And Bob Dole used his own name, not some mysterious cipher.

Morna Hooker ponders, "If the phrase was a common expression for 'I' in Aramaic, then the use of the barbaric Greek phrase [*ho huios tou anthrōpou*] seems an inexplicable blunder; the fact that it was thought necessary to use this translationese suggests that there was already something a little unusual and special about the Aramaic phrase [*bar enash*], even in an Aramaic-speaking community."[9]

Ulrich Luz states the case even more strongly. "Son of the man," he says, is a strange and even mysterious expression without an obvious meaning for the Syriac-speaking person in Syria, where Matthew was probably written. It appears nowhere outside the Gospels. In short, at the level of the colloquial language, the expression "the son of the man" was for everybody a very strange, even mysterious expression. "For Matthew's readers the expression 'the son of the man' was part of their own Christian insider language. They only, not the outsiders, knew about the son of the man, his destiny and his future, and Matthew knew that they knew."[10]

So also, in John 9:36 and 12:34, Jesus' hearers, who well knew the idiomatic translation of "the son of man" as "human being," were baffled by the use of the expression as a title or nickname of Jesus.[11] In fact, all "the son of the man" sayings in the Gospels could be rendered by "I" if the so-called apocalyptic passages were regarded as Jesus speaking of himself and not of another. The easy way out, chosen by some scholars, is simply to opt for mistranslation, and to regard "the son of the man" as nothing more than an indirect form of self-reference.[12] Why, then, did the evangelists not use

"I" consistently, since they unmistakably thought "the son of the man" meant "I" in at least some cases? Jesus is depicted as showing no hesitation whatever in using "I"; he does so scores of times. "I" could have appeared in all the son-of-the-man sayings and we never would have guessed that "the son of the man" once stood there. We can scarcely argue that "the son of the man" is a mistranslation. Anyone capable of rendering a sentence from Aramaic into Greek would know that "son of" is an idiomatic expression simply meaning membership in a class. So why was "the son of the man" preserved at all?

Philipp Vielhauer and others take the most extreme position. They simply dismiss all son-of-the-man sayings as creations of the early church.[13] I find it inconceivable that churches that made no use of the son-of-the-man figure in other contexts would have invented some eighty-four references to it, spread about evenly among all four Gospels, all of them (with one exception) with definite articles.[14] At the time the Evangelists wrote the Gospels, the more exalted christological titles (Messiah/Christ, Lord, High Priest, Son of God, God) were already fully deployed and served as the basis both for christological reflection and liturgical celebration. So why would the church create so many son-of-the-man sayings at a time when no one, so far as we know, was using that expression of Jesus? There must have been a critical mass of authentic sayings with the potency to trigger creative additions to the fund of existing sayings. Had the church invented all of the son-of-the-man sayings, would not the preference have been to use *no* articles in order to create a proof from prophecy that pointed directly to the anarthrous (lacking definite articles) phrase in Ezekiel and Dan. 7:13?

We can list a few things that the "son of the man" is not. As we shall see, in the time prior to Jesus it was not the title of an apocalyptic figure expected to come to earth to judge and redeem humanity. The capitalization that one encounters in Bibles and scholarly writings give the false impression that the "Son of Man" is a title. But the translators have added the capitalization. There is no capitalization in the Hebrew or the Greek texts of the Bible (except in the case of uncials, which are manuscripts written all in capital letters). Nor was the pre-Christian "son of the man" a messianic deliverer.[15] It had not been amalgamated with the Suffering Servant of Isaiah 53. It was not a heaven-appointed judge who would preside over the last judgment.

Douglas R. A. Hare concludes that the Aramaic "son of the man" (*bar enasha*) was not a title but a nickname. Its use as a modest form of self-reference began with Jesus, but apart from John it had no theological content. Hence its neglect by the churches.[16]

My response will begin where Hare's leaves off: rejecting with him the idea that "the son of the man" was a pre-Christian title, but searching for the meaning Jesus himself might have found in the phrase.

This much should be clear: Jesus did not use "the son of the man" as a self-deprecating expression of humility. If there is anything Jesus was not, it was modest. Few people ever spoke with such unmediated authority, or made a higher claim than Jesus': that he was ushering the Reign of God into the world. Later I justify my belief that "the son of the man" functioned as a catalyst for personal and social transformation. I argue that the expression "the son of the man" is an allusion to Ezekiel, and that "the man" in that phrase is the divine figure on the throne who calls Ezekiel "son": the "son" of the Human One seated on the throne. After Jesus' death, that archetype was writ large as the "second coming" of Jesus. We will come to all of that in due time. But first we need to set Jesus' use of this strange third-person self-reference in its Old Testament and intertestamental context.

A. The Human Being in Ezekiel

Every speaker of Hebrew knew that "son of" is a Semitic idiom that means membership in a class. Thus "a son of the quiver" is an arrow (Lam. 3:13), a "son of the herd" is a calf (Gen. 18:7), and a "son of a year" is a one-year-old (Gen. 17:12). Joshua and Zerubbabel are "sons of oil," that is, anointed ones (Zech. 4:14). This idiom was used in scores of ways in the Hebrew Bible, and the translators never treated it literally ("son of"), but always rendered it with an appropriate English expression.[17]

Always, that is, with one exception: the phrase "son of man." Idiomatically, the phrase simply means "human being." But the pressure of theological reflection surrounding Jesus' use of the expression has, until recently, led translators to leave the phrase in its confusing idiomatic form. Newer translations of the Hebrew Scriptures now consistently render the expression in good English: "mere man" or "mortal man" (TEV), "a human being" or "O man" (REB), "mortal(s)" or "the one" (NRSV). However, even these versions still persist in translating "the son of man" literally when they come to the New Testament, setting one or both nouns in capital letters and deleting the second article.

The Hebrew expression translated "son of man" is *ben 'adam* (*bar enash* in Aramaic, *ho huios tou anthrōpou* in Greek). In English, "son of the man" comes across as doubly sexist. I will try to mitigate the male bias by substituting more neutral terms that refer to human beings generically, such as "child of the Human," "Humanchild," "the human one," and so on. Most frequently, however, I have translated it as "Human Being," following Herman Waetjen, since that expression seems best to catch the sense of something transcendently human yet within our God-given capacity.[18] I will also use terms that depict the Human Being as explicitly feminine or female. We already see a tendency in that direction in one Ethiopic expression for son of man: "son of the offspring of the mother of the living." We might then render "son of man" by such English expressions as "Wisdom's Child" or Sophia's Child." Use of a feminine or female paraphrase for the wholly male "the son of the man" is not only legitimate, but imperative. Legitimate, because every translation is an interpretation, producing a new reading informed by its modern context. Imperative, because the very humanity to which we aspire cannot be realized when women are denied their rights and men neglect their own feminine aspect.

I also use Paul Tillich's expression, "the New Being," though it does not connote the parent/child, God/human relationship. But it does suggest openness to transformation through the encounter with the other—other persons, other traditions, and God as the Other. The New Being is perpetually becoming, and that is consistent with the Human Being.

In Ezekiel and Daniel, the son of man took on a complex of meanings that changed the expression into the enigma that it has remained until today. The proper place to begin, then, is with Ezekiel. No other book of the Bible approaches Ezekiel's ninety-three references to the Human Being (son of man). In Ezekiel's inaugural vision of the divine throne chariot in chapter 1, we encounter one of the most significant visions in the Bible; indeed, it is one of the most influential visions in all of human history. For more than a century it has been the custom of scholars to atomize Ezekiel in general, and chapter 1 in particular, into a hodgepodge of sources stuck together with glue and baling wire. In the process, scholars came to regard the vision of Ezekiel as merely a literary device patched together over centuries and thus reflecting no actual experience of Ezekiel.[19]

Most recent scholarship has abandoned that approach. The vision is so unique, unparalleled by other documents within the Bible or by precedents outside it, that it seems the better part of wisdom to let it stand as it has come down to us, and to ask whether it makes sense when taken as the account of an actual experience. No doubt there were later additions and repetitions. In this study, my interest lies in the use of "the son of the man" in the Jesus tradition, and that tradition would have taken Ezekiel's vision as an inspired unity.

Materialists in our culture generally regard visions as hallucinations. In biblical times, however, visions were regarded as sources of information that ranked higher than other sources, because they revealed the inner essence of reality.[20]

Ezekiel's vision is central to Jewish mysticism. No doubt the vast majority of the texts that constituted that mystical tradition are now lost to us, but we still have Isaiah 6; 1 Kings 22:19; Ezekiel 1; 3:22-24; 8:1-4; 10; *1 Enoch* 14; Daniel 7; *Songs of the Sabbath Sacrifice* and *Pseudo-Ezekiel* from Qumran;[21] Paul's vision of the third heaven in 2 Cor. 12:1-10; Revelation 1; 4–5; 14; *Similitudes of Enoch (1 Enoch 37–71); Life of Adam and Eve* 35; *2 Enoch; Apocalypse of Abraham; Visions of Ezekiel; Hekhalot Zutreti; Hekhalot Rabbati; Ma'aseh Merkabah; Merkabah Rabbah; Shi'ur Qomah; b. Hagiga* 14b; *3 Enoch*; and from there to medieval Kabbalah, the *Zohar,* Isaac Luria, and modern Hasidism—an unbroken chain of esoteric traditions lasting 2,500 years.[22]

Ezekiel 1 is so overwhelming in its surplus of powerful symbolic images that the rabbis only permitted mature persons to read this chapter, and then only in the company of a person who was older and wiser.[23] A saying, often repeated in Jewish lore, stated that four Jewish mystics succeeded in ascending to heaven and viewing the divine throne chariot that Ezekiel describes. One went mad, one became a heretic, one died, and only Rabbi Akiba returned in his right mind.[24] These popular warnings indicated profound respect for the raw psychic power of the spiritual world. These mystics recognized that these archetypal images and symbols were not just a manner of speaking, but that they were capable of transforming—or unhinging—those who encountered them.

The immediate political context for Ezekiel 1 is crucial to understanding the vision. It was 593 B.C.E. Ezekiel was by the River Chebar in Babylon in the fifth year of the exile of King Jehoiachin and the bulk of the Jewish aristocracy. Those remaining in Jerusalem, who had escaped exile, persisted in believing that they had weathered the worst, and that the exile of their leaders had diverted the attention of the empire away from tiny Israel. But "tiny Israel" was located on the land bridge between the Middle East and Egypt. Israel thus was critical to the geopolitics of any empire of that region and period. Whoever controlled Palestine was poised to attack any of the major rivals to political control. Six years after this vision, in 587, Zedekiah, the new king of Judah, revolted against Babylon and brought about the destruction of Jerusalem, including the razing of the temple and the walls of the city. Israel had grown accustomed to localizing Yahweh in the Jerusalem Temple, however expansive the divine reach might be from there. But now Ezekiel was in exile, in a foreign land presided over by Marduk, the god of Babylon, who had, to judge by history, defeated Yahweh. It was a time of crisis for Israel. It fell to Ezekiel to reveal to his people that Yahweh was sovereign and could speak and intervene in a foreign land, even without the temple. As Bruce Chilton comments, because Ezekiel saw the throne of God as heavenly rather than earthly, and as moving rather than static, he was able to have his vision in exile in Babylon rather than in the holy land.[25] Ezekiel's vision in exile comes, then, at one of the critical points in Jewish history, when the very survival of faith hung in the balance.

B. Ezekiel's Vision

At the heart of Ezekiel's vision is this astonishing statement:

> And above the dome over their heads there was something like a throne, in appearance like sapphire; and seated above the likeness of a throne was something that seemed like a human form (*'adam*). Upward from what appeared like the loins I saw something like gleaming amber, something that looked like fire enclosed all around; and downward from what looked like the loins I saw something that looked like fire, and there was a splendor all around. Like the bow in a cloud on a rainy day, such was the appearance of the splendor all around. This was the appearance of the likeness of the glory of the Lord.
>
> When I saw it, I fell on my face, and I heard the voice of someone speaking. He said to me: O mortal ["son of man"], stand up on your feet, and I will speak with you. (1:26—2:1)

This is one of the most understated visionary reports ever recounted. Against all tendencies toward exaggeration, Ezekiel goes out of his way, redundantly, to stress that he is doing the best he can to describe the indescribable. Yet he knows that his words are not enough, that he cannot do the vision justice, that his descriptions bend and break while the experience races ahead of language. A fictionalized account would have been full of certainty and precision; Ezekiel qualifies virtually every word of his report.[26]

1. God as the Human One

When at last the vision breaks to the center, the qualifications and hesitations stumble over themselves: "And above the dome over their heads there was *something like* a throne, *in appearance like* sapphire; and seated above the *likeness* of a throne was *something* that *seemed like* a human form" (1:26).

And this is the revelation: God seems to be, as it were, human.

This is not just a figure of speech. Israel was thoroughly familiar with figures of speech and never confused them with reality. If you had asked Israelites if God was walking in the Garden of Eden in the cool of the day because the noonday heat was disagreeable (Gen. 3:8), they would likely have dismissed the question as impertinent: Of course not, that is only a figure of speech.

But Ezekiel is not beholding a figure of speech. God really seems to be turning a human face toward Ezekiel. Whatever else God might be in the wildness of nature and the blackness of interstellar space, when God wishes to manifest divine reality to Ezekiel, it is in "the likeness as it were of a human form."[27]

Obviously God is not just human. In the vision, three of the four faces of the cherubim are animals: eagle, lion, ox. Nature symbols are used to speak of nonhuman aspects of God or as representatives of all creation. The last thing our world needs today is another anthropocentric theology that ignores the violence being done to God's creation. We should not confuse anthropocentrism (a human-centered relationship to the world) with anthropomorphism, which is imaging God as human. In place of anthropocentrism, we need anthropocosmism (human relatedness to the cosmos).

What does it mean to say that God is revealed as human? Why does God turn a humanlike face to Ezekiel? Perhaps because becoming human is the task that God has set for human beings. And human beings have only a vague idea what it means to be human. Humanity errs in believing that it is human. (It also, Amy-Jill Levine reminds me, errs in believing that it is divine!) We are only fragmentarily human, fleetingly human, brokenly human. We see glimpses of our humanness, we can dream of what a more humane existence and political order would be like, but we have not yet arrived at true humanness. Ezekiel's vision intimates that only God is, as it were, really Human, and since we are made in God's image and likeness, we are capable of becoming more truly human ourselves.[28] Even if we do not as yet know what true humanity is, we already know well what inhumanity is.[29] As Gerd Theissen notes, people were once especially eager to find the "missing link" between primates and human beings. Now, however, it is dawning on us that we ourselves could be that "missing link."[30]

Furthermore, we are incapable of becoming human by ourselves. We scarcely know what humanness is.[31] We have only the merest intuitions and general guidelines. Jesus has, to be sure, revealed to us something of what it means to live an authentic human life. But how do I translate that into my own struggles for humanness? Jesus never married, raised children, dealt with the second half of life, or faced the problems of the twenty-first century. So what am I to do? Metaphysically speaking, God is the ultimate mystery, but to myself I am an even more impenetrable mystery. Who am I? I have accepted my parents' answers, my culture's answers, the answers of mentors and peers and colleagues. But how do they know? What are the exact outlines of my true form? How can I find out, unless God reveals it to me? For who else could possibly know what is stored in the divine image inside me, except that One who is the divine image inside me?

As the Sufi poet and philosopher Ibn 'Arabi writes, speaking for God:

> "If then you perceive me,
>   You perceive yourself.
> But you cannot perceive me
>   Through yourself.
> It is through my eyes that you see me
>   And see yourself.
> Through your eyes
>   You cannot see me."[32]

Or, as Elizabeth Howes commented to me, "When I work to become human, is it not God in me that is striving to become human?"

So this is not Operation Bootstrap, trying to lift myself into my own potential. We must, it is true, be constantly attentive to the clues being provided, oh so gradually, in prayer, in scripture, in worship, in preaching and silence and dreams and meditation—and, yes, also from our parents, our culture, our mentors and peers and colleagues. And perhaps, above all, from our enemies.[33] So the journey is conceived, executed, and consummated in God's grace by the promptings of the *imago Dei* within us; by the nudges, glimmerings, and insights that further that journey; and finally, by the transformative power of God in the revelation of who we really are in the consummation of all things. As one of the most remarkable lines of Scripture puts it, "Beloved, we are God's children now; what we will be has not yet been revealed. What we do know is this: when the Humanchild ["he," or "it" NRSV] is revealed, we will be like it, for we will see it as it is" (1 John 3:2).[34] Or, as Paul put it in Rom. 8:29, God destined us to participate in the form of the image of his Beloved, "in order that he might be the firstborn within a large family."

Ezekiel's vision comes to him toward the beginning of the Babylonian captivity. A short time later, the creation story in Genesis 1 was being developed in exile as an answering rebuke to the Babylonian creation myth, the *Enuma Elish*. In the Babylonian myth, human beings are created from the blood of a murdered god in order to serve the gods. Genesis 1 asserts, to the contrary, that all creation is good, and that human beings are created in God's image:

> Then God said, "Let us make humankind in our image, according to our likeness; and let them have dominion . . ."
> So God created humankind in the divine image, in the image of God, God created them; male and female God created them. (vv. 26–27; see also 5:1; 9:6)

Bill Wylie Kellermann comments:

> Human beings are the image of God. Here is an idea so incredibly subversive it may be the most politically loaded claim of all. Who in Babylon, not to mention virtually the whole of the ancient world, was the image of god? The King, of course, who stands in for [Babylonian god] Marduk in the creation pageant, and whose authority is annually legitimated. Who, however, is in the liturgy of Israel? Humanity. Women and men. Human beings in community. This is a subversion and affront to every imperial authority. It's practically anarchism. In this counter-story, human beings are not from the blood of a murdered god, created as slaves of the state. They are made for freedom and responsibility.[35]

And because humans are like God, and God is like humans, the shedding of human blood is prohibited (Gen. 9:4-6; Ezek. 33:25). Our being in the image of God thus has ethical consequences.[36]

Gerhard von Rad suggests plausibly that Genesis 1 is directly prompted by the revelation God gave Ezekiel, and that it is the first elaboration of it.[37] Scholars have long noted that Genesis 1 is too rational and abstract to really be a myth. It was a polemic made possible by the unprecedented breakthrough of Ezekiel's vision.

To be in the image of God is to be of the same stuff, the same essence, the same being, masculine and feminine, as God. God is androgynous in

Genesis 1, encompassing the sexual opposites. If Ezekiel's vision is in some way the experiential source for Genesis 1, then we would expect to find some trace of the same androgyny in Ezekiel 1. And indeed we do, though scholars have stared right at the phenomenon without recognizing it. Throughout the vision there are feminine plurals of verbs, and feminine pronouns are used of the "living creatures" where one would have expected masculine forms exclusively. Almost one-third of these verbs and pronouns—12 out of 45—are feminine. This vacillation is most pronounced in Ezek. 1:9-11, 16, 18, and 23-25.[38] Walther Eichrodt comments that no one has been able to provide an adequate explanation for the strange oscillation between masculine and feminine suffixes in Ezekiel 1.[39] Perhaps the explanation lies like an open book before us: if Ezekiel is seeing the Fully Human Being, that being must encompass all that comprises such fullness, and that means both male and female are in God. The writer(s) of Genesis 1 had no difficulty in seeing that. It has taken us considerably longer.[40]

To say that we humans are made in the image of God, male and female, means that we are somehow "like" God in our mundane existence. But we are not yet fully human. For now, we are only promissory notes, hints, intimations. But we are able to become more human because the Human One has placed the divine spirit within us (Ezek. 37:5, 14), which will remove our heart of stone and give us a heart of flesh (36:26).[41]

If God is in some sense true humanness, then divinity inverts itself. Divinity is not a qualitatively different reality; quite the reverse, *divinity is fully realized humanity.* Only God is, as it were, Human. *The goal of life, then, is not to become something we are not—divine—but to become what we truly are—human.* We are not required to become divine: flawless, perfect, without blemish. We are invited simply to become human, which means growing through our sins and mistakes, learning by trial and error, being redeemed over and over from compulsive behavior—becoming ourselves, scars and all. It means embracing and transforming those elements in us that we find unacceptable. It means giving up pretending to be good and, instead, becoming real. Are not the deepest reaches of our humanity born of our wounds, even of our sins (though one hesitates to say it, for fear the ego* will use it as justification for continuing in destructive behavior)? In this vision, then, the "one in human form" represents the archetypal image, "as it were," of fully human being, reaching out to Ezekiel with a seemingly impossible task: that of becoming human.[42]

Eastern Orthodoxy has long taught that the goal of human existence is to become "divinized." I have deep respect for the spiritual disciplines that the Orthodox mystics have developed in order to further this growth into God.

Somehow the Eastern churches have succeeded in hedging divinization with a received wisdom that prevents inflation on the part of the mystical adept.[43] But I have no idea what "becoming divine" signifies. When people say Jesus is divine, or the Son of God, or God, I have nothing in my experience that can help me comprehend what they mean. It sounds too much like the language of Greek polytheism, in which gods impregnated mortal women, who bore beings who were half human and half divine. The interminable debates about the two natures of Christ seem to me totally off the mark. They strike me as an irrelevancy carried over from a worldview that, for many, is now defunct. Worse, such debates are a stumbling block to dialogue with other religions. I do not know what the word "divine" signifies. But I do have an inkling of what the word "human" might entail, because we are made in the image of God, the Human One, and there have been exemplary human beings, in our tradition and that of others.[44] What the disciples wondered was not what kind of divine being Jesus was, but "what sort of human being is this?" (Matt. 8:27). In William Stringfellow's superb epitome, "What it means to be a Christian is, wonderfully, just synonymous with what it means to be no more and no less than a human being."[45]

I realize that the language of divinity is second nature to many people, and I honor the sincerity of their religious convictions. I am not promulgating new doctrines or making claims for the "truth" of these reflections. I intend them merely as signposts along a "new-ancient" path, a neglected but fresh alternative for those who, like myself, are not satisfied with current alternatives.

Central to the Eastern Orthodox tradition is a statement by the church father Athanasius that Christ became as we are that we might become as he is.[46] This has usually been interpreted to mean that Christ became human that we might become divine. We might hear it saying rather that Jesus became like us—people living within the constraints of earthly reality—in order that we might become like him—fully human. But that way of speaking is still too mythologically literal for me. It still imagines Jesus coming down from heaven to earth in order to incarnate God. I would prefer to say, Jesus incarnated God in his own person in order to show all of us how to incarnate God. And to incarnate God is what it means to be fully human.[47]

Call it what we may, the vision that Ezekiel encountered by the River Chebar exudes symbols of wholeness. We can attempt to decipher some of these symbols, however woodenly. The entire vision seems to form a mandala. Within it are the four living creatures at the four corners or four directions, representing domestic animals, wild animals, birds, and humans. The wheels, dome, and rainbow may be seen as circular symbols of wholeness.

The eyes could signal consciousness. Fire is dynamism, power, energy, life. The central figure is a symbol of human wholeness. The rainbow brings promise and the fullness of the spectrum. The alternation of feminine and masculine endings, as we saw earlier, suggest the integration of the opposites. Finally, by the presence of sun-god imagery (the fiery body), God's sovereignty over the cosmos is stressed. The panoply of symbols functioned, for Ezekiel, as a symbol of the Self. He need not have been aware of these meanings for them to be operative. The mandala (spontaneous patterns of opposites and fourfoldness in a structure of wholeness) *imposes* symbols that strive toward harmony and synchrony. What Ezekiel knew beyond a shadow of doubt was that he had entered the world of the Spirit and was being shown unfathomable mysteries, against which these symbols pale and shatter.

However, we risk losing the numinous reality under a barrage of words. Ezekiel is not struck by an interesting new idea. He is, rather, struck to the ground. The vision overwhelms him, like a blow to the solar plexus. And the God who has overwhelmed him now orders him to his feet. God, apparently, will not converse with human beings who are prostrated.[48] That which addresses us insists that we stand our ground. God will not speak as to an inferior or tolerate a servile mentality. The Spirit enters Ezekiel to embolden him to face this awesome Reality.

2. Ezekiel as Child of the Human One

When the One-as-it-were-in-human-form now addresses Ezekiel, he does so as a parent to a child: "*Ben 'adam* ["child of the Human One"], stand up on your feet and I will speak with you."[49] *Ben 'adam* could also be translated "son of Adam," so that serious wordplay is involved: the human child is also the child of the Divine Human. "Child of" thus stresses the intimacy of their relationship.[50]

As a "chip off the old block," this offspring of the Human will henceforth not be addressed by his given name, but only as the child of the Enthroned One: *ben 'adam*. In the moment that one faces the Glory of God, the Child of the Human is born. To see God as Human is to begin to become what one sees, for our image of God creates us. What is born is a person able to face and to carry this numinous power. Ezekiel has received a name for what emerges when a person withstands God's glory without disintegrating, fleeing, or becoming inflated. The Human Being is thus related somehow to the divine image (*imago Dei*) as an aspect of the Self archetype.[51] This divine image is that within us that has existed as potential from the beginning but that has not yet come to conscious awareness and accessibility. By addressing the prophet as Human Being, God shows that humanizing humanity is one of God's central concerns.

This process of humanizing humanity constitutes the anthropic revelation, that is to say, the revelation of what humanity is meant to be.

Strikingly, Ezekiel's openness to the Human One does not make Ezekiel a superman. Ezekiel is not an ideal figure whom anyone would want to emulate. He is cranky, abrasive, extremist, and offensive. But those very traits make it possible for him to undertake the thankless and abysmal task that God is about to lay upon him. Here we begin to grasp a notion that runs against the natural desire for perfect models and exemplary people, something that Second Isaiah knew ("he had no form or majesty that we should look at him, nothing in his appearance that we should desire him," 53:2) and that comes into complete focus on the cross. What draws us to the sufferings of God's messengers is not perfection but broken wholeness. It is in the crucifixion of our idealized self-images that we discover our true being, which includes those aspects that we would rather disown.

Ezekiel needed such an overwhelming vision. For he was being sent as a prophet to a rebellious people who would not listen.

> He said to me, Humanchild (*ben 'adam*), I am sending you to the people of Israel, to a nation of rebels who have rebelled against me; they and their ancestors have transgressed against me to this very day. The descendants are impudent and stubborn. I am sending you to them, and you shall say to them, "Thus says the Lord God." Whether they hear or refuse to hear (for they are a rebellious house), they shall know that there has been a prophet among them. (Ezek. 2:3-5)

Ezekiel's community of accountability and support has shrunk to one—the Creator of the ends of the earth. This vision sustains him in the face of his own people's nonresponsiveness. God gives him an adamantine forehead, harder than flint, to resist the stubbornness of his equally hardheaded people (3:8-9). He is not God's ventriloquist-dummy, mouthing the words God speaks through him. Rather, as son of man, he is to "eat this scroll, and go, speak to the house of Israel" (3:1). Ezekiel is to swallow God's words, digest them, and articulate them in his own words. He does not open his mouth and let the words pour forth in a mantic trance. Rather, he apparently *writes* his prophecies, and then presents the carefully considered result to the people.[52] God is not speaking *through* the prophet, but speaking *to* the prophet, who then must present, as exactly as he is able, God's word to a recalcitrant people. Yet Ezekiel frequently closes a sentence or paragraph with "I Yahweh have spoken (it)."[53]

Ezekiel is thus the recipient, not the source, of the authoritative word. And this, says Ellen Davis, served him well in speaking an unwelcome word to rebellious Israel. By portraying himself as a listener rather than as an initiator of speech, Ezekiel emphasizes the divine initiative in the communication. Repeatedly we are reminded that Ezekiel is the suffering vehicle, not the originator, of this message.[54]

As Child of the Human, Ezekiel is thus a representative and intermediary between God and the people. Here we can take the liberty of capitalizing "Man" since it refers to God. The "son of Man" seems to be that aspect of Ezekiel capable of discerning and transmitting what the Human One intends for humanity. It is, as it were, prophetic receptivity.[55] The fragile, finite earth creature that is exalted with glory and honor in Psalm 8 is here charged with a mission from God to the "children of the Human One" (*bene 'adam*, 31:14) who go down to death.[56]

Commentators ancient and modern have stressed that what Ezekiel saw on the throne that day was not the divine totality, but only "the appearance of the likeness of the Glory of the Lord" (1:28). God's Glory in rabbinic Judaism was a hypostasis for God, merely a single aspect of a reality too powerful and complex for any human to endure.[57] But the Glory is not a substitute for Yahweh; it *is* Yahweh in special proximity to Israel.[58] As Dan Merkur observes, hidden within the Glory of the Lord is what alone truly cannot be described in words: the ineffable, hidden Godhead. But the mystic is unable, *during the experience*, to appreciate that distinction.[59]

Since raw holiness would destroy a person, God condescends to show, as it were, only that of God that we fragmentary humans can bear, comprehend, and assimilate. God is like the high-voltage power lines that originate at a generating station. Touch them, and we fry. We need a transformer that can reduce the voltage to something usable. By calling the figure on the throne the Glory of God, the Jewish mystics were acknowledging that what they were experiencing was not God in all God's fullness, but God in a form that aspiring human beings can take in without being overwhelmed.[60] The God beyond all manifestation is not only "that than which nothing greater can be conceived" (Anselm), but greater than can be conceived (John Hick). What the mystics saw, like Ezekiel, was the human face of God, God as humanity needs to know God in order to become what God calls us to be.[61] We become what our desire beholds.[62] So the mystic is one who chooses to seek the God who freely offers us the gift of our own humanity, not as something to be attained, but as pure revelation.[63] God is, as it were, a mirror in which we find reflected our own "heavenly," that is, potential, face. As the exultant seventeenth *Ode of Solomon* puts it, "I received the face and form of a new person."

The Renaissance philosopher Montaigne quipped that if horses could make images of their gods, their gods would be horses. That barb dug deeply in the side of theologians, but it need not have. Of course horse gods would look like horses and human gods like humans.[64] Just as one must speak French if one wishes to be understood by those who speak only French, so God speaks as a human being to human beings.[65] Of course, the face God turns toward us is not the incomprehensible and ineffable totality of God, but only that countenance that can coax the human species toward its fulfillment. Ezekiel saw God as Human, yet no one can see God and live: here any image is betrayal, and yet we cannot do without images. As Edmond Barbotin puts it, "God is so great and my representation of God so deficient that the latter can only be a lie. To make God visible, accessible to my eyes, is necessarily to deny and annihilate God. In short, God is the one I most desire to contemplate and the one who most stubbornly eludes my gaze."[66] The Glory of God that Ezekiel beheld was merely the mask of God. That was all he could stand, and all that he needed.

In the vision, however, Ezekiel does not experience God as clear and distinct. The Human One on the throne is like a shadowy silhouette engulfed by fire (1:27). The divine mystery of the humanness of God is not, then, fully disclosed to Ezekiel, but rather compounded into the final human mystery. The greatest danger is that the vision's numinosity will degenerate into dogmatic certainty by turning the supercharged *experience* into a religious *idea*. Does this suggest that God is also in process of becoming? That God is, reciprocally, wanting to take on human form, wanting to incarnate in us?[67]

But what if Ezekiel's vision was merely a hallucination? What if God, and all theistic religion, is merely a massive projection of our own selfhood onto the heavens? Is it possible that the humanness Ezekiel saw at the heart of the universe was only a mirror reflecting his own face?

This was the challenge hurled at religion in 1841 by the philosopher Ludwig Feuerbach, a challenge so lethal that most theologians, even to the present, have chosen to ignore it.

3.   Feuerbach's Challenge

euerbach's famous dictum is that humanity empties itself into transcendence.[1] By that he meant that God has no real existence, but is merely the projection of human values and capacities onto an imaginary, supernatural figure. The divine being is nothing else, then, than human beings writ large. Consciousness of God is self-consciousness, and knowledge of God is self-knowledge. All the attributes of the divine nature are, therefore, attributes of human nature. In Van Harvey's terse summary, "What is worshiped as divine is really a synthesis of the human perfections. Theology is anthropology and, therefore, the hidden meaning of Christianity is atheism."[2]

This process of projecting our own nature onto the Godhead is not harmless, Feuerbach argued. For the higher God is exalted, the more human beings are diminished. To enrich God, humans must become poor. That God may be all, humans must be nothing. Believing in God means remaining in an infantile state, preyed on by religion. If God exists, humanity cannot be itself. People desire to be nothing in themselves so that they can worship God as everything. Thus the real world is impoverished, and God is enriched, as humanity empties itself into transcendence.

All the best powers of humanity we lavish on a Being who needs nothing. Thus humanity sacrifices human beings to God. Religion sucks away the best forces of morality and causes people to evacuate their own highest powers and to locate them in God, thus abandoning the use of these powers for themselves. People give up their own personality and imagine God as an almighty, unlimited Person. They condemn egoism in human beings and then worship God as a selfish, egotistical being who seeks in all things only the divine honor, denying to others as vices qualities of egocentricity that they find exemplified in superlative degree in God. The religious task of the modern world is thus, according to Feuerbach, to withdraw the projections on God and to find divinity in ourselves.

Humanity first unconsciously and involuntarily created God in its own image, and afterward claimed that God had created humanity in God's own image. God is what individuals ought to be and will be. Consequently, Feuerbach sought to found a religion of humanity that would worship the human freed from the tyranny of the divine.

In truth, Feuerbach exclaims, human beings are the measure of God.

A. Evaluating Feuerbach

Nineteenth-century theology was unable to refute Feuerbach. The elements of an adequate response to his challenge were not yet on the intellectual horizon. So theologians hunkered down and hung on, as Feuerbach's ideas became the spirit of the age. Most twentieth-century theologians treated Feuerbach as if he had never lived. Of the few that evaluated Feuerbach's challenge was Karl Barth, who ended by calling Feuerbach's work "something quite extraordinarily, almost nauseatingly, trivial."[3]

In fact, Feuerbach was largely right. For all too many people, religion *is* an evacuation of their best qualities and powers into Godhead. People *do* empty themselves into transcendence. Why else did so many churches abandon their ministry of spiritual healing, treating the power to heal as a special dispensation enjoyed only by Jesus and the apostolic era, or mere fables created by the church? Likewise, the doctrine of sin has been misused to convince believers that goodness is only in God, that there is no good, no health, in them.

There are, to be sure, defective elements in Feuerbach's argument. The optimism of the nineteenth century blinded Feuerbach to human evil. Like others of his time, he seems to have believed that humanity would outgrow evil through evolution and education. His statement that human beings are the measure of God is not merely presumptuous, but naive.[4] Barth fulminates: It is the most illusory of all illusions to suppose that the essence of God is this weak, minuscule, yet arrogant human species. There is something laughable in confusing God with these puny creatures, who even in their most intimate relation with God are and remain liars.[5]

In light of Ezekiel's vision, humanity cannot be the measure of all things, much less of God, because we are not yet human. We do not even know what humanness is. God alone can reveal to us the mystery of our being. Feuerbach had it upside down. According to Dietrich Bonhoeffer,

God is not God at the price of emptying me of my humanity; humanity does not consist in letting oneself be sucked dry by a divine vampire! God does not exploit my weakness, but is present precisely in weakness, and gives us strength in our weakness. Authentic Christianity should leave people stronger, not dehumanized.[6]

Hence we may say that *God* is the measure of all things. And God is engaged in an eons-long project of drawing humanity forward toward its true potential and destiny (or pushing us from behind, or prompting us from within). We are part of a self-surpassing system that we scarcely comprehend. We do not know how to transform ourselves. If there is no God, there can be no humanity, for God alone is human.[7]

Indeed, it is God that lures us toward our transformative possibilities. Left to ourselves, we would go on repeating the past. Our given potentiality, like that of the acorn, is always merely to repeat the past, to be and do what we have always been and done before. God presents the "heavenly" possibilities as a challenge to go beyond our conditioning and habits, our collusion in oppression or being oppressed, our inertia, fear, and neuroses. God offers the heavenly possibilities for creative novelty, and we can accept wholly, or accept in part, or reject completely and go on repeating our past.

Again, Feuerbach overshot by seeking to destroy the archetypes of the divine, rather than withdrawing the projections and continuing to relate to them. As Jung insists, the archetypes are not something we make up. They thrust themselves upon us from the unconscious. Feuerbach's excessive rationalism undermined his correct intuition that human beings cannot live without religion. He sought to demystify the bread and wine of the Eucharist by treating them as the wonderful elements of nature that they are, stripped of all numinous and sacramental power. But powerful archetypes never go away; they merely go underground and work on us unconsciously, as Jung has shown. Feuerbach's failure to grasp this point led to the collapse of his attempt to create a religion of humanity, since he had destroyed the sole means by which such a religion might flourish. Indeed, we might say that Feuerbach erred by trying to create a religion for the ego when he was in fact dealing with the ego-transcending Self. Such a religion can only be idolatrous, since the ego is made equivalent to the God within. As Jung sarcastically notes, "Through the negation of God one becomes deified, i.e. god-almighty-like, and then one knows what is good for mankind."[8] In myths, on the contrary, becoming human is always a miracle, an unexpected, graceful intervention.

Finally, Feuerbach considered projection as wholly negative. But projection is one of our best ways to learn about the world, God, and our own unconscious. To Feuerbach we can thus reply: Yes, by all means, let us withdraw the projections. When we do so, however, we do not find ourselves alone in a universe without God, but rather related meaningfully to God in every atom of spirit-matter.

When we withdraw the projection of our own parents onto God, for example, we purify our God-image* from contamination by our earthly parents. But we are not deprived of our image of God as Father/Mother; rather, we are able to let ourselves be parented by God without the fear of dependency, suffocation, or whatever else may have characterized negative experiences of our parents. I was raised in a very liberal church in which hellfire and damnation were never mentioned. But I still lived in dread of my parents' displeasure and heaped myself with guilt for not being better. I can recall the tremendous sense of relief when, as a seminary student, I discovered that the "wrath of God" in Pauline theology was being forced to accept the consequences of my own actions. "God gave them up" in Rom. 1:18-32 meant that God's wrath was impersonal; God did not lose God's temper and threaten us, but simply required us to reap what we sowed. Recognizing that made it possible to remove the parental projections of wrath that I had laid on God, and to decontaminate my God-image to that degree. And it also made it possible, gradually, to reconstitute my relationship with my parents on an adult basis.[9]

In short, Feuerbach was not in error when he asserted that we project aspects of ourselves onto God. He was simply working with an attenuated theory of projection, one that would not be rounded out until the development of depth psychology in the twentieth century.[10] And he was possessed by an idolatrous view of humanity that cut human beings off from the ground of true humanness.[11]

"Be careful how you describe the world," said one physicist. "It *is* that way." In our Heisenbergian universe, in which the objective world already includes the subject, we are already related to what is to be known. Thus it is impossible to say anything about nature that is not also a statement about oneself. This is because, like the atoms of which we are made, each person is coextensive with the universe.[12] We are not like billiard balls bumping against other isolated and hard-bounded entities. Rather, we are concentrations of energy localized in a body whose electromagnetic and heat shields and thoughts radiate out toward the farthest reaches of the universe. Hence, concludes physicist Brian Swimme, a study of the universe is a study of the self.[13] According to the anthropic cosmological principle, it is not just that humanity is adapted to the universe, but that the universe is adapted to the emergence of human consciousness.[14] As Hildegard of Bingen put it, "Now

God has built the human form into the world structure, indeed even the cosmos, just as an artist would use a particular pattern in her work."[15] That is, *we begin not with individuality but relatedness.* We are not individuals but interbeings, and the goal is not individualism but individuation.*

But this is also true of our relationship with God: it is impossible to say anything about God that is not also a statement about oneself. Calvin therefore began his *Institutes of the Christian Religion* with the astonishingly prescient assertion that there is no knowledge of self without knowledge of God and no knowledge of God without knowledge of self.[16] Every statement about God is simultaneously a statement about ourselves. This means that we are projections of God, functions of God, and that God is a function, a projection of us.[17] Consequently, our perceptions of God *are* projections, as Feuerbach thought. But we can become conscious to some degree of our projections, work with them, and learn something new both about ourselves *and* about God. God is in transformation with us. Knowing God is thus no different in kind than knowing anything or anyone else with whom we are in relation.[18]

In our better moments, we may perhaps not only create God in our own image and likeness (which we undoubtedly do), but we may allow ourselves to be created in the image and likeness of the Ultimate in moments of peak insight, mystical visions, sexual or spiritual ecstasy, deep theological reflection, or struggles for social justice.

Rather than emptying ourselves into transcendence, then, we may now discover God at the core of our inmost beings, as the power of Being itself. Whereas many theologians localized the power of spiritual healing in Jesus or God, we may now experience that same healing power working through us. Whereas we once believed that prophecy was dead in the modern world, we may now recognize God speaking an authentic word to us and through us today. Whereas we once regarded the mystics as rare and solitary athletes of the Spirit, we may now acknowledge everyone's capacity to become mystics. Whereas we once waited for God to bring peace to the world, we may now accept the power of God in our depths to make peace through active nonviolence. Instead of imagining God as the capstone on a pyramid of political, military, and economic Powers that maintain the status quo for the benefit of the few, we may now see God empowering the poor and the powerless to take history into their own hands in the struggle for justice.

Are we then, in the final analysis, simply creating God in our own image? Are we deluding ourselves by means of the imagination? We are not deluding ourselves, but it *is* "all our imagination." That is the only way the experience of God happens.[19] "Imagination does not [always] *construct* something unreal, but [sometimes] *unveils* the hidden reality," writes Henry Corbin.[20] "It is not that we personify, but that the epiphanies come as persons," says James Hillman.[21] In his play *Saint Joan*, George Bernard Shaw pens a revealing exchange, which can be epitomized thus:

> JOAN: God speaks to me.
> ROBERT: That's just your imagination.
> JOAN: Of course. That's how God speaks to me.[22]

Or, to put that exchange in more modern terms:

> SKEPTIC: You project your own meanings onto the universe.
> SEEKER: Yes, I know. That's why the universe brought us into being—in order to project meanings onto the universe.

Feuerbach had himself said, "Imagination is the original organ of religion,"[23] but he was unable to grasp the positive meaning of his insight.

The realm of the imagination, or what I prefer to call, following Henry Corbin, the imaginal realm, produces a third kind of knowing, intermediate between the world of ideas, on the one hand, and the object world of sense perception on the other. The imaginal possesses extension and dimension, figures and colors, but lacks full materiality and hence cannot be perceived by the senses. In dreams and visions, for example, we perceive the action *as if* it were staged on the physical plane, but it is not. This intermediate world of images and archetypes can be known only by the "transmutation of inner spiritual states into outer states, into vision-events symbolizing with these inner states."[24] Concrete symbolization, such as temples, rituals, and myths, may help us to *find our interiority outside ourselves*, as Henry Corbin puts it. We may falsely assume that these images are subjective creations of our psyches, or pseudo-objective delusions, like hallucinations. But we do not make all of them up. We imagine them, to be sure, but something real evokes our imagination. We discover our body as "temple" by going to a temple. Yet the temple (or synagogue or church or mosque) remains valuable, due to its continuing, if spotty, power to evoke the numinous over and again.

The imagination is thus the organ that puts one in contact with spiritual realities perceptible to each individual, according to the dominant images of the person's religious and cultural affiliation.[25] The medieval mystic Hananel, commenting on the vision of God in 1 Kings 22:19; Isa. 6:1; and Exod. 24:10, writes:

It is clear to us that the vision spoken of here is a vision of the heart and not a vision of the eye. It is impossible to say that an image of God is seen through a vision of the eye. . . . It is possible to say that one sees through a vision of the heart the image of the glory but not through an actual vision of the eye, for the verse states explicitly, "When I spoke to the prophets and through the prophets I was imaged" (Hosea 12:10).[26]

The vision of the heart is not intellectual but imaginative. "Not only is the imagination not to be seen as subordinate to reason . . . but it is elevated to a position of utmost supremacy; it is, in effect, the divine element of the soul that enables one to gain access to the realm of incorporeality."[27] Because the incorporeal light is figured within the imagination in corporeal forms, the metaphysical problem of anthropomorphism disappears, for the locus of the iconization is in the imagination of the visionary. The social location, culture, and education of the visionary will provide at least some of the symbolic "vocabulary" that makes the archetypal images indigenous to a particular society or subgroup.

Unless the imagination is recognized as autonomous to a high degree, we trivialize the divine encounter. We do not simply create God with our images; rather, our images are precipitated not only from deep within us, but from beyond our personal unconscious. Medieval Jewish mystics called that place "the roots of soul"—a deep, underground world of archetypes that has encoded the experience of the species from the beginning. It is the recovery of the imaginal that makes possible both the reenchantment of nature and the recovery of soul, in ourselves and in things.[28]

B. On Anthropomorphism

Theologians have sometimes tried to evade the implications of Ezekiel's anthropomorphic language about God by arguing that God is ultimately unknowable. Thus, some argue, God can be talked about only in analogical or symbolic terms, "as if" God were human, though obviously God is not. Of course, we cannot know God in God's fullness; our images of God are only fragile approximations, and the divine Godhead vastly transcends our capacity to comprehend it. But that fact underscores how indispensable these approximations are. When we say that God is "like" a loving parent, we are saying that it is consistent with the image of a loving parent, though God's love surpasses anything we have known. To say that God is Human, then, is to say that whatever God is in the abyss of divine mystery, it is consistent with what Ezekiel saw and with what Jesus attempted to live out. We cannot, then, argue that we are speaking only by analogy, or we open the possibility that God is not *really* "like" a loving parent or the fullness of what it means to be Human.[29] The God who is beyond our knowing is not different from the God known by revelation, but only more so. We do not need to get "beyond" anthropomorphisms, because God manifests anthropomorphically; or, if you prefer, we are theomorphic (made in the likeness of God, the Human One). We can relate to God as human beings because God is truly Human.[30]

Anthropomorphism is indissoluble from religion because many primary religious experiences come to us in dreams and visions, and, as Jung has pointed out, the form these experiences take usually involves human beings. When someone declares, "I saw Jesus" or "God" or an "angel," she means that she really did see such a figure, aided by a religious tradition that provided instantaneous meaning to the vision. Without such a tradition, a person might be unable to exploit the potential meaning in the experience.[31]

The attempt to avoid anthropomorphism in reference to God often leads to images drawn from lower forms of complexity, even from inanimate objects. Religions have used animals (theriomorphism), snakes (herpomorphism), mountains (montanamorphism), plants (floramorphism), or trees (dendromorphism) to represent the divine. Yahweh, for example, is described theriomorphically as a lion (Hos. 5:14). All these forms can, within limits, serve as symbols of the Giver of Life. Any creature is capable of being a theophany. Whether a flower in a crannied wall or the nighttime sky, God can be unveiled as Creator in the beauty and terror of nature. My point is that the attempt to *avoid* anthropomorphic images often leads to the substitution of other images that may be less representative of the image of God in which we are created. Unfulfilled and fickle as we are, we are more like God as the Human One than we are like mountains, though we are made of the same basic stuff as mountains. Conversely, God can be said to be more like a person than an oak tree—though, of course, God's creativity can be seen and celebrated in a mountain or an oak, and, in our environmentally threatened world, perhaps seeing God manifested in a mountain or an oak might be particularly appropriate. The point, as Jung saw, is that "we can perceive God in an infinite variety of images, yet all of them are anthropomorphic, otherwise they wouldn't get into our heads."[32]

Israel was forbidden to make any visual image of God for fear that it would worship the creature rather than the Creator.[33] But it never confused that command with the use of anthropomorphic language. There can be no objection to abstract non-anthropomorphic images such as Harmony (an image drawn from wave mechanics), Spirit ("wind," from meteorology), Energy (from thermodynamics), or The Force (from the movie *Star Wars*). I sometimes employ them myself. At times our personal images of God are so contaminated by bad experiences that they are worse than useless. There is always the danger that anthropomorphisms will privilege male imagery, or evoke experiences of abusive parents. But missing in all these non-anthropomorphic images are human qualities: love, compassion, consciousness, intentionality, regard, relationship, purpose: in short, personality. An implication of the Heisenberg principle is that even when we think in nonhuman terms about God, we cannot do so without taking into account the human observer's impact on the field of observation. Thus, even inanimate objects are invested with personality when they are made God-images. The "Rock of Ages" in the old hymn has a "wounded side" from which flows water and blood: it is the crucified Jesus.

Anthropomorphism is inevitable if for no other reason than that human beings in every culture persistently report having heard God speak. They have discovered themselves forgiven. They know themselves loved from the very bosom of the universe (if I may speak anthropomorphically). If God has a voice, forgives, and loves, God must be personal, perhaps even a Person. As the physicist/theologian John Polkinghorne notes, it is less misleading to speak of God as personal than as impersonal, though both ways are inadequate.[34]

Recent brain studies provide confirmation that the brain inevitably interprets the world and God in human terms. According to James Ashbrook and Carol Rausch Albright, the humanized brain is necessarily a humanizing brain; the mind-producing brain compels us to deal with our universe as a humanlike reality. *"The brain necessarily humanizes all of its perceptions,"* so that it cannot help perceiving God that way as well. But this is not simply projection; humanity is oriented to human reality and motivated to make sense of what it observes in human terms.[35]

Physicist Edward Harrison sees it this way: "We cannot doubt the existence of an ultimate reality. It is the universe forever masked. We are a part or an aspect of it, and the masks figured by us are the Universe observing and understanding itself from a human point of view.[36] As historian of science Anne Harrington puts it, we live in a universe that gives birth to humanizing, and the human brain is set up so that we are incorrigibly anthropomorphic in our efforts to make sense of reality. We are wired to recognize faces, to want and seek ordered patterns, emotional connection, and larger personal meaning in the world, and some of us discover a "human face" in our encounter with the cosmos, too.[37] Or, as the anthropic cosmological principle puts it, the universe that astronomers perceive seems to have been designed to produce astronomers to perceive it.[38]

But Ashbrook and Albright press the case for anthropomorphism even farther. Since reality is unavoidably mediated by the lens of the human, "reality itself is *actually* humanlike. Put another way, the human brain-mind and the larger reality share a fundamental likeness. People can only perceive things in a humanlike way—*and* any reality that we perceive must of necessity be humanlike." While it may be true that humans construct not only reality but their images of God, one may contend that such constructs are not inaccurate. "The inner representations of God and reality and their outer referents are intricately related."[39] This correspondence made it possible for Jung to insist—correctly, I believe—that when he speaks of God, he refers to an anthropomorphic archetypal God-image, and does not imagine that he has said anything about a metaphysical "God." This correspondence is also what makes it possible for mystics of widely disparate religions to directly apprehend what Paul Tillich called the Ground of Being, and to tell what is recognizably the same story despite the frailty of human language.

Guild for Psychological Studies therapist John Petroni agrees that while for him, as for me, God must be personal, in his practice he finds that the opposite is true: many experience God as impersonal.

> People have dreams of Light, a circle, a square, or a mandala that have numinous, godlike power. What I find, as I look in dreams for images of the Self, is that animals are very prominent. This often represents the instinctive side of the Self which we find historically in the animal representations of Yahweh, Christ, and the ancient gods. I do not find much in the way of human images of God in modern dreams. Many from the Christian tradition are finding that Christ no longer is a numinous image for them. Whereas once Christ was in the center, they are left with an "empty center" (Jung), which is terrifying.[40]

I believe that there is one surprising place, however, where that image is alive and thriving: in the three-century-old quest for the historical Jesus. As I said earlier, that quest has been unconsciously driven by the desire for personal individuation. And that powerful incentive has been mythologically depicted (all unconsciously!) as the myth of the human Jesus. Perhaps we have been looking for God in the usual places—dreams, fantasies, drama, culture, devotional literature, theology—when, all the time, the numinous energy of a quest for the Holy Grail has been publicly manifest in the prodigious outpouring of studies on Jesus. I cannot prove it, but I believe that more has been written on Jesus than on any subject in human thought. Whole libraries are devoted to that theme. Many scholars have been grasped by the image of Jesus, perhaps without even sensing the sacred dimension of their quest. This book is itself a probe that attempts to discern whether that quest has in fact struck something huge and metallic, something archetypally real that breathes the promise of spiritual revolution.

Karen Armstrong makes this sage comment about anthropomorphism: "The personal God reflects an important religious insight: that no supreme value can be less than human."[41] Obviously, God is not just like us; in Ezekiel's vision, God's human form is clothed in incandescent fire. But, comments the philosopher Martin Buber, human beings cannot approach the divine by reaching beyond the human; they can only approach it by being human. To become human is why individual persons have been created.[42]

God will forever remain a mystery, forever beyond our grasp or comprehension. That, however, is precisely why God condescends to grant visions of God's Human face. When Ezekiel sees the Glory of God, he is seeing not just his own face in a cosmic mirror, but the revelation, or intimation, of the Humanity of God. That is how God coaxes us toward the fullness of our own humanity. Thus the visionary poet William Blake could write:

> God appears & God is Light
> To those poor Souls who dwell in Night,
> But does a Human Form Display
> To those who Dwell in Realms of Day.[43]

C. We Are the Seer and the Seen

The philosopher George Berkeley said, "To be is to be perceived" (*esse es percipi*). (To which Amy-Jill Levine retorts, "To be is also to perceive!") A truth in Ezekiel's vision of the wheels within wheels "full of eyes all around" (1:18) is that we are not the only watchers. We are ourselves, says James Hillman, the subject of others' gazes. We are on display. We are not the judge or the measure of all things, but part of the field being observed. We do not just observe ourselves observing. We are being observed, and by powers and persons that are prepared to commune with us.[44] Thus the eye of God fell upon Hagar, fleeing to the wilderness to escape the cruelty of Sarah (and God, and Abraham). When God blessed her with the promise of a son by Abraham and descendants beyond counting, she named the Lord who spoke to her *Elroi*, "God who sees," and the well where this took place, *Beer-lahai-roi*, "the Well of the Living One who sees me" (Gen. 16:13-14).[45] That which is alive in the universe sees us.

The final answer to Feuerbach, therefore, is prayer. That which we can only imagine, that beyond all imagining, wants to hear from us, so to speak: it wants us to meet its gaze with words, with feeling, with love. Prayer is thus, in Corbin's view, "the supreme act of the Creative Imagination."[46] Only theologians are highly fastidious about the One to whom they pray; most people are a bit confused. Christians pray to God, to Christ, to Jesus, to Mary, to saints. Peoples of other religions pray to their representations of deity. Many Christians are bothered by the idea that prayers might be answered when prayed to the wrong source. But it appears that people all over the globe pray and find it helpful to do so. The universe seems to be, at least some of the time, a richly answering habitat.

The charge that humans create God-images is thus not devastating, though perhaps "co-creates" would be better.[47] Of course we do create such images—and we also create self-images, worldviews, and other perceptual constructs for feeling our way around in the opacity of reality. But, John Petroni reminds me, with the really powerful images—those that deserve to be called archetypal—we do not so much create them as suffer them. They impinge on us without our consent and often without our wanting. Despite our desire to be in control of our lives, these images happen to us, to an extent far beyond our awareness, at the intersection of vast and invisible forces that leave us blighted, bereaved, or blessed, and we often have little say about the outcome.

As is often the case with enemies, Feuerbach, one of the most powerful opponents the church has encountered since the second-century pagan philosopher Celsus, turns out to be a friend of the truth. His profound reflections on religious projection could not bear positive theological fruit for a century and a half. Now his insights can be seen for what they were: a prescient intuition into the dynamics of the God–human relationship. If he was unable to grasp the positive aspects of projection, that is not so much his deficiency as a testimony to how far he was ahead of his contemporaries. Let us then embrace our brother Ludwig Feuerbach, who suffered much at the hands of Christian censors, and whose atheism was the tragic personal cost of a knowledge too far in advance of wisdom: not just his wisdom, but that of a species.

D. From Feuerbach to Berdyayev

In a time of ecological crisis, when we are becoming increasingly aware of the anthropocentrism of Western religions, some readers may be uncomfortable with all this talk of humanity. Am I not limiting God's purview to a narrow concern for happiness and survival? Is the rape of the earth not the consequence, at least in part, of a religious attitude that regarded human beings as God's sole concern?

The problem, paradoxically, is not too much anthropology, but not enough. We have held an attenuated view of the human as only another object in a world of objects, and this is what has caused us to treat the world as an object to be used and consumed. Human beings today can no longer regard themselves or other creatures, or even the earth itself, as objects possessing purely instrumental value. Since we are coextensive with the universe, and can say nothing about God or nature that is not at the same time a statement about ourselves, we must learn to think of ourselves as the universe reflecting upon itself. Every particle of matter in us was produced in the process that led to the creation of the universe. We are cosmic by our nature, children of the universe. The universe has spawned persons because it is itself personal. Human life has begun to emerge because the heart of reality itself is Human. In the words of that seminal thinker Owen Barfield, "[I]n the course of the world's history, something like a Divine Word has been gradually clothing itself with the humanity it first gradually created"—so what was first spoken by God may eventually be respoken by human beings.[48]

Even the most crass materialist believes that in human beings are exceptional resources for knowing the world. Our microcosmic nature enables us to know the macrocosm. We are small universes: this is the basic truth that precedes the possibility of knowing and of science itself.[49]

The forgotten prophet of the anthropic revelation is Nicolas Berdyayev, a philosopher who lived through the Russian Revolution and who was subsequently exiled for his open resistance to the Communist regime. As early as 1914, he predicted that humanity was on the eve of an anthropological revelation.[50] The final *human* mystery, Berdyayev saw, is the birth of God in humanity. But there is a final mystery of *God* as well: the birth of humanity in God. Not only does humanity have need of God, but God has need of humanity.[51] There is a summons, a call in the human self, for God to be born in it. But there is also God's call to the self to be born in God.[52] In God is hidden the mystery of humanity and in humanity the mystery of God. In language drenched with references to divinization and the Christ, Berdyayev nevertheless describes what I have been calling the Human Being. In its religious depths, he says, the anthropological revelation is the revelation of Christ as fully human, as the Absolute Human within us. But the Fully Human was not completely and finally revealed in the appearing of Christ the Redeemer, says Berdyayev. The creative revelation of humanity is a continuing and completing revelation of Christ, the Truly Human Being. The anthropological revelation dawning on us today is at once fully human and fully divine: in it humanity is deepened to the point of divinity and divinity is made visible to the point of humanity.

> God reveals [Godself] as Humanity. Humanity is indeed the chief property of God, not almightiness, not omniscience and the rest, but humanity, freedom, love, sacrifice. . . . God is humane and demands humanity. Humanity is the image of God in [human beings]. . . .[53]

Christianity, Berdyayev felt, has never revealed in its fullness what one might dare call a Christology of humanity, that is, the secret of humanity's divine nature. The task of humanity's religious consciousness is to reveal the christological consciousness of humanity—indeed, of the cosmos. Only the mystics, transcending all times and seasons and religions, have glimpsed the truth of the Christology of humanity. The Christology of humanity, the reverse side of the anthropology of Christ, reveals in humanity the genuine image and likeness of God, the Creator.[54]

Berdyayev expresses a similar eschatological consciousness to that in 1 John 3:2—"We are God's children now; what we will be has not yet been revealed. What we do know is this: when he is revealed, we will be like him, for we will see him as he is." Now we can see that statement for what it is: the anthropic revelation. Our failure to recognize and incarnate the anthropic revelation has dire and predictable consequences.

Several writers have puzzled over the Bible's lack of an anthropology. No anthropology can yet be written, however, because humanity is not yet human. The Bible displays, rather, the failure of anthropology: rebellion against our divine destiny. But Jesus did not carry his cross and suffer crucifixion so that we can escape. We are cornered by the supreme power of the incarnating Will. God wants to become human, *even if God rends humanity asunder.* We are threatened with universal genocide if we do not undergo an inner, spiritual death to that in us that causes our destructiveness.[55]

Karl Barth showed his grasp, in a more cautious but affirmative way, of the anthropic revelation. In his book, audaciously entitled *The Humanity of God*, he writes:

> It is precisely God's *deity* which, rightly understood, includes [God's] humanity. . . . It is when we look at Jesus Christ that we know decisively that God's deity does not exclude but includes [God's] *humanity*. . . . God is *human*. . . . genuine deity includes in itself genuine humanity. . . . [56]

Before turning to Jesus' statements about the son of the man, we need briefly to survey the phrase's other biblical and extracanonical appearances as part of the effort to understand it.

4. Other Biblical and Extrabiblical References to the Human Being up to 100 C.E.

Most of the rest of the son-of-man sayings in the Hebrew Bible simply mean "human being." But there are a few significant canonical and extracanonical sources as well.

A. Psalm 8

> When I look at your heavens, the work of your fingers,
> the moon and the stars that you have established;
> what is man (*'enosh*) that you are mindful of him,
> the son of man (*ben 'adam*) that you care for him?[1]

The "human being" or "mortal" ("son of man") here is paradoxical: at once infinitesimally small, and yet lower only than God. This paradox embraces all that will later be ascribed to the New Testament "son of man": he has nowhere to rest his head, yet he is now seated at the right hand of God. As Bruce Chilton observes, "The psalmist obviously includes himself in the category of human beings for whom God's care comes as a miracle. The psalmist is not talking about himself alone, however, but of people in general."[2] The importance of Chilton's insight will become increasingly clear as we go along.

B. Psalm 80

Israel was a vine that Yahweh brought out of Egypt and planted in Canaan. Why, then, has Yahweh allowed it to be ravaged by the nations?

Turn again, O God of hosts; look down from heaven, and see; have regard for this vine, the stock that your right hand planted. . . . But let your hand be upon the one (*'ish*, "man") at your right hand, the one (*ben adam*, "son of man") whom you made strong for yourself. Then we will never turn back from you. . . . (vv. 14–18)

Who is the "man" here? It might be a king of the line of David, or a messiah who will come in the future, or a prophecy of the coming of Jesus. But most likely it is Israel, the "vine."

We will have occasion more than once to note this oscillation between individual and corporate in the use of the expression "the Human Being."[3]

C. 1 Enoch 14

Several decades, at least, before Daniel, around 185 B.C.E., another vision of the divine throne chariot was recorded, this one in the name of the ancient ancestor Enoch (*OTP* 20–21). Here we find another vision of the divine throne chariot: "And the Great Glory was sitting upon it." The central figure is clearly in the shape of an *anthrōpos*, and despite the author's claim that no mortal can behold the enthroned Glory, that is precisely what Enoch does.[4]

D. Daniel 7

Two decades later, around 167 B.C.E., Antiochus IV Epiphanes, king of Syria, attempted to proscribe the Jewish religion. He was defeated in what proved to be one of the most successful revolts in Jewish history. Under the pressure of that crisis, the author of Daniel 7 presented to the world a new mutation in God-consciousness. It marked the revelation of a new archetype: humanity was seen to be moving into Godhead.[5]

Most of Daniel 1–6 is fanciful and falls under the category of edifying tales. Daniel 7 seems to mark a genuinely revelatory moment in humanity. Daniel 7 signals an archetypal movement in the psyche of the writer and the nation Israel—a movement clearly marked by the account's numinosity and its enduring impact on spirituality. Godhead is here undergoing a transformation toward the emergence of future possibility, rendered symbolically by the drawing of humanity toward the divine and its receiving dominion over the bestial empires.

Consequently, it makes no difference whether Daniel 7 was a real dream or a vision, or how it was composed. Something new was being been born in the period's collective psyche, and it is to that psychic reality that we must attend.

> As I watched, thrones were set in place, and an Ancient One took his throne, his clothing was white as snow, and the hair of his head like pure wool; his throne was fiery flames, and its wheels were burning fire. A stream of fire issued and flowed out from his presence. A thousand thousands served him, and ten thousands times ten thousand stood attending him. . . . (7:9-10)

After the fourth beast (the Seleucid, or Syrian, Empire) is destroyed, and the other nations (the three beasts) are subjugated (7:11-12), another figure appears:

> As I watched in the night visions, I saw one like a human being (*bar enash*, the Aramaic equivalent of the Hebrew *ben adam*) coming with the clouds of heaven. And he came to the Ancient One and was presented before him. To him was given dominion and glory and kingship, that all peoples, nations, and languages should serve him. His dominion is an everlasting dominion that shall not pass away, and his kingship is one that shall never be destroyed. (7:13-14)

Why has the Human One of Ezekiel become the "Ancient of Days"? Some scholars suggest that this vision reflects the motif of the senescent god being violently replaced by a younger god, as in the myth of Baal supplanting El in the Ugaritic texts.[6] Quite apart from the unlikelihood of a Jew borrowing the mythology of the oppressing Seleucid Empire during wartime, Daniel's "one like a human being" is not offered a throne, nor does the Ancient One relinquish sovereignty. Rather, the divine Ruler gives earthly dominion to this humanlike figure. The "Ancient of Days" continues to act in the capacity of divine ruler and executes judgment against Israel's enemies with no assistance from the one in human form (7:22). There is really no precedent for Daniel's vision.[7]

The problem that Daniel 7 poses is the identity of this "one like a human being" (7:13). In the verses that follow, this individual seems to be clearly identified with the people of Israel, or at least a remnant of it: "But the holy ones of the Most High shall receive the kingdom and possess the kingdom forever" (7:18); Antiochus "made war with the holy ones and was prevailing over them" (7:21); "judgment was given for the holy ones . . . the holy ones gained possession of the kingdom" (7:22); Antiochus will "wear out the holy ones of the Most High, and shall attempt to change the sacred seasons and the law; and they shall be given into his power" (7:25); "kingship and dominion . . . shall be given to the people of the holy ones of the Most High" (7:27).

A variety of theories have been proposed about this humanlike figure's identity. Some argue that it is Israel,[8] others Michael, the guardian angel of Israel,[9] others a messiah, and others God (in the Greek translation of the Hebrew Bible, the one like a man comes, not *to* God, but *as* God).[10] Early Christians seeking scriptural confirmation that Jesus was eternally in God's plan saw Jesus prefigured here.[11]

All of these options have a degree of plausibility, and none can be soundly refuted. The debate has been inconclusive for a simple reason: exegetes have been treating a symbol as a sign. All scholars recognize that "one like a human being" (*kebar 'enosh*) in Dan. 7:13 is a simile, not an identification. But many, having noted this in passing, promptly seem to forget it and treat the expression as a title. It is not a title in Daniel, nor is it a name or a role or a person. Since the figure appears in a night vision (that is, a dream), we should treat it as we would the symbolism in any dream: as polyvalent, suggestive, opaque, and finally as nonreducibly strange. Even in a specific context, symbols often remain ambiguous.

Who or what, then, might this figure be? The philosopher Paul Ricoeur cautions that we should resist giving too univocal a meaning to the "one in human likeness"; the very expression seems to want to preserve a "space of hesitation." We must leave a bit of play to allow several concurrent identifications.[12] It is not clear, for example, whether this humanlike figure is a human being given unprecedented authority, or some other kind of being with certain human features.[13] The ambiguity of this figure indicates that the author *did not know* who or what it was. When Daniel comes back to consciousness at the conclusion of the dream, he has to ask for interpretive insight. That perplexity suggests that we are dealing with an actual unconscious process in a real person's mind.[14] At the least we can say that, in a political context where Jews were being forcibly converted to paganism, Daniel is reaffirming his faith that God intends to replace the bestiality of the conquest states with a more humane arrangement: nations will be ruled by human principles and humane leaders rather than by the predatory empires that had so long held sway.

The focus of the new archetypal reality revealed here seems to be the movement of the human toward God. In Ezekiel we saw God manifest as the Human One, and Ezekiel as God's mediator, the offspring of the

Human, the Humanchild. Now in Daniel another great step is taken: God is calling the human (with a little "h," actual, puny, fragile mortals) from the periphery to the center. The writer is careful not to identify with the archetype. The figure is archetypally human—something akin to humanness as such. This explains the confusion over the identity of this figure: its identity is still emerging. This vision declares that something in human beings is still only virtual, only potential. Ezekiel, who first grasped, or rather was grasped by, the revelation of this new spiritual movement in the psyche, had been completely identified with it, so much so that his personal identity was submerged: he essentially ceased to be Ezekiel and was addressed by God only as the Human Being.

We might contrast Ezekiel and Daniel by saying that, in Ezekiel, we see God becoming closer to humanity, seeking incarnation, while in Daniel we see humanity approaching God, seeking transformation. The offspring of this mutual attraction is the Human Being.

As Ezekiel presents it, God, as it were, wants to leave the realm of the purely abstract, archetypal, and divine, and become human in the earthy, mundane sense of the term. The eternal and universally Human One wants to become mortal, to be clothed in time (the "Ancient of *Days*"), to submit to the limitations of existence in order to manifest itself more concretely.[15] The Human wants to actualize within mortal flesh. That divine longing is now matched in Daniel by the human longing to draw nearer to God, to realize the divine likeness of the image of God, to transcend the bestiality of the Domination System, and to discover in the Eternal the capacity for a genuinely humane politics and society. It should be clear that these statements are not historical, but represent the early emergence of the "myth" of human being. Daniel's "one like a human being" is "proto-incarnational,"[16] in Robert D. Rowe's expression, an intimation of the full humanness to come. Christianity developed that myth one way, Judaism another, and Gnosticism still another, as we shall see.

E. Ezekiel the Tragedian

The Exodus by Ezekiel the Tragedian (*OTP* 2:811-12), a play written in the Greek style by a Jew in the first part of the second century B.C.E., depicts God as "a Man (Greek *phōs*) of noble mien, becrowned," seated on a throne so great that it touched the clouds (or corners) of heaven. A wordplay reveals the influence of Ezekiel 1, for *phōs* means "man" while *phôs* means "light" or "glory"; thus, God is the Man of Light.[17] That God is depicted as Human here indicates that this drama is an elaboration of the throne mysticism of Isaiah 6, Ezekiel 1, and Daniel 7. What is tersely indicated in the drama of Ezekiel the Tragedian is exhaustively developed in the Similitudes of Enoch.

F. The Dead Sea Scrolls

"Son of man" appears in the singular three times in 4QPseudo-Ezekiel (4Q385–386), two of them in an approximate rendition of Ezekiel 37, in which the "son of man" is addressed as a prophet by God. The third is striking in that God addresses a *contemporary* prophet as "son of man," indicating that the spirit of prophecy was not dead, and that at least this prophet continued to speak (or, more accurately, to be addressed by God) using that same expression from Ezekiel. The three uses take place in the context of a vision of the divine throne chariot. Elsewhere in the Scrolls, "one born of woman" is used in place of "son of man."

"Sons of man" appears a score of times or more, almost always with the plain meaning "people." In one passage, however, it is said that God will call out from among the "sons of man," a "community of the gods like a holy congregation in the position of eternal life and in the lot of his holy ones." This use of the term echoes "the holy ones of the Most High" of Dan. 7:18 and continues the collective or corporate dimension of the Human Being, except that here the community is virtually deified.[18]

G. The Similitudes of Enoch (1 Enoch 37–71)

Somewhere between 50 and 100 C.E., a book of "parables" or "similitudes" appeared in Israel, ascribed to Enoch (*1 Enoch* 37–71; *OTP* 1:29-50). R. H. Charles placed the Similitudes as early as 105–61 B.C.E.[19] But at Qumran, the eleven different copies of *1 Enoch* included every chapter except those of the Similitudes. The absence of any trace of the Similitudes at Qumran led J. T. Milik to propose a date after 70 C.E. and perhaps as late as 270 C.E.[20] Virtually no one accepts the later date. The Society for New Testament Studies Pseudepigrapha Seminar that met in 1977 and 1978 reached a consensus that the Similitudes date from the first century C.E.[21] The later New Testament books seem to reflect not only knowledge of Enoch, but actual dependency, especially by Matthew, Jude, and Revelation.[22] None of the early epistles reflects the Similitudes, and Mark has only one possible parallel.[23] All of the parallels to the Similitudes in the Gospels appear to be additions by the evangelists. None of the parallels, early or late, seems to be the work of later scribes assimilating the Similitudes to Christian writings. If there is textual influence, it seems to be from the Similitudes to the New Testament, not the other way around. There is no trace of Christianizing in the Similitudes. In chapter 71, Enoch is identified as the son of man, an identification no Christian would ever make.[24] So a date is needed for the publication of the Similitudes that explains its absence in the earlier strata of the New Testament and its presence in the later writings. Any time from 50–100 would be adequate. The Similitudes were thus unknown to Jesus, but familiar to at least some Christian writers in the second half of the first century.

"Son of man" appears in the Similitudes sixteen times, and is represented by three different expressions (an asterisk indicates that the term appears with a demonstrative pronoun ["*that* son of man"]):

> *walda sab'e* — 46:2(B* and C), 3*, 4*; 48:2*; 60:10. Literally, "son of people"; it is more abstract ("humanity") and universal ("human beings") than the other terms.
>
> *walda be'esi* — 62:5*; 69:29*, 29*; 71:14. A male person.
>
> *walda 'eg^wula 'emmaheyyāw* — 62:7, 9*, 14*; 63:11*; 69:27*; 70:1*; 71:17*. Literally, "son of the offspring of the Mother of the Living" or "son of Eve's offspring"; it is more individual, particular, and specific.[25]

The Human Being in the Similitudes has developed further from its origins in the Psalms, Ezekiel, and Daniel. Here it has become a heavenly human being endowed with key attributes of God. It is born of the mother of human beings, but is a prototype (or parable) of the Ancient of Days (46:2). Yet the description of God and the Human Being continues to be inspired by Ezekiel and Daniel: "I saw the One to whom belongs the time before time. And his head was white like wool [Dan. 7:9], and there was with him another individual, whose face was like the appearance of a human being [Dan. 7:13]." The attributes of this one-in-human-form have become those of a heavenly being of unsurpassable greatness. He is an exemplar of righteousness, a revealer of heavenly secrets, and a conqueror of the enemies of God. He will remove kings from their comfortable seats and the wealthy and oppressive from their positions of power (46:3-8). All the earth is to fall and worship before him (48:5). He is the preexistent (or at least foreordained) Chosen One, the revealer of God (48:6-7), the Messiah (48:10), the Righteous One (38:2), the Elect One (frequently.) He will sit on the throne of the Lord of the Spirits.

Even this partial listing demonstrates that the "son of man" in the Similitudes is a human figure of power and authority such as no one had before conceived. This Human Being is scarcely distinguishable from God. In its first occurrence in the Similitudes, "the son of man" echoes Ezekiel and Daniel with their "in human form." Subsequent uses of the expression employ the demonstrative (*"that* son of man") as shorthand for *"the person like a human being whom I mentioned above."*[26] The translator has used three different Ethiopic expressions to render "son of man," evidence that the phrase was not a recognized, traditional, or fixed title.[27] Rather, "that son of man" is an archetype of emergent humanity, building further on its archetypal sense in Ezekiel and Daniel.

The Similitudes continue God's voluntary abdication of power and authority to human beings. It is not self-evident that the role of judge and savior should be given to an exalted human being. Final judgment was not only a prerogative of God, but part of God's self-definition and identity. Judgment was something God could do impartially and adequately. Why then is God, as it were, pushing off this responsibility on humans? Why (for it is necessary to say it both ways) are humans usurping the sole prerogative of God?

What revolution is going on in the God concept, that human beings are being given greater and greater authority and responsibility, not simply on earth, but in the spiritual realm as well?

If the Similitudes were written in apocalyptic Jewish circles at about the same time as the birth of Christianity, it becomes apparent that similar archetypal motifs throughout the culture were edging toward collective consciousness. Like the stifling humidity that precedes a thunderstorm, the air was charged with phantoms of the imagination, longings given visionary form, deep images that could no longer be contained bubbling up from the unconscious. Something new was constellating, some unprecedented God-hunger was manifesting. There was a desire to make good on the ancient prophecies of God's Spirit in the human heart. The Spirit would be poured out on all flesh (Joel 2.28). A coming deliverer and revealer and redeemer would make right all that was wrong, personally and politically, in Israel and the entire world. That these longings were manifested simultaneously in a variety of Jewish enclaves indicates that more was afoot than merely the idiosyncratic beliefs of marginal cults. The same longing is evident in Virgil's *Fourth Ecologue*, with its messianic, even utopian proclamation of the "good news" of Augustus's birth as the savior of Rome and the bringer of peace to the world: "Now is come the last age . . . the great line of the centuries begins anew. Now the Virgin returns . . . now a new generation descends from heaven on high . . . smiles on the birth of the child, under whom the iron brood shall first cease, and a golden race spring up throughout the world. Thine own Apollo now is king!"[28] Indeed, the divinization of the Roman emperors was itself one of the most significant examples in that period of human figures being elevated to divinity.

Something was about to happen to humanity *as a species*. A new mutation was seeking to emerge. The womb of the world was pregnant with God waiting to be born in a human, as a human, as human.

Humanity had until then not developed a sense of species, unlike all other species, and it has not done so yet. The Sufis speak of the Holy Spirit as the angel of humanity, coaxing humanity toward some kind of corporate integrity. They too are aware of a deficit in humanity that could allow us to turn on each other with ferocious violence. Emerging at the turn of the eons was the realization that the human species had an inadequate sense of itself *as a species*.[29] Hence the incomparable savagery of human beings toward others of their species. The occasional intraspecies violence of a few animal groups is nothing compared to the pogroms, lynchings, mob scenes, wars, revolutions, vigilante actions, persecutions, "ethnic cleansings," and genocides perpetrated by human beings on each other. It is unmistakably clear that human beings must develop a communal sense that incorporates all members of the species. Humanity is not yet humane. We are not talking about some far-off utopia, when sin and evil will be no more and the lion will lie down with the lamb. We are dealing with the need for practical nonviolent solutions to the conflicts that plague humanity here, now, in our time.

The Similitudes of Enoch constitute an independent witness to the massive yearning in the depths of that age for the transformation of human beings into genuine humanness: to become more like God, the Human One. From the side of God, that same ferment indicates God's longing to incarnate, to rectify the injustices in human affairs, to bring to human consciousness the transcendent possibilities that people squander on lesser goals and delights. The Similitudes are a testimony to that hunger become ravenous.

But in the Similitudes the "Human Being" is still heavenly, virtual, potential. It is not incarnate in a person or community. It thus remains totally in the future, unattainable in current life under the Domination System that it so vigorously deplores. The Similitudes, thus, are apocalyptic in the passive sense. There is nothing for the saints on earth to do now, no program of liberation, no responsibility to be assumed, no countereffort of opposition, no intercession against the Powers. History is abandoned. There is no salvation within history, only beyond it. Everything remains purely mythic, and while apocalyptic myths can provide catharsis, they seldom challenge people to action. Missing is the ego of actual human beings, placing questions, demanding decision, calling people to transform their lives and their world. The valid urgency of the apocalyptic situation remains projected outside history, and the Powers get off unscathed.

The Similitudes of Enoch could never have been written by anyone affected by the life of Jesus, with his message of the inbreaking of God's domination-free order into a world organized for oppression. This is the tragic irony: that the Similitudes of Enoch, which might have represented a transition toward the full incarnation of God in human beings, was instead to provide the later books of the New Testament (Matthew, Revelation, and Jude) with resources by means of which the message of Jesus was apocalypticized and its sociopolitical impact compromised.

H. 4 Ezra

Brief mention should be made of *4 Ezra* (*OTP* 551–53). Written around the end of the first century C.E., this apocalypse features a messianic figure described as "something like the figure of a man," "the man," and "the same man." Three times he is also identified as "my [God's] son." The first description clearly evokes Dan. 7:13's "one like a human being," as does his flying "with the clouds of heaven." "The man" here is equivalent to Paul's translation of "son of man" with *anthrōpos*. The description of the man appearing in a night vision and emerging from a stormy sea suggests the revelation of an unconscious content — one more instance of the inbreaking of an archetypal image of the *anthrōpos*.

I. Odes of Solomon

An additional son-of-the-man saying is almost never mentioned, from a Christian source almost unknown to Christians: the *Odes of Solomon*. This is a collection from around 100 C.E. of quite orthodox but extremely sensual hymns, which may account for their neglect or even suppression.[30] It was rediscovered by Rendall Harris in 1909, but largely ignored ever since. The reference to the son of the man is in Ode 36:3, 5:

> (The Spirit) brought me forth before the Lord's face,
> and because I was the son of the man,
> I was named the Light, the Son of God. . . .

> For according to the greatness of the Most High, so she made me,
> and according to his newness he renewed me."

Spirit/Sophia continues:

> I fashioned their members,
> and my own breasts I prepared for them,
> that they might drink my holy milk and live by it. . . .
> For my work are they. (8:14, 16)[31]

But whose breasts?

> And I was carried like a child by its mother,
> and he gave me milk, the dew of the Lord. (35:5)

No, that is not a mistake; the Father has breasts and nurses his children.

> The Son is the cup,
> and the Father is he who was milked;
> and the Holy Spirit is she who milked him;
> Because his breasts were full,
> and it was undesirable that his milk should be released without purpose.
> The Holy Spirit opened her bosom, and mixed the milk of the two breasts
> of the Father. (19:2-4)

No doubt the confusion is caused by the author's androgynous image of the Godhead, which leads to an interesting trinity of Father, Mother, and Child. But that is not all.

> As the eyes of a son upon his father,
> so are my eyes, O lord, at all times toward you.
> Because my breasts and my pleasure are with you. (14:1-2)

> For the Most High circumcised me by his Holy Spirit,
> then he uncovered my inward being toward him,
> and filled me with his love. (11:2)

In fact, the whole of the *Odes* stands under the ensign of love:

> I love the Beloved and I myself love him,
> and where his rest is, there also am I. (3:3)

These ecstatic love hymns are legitimate descendants of the Song of Solomon. I find myself wishing that Christian theology had moved more in this direction and less in that of an all-male Trinity, a dark and abusive blood-atonement theory, and an at times doctrinal and moralistic rigidity.

J. Conclusion

Apart from Ezekiel and Daniel, "son of man" is used in the Hebrew Bible almost exclusively in synonymous parallelism, meaning simply "mortal human being." In the pseudepigraphical Similitudes of Enoch, it has taken on a numinosity and exaltation that gives it a unique meaning. *First Enoch* 60:10 shows that the precise usage of Ezekiel continued, but rarely; instead of mere human mortality, "son of man" now indicates special divine election. So while the expression in the Similitudes of Enoch is not a title in the usual christological sense, and while we cannot speak of a "son-of-man expectation" existing anywhere in the first century, far more is riding on the term than simply "human being." The phrase had virtually ceased to possess its original idiomatic equivalence to "human being," and had taken on the grandeur and destiny implicit first in Ezekiel and then in Daniel (though Psalms 8 and 80 had prepared the way). So while it is not quite accurate to say that the Similitudes of Enoch do not witness to a "son-of-man concept" in Judaism, there was recognition that the phrase now denoted a human being that stood in a special relationship with God as the mediator between God and Israel. There is no pre-Christian expectation of a distinct figure bearing the title "son of man." But there was at least the sense that this figure possessed the prophetic authority that God bestowed on Ezekiel and the "one like a human being" of Daniel, and that this figure would play a role in the restoration of Israel's independence.

In Daniel, this figure also has mythological qualities. The phrase no longer denoted simply God's prophet, as in Ezekiel, but is a human being exalted to heaven, to the presence of God. The figure is thus endowed with numinous power. Frederick Houk Borsch is one of the few to have recognized that "there may be something almost archetypal about the basic conceptions involved" in the son-of-the-man figure.[32] The phrase no longer designates a mere mortal, but a heavenly humanlike figure receiving almost infinite political power. In the Similitudes of Enoch, this apotheosis of the human reaches its apex when the human Enoch is upgraded to the angel Metatron.

Once Daniel and the Similitudes of Enoch had thus exalted the Human Being, it would be difficult to use the expression in the old, mundane way. That Jesus favored the mundane use is remarkable and speaks against his having been influenced by the Similitudes of Enoch. Nor is it likely that the mundane son-of-the-man sayings were creations of the early church. The church was preoccupied precisely to stress Jesus' exaltation.

When Jesus appeared on the scene, the collective unconscious of the age was fully prepared. His life tapped into the massive psychic upheaval that was affecting numerous groups, not only in Judaism, but in the Mediterranean world generally. Something seismic was about to happen, and Jesus stood at the epicenter.

Part Three

The Human Being: Pre-Easter Sayings

W
e now turn to the son-of-the-man sayings in the Gospels. In the analysis that follows, I use historical-critical tools where they apply, as discussed in chapter 1. But by far the greater emphasis lies in trying to understand what Jesus (or his successors) meant by this mysterious expression. The primary task, then, is creative interpretation. I want to know what these sayings might contribute to the myth of the human Jesus. But because that myth is historical in its orientation, it is necessary to create at least a plausible picture of Jesus that is backed by warrants in the texts. The myth of the human Jesus—that is, the myth of the son of the man, the Human Being—offers us a means to create a new Christology "from below." In some cases I have gone to some lengths to reinterpret texts that I believe have received rough treatment at the hands of scholars. I have made the case for the authenticity of some of the son-of-the-man sayings, even though I place truth above historicity. I see truth and historicity as complementary. Even if the church created all the son-of-the-man sayings, these sayings would still represent the church's earliest Christology. In short, the myth of the human Jesus requires that we decide whether Jesus' sayings about the son of the man are true, whether he said them or not.

Perhaps it would be helpful to divide the son-of-the-man sayings into categories. A long tradition of scholarship distinguishes the Human Being sayings in the Gospels into three groups: sayings about the son of the man as a present reality, sayings about its suffering, and eschatological (futuristic) sayings about its coming again. Norman Perrin further divided the last category into two: the ascension to the right hand of God, and the return of the son of the man at the end of time.[1] These four categories are purely arbitrary and "modern." The so-called present Human Being is bound to suffer; the two cannot be separated, for the Powers That Be cannot tolerate authentic human beings who will inevitably challenge their power (and an authentic human being can be expected to challenge the Powers). Likewise, the "present" Human Being is eschatological to the core; the inauguration of the new humanity is revealed in the ministry of Jesus, and that new humanity is the future of the species. Jesus' present *is* the human future. The "coming" of the Human Being in the future will be the culmination of the Human Being revealed by Jesus, exalted to sublimity by Jesus' ascension into the realm of what physicists are calling nonlocal reality—or, if you prefer, the realm of the archetypes, or the imaginal plane, or what John's Gospel simply calls "eternal life."

I suggest a different, equally arbitrary set of categories that can be most easily grasped by means of diagram 1. The large, overarching umbrella is the son-of-the-man motif in the Gospels. Following Marcus Borg's distinction between pre-Easter and post-Easter sayings of Jesus, we can call the secondary umbrella on the left the pre-Easter son-of-the-man material: the earthly, human, living, suffering, dying son of the man. The secondary umbrella on the right is the post-Easter son-of-the-man material. It is subdivided into two umbrellas, smaller yet. The one on the left represents the movement of Jesus as Human Being into the archetypal realm, into Godhead. I have labeled it "Ascension," though it also includes an eschatological element: an open future with God. The mythic movement here is "up." Its paired opposite, the small umbrella on the right, is "apocalyptic" son-of-the-man material. It concentrates on the "Second Coming" of Jesus at the end of time. The mythic movement here is "down." Here I follow Perrin by accepting his distinction between Jesus' ascension and his return. No tight division is possible between pre- and post-Easter sayings. Some of the "pre-Easter" sayings seem to have been added by the church. Some of the "ascension" sayings may go back to Jesus' thoughts on his own personal myth and the cosmic future, as he created the story of his life in fidelity to the urgings of God. Luke 12:8-9 might be an example. Both pre- and post-Easter sayings about the son of the man contain reflections on traditions as early as Psalm 8, Ezekiel, and Daniel, which were themselves already archetypally rich.

We turn, then, to the pre-Easter son-of-the-man sayings.

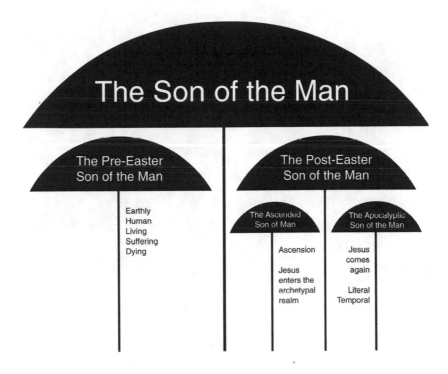

DIAGRAM 1: Categories of the Human Being

5. Jesus and the Human Being

number of scholars early in the twentieth century were convinced that the biblical "son of man" was an offshoot of Iranian mythology about an "Ur-mensch," or Primal Man.[1] Subsequent research has exposed the synthetic nature of this "myth," which never existed in the form proposed. Despite the absence of such a hypothetical myth in pre-Christian sources, however, there is something irreducibly mythic about this enigmatic "son of man." It glows with a halo of overdetermined meaning. It possesses singular numinosity, but has no story. There is no drama of creation, redemption, or the founding of a people; there is no narrative, no pattern. We seem to have a mythic figure without a myth. It was the seminal contribution of Elizabeth Boyden Howes to develop the insight that the "son of the man" was not a title, nickname, circumlocution, or myth, but an *archetypal image*. As such, she saw, the image functions as a symbol of wholeness, less august and almighty than the Messiah or Christ, more mundane and daily than the heroes of myth. She saw the image more as a catalytic agent of transformation in the service of the Self than as a symbol of the Self as such.[2]

We turn first, then, to an examination of the son-of-the-man saying in the story of the plucking of grain on the sabbath.

A. Plucking Grain on the Sabbath: Mark 2:23-28 // Matt. 12:1-8 // Luke 6:1-5

[23]One sabbath he was going through the grainfields; and as they made their way his disciples began to pluck heads of grain. [24]The Pharisees said to him, "Look, why are they doing what is not lawful on the sabbath?" [25]And he said to them, "Have you never read what David did when he and his companions

were hungry and in need of food? [26]He entered the house of God, when Abiathar was high priest, and ate the bread of the Presence, which it is not lawful for any but the priests to eat, and he gave some to his companions." [27]Then he said to them, "The sabbath was made for humankind, and not humankind for the sabbath; [28]so the son of the man is lord even of the sabbath." (Mark 2:23-28)

This passage has been regarded as inauthentic by a number of scholars. Their reasons include the fact that not Jesus' behavior, but that of his disciples, is being criticized, suggesting a setting in the early church in its controversy with Judaism over the law; the example of David depends on David's violating the law, whereas Jesus has done nothing; David did not act on a sabbath; David took the initiative on his followers' behalf, whereas Jesus' disciples act on their own; no reason is given for the Pharisees' presence in a field on a sabbath; in v. 28 one's relationship to Jesus determines one's right to break the sabbath, rather than one's special needs; "and he said to them" in v. 27 is usually the mark of a suture between independent traditions.[3]

Each of these objections has counterobjections. A teacher going to bat for his disciples is scarcely unusual in any age, but especially in a movement as controversial as Jesus'. David had to have acted on a sabbath, since the sabbath was the only day that Ahimelech (Mark erroneously reads "Abiathar") would have had only the shewbread available for feeding David and his companions. The appeal to David's example, while not exact, was nevertheless a real parallel, in that regulations meant to safeguard something holy (the shewbread) were set aside for David and his men, just as regulations meant to safeguard something holy (the sabbath) are now set aside for Jesus and those with him.[4] Pharisees would not have had to walk out to the fields since the fields ran right up to the houses in Galilean villages; fields commonly had public pathways running through them (*m. B. Bat.* 6:7), and one could avoid violating the sabbath rule against traveling more than two thousand cubits between villages by taking shortcuts through the fields (*m. 'Erub.* 4:7; *m. Sotah* 5:3).[5] Hellenistic Jewish and Gentile Christians seem to have left the issue of sabbath observance behind quite early (it is not an issue in the Pauline correspondence or in the rules set down for Gentiles in Acts 15:29). Besides, the text assumes the validity of the sabbath; had the church created the narrative, they would more likely have made it a contest between the Jewish sabbath and the Christian "Lord's day," or Sunday. The earliest Christians kept the sabbath; any controversy would be over the proper interpretation of the law. Later Christians did not keep the sabbath at all.[6] And as for the phrase "then he said to them," this might simply be a rhetorical device to heighten the solemnity of the saying that follows; Luke retains it even though he drops Mark's v. 27. The objection that v. 27 refers to humanity in general, while v. 28 deals just with the authority of Jesus, presupposes the identification of Jesus with the son of the man, and that is precisely what I am contesting here.

If v. 27 refers to human beings in general ("the sabbath was made for humankind, and not humankind for the sabbath"), then, says Oscar Cullmann, we would expect v. 28 also to say that humanity in general (here, "son of Adam" might fit) is lord of the sabbath, since the sabbath was made for the sake of human beings.[7] That construction would then feature synonymous parallelism between the terms "human" and "child of the human" as we find it in the Hebrew Scriptures, especially the Psalms. Reverse synonymous parallelism is what we have, once we abandon the notion that "the son of the man" here is a christological title.

The disciples, whom Mark often portrays as dunces, are depicted here as having grasped the authority that Jesus had engendered in them, or, rather, that he had helped them discover in themselves. They had made no provision for meals on the sabbath, though they obviously knew it was coming. But being part of Jesus' peripatetic retinue made such preparations difficult, if not impossible. Jesus is shown backing up their actions by a statement giving them even more magisterial authority.[8] Even if we conclude that the followers of Jesus fabricated this story, the result is the same: unauthorized disciples of Jesus discover the power latent within them to become "lords of the sabbath."

Elsewhere, the disciples are shown assuming the same authority as Jesus. As the Human Being, Jesus places himself above the practice of fasting (Matt. 11:18), and his disciples claim the same authority for themselves (Mark 2:18-20). The Human Being is not alone in having left home to preach the kingdom (Luke 9:58); his disciples have done so too (Mark 10:28). The Human Being is persecuted (Mark 9:31); so are the disciples (Matt. 10:19).[9] That some of this information reflects later church practice is undeniable. But I can only regard the sheer sovereignty exercised by these untutored peasants as a consequence of the creative impulse of Jesus, whether all of these sayings go back to Jesus or not.

Furthermore, Jesus is not making claims about himself in this narrative. In appealing to the behavior of David, Jesus does *not* make an argument from the lesser to the greater: if David could take the law into his own hands, how much more *the Son of David?* Instead, the focus shifts to the son of the man (compare Mark 8:29, 31). Not David's status, but only David's need and the need of his companions is appealed to. The assertion that the sabbath was made for humankind, not humankind for the sabbath, seems to place human need over divine law. A statement like this could lead to endless mischief; no wonder both Matthew and Luke, and some manuscripts of Mark, omit it![10] Not only that, but a son of the man can even violate the tradition's understanding of the role of the son of the man: "Happy is the man (*'enosh*) who does this [maintains justice], the son of man (*ben 'adam*) who holds it fast, *who keeps the sabbath, not profaning it*" (Isa. 56:2). Yet this Galilean "son of the man" and his followers have no scruples about interpreting the sabbath according to need, since they are "lords of the sabbath." Jesus might seem to be saying that humanity is the measure of all things. If so, it would take little to refute him. Humanity is alienated from the cosmos, a wolf at the throat of its neighbors, a rebel against God and the requirements of the ecosystem, and a threat to every living species. Humanity can least of all be the measure of all things! It is not humanity as such, but the Human Being that is the lord even of the sabbath.

What constituted a sabbath violation was the focus of ongoing debate in Judaism. Many liberal rabbis would have agreed with Jesus that human need takes precedence over sabbath observance.[11] The only question, then, would have been whether the disciples' need was serious or trivial. Jesus is not condemning the law here, or abrogating it, or declaring himself and his followers above the law and beyond good and evil. The passage assumes that keeping the sabbath is normative. The question is not whether to keep the sabbath, but when and how.

Jesus presses behind the issue of obedience and examines the origin of the sabbath itself. Why did the first Hebrews celebrate the sabbath? Was it in order to fulfill a commandment, or to give former slaves, who had never known rest, a day of rest each week (Exod. 5:12-15)? In the later creation story of Genesis 1, even God enjoys a day of rest; sabbath is part of the rhythm of the cosmos. Therefore it is not an onerous obligation but a blessed gift, one that Judaism has now given to the world. Jesus honors its purpose, but reminds his hearers that the sabbath was itself created to serve the needs of human beings, not human beings to serve the sabbath.

Jesus drives to an apprehension of what it means to keep the sabbath, within and out. To operate out of consciousness of the Human Being, which by definition indicates that *more* than personal need is involved, is to function out of the heart of the sabbath. If only need is involved, one breaks the law without understanding the depth of the sabbath.[12] If this is the most sacred of all Jewish institutions (since the sabbath alone was created on the seventh day), then one can say, "Institutions have been created to serve human beings, not human beings to serve institutions."[13]

A Jewish saying from a later period states, "The sabbath is delivered to you, and you are not delivered to the sabbath."[14] But I suspect that few rabbis would have considered the plucking episode to be an occasion serious enough to warrant sabbath suspension. If everyone began to behave this way, it would not be long before the sabbath was ignored in all but name — as has happened in our own time. Why then does Jesus defend the disciples' behavior?

On this occasion, they have placed the urgency of proclaiming Jesus' gospel to all Israel above the preparations for the sabbath, and so they do what the very poor are allowed to do: to pluck and eat standing grain by hand, but not to gather it in their pockets (Deut. 23:25; b. Meṣiʻa 87b). Technically, they were reaping, an activity prohibited on the sabbath. But the disciples judged, with the freedom in which they had been established before God by Jesus, that the infraction was too trivial to count.

But was it? Numbers 15:32-36 recounts an episode during the Exodus when a man who was gathering sticks on the sabbath was stoned to death, showing how seriously Israelites regarded such infractions.

How then does one prevent this freedom from turning into antinomian license? The world has witnessed to the breaking point the narcissistic insistence that the individual's needs transcend all other considerations in the universe. Once need has been elevated above law, law is subject to infinite qualification, until anarchy prevails. What does it mean, then, that the Human Being is lord even of the sabbath?

The sabbath was indeed made for everyone, but not everyone knows how to keep the sabbath. The Human Being knows, because the Human Being in us can know what God wants. Laws structure freedom. If we are serving that which the law serves, then we have freedom of choice, even if it means breaking the law (or, as here, interpreting for oneself what constitutes violation of the law). But if we are not serving that which the law serves, then we are obligated to obey the law. Law deals with the unredeemed aspect of persons, and insofar as we are all unredeemed, to that degree we are and must remain under law. So this freedom is the opposite of lawlessness (Howes).

One very valuable Greek manuscript of the New Testament, Codex Bezae (D), has a surprising reading after Luke 6:4, just before the statement about the Human Being being lord of the sabbath: "On the same day he saw someone working on the Sabbath and said to him: ʻanthrōpe (Human Being), if you know what you are doing, you are blessed; but if you do not know, you are cursed and a transgressor of the law.'"

This comment is remarkable for its positive evaluation of work. The Greeks despised manual labor and handed it over to slaves; those who entered the study of philosophy were required to give up work. In the Bezae saying, work is not only *not* inconsistent with the sabbath, but can even be considered to merit divine blessing.[15] Ernst Bammel notes the uncharacteristic assumption that an unlettered peasant might be able to know the will of God in a concrete situation, or that she might be capable of interpreting the law for herself. Equally striking is that Jesus is not shown formulating his own opinion. He neither denounces the law nor imposes a new rule. No direct information is given about the position Jesus himself takes, nor is advice given to his hearers. "It is exactly the point where the historic Jesus stood which is brought out in the saying. The Law is not declared null and void, but freedom and independence are required and demanded for those who have an inkling of God—the very independence that led to Jesus' downfall and condemnation."[16] This apocryphal saying in Codex Bezae implicitly critiques all human institutions, calling them back to their created purposes, and it continues the creative impulse of Jesus by freeing people to become human. I regard the Codex Bezae story as true whether Jesus said it not.

Jesus does not call on his disciples to let conscience be their guide, because their consciences had long since taken on the conventional values of society. In most cases, conscience is nothing else than the cultural superego. (One thinks of Huckleberry Finn grappling with his conscience over whether to turn in the runaway slave Jim. All the data in his conscience represented the internalized values of Southern slaveholding, so that his decision to save Jim is made in violation of everything that his conscience has been taught is right.[17] But that must mean that there is a transcendent dimension to conscience that is not socialized, but that represents the ineradicable image of God in us. Huck responded out of that higher impulse.) The Human Being is not the offspring of the Domination System, or of this old and fading order. It is something of God within us, "that aspect of the Self which has about it the moral quality of being able to function through the ego in concrete everyday decisions" (Howes).[18] The Human Being seems to be encoded with the specificity of the *imago Dei* in each person, in a non-standardized form capable of infinite variation within fixed patterning. "To be oneself means to realize God's idea of one's self."[19] The religious task of the ego is to encourage the growth and nurturance of this inner element of discernment. Jesus responded to what God was doing in the outer reality, but he was able to do so only because he was responding out of something deep inside himself as well.[20]

We need sabbaths in order to foster the Human Being within. If we are not in touch with the Human Being, then nothing is lord of the sabbath, and we lose relatedness to the sabbath as a healing interval in our lives and communities. Perhaps the Human Being is most especially lord of the *sabbath—*

of the centering, renewing spaces in which our lives get restored and related again to the Source. The man who is plowing, *if he knows what he is doing,* is not an anarchist violating the law; he may in fact be *keeping* the sabbath.

To place so much premium on consciousness is terrifying. Are we to weigh every decision in the light of the Human Being? Might Jesus have also said (or might we): "On the same day he saw someone *keeping* the sabbath, and said to him: Man, if you know what you are doing, you are blessed, but if you do not know, you are cursed and a transgressor of the law"?

What then can we say about the Human Being in the plucking story? The son of the man cannot simply be a name for Jesus, for it is not Jesus but his disciples who show themselves to be "lords of the sabbath." Thus, the son of the man here cannot represent "I" or "this fellow" either. It could mean "I and anyone else like me," but that leaves us without any idea of the expression's *content.* The Human Being here exhibits a breathtaking authority, an authority fearlessly assumed by a common artisan and by his motley band of disciples. The scandal, says José Cárdenas Pallares, is that Jesus places the whole of the law in the service of a few poor people, subordinating the law to the welfare of any human being who is hungry and in need. "For Jesus nothing, not even the most sacred law, may be allowed to obstruct the liberation of the human being." After all, the law of Moses was originally intended for the benefit of an oppressed slave people.[21]

The sabbath was the most revered practice in Israel. It had more weight than all the other commandments of the law combined.[22] If the Human Being is lord even of the sabbath, then it is in principle lord of every law touching the lives of humanity. It knows not only what we need, but the fullness toward which God is drawing us.

Elizabeth Howes comments:

> [T]he term "Son of man" is related to but is not the same as the archetype of the Self. . . . It was used by Jesus to describe the main image which dominated his life and which can be found by others, as it describes in a rather rare way the Self as it operated through him. The "Son of man" phrase describes the Self *at work in concrete life,* a Self lived existentially, not as a hope or a vision; but it is not the same as the Self. We have thus a picture of God coming into humanity lived as the Son of man by Jesus.[23]

Thus Jesus could speak of himself as the Human Being, but also of anyone else (the peasant plowman, for example, or Jesus' grain-plucking disciples) who could respond out of the higher self, even if it violated current morality. Such sovereign freedom, placed in the hands of the underclasses, inevitably strikes terror in the hearts of those entrusted with the tranquillity of society. The dramatic location of the initiation of the death plot against Jesus, only a few verses after the story of the plucking of the grain in Mark (3:6), may or may not be chronologically exact, but it is logically appropriate.

It was not simply the religious and political authorities, however, who trembled at the human cost of such freedom. Some in the early churches also blanched at so much moral discretion being placed at the disposal of common people. I have already noted that Matthew and Luke omit Mark 2:27 ("the sabbath was made for humankind . . ."), and so do a few manuscripts of Mark itself. By deleting that verse, Matthew and Luke have converted the saying into its opposite: the assertion that Jesus *alone* as son of man is lord of the sabbath. Once "the son of the man" had been flattened into a mere equivalent of Son of God and Christ/Messiah, no other reading seemed possible.

Matthew additionally enhances the christological centrality of Jesus by inserting, "Or have you not read in the law that on the sabbath the priests in the temple break the sabbath and yet are guiltless? I tell you, something greater than the temple is here" (12:5-6). Whereas special *need* had originally justified the breach or suspension of the law, now one's relationship with a special *person* does so—a person endowed with a transcendent authority shared by no one else.[24]

Once all authority becomes vested only in Jesus, however, what happens to the sovereign freedom that he evoked in his disciples? What becomes of the freedom to "judge for yourselves what is right" (Luke 12:57)? It is indeed awesome how Christology has been used to avoid the clear intent of Jesus! So the astonishing freedom of the Human Being was sabotaged in the interests of institutional harmony and rule by law.

And Feuerbach chuckled.

B. The Healing of the Paralytic: Mark 2:1-12 // Matt. 9:1-8 // Luke 5:17-26

[1]When he returned to Capernaum after some days, it was reported that he was at home. [2]So many gathered around that there was no longer room for them, not even in front of the door; and he was speaking the word to them. [3]Then some people came, bringing to him a paralyzed man, carried by four of them. [4]And when they could not bring him to Jesus because of the crowd, they removed the roof above him; and after having dug through it, they let

down the mat on which the paralytic lay. [5]When Jesus saw their faith, he said to the paralytic, "Son, your sins are forgiven." [6]Now some of the scribes were sitting there, questioning in their hearts, [7]"Why does this fellow speak in this way? It is blasphemy! Who can forgive sins but God alone?" [8]At once Jesus perceived in his spirit that they were discussing these questions among themselves; and he said to them, "Why do you raise such questions in your hearts? [9]Which is easier, to say to the paralytic, 'Your sins are forgiven,' or to say, 'Stand up and take your mat and walk'? [10]But so that you may know that the Son of the Man has authority on earth to forgive sins"—he said to the paralytic— [11]"I say to you, stand up, take your mat and go to your home." [12]And he stood up, and immediately took the mat and went out before all of them; so that they were all amazed and glorified God, saying, "We have never seen anything like this!"

This seemingly simple account is the focus of a complex debate about its historicity. Many scholars believe that Mark 2:5b-10 has been added, thus turning what was a simple healing narrative (1-5a, 11-12) into a compound healing-and-conflict story. The alleged insertion is full of Markan vocabulary; the repetition of the phrase "he said to the paralytic" in 5a and 10b has the appearance of an editorial link; the transition between 10 and 11 seems awkward; the universal acclaim at the end of the story ignores the scribes, who were most certainly not mollified, and takes account only of the act of healing, not the forgiveness; and the implication that the man's sin had caused his sickness seems at odds with Jesus' attitude elsewhere (e.g., Luke 13:10-17). The most influential argument against the passage's integrity, however, pertains to its form: two discrete forms are juxtaposed, a healing story (regarded as primitive) and a conflict story (assumed to reflect later church struggles with the Jews).[25]

These arguments, however, are not conclusive. Markan vocabulary appears in vv. 1-5a as well;[26] the repetition of "he said to the paralytic" is good storytelling technique (see Exod. 4:4); the putative "awkwardness" of the transition from vv. 10 to 11 escaped the notice of both Matthew and Luke, who faithfully reproduced it while freely making other changes to improve or condense Mark; the acclaim at the end that ignores the scribes also is repeated by Matthew and Luke, who apparently enjoyed the total eclipse of Jesus' opponents, even though the opponents' unabated hostility would very shortly lead to a death plot (Mark 3:6 par.); and Mark probably intended the crowd's amazement to include the act of forgiving sins. The structure of this passage also argues for its integrity as a unit.

Ched Myers notes a neat echoing that no one else, to my knowledge, has seen:

A   C 2:2 Jesus was *teaching* them the Word . . .
B   D 2:6 Scribes were *reasoning* in their hearts . . .
B   C 2:7 Scribes: "Why does this man *teach* this?"
A   D 2:8 Jesus: "Why do you *reason* thus in your hearts?"[27]

Note the ABBA structure of the speakers (technically known as "chiasmus") coexisting with the CDCD sequence of the verbs. For this structure to work, however, v. 2 (the healing) must have coexisted with vv. 6, 7, and 8 (the controversy) from the beginning, for the structure of the saying is not a redactional superimposition but is intrinsic to the narrative. And v. 9, which is in the heart of the conflict story, refers to the contemplated healing.[28] Are we to ascribe this tight construction to the chance juxtaposition of two in-dependent narratives, or to the redactional work of a scribe (Mark) who is al-ready roundly accused of making awkward transitions in vv. 5 and 10? This passage has suffered from the worst kind of form criticism, which simplisti-cally separated the healing narrative from the controversy story.[29] There is no doubt that such forms are standard. But if the healing precipitated conflict, then the two forms naturally belong together. And we know from other sto-ries (including the Fourth Gospel's independent version of the same story, John 5:1-18) that Jesus' healings created enormous controversy. The Gospel "forms" are not Procrustean beds into which every lively and unpredictable story must be crushed, but "typical" frameworks that are not always appro-priate. They are not causes but effects.

It is worth pausing over the form-critical issue, because this text has been something of a showpiece for the form-critical approach. Let me tell a brief healing story. "A boy was beaten up, received multiple injuries, and was rushed to the hospital, where the doctors had to take forty-six stitches to sew him up. After some days in the hospital they released him, still a bit groggy, but mending." There you have all the elements of a healing narrative: de-scription of the problem, encounter with the healer, the healing act, and evidence of healing. What I did not tell was that he was a twelve-year-old black boy in Harlem, and the injuries were delivered by three white police-men, and that their brutal beating of him set off furious protests, including the trashing of some stores, a march on precinct headquarters, and charges from black leaders.

So there you have it: a healing story *intrinsically* yoked with a conflict story. This happens all the time. Jesus' healings seem to have created con-

troversy on more than one occasion. To recall an early criticism of the extension of form criticism beyond its capacities, "Judgments of form cannot
lead to judgments of historicity." To which we might add, the story should
suggest the form; the form should not be imposed on the story. When form
criticism does move from judgments of form to judgments of historicity, it
invariably becomes impaled on circular reasoning: this passage reflects a hypothetical community, which in turn is seen as creating this passage to meet
the needs of that community. The enigmatic is explained by the imaginary.
The capacity to fantasize plausible contexts in the early church's life does
not make them historical.

Most significant, however, are the data from the independently transmitted story of a healed paralytic in the signs source of John's Gospel.[30] Here
we find the almost identical words ("Jesus said to him, 'Stand up, take your
mat and walk.' At once the man was made well, and he took up his mat and
began to walk," John 5:8-9a). In addition, the man's illness is associated with
his having sinned ("Do not sin any more," John 5:14), and the healing story
is subordinated to a conflict narrative (5:1, 9b-47). In the center of that conflict, Jesus says that the Father "has given him authority to execute judgment, because he is a son of man" (5:27). Only this once is the phrase
anarthrous (lacking definite article). Apparently John believes that this authority has been given to *everyone* who will claim it. This is very similar to
Mark 2:10 ("the son of the man has authority on earth to forgive sins"). Most
scholars believe that John's Gospel was written independently of the Synoptic Gospels, though drawing on common traditions.[31] If so, then it must have
used a source in which the healing narrative and the conflict story were already joined.[32]

This is the only "son of the man" saying connected with forgiveness (or
with healing, for that matter). If Jesus had not made that connection, how
would it have occurred to people in the early church to do so? Some argue
that the church wished to authorize its right to declare sins forgiven by drag-
ging in the son of the man title; but that assumes that they were already declaring sins forgiven (and that the son of the man was a title). How did they
get started, if it was not Jesus' own initiative? The scandal is exacerbated by
the fact that, not just Jesus, but also his followers, were authorized to declare
the sins of people forgiven. And the three Synoptic Gospels concur that
these scribes regarded Jesus' declaration of forgiveness at least as unambiguous blasphemy.[33]

The collective implications of this story are made most clear by Matthew,
who ends his version with the statement, "and they glorified God, who had
given such authority to *human beings*" (9:8). We would have expected

Matthew, of all the evangelists, to conclude that sentence with "Jesus" or "the Christ." Matthew clearly understands the term as collective. (The Greek term *anthrōpois* here is equivalent to the Hebrew *benê 'adam*, "sons of man.") Any person who knows that God forgives sins has the authority to declare another person's sins forgiven. They would know this ostensibly because they had experienced it. Matthew no doubt was thinking about the church as the community that had received this revelation, but it would in principle include *anyone* who knows this revelation to be true. Matthew believed that Jesus intended to share this authority to forgive with his followers. That much is clear from Matt. 16:19 and 18:18, as well as 9:8. The authority to heal and exorcise was also given to the disciples (Mark 6:7-13 par.; Luke 10:9, 17-20).

According to Matthew, then, "the son of the man" in this narrative is not limited to Jesus, but indicates any person who "knows" God's will regarding forgiveness, indeed, who knows God's very nature, that God is, at the core, forgiving. This forgiveness is not attained or earned. One does not, as in both Jewish and Christian liturgies, need to repent first before receiving words of absolution. Jesus does not offer forgiveness to those who repent and promise to do works of restitution. He declares people forgiven before they repent, as in this story. There were, in that society, people who were by trade or ill fortune categorically incapable of doing works of restitution (toll collectors, prostitutes, shepherds, attendants at bathhouses, weavers, tanners, robbers), who were regarded as sinners because of their occupations. To these he declares: Your sins are forgiven (Luke 18:9-14)! Now you can repent! As Mark summarizes Jesus' message, "The time is fulfilled, and the kingdom of God has come near; repent, and believe in the good news" (Mark 1:15). Repentance is possible because God has drawn near in the proclamation of Jesus.

We must cling to Matt. 9:8 with all our might, because it is one of the few passages in which we can know unequivocally that at least one of the evangelists understands the Human Being in a collective sense.[34] It is not then merely a title for Jesus, or a form of humble self-designation, or a circumlocution for "I," though it would be possible to understand it as "I and anyone else like me." But even that is too limiting. The early Christians had the clear sense that the Human Being is not restricted to Jesus, but that it is an authority they are permitted to assume themselves: the authority to heal and to forgive sins. Perhaps that is why Jesus does not say, "But that you may know that I am the son of the man . . ."

This is the point T. W. Manson made in 1931, though few endorsed it. Arguing from the explicitly collective nature of *ben 'adam* in Psalm 80 and *bar enash* in Dan. 7:13, Manson suggested a "communal interpretation" of the Human Being. The "son of the man" is "an ideal figure and stands for the manifestation of the Kingdom of God on earth in a people wholly devoted to their heavenly King."[35] Jesus' mission was to create the kingdom of the saints of the Most High—a fully human community that honored the integrity and uniqueness of all people. Jesus and his disciples *together* "should be the Son of Man, the Remnant that saves by service and self-sacrifice, the organ of God's redemptive purpose in the world."[36] "He and they together, so long as they adhere to him, constitute the 'Son of Man'. . . . 'Son of Man' should be read throughout and understood to connote 'the people of the saints of the Most High' and to denote Jesus and his disciples."[37] When Jesus speaks of the sufferings of the Human Being, then, he means something in which he and his followers would share (Mark 8:34-35). "By dying Jesus has brought the Son of Man into existence, given to that dream-figure a body, a local habitation, and a name. It is the Church, his own body, of which he is the head."[38]

Manson's ideas won little acceptance largely because he was unable to provide sufficient textual evidence for his corporate–Human Being concept. In a peculiar form of self-immolation, he dismissed the two texts that support his thesis most powerfully: Mark 2:1-12 and 2:23-28.[39] I have already demonstrated that Matthew understood the Human Being corporately in 9:8; this is a rare fact about which there can be no doubt. And the authority exercised by the *disciples* is what Jesus refers to in Mark 2:23-28. Armed with these two texts, we are able to make Manson's case for the collective son of the man more strongly than Manson himself.

The story of the paralytic furthers the sense of sovereign authority that we found in the account of plucking the grain on the sabbath. Surprisingly, in contrast to Ezekiel, Jesus never appeals to God's authority to authenticate his mission. He never says, "Thus says the Lord." In Mark 11:27-33 par., a conflict narrative of highest authenticity, Jesus is depicted as *refusing* to claim divine authority for his mission. This attitude is counter to the trend of the developing church. He clearly implies that his authority is "from heaven," but will not say so, indicating only that it has the same source as John's. This exalted evaluation of John is also opposite the church's tendency (Matt. 11:11b // Luke 7:28b; John 3:27-30). There was no reason for such reticence by Jesus; the long history of prophets in Israel had more than adequately prepared Jews to take seriously a person who claimed to speak on behalf of God, saying "thus says the Lord." That Jesus *never* appealed to God's authority for anything he said or did is as remarkable as the divine authority that clearly shines through his words and deeds.

We must not overlook the implications of his reticence. He refused to stake the truth of his ministry on external authority, even God's. He spoke, as Mark reports people as saying, with authority, and not as the scribes (1:22). The scribes worked from texts, exegetically—like Christians! They appealed to Scripture to buttress their arguments—like Christians! (Feuerbach would have loved it!) But Jesus simply spoke with authority. And he taught his disciples to do the same.

Why then does Jesus say that the Human Being forgives, instead of God forgiving (as his entire tradition would lead us to expect)? Apparently the Human Being is authorized to act on God's behalf. Jesus does not contemplate a God outside the universe intervening to heal the paralytic, but as a power that can be evoked in suffering human beings themselves. That power is put into action by faith-acts: take up your bed and walk! What Jesus says arouses the Human Being in the other. Jesus knows that the Human Being has its locus in himself, but it also has its locus in the paralytic. The Human Being seems to function as the mediator of God's intent for our becoming whole.

When the church ceased to read the reference to the Human Being here as universal empowerment to forgive sins, and took it instead as a christological title more or less equivalent to Christ and Son of God, the authority to declare people reconciled to God ceased to be common property of the New Humanity established by Jesus. Instead, it became the sole prerogative of Jesus and, through ordination, of those who continued to represent him as the official leaders of the church. With ordination, the rank-and-file members were stripped of the authority to declare others forgiven on behalf of God. The "laity" became passive recipients of grace and thus emptied themselves once again into transcendence.

C. Foxes Have Dens: Luke 9:58 // Matt. 8:20 // Gos. Thom. 86

> And Jesus said to him, "Foxes have dens, and the birds of the sky have nests; but this mother's son has nowhere to rest his head." (SV, modified)

This is the only son-of-the-man saying that has multiple independent attestation (Q and Gos. Thom. 86).[40] It appears to be authentic. The problem is making sense of it.[41] Is it a disguised political swipe: foxes ("that fox [Herod]," Luke 13:32) have their lairs, and those marching under the Roman eagle (Luke 17:37) have their encampments, but the human and humane ruler is deemed "a worm and no man," and denied his proper homage and habitation?[42] It is not difficult to imagine Jesus giving expression to the hardships imposed by his itinerant mission. But why would he or his disciples have repeated what looks like a self-pitying complaint, and why would it have been preserved in collections of sayings intended to challenge others to a permanent commitment toward God's rule, whatever comes?[43] "For Jesus to use the mere lack of a bed to call his own," says Mahlon Smith, "even if it was a fact of his chosen lifestyle, to declare that vermin and scavengers had more than he, makes him seem not only bitter but petty."[44] "If you can't stand the heat, stay out of the kitchen!" Besides, we do know that he had a home in Nazareth (Mark 1:9) and, later, Capernaum (Mark 2:1).[45]

Nor is it plausible that Jesus was a Cynic sage complaining of hardship. Superficially at least, Jesus and his disciples may have resembled the Cynic philosophers who wandered the world barefooted, sleeping on the ground, with only a threadbare cloak, a begging bag, and a staff. Yet the Gospel writers seem to be deliberately depicting the disciples as "anti-Cynics," in Richard Horsley's apt characterization: no purse, no bag, no staff, no sandals; and "greet no one on the road."[46] The Cynic Diogenes (d. 323 B.C.E.) liked to proclaim himself

> Without a city, without a home, bereft of fatherland,
> A beggar and a vagabond, living from day to day.[47]

There are other similarities: voluntary poverty; indifference to what one eats or drinks; unconcern for etiquette; rebellion against law and custom; simplicity; rejection of fame, family, social distinction, and respectable clothing; a significant role for women; iconoclasm; missionary zeal to convert and proselytize; wandering disciples; subversion of existing authorities; occasionally a large response among the poorer classes; and persecution and martyrdom at the hands of the emperors Nero and Domitian. Some similarities are due to the same type of lifestyles. For example, the Cynic Crates writes, "I don't have one country as my refuge, nor a single roof, but every land has a city and house ready to entertain me" (compare Mark 10:28-30).[48]

The differences, however, are glaring. Most of the Cynics had no god, and the rest, at best, expressed indifference or atheism. Among the Cynics there was no worship; no mysteries; no rituals; no healings; no exorcisms; in most cases no prayers; no dogmas; no punishments after death; no eschatology; no anthropomorphisms; little concern for community; the use of put-downs, sarcasm, shaming, and derogatory laughter; deliberate provocation to shake hearers out of complacency, such as public masturbating, urinating, farting, spitting on people, defecating, and copulating; defense of cannibalism, incest, and free love; self-mastery and self-sufficiency as opposed to dependence on God; living according to nature rather than custom; the wearing of filthy garments and the refusal to take baths; unconcern for where one sleeps, or how one satisfies one's sexual desires; and behind all these practices, the quest for freedom and happiness.[49] No doubt some Cynics lacked the brass to offend deliberately; some were more pious, some even referred to God as Father of all.[50] But the Cynic reputation was not built on etiquette.

On top of these observations is the difficulty of determining what documents can be regarded as Cynic, and which contain authentic Cynic statements. Derek Krueger faults scholars who wish to portray Jesus as a Jewish Cynic preacher for sanitizing the bawdy aspects of Cynic behavior. "It is not surprising that studies attempting to draw parallels between texts about Diogenes and texts about Jesus are unlikely to focus on stories of Cynics' spitting, farting, or defecating."[51] Besides these points, by making Jesus a Cynic sage, these scholars take him out of his natural Jewish milieu of prophets and wisdom teachers, exegetes and rabbis, and place him in a Greco-Roman context. The result is a Jesus who is more philosopher than preacher, more loner than leader, more humanist than *hasid*.[52] The result is a very un-Jewish Jesus.[53] Christians and even Jesus might have borrowed aspects of generalized Cynic behavior and teaching. But I doubt it constituted a very high degree of borrowing.[54]

More must be at stake in this saying about homelessness than simply grumpiness. Arthur Dewey suggests that we are missing the joke, and that Jesus is having some fun at our expense: "Ah yes, that son of man who exists at the pinnacle of creation, as Psalm 8 avers—and not a cot to sleep on!" Jesus neither identifies with nor dissociates himself from the Human Being here. He can speak as if the Human Being were he, as if it were other than he, as if it included his disciples, or as if it included this prospective disciple.[55] The title demands as much of them as it does of him. Here again we see indications that the Human Being could denote Jesus and, at the same time, have a collective meaning that took in those following Jesus' way. He does not say, "*I* have no place to lay my head," nor "*I the son of the man* have no place to lay my head," but "the son of the man has no place to lay its head." Insofar as Jesus, and others, live the existential uncertainty of the Human Being, they have incarnated it. Such incarnation can be the realization that we can live out of an interior center, secure yet flexible, capable of enduring tension, with a tolerance for ambiguity, anxiety, and conflict, traveling like turtles with our homes on our backs.[56] Dogmatic religion exists to protect people from this anxious, insecure openness to the possibilities of the moment.[57]

Whatever else it signifies, the Human Being represents the urge to actualize the self, inner and outer. The Powers are what prevent our becoming. The Human Being is the lure toward our becoming. The Reign of God—God's domination-free order—is the goal of our becoming. Becoming means fidelity to the uniqueness of our own selves. As Jung put it, "Personality is the supreme realization of the innate idiosyncrasy of a living being."

> To develop one's own personality is indeed an unpopular undertaking, a deviation that is highly uncongenial to the herd. . . .To the [person] in the street it has always seemed miraculous that anyone should turn aside from the beaten track with its known destinations, and strike out on the steep and narrow path leading into the unknown. Hence it was always believed that such a [person], if not actually crazy, was possessed by a daemon or a god.[58]

Were such persons crazy? Or were they merely stubborn seekers following the impulse of the Human Being, who has no place to lay its head?

D. Blasphemy against the Human Being: Luke 12:10 // Matt. 12:31-32 // Gos. Thom. 44

> And everyone who speaks a word against the son of the man will be forgiven; but whoever blasphemes against the Holy Spirit will not be forgiven.

On the basis of dissimilarity alone, this passage should be judged authentic, since Jesus does not demonize his opponents, as the church was later to do, even in the Gospels (Matthew 23). Furthermore, Jesus does not treat "speaking against" or blaspheming the son of man as unforgivable, in contrast to the later tendency of the church. Mark has changed "the son of man" to a plural, so as to avoid the suggestion that it is permissible to curse the Human Being. As far as Mark is concerned, it is not permissible. It is inconceivable that a church that regarded Jesus as "*the* son of the man," exalted to the right hand of God, the judge of the world, the Messiah, Son of God, and God, would *invent* a saying as mischievous as this. As James D. G. Dunn suggests, a prophet might dare to blaspheme Jesus on the authority of the risen Christ, but no church would have recognized it as an authentic prophetic saying. We know exactly how they would have responded, because we have their response: "No one speaking by the Spirit of God ever says 'Let Jesus be cursed!' " (1 Cor. 12:3).[59] So while we can imagine the uses to which such a saying could be put after it was accepted into the tradition, I find it difficult to imagine any other source for the saying itself but Jesus.

In the Markan framework, which Matthew follows, Jesus has been accused by a deputation of scribes from Jerusalem of "having Beelzebul." This charge is not one of possession, but of possessing: he is alleged to have brought a demonic spirit under his power to do his bidding. We can see from the Greek Magical Papyri what this entailed. A magician acquires an "assistant" (variously referred to as a demon, angel, or god) who is adjured to obey its master in every regard. "He [the spirit] sends dreams, he brings women, men . . . he kills, he destroys, he stirs up winds from the earth, he carries gold, silver, bronze, and he gives them to you whenever the need arises." This demon also "stops very many evil [demons]"—just what the scribes charge Jesus with doing. The scribes are, in short, accusing him of evil magic, and of using evil powers to gain control of people—a power the papyrus expressly promises: "And you will be [worshiped] as a god since you have a god as a friend."[60]

To this charge, Jesus gives a series of devastating rebuttals that probably had no effect. Of interest for our purposes is what he does *not* say. He makes no appeal to any divine or messianic status or authority. He unambiguously regards himself as the one who brings the Reign of God, but he just as clearly indicates that he does so, not by his own power, but by the "finger of God," the power of the Holy Spirit.[61] He does not reverse the argument against his opponents and insist that they are the ones in collusion with the devil. Nor is there the slightest suggestion, notes Douglas Hare, that the vilified son of the man is destined to become a heavenly figure, the eschatological judge, who will give these detractors their comeuppance.[62] On the contrary, Jesus tries to explain the illogic of their position and—amazingly—concedes them the right to criticize and even blaspheme the Human Being ("every one who speaks a word against the son of the man will be forgiven"). He simply adds the warning that they should look to their own souls to see if they are not perhaps themselves the blasphemers, despite their sincere "defense" of God. He thus avoids satanizing his opponents, remaining open to the possibility of their transformation, convinced that the God who heals the sick and casts out demons can even convert those who defend God. He makes his case by a series of statements that assume his hearers' capacity to recognize the truth when they are shown the truth: "How can Satan . . . If a kingdom . . . if a house . . . if Satan has risen . . . if I cast out demons . . . if it is by the Spirit . . . how can one enter?"

His hearers' case against him, however, is pretty persuasive: the devil, in order to deceive people, has raised a false prophet and given him power over demons. Why shouldn't Satan sacrifice a few demons if thereby he can gain a kingdom? The position of the investigatory commission is understandable:

they recognize Jesus' power, sense its numinosity and fascination to the crowds, judge his ministry to be destructive to the ancestral religion, and therefore infer that his inspiration is Satan. But rather than confronting Jesus, they "were going around saying" (*elegon*, imperfect, Mark 3:22) their charges to the people, behind his back.

Jesus' refusal to deny their charge outright is astonishing. Does it mean that he is willing to acknowledge that he might have a malevolent element at work in him ("No one is good but God alone," Mark 10:18)? If so, one might conclude that he saw the same sinister element at work in everyone; this at least is the memory of the Johannine community (John 2:24-25). This vivid sense of the universality of sin could be the presupposition of his teaching on loving enemies. He is clear that, in the name of the Human Being, he can make wrong decisions. Decisions are fallible. Therefore one may speak against the Human Being, precisely because it is not identical with the Holy Spirit.

It is curious that he does not say, "Every one who speaks a word against *me* will be forgiven."[63] He could easily have referred to himself directly. There was no reason of modesty or humility to disguise himself by a third-person reference, since the passage makes no claims about him. Quite the opposite—the Human Being, whatever it is, can be blasphemed. Jesus surely saw his mission as part of a process of transforming life. He attempted to live by the power of the Holy Spirit within him (Matt. 12:28 // Luke 11:20). His choice of "the son of the man" instead of "me" here means that we have three entities to account for: Jesus, the Human Being, and the Holy Spirit. Jesus resists identifying either with an emergent archetypal image of what it means to be human (the Human Being) or with the immanent power of the life-transformative process (the Holy Spirit).

But why then is it permissible to blaspheme the one and not the other? In the terms of modern depth psychology we might say it is because the Human Being is not the Self. The latter is the totality, the complete human integrated with all that is. Psychologically speaking, the Self is indistinguishable from God (though not theologically speaking!). The Human Being seems to be more mundane, more a process of emerging consciousness than consciousness itself. It is, as it were, a mediator between the Self and the ego, seeking to bring the depths of the Self to consciousness, on the one hand, and to keep the ego faithfully attending to the Self's longing to incarnate on the other. The Human Being pursues the will of God through trial and error and consequently is bound to make mistakes. Therefore the Human Being may be "spoken against," even corrected or condemned.

The Holy Spirit, on the other hand, is the divine immanence urging us toward our full humanity. In this text, specifically, blasphemy against the Holy Spirit is consciously calling good evil. Sin is the opposite: calling evil good. Everyone does the latter, says Elizabeth Howes, and this passage assures us that all such sins are forgiven. But to consciously recognize the good and to damn it as evil so devastates the moral sense that one may never recover.[64] The architects of Nazism possessed a moral sense so atrophied that most of them later were unable to repent. Blasphemy against the Holy Spirit must be extremely rare. In blasphemy, one cuts off the possibility of forgiveness, because forgiveness flows from an interaction with the Source; blasphemy is calling the Source itself evil.

This passage about blaspheming the son of the man has, unfortunately, been used to terrify people who are only too certain that whatever sin they have committed is precisely the unnamed "unforgivable sin." But Jesus is not talking about sin here; that one is anxious shows that the moral sense has not been destroyed. Anyone who can feel guilt can still repent. Even more insidious has been the use of this saying to damn the Jews, who rejected Jesus and had to be disposed of so the church could assume their role as God's chosen people. Tragically, churches have all too often ended up in the same role as the scribes in this story, defending "God" and "religion" against "blasphemers" and "heretics." How sad, when so often these "sinners'" only sin was to call the churches to look at their apostasy, a call coming from the one who taught that it was forgivable to badmouth the Human Being.

E. A Glutton and a Drunkard: Luke 7:31-35 // Matt. 11:16-19

> To what then will I compare the people of this generation, and what are they like? They are like children sitting in the marketplace and calling to one another, "We played the flute for you, and you did not dance; we wailed, and you did not weep." For John the Baptist has come eating no bread and drinking no wine, and you say, "He has a demon"; the Human Being has come eating and drinking, and you say, "Look, a glutton and a drunkard, a friend of tax collectors and sinners!" Nevertheless, wisdom is vindicated by all her children.

This passage certainly belongs to the myth of the human Jesus.[65] In the first place, it is intrinsically improbable that the early church would have created a tradition in which Jesus is labeled a "glutton and drunkard" and not also have included a vehement *denial* of that charge. But Jesus seems to *accept* the charge, and even, in a perverse sort of way, revels in it.

Second, this saying subtly balances Jesus' solidarity with John and his marked differences from John in a way that is nonpolemical. John and Jesus are portrayed fighting on a common front on *equal* terms, but in opposite ways. This runs counter to the tendency, already in Q but present in all four Gospels and Acts, to circumscribe John's role and to establish his inferiority to Jesus.[66]

Third, there is no reason to doubt that Jesus ate with tax (toll) collectors and sinners. There are too many references to them in the Gospels (twenty-five!).[67] Jesus' friendship with tax collectors and sinners was scandalous and an embarrassment to the church. There is no conceivable reason why the church would have manufactured Jesus' contact with socially stigmatized people and every reason to see in that behavior something characteristic of his companionship with the marginalized. The church was simply unable to maintain this radical aspect of Jesus' ministry for any time. Paul is already struggling over who can be included, who excluded, from the community and its meals (1 Cor. 5:9-13; 6:9-11).

Fourth, "a glutton and a drunkard" is the precise charge leveled against a rebellious son in Deut. 21:20, and it is the prelude to his being stoned to death.[68] By applying the expression to Jesus, his opponents imply that he deserves to be stoned. But that is not the way Jesus was executed. So why would the church have invented an allusion to Jesus' execution if it was not the manner by which he was actually killed? Therefore, this passage has a claim to antedate the death of Jesus.

Fifth, one of the earliest evaluations of Jesus by some branches of the early church may have been based on the figure of Wisdom in the Book of Proverbs. Luke reflects that early belief, in which Jesus is not identified with Wisdom, but is merely one of her children, twinned with John, who is therefore portrayed as Jesus' equal (7:35). Both are prophets sent by Wisdom and rejected by the rulers.[69] Matthew changes the phrase to "Wisdom is justified by her *deeds*," suggesting that Jesus is himself Wisdom incarnate. Luke has no interest in a Wisdom Christology, so the presence of this saying in his Gospel must mark an early tradition.

Sixth, the passage can be retranslated into Aramaic poetry featuring the *kina* or lament meter: a three-beat cry answered by a shorter two-beat echo. There is also a rhyming wordplay between *raqqēdtūn* ("dance") and *arqēdtūn* ("lament").[70] And there is antithetical parallelism in Luke 7:33-34. This would suggest a Palestinian, or at least Aramaic, origin for the saying.

Seventh, there are a staggering number of references in the Gospels to meals. Jesus seems to have had a predilection for table fellowship and good times. He comes across here as humorously self-ironical and paints a

"Falstaffian" (if you will pardon the anachronism) image of himself—an image assiduously avoided by later church iconographers.

There are, however, several negative arguments as well. The first is the lack of integration between vv. 31-32 and 33-35. The structure is:

THIS GENERATION = CHILDREN CALLING

A	Counter A
we piped	*you did not dance*
B	Counter B
we wailed	*you did not weep*
A'	Counter A'
For John was ascetic	*he has a demon*
B'	Counter B'
Jesus ate and drank	*a glutton and a drunk*

The problem with this otherwise beautiful structure is that "this generation/children" are doing the piping in v. 32, whereas John and Jesus are doing it in vv. 33-34. The problem may have been created by inadequate integration of a folk adage in v. 32. In any case, the saying is confusing. Since it is already found in Q, the Q community or its predecessors may have joined the two pieces infelicitously. Verses 33-35 would then at least antedate Q.

The Q source shows no awareness of contradiction, so perhaps it focuses on a different logic, as captured by Patrick J. Hartin:

> PREMISE 1: The children of this generation opposed John and Jesus.
> PREMISE 2: John and Jesus are the children of Sophia.
> CONCLUSION: The children of this generation oppose Sophia's children.[71]

A second problem is the statement that the son of man "has come." Does this indicate Christian reflection on Jesus' coming from God? Rudolf Bultmann, who has reservations about these verses, nevertheless grants that "there are no possible grounds for objecting to the idea that Jesus could have spoken in the first person about himself and his coming; that need be no more than what befits his prophetic self-consciousness."[72] Jeremias believes that the underlying Aramaic *'atayit* has nothing of the intentionality of later reflection, but simply means "it is my task."[73] "Came" is also used of John

(Matt. 11:18; 21:32); for both figures, the word simply implies vocation. The Scholars Version of the New Testament paraphrases "come" in Mark 1:38 as "that's what I came for," and in the present passage as "John the Baptist appeared on the scene. . . . The son of Adam appeared on the scene."[74]

What then shall we make of Jesus' use here of "the son of the man" (or of Wisdom's child, Luke 7:35)? It could be a circumlocution for "I"; it could be a third-person self-reference with a gesture ("this fellow," pointing to himself). It could *not* be the equivalent of "a human being" or "mortal" or "I and anyone else in my situation," since Jesus' speech points specifically to the actions of Jesus alone.[75] But we learned from earlier passages that this identity need not be without remainder. Jesus could refer to himself as the Human Being, but he could also be referring to the gathered community. Logically, A (Jesus) is B (the Human Being), but B is more than A.

The "Human Being" here is virtually identical with Divine Wisdom in Wisd. Sol. 7:27:

> Although she is but one, she can do all things,
> and while remaining in herself, she renews all things;
> in every generation she passes into holy souls
> and makes them friends of God, and prophets.

Wisdom is a catalytic agent, who changes things without herself being changed, and who inspires the prophets. So Ezekiel, John, and Jesus are all her children, all of them prophets, all of them catalysts of change.

Jesus portrays himself here, mockingly, as a bon vivant who enjoys good food and drink. But he is not necessarily admitting to debauchery. This may be what Frederick Danker calls an "opposition logion," in which Jesus takes the complaint of an opponent and turns it into a self-affirmation.[76] The issue is not really culinary excess but eating with people deemed social inferiors, pariahs, outcasts, and deviants. Jesus seems to wish to make the point that his behavior is not simply whimsical, or rebellious, or counter-cultural posturing, but that it is a direct consequence of his divine calling. "The Human Being has come eating and drinking"—and "come" here refers to his divine destiny—because his meals with the marginalized and rejected are a manifestation of God's domination-free order as a present reality. Wisdom's Child is God's emissary sent to those never invited to the banquet (Luke 14). The Human Being "comes" among them as an archetypal mutation, as an eruption of joie de vivre from the center of a celebratory universe, and all are invited. Jesus comes out of that side of Judaism that could later declare (here, rather heavy-handedly), "We will have to give account on the judgment day of every good thing which we refused to enjoy when we might have done so."[77]

Most amazing about Jesus here is that he not only is unafraid of pleasure, but that he is willing to risk his life for this kind of happiness with these kinds of people. For his effort, he is branded a "disobedient son," a "glutton and a drunk," an expression that, as we saw, implies the penalty of stoning. Jesus proudly accepts the reproach and ascribes the genesis of his behavior to Wisdom herself, whose child he unapologetically is. But he does not claim that he alone has truth. John the Baptist came following an ascetic path, and that is one of Wisdom's ways as well. The problem with "this generation" is that it is prepared to follow neither path, but petulantly pouts, seated firmly on the ground, demanding that its prophets do their bidding. They will answer neither John's call to repent nor Jesus' invitation to the messianic feast that has already begun, even under the conditions of the domination system.

God's all-inclusiveness explicitly includes God's feminine or female aspect here: the figure of Wisdom. Luke preserves the earlier tradition, in which Jesus and John are both Wisdom's children. Matthew identifies Jesus with Wisdom, thus replacing her with the male Jesus. Elsewhere Wisdom is crowded out by the male Logos (Col. 1:15-20; John 1:1-18). This masculinizing of the Godhead meant the suppression of the female aspect of Wisdom in the Godhead. This process took place alongside the general devaluation of the feminine and of females in Christianity. In the long run, Christian churches would abandon the Wisdom tradition's acceptance of ambiguity and inclusiveness in favor of an all-male Trinity and a rigid orthodoxy.[78] Consequently, churches are often the last place where most "tax collectors and sinners" feel welcome or wanted.

F. The Human Being Refuses Signs: Mark 8:11-12 // Matt. 16:1-4; Luke 11:29-30 // Matt. 12:38-40

> The Pharisees came and began to argue with him, asking him for a sign from heaven, to test him. And he sighed deeply in his spirit and said, "Why does this generation ask for a sign? Truly I tell you, no sign will be given to this generation." (Mark 8:11-12)

Here Jesus refuses any kind of sign that would externally authenticate his divine mission. If he has already, right before the people's eyes, healed the sick, cast out demons, and brought an authoritative message from God, what sort of "sign" could surpass these? So he refuses. Q, however, has a different form of the tradition:

> When the crowds were increasing, he began to say, "This generation is an evil generation; it asks for a sign, but no sign will be given to it except the sign of Jonah. For just as Jonah became a sign to the people of Nineveh, so the Son of Man will be to this generation. (Luke 11:29-30)

Specifically, Jesus identifies his preaching of repentance with Jonah's. "The Son of Man *will be* to this generation what Jonah was to the Ninevites, namely, a sign, and he will be the *only* sign to be given to it," writes A. J. B. Higgins. Consequently, Higgins sees no essential difference in meaning between the prediction of the sign of Jonah in Q and the refusal of any sign at all in Mark 8:12.[79] The point seems to be that one's standing in the last judgment will be determined by one's response to Jesus' preaching of repentance *now*, in "this generation." Wisdom's Child will not come in the future to judge; rather, he is the present standard by which one will be judged in the future. Repentance—literally "getting a new mind," a mind that goes beyond one's old ways of thinking—is the doorway to the dawning Reign of God. It is not possible to stand outside the door and to view God's Reign, and then, if it prevails, to throw one's lot with it. Rather, Jesus challenges his hearers to risk everything in the knowledge that one's present life has reached its end, and that a new life and new world await on the other side of the door; one simply must leave that old life behind.[80]

One can understand Jesus fully identifying himself here with the Human Being. But it is also possible that Jesus sees the emergence of the Human Being as one of the significant new events in his ministry As the Human Being's bearer and revealer, he can identify with it, but not exclusively. As we have seen, the disciples too are a part of this disclosure. Hence—as Adela Yarbro Collins points out—in the verses that immediately follow, the formulations "some*thing* greater than Solomon" and "some*thing* greater than Jonah" are somewhat surprising. We expect "some*one* greater" than Solomon and Jonah, namely, Jesus, the son of man.[81] But Jesus does not point to himself. That is why he refuses to do a "sign." He is only the bearer of Sophia's Child. And yet he also cannot deny that he incarnates that new reality, so much so that he can virtually use it as a nickname for himself, in a way similar to Yahweh's use of the phrase for Ezekiel. Jesus thus identifies himself as a prophet like Ezekiel and like Jonah, divinely authorized, needing no external qualifications or credentials, no ordination or diplomas. But what a difference between Jesus declaring that he *himself* is

greater than Solomon or Jonah, and declaring that what he bears and embodies—the Human Being—is greater.[82]

G. The Human Being Serves:
Mark 10:35-45 // Matt. 20:20-28 // Luke 22:24-27

> [W]hoever wishes to become great among you must be your servant, and
> whoever wishes to be first among you must be slave of all. For the Human
> Being came not to be served but to serve, and to give his life to liberate [or
> "ransom"] many. (Mark 10:43-45)

The sayings about the first becoming the last and on service are among the
most frequent in the Jesus tradition.[83]

The context of the son-of-man saying here is the power play of James and
John, who want top billing when Jesus assumes kingly power. He rejects
their appeal, reminding them that the seating plan is the province of the
Host, not him. Perhaps as we read this text today we should employ poetic
license and imagine that, in the Realm of God, everyone will be sitting
around with no head table and no assigned seating whatever!

What gives pause is the miscomprehension of Jesus' ministry that these
disciples' request betrays. The outrage of the other disciples when they hear
of it shows that they harbored the same ambitions.[84] (Matthew is so alarmed
at the obtuseness of James and John that he makes their mother the source
of the request; but his failure to edit out the plural "you" in 20:22 reveals that
the disciples themselves are the culprits.)

Tödt believes that the reference to the son of man's giving his life to liberate many (Mark 10:45b) is secondary, though early, Palestinian tradition,
because it is inharmonious with the context. Jesus is calling the disciples to
reverse the customary power relations of society. In this, they are to imitate
his behavior. But they cannot give their lives as ransoms for many, as the son
of the man does. That has been accomplished in the cross, once for all. The
ransom reference, Tödt believes, has thus probably been introduced by the
church under the influence of Isaiah 53.[85]

Tödt's argument presupposes a blood theory of atonement, a Christology in which the son of the man is identical with Jesus, and the belief that
"ransom" refers to Jesus' crucifixion. But this study questions precisely those
assumptions. "Ransom" draws its metaphorical power, not from crucifixion,
but from slave manumission. The idea is that of liberating people from

bondage to the Powers That Be.[86] That *is* a behavior that Jesus' disciples can imitate. Insofar as the disciples did carry forward Jesus' struggle to liberate people from the Domination System, they too could participate in the Human Being as a corporate entity.

The word "ransom" (*lutron*) is used only in this passage and in the passage's Matthean parallel in the Synoptic Gospels, but its background is the biblical hope that God would redeem the people. Jesus' disciples had been grasped by that hope, says Hooker; that hope was one with the inbreaking of God's reign into the world, with the restoration of Israel, with the new era visualized by Daniel 7, and with the "good news" that Mark proclaimed at the beginning of his Gospel. "It is, in fact, the message of the whole ministry of Jesus," who restores the sick to wholeness and casts out demons by the finger of God.[87]

It is not enough that people should be liberated from the Powers. They must also be made whole in order that they might help others become whole. We are not just liberated *from* something, insists Chris Rice, but also *to* something: the Beloved Community, which embraces freed oppressed and redeemed oppressors.[88] Unfortunately, liberation alone can lead to group empowerment as its own end: black power that excludes white allies, women-only churches and classrooms, reverse racism, ethnic cleansing, and intranational fratricide. Much as some of these empowerment efforts have helped to liberate oppressed people, their failure to liberate *from*, without liberating *to*, has created new separatisms and even genocide. Liberation from, alone, is an idol. Full liberation involves exorcism of the internalized values and presuppositions of the Domination System, and healing from the wounds inflicted by the crushing of self. Liberation *to* requires becoming part of a sustaining community that welcomes even the former enemy. We are liberated in order to liberate. The ultimate service, then, is to give one's life for others. "Far from introducing a foreign concept into the verse, therefore, the word *lutron* expresses the supreme example of the 'service' that is spoken of in vv. 43-5."[89]

Later, as the archetype of the Human constellated around the life, death, and resurrection of Jesus, "service" became invested with increased profundity. What may have begun as Jesus' own reflection on his vocation became a new criterion for humanness and a cornerstone in the emerging myth *about* Jesus. The Human Being who had no place to lay his head, and who changed the definition of greatness, had become a universal standard of human values. In the process, this saying may have attracted to itself the Suffering Servant of Isaiah 53, adding depth to what it means to serve.

Whether or not Jesus articulated the earliest form of this saying, it reveals an understanding of existence consistent with what Jesus expresses elsewhere.[90]

As to the historicity of the reversal formulas (first/last) and the service sayings, they have often been treated as pertaining only to the church or, at the earliest, to the disciples. But Richard Horsley points out that the governance of society generally is at stake ("kings," "those who rule over the Gentiles," "their great men," "those in authority over them"). Jesus commands his followers to repudiate the patriarchal social-economic-political hierarchy that constituted institutionalized injustice. One who would be "great" or "first" would have to be a "servant" — "which meant in effect there could be no great kings and high officials at all in the renewed Israel."[91]

In this passage, Jesus is depicted as dealing gently with the disciples' projection of worldly power onto him. He challenges them to take up the cup and baptism of suffering, and to leave the outcome to God. He points beyond himself to the Source, as if to say: Instead of centering your devotion on me, can you be devoted to what I am devoted to? They sense power in him, far greater than any they have experienced, and they want to share in that power, not by finding it deep within themselves, but by riding Jesus' coattails into office.

Jesus' death at the hand of the Powers would serve to expose the Domination System for what it is: a massive engine of greed and covetousness fueled by the sweat of unjustly treated workers and the blood of innocent victims.[92] The deaths of Jesus and of some of his disciples would "ransom many" by unmasking the Powers and revealing their defection from their divine vocations. The redemptive suffering of the few would show others a new world of power relations in which "success" is measured by the capacity to help liberate others, not out of emptiness, but out of the fullness of the Human Being. Thus, against the drift of later Christology, the book of Revelation depicts Satan's expulsion from heaven as the work, not of Jesus, but of Jesus' followers, who, in heavenly collaboration with Michael and his angels, "have conquered him [the Dragon, Satan] by the blood of the Lamb and by the word of their testimony" (12:11).

How easy it is to turn the *experience* of dying to the Powers (symbolized by the cup and baptism, Mark 10:38-39) into sacraments, in which we repetitiously remember Jesus' dying for us without necessarily dying to the Powers ourselves. (The churches' liturgies of baptism and Eucharist could easily be rewritten to make explicit this liberating element.)[93]

People do not give up their dreams of power lightly; James and John show us that. And yet power is itself not the problem, but how we relate to power, what kind of power, and to what ends we put power. Community organizer Greg Galluzo remarks that power is a sign of God's presence, and where power is absent, evil will be perpetrated. Hence, the more people who have power the better.[94] Power can mean the capacity to dominate (Mark 10:42), or the power to prevent domination (10:43-45). Christians have projected so much power onto God that there is little left for themselves. We have rightly understood that an unredeemed ego cannot be trusted to exercise power responsibly, that the ego must be mortified so that the power of the Holy Spirit can act safely through us. But many have heard that formulation as an avoidance of power altogether, fulfilling Feuerbach's objection by emptying themselves of their own most integral powers.

The gospel comes with power: "For the kingdom of God depends not on talk but on power" (1 Cor. 4:20).[95] Christians are taught not to be ambitious, but to be self-effacing servants of the Lord. But, asks Elizabeth Howes, was Jesus not ambitious? Did he not aspire to end oppression and to replace it with the kingdom of God? Did he not want to open people to true living in the fullest sense, to unite them with his heavenly Abba, to reveal to people that they are infinitely beloved of God? Was it not his ambition to actualize the Human Being in himself and others fully, to embody his vocation, to use himself completely for God?[96]

Howes continues: Does Jesus serve in order to *find* life, or does he serve because he *has found* life? Is serving a way *to* life, or is service the overflow from having *discovered* life? Christians have too often performed acts of service in order to "earn" eternal life. They attempt to obey Christ, who said they should serve. But Jesus served not in order to get somewhere but because he had gotten somewhere. For him, you do not lose life to serve people, but the reverse: you serve people because you have lost and found your life. You serve out of joy, not obligation. Service is not the way, but a consequence of having found the way.[97]

Ambition can be positive or negative. In his vision of the new order of God, Jesus offers us a way to pour ourselves into an ambition worthy of our lives. And in his critique of domination, he shows us how to avoid the pitfalls of egocentric ambition.

There is a downside to this saying about service. It has been used to keep slaves docile, all in the name of serving God by serving one's master. Many women find the sayings about the great reversal (the first shall be last, and the last first) to be good news, but not the business about being slaves to all. They too long have been forced into the servant role by patriarchal families, churches, and an oppressive economic system. (Perhaps it is significant,

then, that Jesus' advice was issued to *men* who aspired to greatness and dominion.) The reversal of first to last and last to first has nurtured fantasies of
revenge rather than promoting all as *equal*.

What then is the son of the man in Mark 10:45 ("For the Human Being
came not to be served but to serve, and to give his life as a ransom for many")?
What we receive is a new image of human beings, ransomed from what possesses, oppresses, or depresses us. We are delivered from ladder-climbing and
from getting ahead, liberated to be responsive to the needs of each other. In
this epochal reversal, power itself is cleansed of its association with might, the
elite, sovereignty, ranking, and stratification. A new human order is established in which the ambition to excel, to transcend our limitations, and to develop our full potential is purified of the desire to be on top.

Jesus' saying about serving and giving also preserves the individual/col-
lective complementarity that we often see in reference to the Human Being.
As Morna Hooker writes:

> In this pattern [of service and suffering for others] Jesus and his followers are
> inextricably bound together: the necessity which is laid upon the Son of
> man is laid also upon the disciple. We must conclude that "the Son of man"
> is either a corporate term (as in Daniel) or a designation for one who is
> closely linked with his followers (as in Enoch).[98]

We saw earlier how that same archetypal image, at about the same time
as the New Testament was being written, burst into the world in the Similitudes of Enoch. The image describes the great reversal that would thrust the
marginalized into the center, when "that son of man" would destroy the
Domination System and put in its place—domination by the elect! We find
the same lust to counterdominate in Daniel, which promises that the "one
like a human being" would receive "dominion and glory and kingship, that
all peoples, nations, and languages should serve him"—everlastingly (Dan.
7:14). Too often the valid critique of domination leads to new forms of domination. That is why the great reversal *must* be held in tension with the sayings on service. Unless our orientation toward power itself is altered, our
schemes for ending domination will usher in new blood-drenched night-
mares of righteous revolution. Jesus both maintains solidarity with the oppressed *and* refuses to endorse their visions of revenge. In his gospel, the
nonviolent God seeks to overcome domination without creating new forms
of domination. What Jesus or the early church comprehended in the expression "the son of the man" in this passage was a self-rectifying movement
that implies a whole new politics. The faltering development of democracy

today remains the battered yet promising prospect of fulfilling the front edge of that dream: a remote but nevertheless significant premonition of the Beloved Community.

H. The Human Being Seeks and Saves the Lost: Luke 19:10

For the Human Being came to seek out and to save the lost.

There is no reason to regard this saying as apocalyptic or inauthentic. Jesus could have said something like this in his encounter with Zacchaeus or elsewhere. Similar words are said in Luke 5:32 and 7:34; see also the variant in Luke 9:56—"For the son of the *anthrōpou* has not come to destroy the lives of *anthrōpon* but to save them." We find similar statements in Matt. 18:11—"For the Child of the Human One came to save the lost," and Mark 10:45—"For the Child of the Human One came . . . to give up his life as a ransom for many." (Compare Ezek. 34:16—God "will seek the lost.") These parallels, of course, do nothing to prove that Jesus uttered these words. They are consistent, however, with the original impulse of Jesus, and deserve to be included in the data bank that comprises the myth of the human Jesus.

This text provokes the question: why did Christianity become such a powerful missionary religion? Judaism was not. A Jew was born a Jew, and while provision was made for proselytes (converts) and "God-fearers" (supporters who did not convert), Jews were largely content to maintain the ancestral religion. So why did Christianity develop such a passion and urgency about converting the world? There is little evidence in the New Testament that the delay of the second coming was a major problem for the church. The notion of saving as many souls as possible before the end of the world presupposes a vivid fear of hellfire for unbelievers. But while there was plenty of fire fear in the New Testament, the focus is on saving oneself, not total strangers. The Zacchaeus story helps us understand at least something of that missionary impulse.

Jesus himself seems to have been the source of the gospel's urgency. According to the account of his baptism, Jesus received a powerful call to preach the reign of God. His calling, to judge from the teachings ascribed to him, included a revelation of the nature of the Domination System and the antidote for it. Compassion for the victims of domination—of poverty, inequality, illness, and possession by the mentality of domination—drove him to keep moving throughout the land and to abandon the normal conveniences of living ("the Human Being has nowhere to lay its head"—Luke 9:58). *Love drove him, not fear of the end of time or the last judgment.* The Spirit of God drove him, and through it the power that flowed from the future, the inbreaking communion of God (Matt. 12:28 // Luke 11:20).

Zacchaeus caught sight of what someone called "the God-possible response." He grasped the incompatibility between his greed and his desire to become a Human Being. Jesus declares, "Today salvation has come to this house, because he too is a son of Abraham. For Wisdom's Child came to seek out and to save the lost." This conclusion places the particularity of "the practice of Jesus"[99] in the universal context of the arrival of God's new order. The Human Being may be a wanderer (Luke 9:58), but it is not lost; rather, it seeks what is lost. To *see* this, and not want to share it, was unthinkable.

I. The Human Being Must Suffer . . .

Thirteen prophecies of Jesus' death in the Synoptic Gospels include the expression "the son of the man," none of them in Q.[100] In four sayings in the Fourth Gospel, Jesus speaks of the Human Being's glorification by being "lifted up" onto the cross. These Johannine sayings scotch any attempt to ascribe this class of sayings to the inventiveness of Mark. Seven of the Synoptic sayings reproduce the phrase "the son of the man will be delivered" or "betrayed" (using the same Greek word, *paradidōmi*), with execution the final outcome.[101] The other six predict that "the son of the man must suffer many things and be rejected" (three times),[102] be "treated with contempt" (Mark 9:12), or simply "suffer" (Matt. 16:21; 17:12). Most of the references to being "delivered" appear in mini–passion narratives, which has led scholars to regard these as predictions created by the church after the crucifixion.[103] Such thumbnail sketches of the outcome of Jesus' ministry would have been ideal for the early preachers, who could detail aspects of the Jesus story and then wind up with brief summaries like this one from Mark 10:33-34—"The son of the man will be handed over to the chief priests and the scribes, and they will condemn him to death; then they will hand him over to the Gentiles; they will mock him, and spit upon him, and flog him, and kill him; and after three days he will rise again." These predictions seem too full of details from the passion narrative to be actual prophecies of Jesus (who apparently suspected, even close to the end, that he might be stoned rather than crucified).[104] Surely we can conjecture that Jesus anticipated being executed without having to affirm the historicity of these full-blown "mini–passion narratives."

However, Catchpole and Hare argue that either Mark 8:31 or something like it must already have been in Mark 8:27-33, for it is inconceivable that any Christian community would have called Peter "Satan" or rejected the messianic title so vehemently. The frequency of son-of-the-man sayings related to suffering opens the possibility that the connection is early. It would have been more natural for the Christian creator of a passion prediction to have attributed first-person language to Jesus rather than this awkward third-person idiom.[105]

Perhaps the "suffer many things" predictions derive from one or more authentic sayings in which Jesus anticipated his death without providing the details (which he could not have known since it had not yet happened). A number of passages make no reference to Jesus' execution, resurrection, or the agents of his death. They simply observe that the son of the man "is to go through many sufferings and be treated with contempt" or "must suffer many things and be rejected by this generation."[106] If we deduct from Mark 8:31 the details of Jesus' execution and resurrection, we have a similar saying: "The Human Being must undergo great suffering, and be rejected."[107] One might also make the case that the *paradidomi* sayings referred originally to Jesus being "betrayed" or "handed over" to the authorities for execution. That Judas's treachery is implied gives this speculation added weight, since the church was not likely to have created a betrayer in its inner circle when the blame could have been laid at the door of the religious leaders and Roman occupiers.[108]

I assume that once Jesus made the decision to go to Jerusalem, he would have regarded his death there at the hands of the authorities to have been virtually inevitable. That he would have expressed this expectation to his disciples is also likely. Numerous troublers of a false peace have anticipated the death that the Powers eagerly visited upon them. There is nothing supernatural about such foreknowledge. Luke 13:31-33 provides a good example of the kind of prediction Jesus must have made: "It is impossible for a prophet to be killed outside of Jerusalem." Hare's conclusion is judicious: "While some of these [suffering-son-of-the-man sayings] are probably redactional, Mark derived his model for speaking of Jesus' passion in this way from earlier tradition. For our purposes it is immaterial which of the sayings corresponds most closely to the model Mark followed. All the sayings equally reflect the tradition (authentic or inauthentic) that Jesus spoke to his disciples about his impending passion in third-person statements employing 'the Son of man.'"[109]

Thus these sayings should be regarded as both authentic and inauthentic: an authentic prediction later elaborated in light of the actual event. That "the son of the man" appears in all seventeen passion predictions is striking. The tradition's insistence on using "the son of the man" instead of the fully sufficient "I" requires explanation. Why is the Human Being in these predictions at all?

Wisdom's Child, the son of the man, seeks to incarnate God in the human species. That Human Being lures people to the fuller humanity that is God, the Human One, and is exemplified by the life of Jesus. But this process is not one to which human beings respond with uniform enthusiasm. Few want to take on the sufferings of God. It is much easier to let someone else carry this dynamic and demanding supernova of soul than to open ourselves to its birth within us. Like a fledgling scratching the inside of its shell, the Child of the Human wants to be hatched in us. But our world finds the Humanchild an intolerable threat. The Domination System is able to survive only as long as it can delude people into believing that it is in their best interests to abandon their best interests. Domination is taught from the start, in the home ("domination" is from the latin *domina*, the one pertaining to a house, or the subduing one). It seduces its devotees into competing for a limited amount of prestige, wealth, and honor in an economy of scarcity, and it reserves the right to pronounce acceptance and rejection. The Domination System is calculated to crush the spirit and to produce predictable and pliant people to staff its economy and armies. The Human Being cracks open the shell of something new. But human beings are terrified by the sound of that scratching deep inside. The sound reminds them of their deprived humanity, which they know instinctively cannot be recovered without painful inner resistance and a massive reaction from the Powers. Drug addicts, multibillionaires, dictators, or perhaps simply bad teachers and domineering bosses—such people are seldom interested in changing, and they know how to deal with anyone who challenges them. To take on those who have power over our lives inevitably will require that one "suffer and be treated with contempt" and "be rejected by this generation."

The normal reaction to the threat of the new is resistance. Jesus' ministry stirred resistance at every turn. Yet he persevered, because resistance can mean, not just rejection, but a last-ditch attempt to quash the new. The vehemence of the resistance may betray an unwanted fascination with the new. (Think of Paul persecuting Christians up to the moment of his transformative vision of Jesus in Acts 9.) Resistance can be the final convulsion of the old order and a harbinger of change. The intent of the regressive pull (the "satanic") is to prevent consciousness; but when the regressive pull encounters consciousness, the resistance can hone consciousness and enable movement forward.[110] So Jesus continued to sow the word, though most of it fell on unreceptive soil, because the few who faced resistance and overcame it provided a miraculous harvest (Mark 4:1-9 par.).

To be in touch with the Human Being, then, is to be vulnerable to suffering at the hands of the collective. Jesus warns people to expect suffering. This reading is buttressed by another saying about the Human Being that also anticipates suffering: "Blessed are you when people hate you, and when they exclude you, revile you, and defame you on account of the son of the man" (Luke 6:22).[111] But here it is disciples generally, and not just Jesus, who are the objects of rejection. Historically, the Human Being in this beatitude has been identified with Jesus. Perhaps we can see it instead as Divine Wisdom pressing for actualization in Jesus and in his disciples. For what is emerging is a new human being who no longer lives from the enticements, blandishments, and threats of the prevailing order. Rather, the new human being offers immediate relationship with the truly Human One, who alone holds the secret of our true nature and the society that could be.

I believe that Jesus himself articulated the necessity that the Human Being must suffer at the hands of the Powers. (And if it was not Jesus, then it was someone else who understood the inevitability of resistance by the Powers equally well, so the saying is true regardless.) Scholars have long pondered what might be the Scripture to which Jesus was referring when he asks in Mark 9:12, "How then is it written about the son of the man, that he is to go through many sufferings and be treated with contempt?" The consensus has been that no such passage exists. But it is in Scripture, wide as a house, in the fountainhead of son-of-man traditions: Ezek. 2:1—3:11. There we hear that the son of man must speak to a nation that has rebelled against God, a people who are like briers and thorns and scorpions, who will not listen to what the son of man brings. The people, the text says, have foreheads of flint and stubborn hearts, and they hate the son of man for telling them a truth they cannot bear. Thus the son of man is rejected and treated with contempt. The whole Book of Ezekiel is an account of the son of man's sufferings and endurance of contempt. So Jesus, as the heir or "son" of that "son of man," Ezekiel, can scarcely escape a similar fate, since he is doing similar things.

True humanity, then, is not defined by the values of the Domination System, in which strength, power, and wealth prevail, and the "beautiful people" rise to the top. A real human being is an accusation against the counterfeit personalities that clutter the magazine racks of our grocery checkout lines, and a challenge to the Powers That Be.

How curious that the Gospels nowhere describe Jesus as possessing exemplary qualities of character and action. No doubt he had such qualities, but the Gospel writers' interest lay elsewhere: in Jesus' attempts to establish a beachhead for a new reality. He is not an exemplar of perfection. He is, instead, a broken figure. Only those alienated by "this world" find him attractive, compelling, magnetic. From the perspective of the "beautiful people"—the powerful, the successful, the achievers, the self-made—Jesus is a loser.

This insight casts a different light on the frequently used expression "it was necessary" in reference to the Human Being's execution.[112] "It was necessary (dei)," in the sense of "inevitable," that "the Human Being *must* be lifted up" on the cross (John 12:34), "that the Human Being *must* be handed over to sinners, and be crucified" (Luke 24:7), that the Human Being "*must* endure much suffering and be rejected" (Luke 17:25), and that "the Human Being *must* undergo great suffering, and be rejected" (Mark 8:31 par.).[113]

What creates the inevitability of crucifixions (and lynchings, disappearances, torture, assassinations, massacres, executions, and rape as state policy) are the requirements of power. Something coldly calculating exists in these forms of state and vigilante terrorism. The actions seldom are carried out in the hot flush of anger, but are usually bureaucratically conceived and executed. The death of Jesus was not "necessary" because God needed Jesus killed in order to save the world. Rather, Jesus was killed because the Powers are in rebellion against God and are determined to silence anyone who slips through their barbed-wire perimeter with a message from the sovereign of the universe. "For the Human Being is going as it has been determined, but woe to that one by whom he is betrayed!" (Luke 22:22). God and Scripture could anticipate Jesus' death, but the Powers themselves are the perpetrators.

The early Christians made the necessity of suffering and rejection a virtue, and celebrated their marginalization by the dominant society. As Ignatius of Antioch (second century) thundered, "The greatness of Christianity lies in its being hated by the Domination System (*kosmos*), not in its being convincing to it."[114] In their experience of the Human Being, Christians had learned what it means to be treated with contempt and to be rejected. They were able to ascribe meaning to that suffering by seeing Jesus as their forerunner in the faith. In turn, they were living out the suffering of the Human Being in their own history. This provides us an insight into Jesus' choice of "marginal" people: they are those whom the dominant and dominating culture has failed to "decompose." That term comes out of Central Europe and the Balkans, where the communist dictators did not employ murder on a wide scale, but aimed rather at what the Stasi, the East German secret police, called the "decomposition" of people. As Roger Cohen describes it, "Decomposition meant blocking people from acting. It meant paralyzing them as citizens by convincing them that everything was controlled. It meant the relentless application of a quiet coercion leading to compliance." For the East German state, it was better to have no activity than an activity out of the Stasi's control. Hence, says Cohen, many Germans in the old East Germany are unable today to act on their own free will. This has left them incapable of taking risks or of acting on their personal initiative.[115] The "New Man" that communism was supposed to produce was systematically decomposed in people's souls. This is only one example out of many in which the Human Being is made to suffer and is treated with contempt.

It is exciting to wallow in the numinosity of the archetypal world, to let one's brain spin with Ezekiel's wheels, or to be caught up, with Daniel, in visions of human possibilities. It is another thing altogether to incarnate this numinous power in the humdrum of everyday life—in the home, at work, in relationships, in the struggle against institutional evil, or with the homeless on the streets. Individuation is, in Jung's terms, the progressive unification of unconscious and conscious, inner and outer, spirituality and social transformation. It is a long and arduous process, and people often mistake the vision of a fuller life (which we are given to entice us onto the path) with its achievement. Wholeness as image and wholeness as reality are two different things. The self actualized is never the same as the self hoped for.

It might be appropriate, then, to end this section on a more personal note by meditating on the ways we reject the Human Being and treat it with contempt. Why, if God is trying to incarnate in me through Wisdom's Child, do I resist it? What would it mean for the way I live if I were in touch with this suffering and rejected aspect of the Human Being? Do I care enough about the integrity of God's new order that I am willing to take on the Powers, even if it means loss of a job, public disgrace, rejection by friends and family, threats, and even death? Why am I reluctant to be "treated with contempt"? What in the Domination System still has the power to silence me, or to keep me in compliance? Can I repudiate the current world order and experience what Paul called "the glorious liberty of the children of God" (Rom. 8:21 RSV)?

For there is a more terrible dimension of resistance: betrayal. Much as it might have liked to, the early church could not forget that the betrayer who handed Jesus to the authorities had come from the inner circle of Jesus' most trusted disciples, "one who is dipping bread into the bowl with me" (Mark 14:20).[116] How was it possible to be with Jesus and then to repudiate everything he stood for? Judas turned his back on everything God had so evidently been doing through Jesus. How was that possible? And why the *kiss?* "Judas, would you betray the son of the man with a kiss?" (Luke 22:48). The horror of that kiss is beyond comprehension. All Judas needed to do was point. Why a kiss?—and no peck this, but a kiss of intense emotion (*kataphileo*)?[117]

"For the Human Being goes as it is written of him, but woe to that one by whom the Human Being is betrayed! It would have been better for that one not to have been born" (Mark 14:21). There is another kind of resistance: one that longs for the fullness of another's being but that despairs of achieving it oneself. For such persons, Jesus represents a living censure and condemnation. Desire draws them to Jesus, but envy poisons their relationship, because they know they can never find such plenitude within themselves. So love turns into antipathy, and the disciple gives Jesus the Judas kiss.[118]

The church eagerly spun tales of retribution in which Judas got what was coming to him (Matt. 27:3-10; Luke 22:3; Acts 1:16-20; John 12:4-6). Those at table on the night before Jesus' execution were wiser. They asked, "Is it I?" Well might I—could I—betray my own highest value? To save my skin, to prevent discovery, or simply for the sake of money, would I betray the Human Being with a kiss? Could I—have I—played Judas to my own destiny?

J. . . . And Be Killed [Mark 8:31]

I find it odd when scholars claim that we have no idea why Jesus was killed, that it might have been an accident, a mistake, or a tragic misunderstanding (Jesus was not really a political messiah, he did not really present a threat to the empire, he was just a sage or teacher refining his own tradition and was at the wrong place at the wrong time, and so forth).[119] None of those "reasons" explains why Jesus was executed. What we do know is that Jesus was perceived as a threat by the Powers That Be. And indeed he was a threat. Building on the words of the prophets, Jesus hammered out the first consistent critique of domination that we know of since the world began. Virtually everything Jesus did or said involved unmasking the Domination System.[120] Jesus was setting the captives free, and the captors were not pleased. Thus his death was consistent with his life. He shows us not just the liberating God, but the consequences of following such a God in a world organized for exploitation and greed: "If any want to become my followers, let them deny themselves and take up their cross and follow me" (Mark 8:34). This means that the earliest theological explanation of the death of Jesus—the "Christus Victor" theory—was *historically correct*. Christ was the "victor" who overcame the Powers by exposing them for what they were, trumping their final sanction, which is death. The Powers wanted him dead. He was not a "sacrifice," but rather the victim of judicial murder. The Gospels are, in their essence, merely a theological elaboration of that historical fact.

What then do we make of the fact that Jesus was tried and executed as an insurrectionist? Traditional Christologies begin by assuming Christ's divinity, and then speak realistically of his coming "down" from heaven to earth as God incarnate to die on our behalf. They then speculate about how Christ's blood washes us from all our sins. Sometimes this is seen as a transaction between Christ and God, in which God's honor is offended by our sins, which are so heinous that not even our own deaths can atone for them. Therefore God sends "his" only begotten son to die in our place. Others speak of Christ ransoming us from the power of Satan by his death. Still others speak of God sending the Son to reveal to us the unfathomable love of God, who sacrifices the one most precious to him in order to convince us that his love is absolute and our forgiveness certain. Or Christ is seen as identifying with our suffering and as our representative before God. All of these approaches begin from on high and depict God either as a cruel tyrant and dysfunctional father (Anselm), or as a more benign father who still treats his son as property at his disposal, whom he can freely offer up to death to win our love. All these views share the presupposition that God had Jesus killed in order to redeem the world. None of them makes realistic sense of the fact that Jesus was executed by the religious and political establishment. Let us recapitulate these positions in greater detail.

1. The Satisfaction Theory of the Atonement

This theory, developed by the medieval theologian Anselm (d. 1109), is usually called the blood-atonement theory. As Richard McBrien puts it:

> Anselm's theory is to be understood against the background of the Germanic and early medieval feudal system. There is a bond of honor between the feudal lord and vassal. Infringement of the lord's honor is tantamount to an assault upon the whole feudal system. A demand for satisfaction, therefore, is not for the sake of appeasing the lord's personal sense of honor but for the sake of restoring order to the "universe" (feudal system) in which, and therefore against which, the "sin" was committed. The feudal lord cannot simply overlook the offense, because the order of his whole economic and social world is at stake. So, too, with God.[121]

Sometimes called the penal or punishment theory of atonement, the point of this theory is that God chooses to intervene so that sinners can avoid punishment even though they are guilty.[122] In pagan cults, the gods were propitiated by those who offered gifts in order to avert the gods' anger or to gain their favor. But Paul declares us incapable of doing anything that can save us. Hence, according to Rom. 3:25, by an act of pure grace, God presents Christ in death as a means of expiation. Believers are saved from God's wrath, then, and reconciled to God not by their own efforts, but by God's own action in and through the death of Christ. But "no effort" translates into human passivity, which emphasizes even more that it is God who does the killing.

This atonement theory turns the crucifixion into a voluntary sacrifice, as if it had been God's idea all along. As Thelma Megill-Cobbler notes, even the softer notion that God allows, but does not desire or inflict the punishment of the child, fits the pattern of abusive family systems (as when a parent passively observes his or her spouse beating their child). God thus becomes the model abuser.

> At their most extreme, penal theories threaten to divide the Trinity, depicting the Father as a vindictive judge, and the Son as the loving savior who is willing that humanity be saved, meekly enduring an undeserved death. Perhaps the Son is for us, but the Father appears to be against both us and the Son.[123]

Anselm's younger contemporary Abelard (d. 1144) rightly protested, "Indeed, how cruel and wicked it seems that anyone should demand the blood of an innocent person as the price for anything, or that it should in any way please him that an innocent man should be slain—still less that God should consider the death of his Son so agreeable that by it he should be reconciled to the whole world!"[124] The problem with the penal theory is that it pictures God as a cruel and unforgiving patriarch, unable to love as a decent parent should, trapped in his own rules that force him to commit a ghastly crime. In that view it is God who needs forgiveness, not us!

In addition, this theory introduces sacral violence back into the heart of Christianity. Jesus is the scapegoat on whom the sins of the world are laden. He is driven out and killed in a charade of justice that means regression to the sacrificial mentality from which Jesus had sought to free people.

Why then have many Christians favored Anselm's theory, especially when there were less vindictive alternatives? Émile Durkheim, I think, put his finger on the reason. He observed that primitive peoples punish for the sake of punishing, seeking neither to strike back justly nor usefully, but merely to strike back. This passion for punishment of offenders subsides only when exhausted by excessive punishment. "A simple restitution of the troubled order would not suffice for us; we must have a more violent satisfaction." The force that the crime encounters is too intense to react with much moderation. Surely a force so powerful must come from a transcendent authority or god.

> [A]t the bottom of the notion of expiation there is the idea of a satisfaction accorded to some power, real or ideal, which is superior to us. When we desire the repression of crime, it is not that we desire to avenge personally, but to avenge something sacred which we feel, more or less confusedly, above us. . . .That is why penal law . . . always retains a certain religious stamp. It is because the acts that it punishes appear to be attacks upon something transcendent. . . .

Now comes the revelatory insight: "Assuredly, this representation is illusory. It is ourselves that we . . . avenge, ourselves that we satisfy, since it is within us and in us alone that the offended sentiments are found."[125]

According to Durkheim, the appeal of the penal theory of atonement lies in the human desire for revenge, masquerading behind a concern for the honor of deity. The penal theory of the atonement seeks to satisfy, not God, but our own need to avenge *on behalf of God*, a need projected as God's own need when it is ours. Hence Christians have preferred a God of cruelty to a God of love. Durkheim's theory also casts light on why Americans cherish the death penalty.

There is also a contradiction, often noted, that both Jesus and those who killed him must have acted according to the will of God, and therefore Jesus' executioners were guilt-free, having only acted on behalf of God.

2. The Love Theory of the Atonement

Abelard had championed an earlier version of this view, which we might call the love theory, or perhaps the revelatory theory of the atonement, or even the sacrificial theory: God reveals God's love for us by sending God's Son to identify with us and to offer his life as proof of the depth of God's love. This is the milieu of John 3:16—"God so loved the world that God gave God's only Son, so that everyone who believes in him may not perish but may have eternal life." The theory is reflected in 2 Cor. 5:14-21, especially v. 19—"In Christ God was reconciling the world to Godself, not counting their trespasses." We find the most elaborate version of this theory in the Epistle to the Hebrews. But this theory still treats God as the initiator of Jesus' death, and still depicts Jesus as the divine Son in heaven who comes "down" on our behalf to demonstrate God's love by his death. However, this wonderfully reassuring theory can be restated in the terms of a Christology from below. As Ernst Bloch puts it, "By the *hubris* of complete surrender, a person has transcended every past idea of God; Jesus becomes a divine love such as had not been conceived in any deity."[126]

3. The Representational Theory of the Atonement

Dissatisfied with the views above, others promulgated the representational theory. In this view, Jesus becomes one of us so completely that he takes on all our sin and becomes the greatest of all sinners. In Luther's typically pungent phrase, "Christ was to become the greatest thief, murderer, adulterer, robber, desecrator, blasphemer, etc., there has ever been anywhere in the world . . . not in the sense that He has committed them but in the sense that he took these sins, committed by us, upon his own body."[127] God and Jesus concur in willing that the Son assume the flesh and blood of those who were immersed in sin. Now Christ is "wrapped up" and "clothed" in our sins. Reckoning him with sinners, the law puts him to death. "In this duel . . . it is necessary for sin to be conquered. . . . in Christ all sin is conquered, killed and buried; and righteousness remains the victor and ruler eternally."[128]

It is as if the judge renders the impartial verdict, whose punishment is death. But to the sinners' amazement, the judge steps over the bench, comes to our side, and takes the judgment on himself. The charge cannot be dropped because our sin is real; the punishment must be undergone, but God in Christ undergoes it for us. Having fully satisfied the demands of the law, Christ frees us from the charge and presents us to God cleansed from all our sins. "For our sake he [God] made him to be sin who knew no sin, so that in him we might become the righteousness of God" (2 Cor. 5:21). "God proves his love for us in that while we still were sinners Christ died for us" (Rom. 5:8). "Since all have sinned and fall short of the glory of God, they are now justified by his grace as a gift" (Rom. 3:23-24).

This view of atonement is an improvement on Anselm, but it still is a Christology "from above," in which God is still responsible for the death of Jesus, however willing Jesus might have been to die. The Gospel evidence is that Jesus was not executed by God, but by the Powers That Be, specifically, the religious authorities and the Romans. God may have been able to work out redemption *despite* the Powers, and even *through* the blind operation of the Powers, but God did not kill Jesus or have him killed or even allow him to be killed, and every view to the contrary depicts God as committing an unconscionable sin.

4. The Liberation Theory of Atonement

A Christology from below repudiates the notion that God killed Jesus. This position is sometimes called the "Christus Victor" (Christ the Victor) theory of atonement, but that expression is itself drenched with the assumptions about power that Jesus repudiates. So I will dub it the "liberation theory" of atonement, for that is what the term "ransom" in Mark 10:45 means ("For the Human Being came not to be served but to serve, and to give his life to *ransom/liberate* many"). It was an absurd literalization that led Origen and Augustine to speak of this "ransom" as a payment Jesus made to the devil in order to win us free. When we speak of someone dying for their country, we do not envision another to whom their life is paid. When someone is liberated from a concentration camp, no payment is made. People are simply set free. Thus Isa. 35:10 — "And the ransomed of the Lord shall return." Again, no payment.

This theory sees that people are both sinners and sinned against. They may be guilty of letting themselves be used to further the interests of the Powers, in exchange for financial and social benefits. They may be guilty of collusion in the repression of other races, classes, and genders. They may be guilty of despoiling the planet and raping its resources. They may exploit workers, abuse family members, violate the trust of loved ones, or harm and even kill others. People do sin, and the popular aversion to that word reveals our reluctance to admit our involvement in evil.

But people are also sinned against. Blacks, Hispanics, gays and lesbians, the homeless and unemployed suffer discrimination. Those who find life unendurable in this System may turn to addictions to ease the pain, further inflicting damage on themselves. Young boys and girls seduced by their priests or clergy, or women who are sexually abused or raped, are made to feel guilt and shame for a sin they did not commit. For all these, the sinners and the sinned against, Jesus comes as liberator. There must be radical transformation both for people and for their systems: a new heaven and a new earth, *on earth*.

Jesus is more than a revealer. By his suffering and death, Jesus identifies with all who sin and are sinned against. Jesus spells liberation for those who suffer at the hands of the Domination System, and by his resurrection Jesus shatters the delusion that keeps people complicit with the Powers, and frees them to free others from bondage. Jesus exposes the scapegoating mechanism by which many innocents have been destroyed, exposing it by knowingly, voluntarily, deliberately taking it on himself—as the text always said! He died, not to satisfy the demands of an unforgiving God, but to break the spiral of violence.

In this view from below, Jesus does not come down from heaven and undergo birth from a virgin's womb. Rather, he experienced rebirth through the baptism of John. Of him we can say, not that God incarnated in him, but that Jesus incarnated God. He did so the same way that we must: by trial and error, by sinning, by learning, by listening, by going one's own path, by risking everything, even one's life. "He *learned* obedience through what he suffered" (Heb. 5:8). In this view, says Ernst Bloch, "the lowly were to be raised up; the cross was to be *smashed*, not to be borne."[129]

Jack Nelson-Pallmeyer suggests an additional atonement theory: what I call "The No-Atonement Theory."

5. The No-Atonement Theory

In this encounter with the paralytic, Jesus simply declared him forgiven. No divine transaction was needed. The son of the man already had the power on earth to forgive sins, and that included *anyone* who knew their sins to be forgiven and who could thus communicate that forgiveness to others (Matt. 9:8). In this view, says Nelson-Pallmeyer, a compassionate God is incompatible with *all* atonement theories. "Atonement theories grow out of the vile and violent portraits of God. They should be placed on the scrap heap of distorted history and theology."[130]

Jesus was not sent by God to die in order to appease a violent deity, nor did he defeat the powers by dying on the cross. His death was not an atoning sacrifice or a way of bringing a scapegoat mechanism to light. It was a political murder meant to sow terror and to undermine hope. His violent death exposes the domination system as oppressive and violent. His resurrection challenges the ultimate power of the system and invites us to be people of God here and now where oppressive systems remain powerful and must be challenged. Jesus teaches us how to live and shows us the risks of living God's compassion in an unjust world.[131]

There is truth in most of these atonement theories. Anselm's is the exception. His blood-atonement theory is beyond being salvaged. Likewise, I find the notion of God causing Jesus' death repulsive, and the thought of a divine being coming to earth anachronistic. But other views of the atonement may have a different effect for different kinds of people, or be of relevance for the same persons at different stages of their lives.

The point is that no religious experience can be made normative for all people. God reaches out to us in love wherever we are and instigates what leads us to wholeness. Each response is divinely tailored to meet our situation.[132]

Perhaps a convict who has committed a serious crime that has caused irreversible harm can only come to believe his sins forgiven through the image of God as the judge who died in his place. Some women may need to be released from shame more than guilt, and delivered from a system that demeans them.[133] They may need the embrace of a womanly God who loves unconditionally and identifies with those on the margins.

The virtue of the multiple images of the atonement in the New Testament is that each communicates some aspect of forgiveness and new life, without a single model being elevated as exclusively correct. Atonement theories are need-specific remedies for the spiritual afflictions that assail us. There can be, in principle, no "correct" or "true" atonement theories, in the exclusive sense, but only the necessary or right atonement theory in the current phase of our lives.

The real issue behind atonement is whether our anthropology is commensurate with our Christology. If we have a high Christology in which Jesus is divine, but a low anthropology in which we see ourselves as weak, sinful, and incorrigible, we will deny ourselves the powers that we see in Jesus. But if we have a high Christology and a high anthropology, as in the Orthodox tradition, we will be inspired, by our image of Jesus, to develop our God-given powers. Similarly, if we have a low Christology in which Jesus is fully human, and a matching anthropology that acknowledges the possibility of our becoming more fully human as well, then that low Christology is also valid. But a low Christology and a high anthropology will lead to arrogance and inflation and the unreflective assertion that we are gods. The inescapable relativity of Christologies, their number and variety, are eloquent witnesses to the high degree of subjectivity involved. You get the Jesus you need. Our needs change over our life span. Our developmental stage will predispose us to the appropriate christological type. The Holy Spirit will be our guide.

K. Conclusion

This concludes the review of son-of-the-man sayings attributed to the pre-Easter Jesus. I am acutely aware that some of my colleagues will remain unconvinced that the texts above go back, even in part, to Jesus himself. However, as I mentioned at the beginning of this chapter, even if the church did create all the son-of-the-man sayings, they would still represent the church's earliest Christology. Thus the Human Being could still serve as the basis for a new Christology from below.

But at such a loss! For the myth of the human Jesus is a *historical* myth. That is the cross, as it were, on which the study of Jesus is nailed, the paradox from which there is no escape. The myth of the human Jesus can have no credibility unless grounded on data that appear to be both factual and true. Otherwise, what authority does the story of Jesus possess? Why should we preoccupy ourselves with Jesus at all? Unless we are gripped by something compelling that we see in him, why waste the time? Two centuries of painstaking effort have not been in vain. True, the quest for the historical Jesus has not presented "Jesus as he really was." Rather, that quest has all along been the largely unconscious search for a Jesus who can bring us to life.

As the Lakota Sioux, Black Elk, commented about his own rich tradition, "This they tell, and whether it happened so or not I do not know; but if you think about it, you can see that it is true."[134]

6.   Jesus and the Messianic Hope

Jesus clearly preferred to speak of himself in the third person, as the son of the man. No other title, nickname, or expectation received his approbation. Most Christians believe that Jesus saw himself as the anointed one ("messiah" in Hebrew or "christ" in Greek, both meaning "one anointed with oil"). By contrast, critical biblical scholars tend to believe that Jesus' followers first made that identification after his resurrection. In either case, however, the result is the same: Jesus is the Messiah or Christ of the Christian church. In time, Christ became for all effects Jesus' last name (as in "Jesus Christ"). Finally people dropped the "Jesus" part altogether, leaving simply "Christ." Thus Jesus and the Messiah were completely amalgamated. In this chapter and the next we consider why he may have refused to consider himself Messiah, and favored instead the mysterious expression "the son of the man."

Before attempting to answer these questions, I need to clarify what I mean by the messianic hope. Often it is understood as the Jewish expectation of a person who will bring deliverance from political oppression. This figure was most often cast in the role of a king from the line of David who would overthrow foreign despots and reestablish Jewish political sovereignty. But occasionally the Messiah was depicted as a priestly figure who would cleanse the temple of unrighteousness and restore true worship. Some groups awaited the prophet like Moses of Deut. 18:15. Jesus is depicted as struggling with these three messianic roles in the longer account of the temptation (Matt. 4:1-11 // Luke 4:1-13).[1]

Often neglected is the broader, cross-cultural context of the messianic hope. In our own day we have had positive messianic figures like Gandhi, Martin Luther King Jr., Cesar Chavez—individuals who have struggled effectively to liberate oppressed people. But there are also pop-cultural messiahs, persons of electrifying charisma who attract masses of fanatical fans: Michael Jordan, Muhammad Ali, the Beatles, Michael Jackson, Marilyn Monroe. Some even are "crucified" messiahs: Gandhi, John F. Kennedy, Bobby Kennedy, King, John Lennon, Selena. Athletes, television personalities, movie stars, billionaires, political figures—all, as larger-than-life personalities who somehow can fill something lacking in our lives, draw on the messianic archetypal image. Then there are those we might call false messiahs (except that their followers regarded them as true): Hitler, Stalin, Pol Pot, Charles Manson, Jim Jones, David Koresh, and others.

We can present the longing for a messiah graphically:

POSITIVE MESSIANIC HOPE

People need help in a hopeless situation.
They feel powerless. Change seems impossible.
They need a leader who can activate their efforts.
They need a hero to whom they can turn for help.
They need someone to liberate them from oppression.
They need help living their full humanness.
They need to recover their self-esteem and identity after having been crushed by oppression.
They need someone to galvanize resistance and to rally the people.
They need someone like Moses who can speak truth to power.
They need someone charismatic and magnetic, who can hold people together for long-term struggle.
They need someone who can help people take responsibility.
They feel inadequate and need someone who does not.
They feel incomplete and need help in becoming more complete.
They need someone to save them.
They need someone who can expose the unjust order.
They want to be vindicated.
They want the excitement, risk, and action that only a spellbinding leader can evoke.
They need someone who can rescue them from their own involvement in an unjust system.

However, there is a downside to the messianic longing as well:

NEGATIVE MESSIANIC HOPE

People want an authority figure to tell them what to do.
They want someone to take responsibility for the mess they have made.

They want someone to change everything so they won't have to change.
They want a strong-armed ruler who will impose on everybody else
    what the leader regards as good.
They want freedom from oppression so they can be oppressors.
They want someone they can idolize and on whom they can project.
They want a cosmic breast, someone to care for them.
They want someone else to do what needs doing.
They want someone exciting who can lift them out of a humdrum
    existence.
They want to feel they are better than others racially, ethnically,
    nationally, and religiously.
They want someone who will lock up the deviants.
They want someone who will take revenge on their enemies.
They want a miracle worker who will dazzle them with her or his
    powers.
They want a conqueror who will violently punish their enemies.
They want someone they can scapegoat and assassinate if he or she
    fails to produce the above.

Christians tend to deal only with the positive side of the messianic longing, which they identify with Jesus as the Christ. We must also deal, however, with the negative side. Throughout history, that negative side has
erupted time and again, with catastrophic results. In the name of Christ,
clergy have for 1,700 years blessed armies fighting for nothing more than
prestige, plunder, and territory. The criminal who was hanged between
thieves now hangs in cathedrals, decked in gold leaf. These are not mere de-
viations from Jesus' values. They are deep tendencies already present in the
cultural unconscious, that, when activated by an unscrupulous or naive
leader, overwhelm Jesus' more austere convictions.

Israel itself, before Jesus, had suffered from the latest episode of kingship. The Maccabees claimed the throne of David, only to become corrupt
and venal themselves. Such pretenders had repeatedly disappointed the
people's hopes. Some Jews wanted nothing more to do with messiahs, and
longed for direct governance by God. Jesus himself seems to have been
acutely aware of the dangers of messianism, and tried to avoid being identified with people's messianic hopes. His attitude toward the messianic is
sharply at odds with that of most Christians.

One of Jung's great contributions was to help us see how, in Christianity,
the Christ-image was completely identified with the Self (understood as
both the totality of the person and the totality of all selves). However, Jung

generally equated Jesus with the Christ, convinced that we can know nothing with certainty about the historical Jesus. The contribution of Elizabeth Boyden Howes was to distinguish Jesus from the Christ and to show how Jesus lived, not just the myth of his own people, but, more centrally, his own myth. He refused to identify with the messianic archetypal image and spoke instead of the son of the man, an archetype of the Human that is disidentified from the Self. Rather, the son of the man acts more modestly as a go-between bridging ego and Self, conscious and unconscious, humanity and God. This was the role played by Ezekiel as son of man. In the current hothouse spiritual climate, a couple of weekend retreats qualifies a person to set up shop as a guru. The lust for spiritual power over others seduces some to identify their egos with God. The lowliness of the Humanchild who has nowhere to lay its head is a timely and much-needed corrective.

Here, then, are a few passages that show Jesus struggling with the messianic longing in Israel.

A. Peter's Obsession (Mark 8:27-33 par.)

Jesus went on with his disciples to the villages of Caesarea Philippi; and on the way he asked his disciples, "Who do people say that I am?" And they answered him, "John the Baptist; and others, Elijah; and still others, one of the prophets." He asked them, "But who do you say that I am?" Peter answered him, "You are the Messiah." And he sternly ordered them not to tell anyone about him.

Then he began to teach them that the son of the man must undergo great suffering, and be rejected by the elders, the chief priests, and the scribes, and be killed, and after three days rise again. He said all this quite openly. And Peter took him aside and began to rebuke him. But turning and looking at his disciples, he rebuked Peter and said, "Get behind me, Satan! For you are setting your mind not on divine things but on human things."

Many scholars regard this text as a fabrication by the early church. Here for the first time, ostensibly, a disciple penetrates to Jesus' identity as the Messiah. I find it inconceivable that the early church would have invented a saying that called its chief leader "Satan"—or, if anyone had done so, that they would have preserved such a memory. This is a curse of astonishing virulence, revealing the attraction the messianic role still holds for Jesus. The story scandalizes Matthew and Luke. Matthew administers an antidote in 16:17-19, declaring Peter's insight a divine revelation and handing him the keys of the kingdom. Luke simply eradicates the rebuke.

In Mark's version of the story, what the crowd is *not* saying about Jesus is most significant. No one thinks that he is the Messiah. Nor does Jesus accept Peter's so-called confession in v. 30; rather, he "rebuked" (*epitimao*) him for it. The same harsh term is used in vv. 32 and 33; hence, v. 30 needs to be rendered with the same passion: literally, "and he rebuked them in order that they should not speak to anyone concerning it/him."[2] If the church invented the tale, why is Jesus' response not like Matthew's acclamation? What Mark gives us is not Peter's "confession," as tradition has named this account, but Peter's continuing *obsession* with the kind of political power Jesus sharply repudiated.[3]

Jesus' apparent reticence about the messianic title is surprising. He gives neither a clear yes nor an unambiguous no. He can scarcely say yes, for the messianic role with which Peter, Satan-like, tempts Jesus involved the violent overthrow of the Roman occupation and the establishment of an autonomous Davidic kingdom. How could Jesus accept that title when he repudiated its content and regarded it as *a satanic temptation?* But how could he reject it outright, for he had to be aware of divine redemptive power at work within and through him. God's kingdom was breaking into the world through his ministry (Matt. 12:28 // Luke 11:20), and he could not deny its reality. He was the bearer of God's liberating and saving power—messianic power—but he refused to identify with it. In the language of depth psychology, he seems intent on keeping his ego disidentified from the Self. He recognized the Christ-image as a numinous factor present in everyone's psyche. He therefore could not identify himself with it as Christianity later did on his behalf. He did not say that he was the Messiah, but he could not deny that the messianic was real and alive within him. Because he had touched this power, he aroused wholeness in others who projected the power onto him. He could not say no to Peter's projection if he wanted to keep the messianic image alive in Peter. Jesus had to hope that Peter would eventually discover the powers of God's reign within himself.[4] In Howes's words, Jesus now knew himself to be a vessel, a container of God's newness, yet he hardly knew what to do with it. To have said no would have denied this new archetypal Reality being born within the disciples.[5]

We might speculate, then, that Jesus did not reject the messianic role simply because he had redefined messiahship in a nonviolent way. Rather, Jesus seems to have been moving messiahship from its projection onto public leaders, however great, to an inner reality whose latent powers everyone must discover for themselves. How conscious he was of this process we cannot know.

B. John's Question to Jesus [Matt. 11:2-6 // Luke 7:18-23]

> When John heard in prison what the Messiah was doing, he sent word by his disciples and said to him, "Are you the one who is to come, or are we to wait for another?" Jesus answered them, "Go and tell John what you hear and see: the blind receive their sight, the lame walk, the lepers are cleansed, the deaf hear, the dead are raised, and the poor have good news brought to them. And blessed is anyone who takes no offense at me."

The tendency of the gospel tradition was clearly in the direction of heightening Christology. Both Matthew and Luke manifest that tendency in their opening lines. Matthew uses "the Messiah" and Luke "Lord" instead of "Jesus," removing any doubt that the story itself may raise as to Jesus' identity. How remarkable, then, that both evangelists independently allow Jesus' answer to stand in all its ambiguity. Why is Jesus not made to say, "Yes, I am the one you have been waiting for; look at all I've done"? Or, on the contrary, "No, I am not the one you have been waiting for; I am just a prophet and healer"? Why is he afraid that John will be "scandalized" (literally, "caused to stumble") by him?

These were not the kinds of acts most Jews usually associated with the Messiah. But they were nonetheless a part of the vision of a redeemed Israel (Isa. 29:18-19; 35:5-6; 61:1). That the Synoptic Gospels do not give John's response indicates that his response was not favorable, for the church would gladly have reported his endorsement if he had made it. (The Fourth Evangelist invents that endorsement by making John the first confessing Christian!)[6]

Why does Jesus throw the decision about who he is back on John, rather than *telling* John who he is? Again, apparently Jesus cannot identify with the messianic role, yet knows himself to be *related* to the messianic powers at work in him.[7] He is moving the messianic image from external military intervention to personal and social transformation, from killing to healing, from power at the top to empowerment from the bottom: the blind, lame, lepers, and deaf are healed, the dead are raised, and the poor have good news preached to them. Jesus shifts from the messianic image of one who intervenes to reestablish Israel, to a new and puzzling view that stands the world's idea of power on its head. He moves from the archetypal image of the messianic to the archetypal image of what he elsewhere calls the son of the man: the Human Being. For a people saturated with messianic hopes, many of them legitimate, his response is a real "stumbling block" (*scandalizo*). Consistent with that inversion, he refuses to tell John unambiguously who he is.

Perhaps he himself does not know, if that entails identifying himself with some preexistent role. John has to decide for himself. Jesus does not claim messiahship because he cannot. People are forever projecting the messianic longing on powerful leaders. Is not the true messianic function to help others discover messianic powers within themselves?[8]

C. Exorcising by the Finger of God (Luke 11:20 // Matt. 12:28)

Jesus cannot deny that the power of God is working through him to inaugurate God's reign in the world: "If it is by the finger of God that I cast out the demons, then the kingdom of God has come to you." What he does *not* say, astonishingly, is that through these exorcisms the *Messiah* has come to them in his own person. Jesus did not preach about himself. Rather, he preached the coming Reign of God in the actual conditions of suffering human beings. His reticence about himself is not due to modesty on his part; indeed, his bold assertion of his role as bringer of God's reign is anything but modest. He has no hesitation in speaking about the coming of God's reign in every act of his that liberates people from oppression, sin, or death. To free people from the powers that possessed them was central to his struggle to undercut the Domination System in all its forms, spiritual as well as physical, personal as well as political. Here again he acknowledges that he himself actualizes, bears, and reveals God's reign, but he refuses to take the additional step of identifying himself as the Messiah. For to do so would have been fatal to the task of awakening and empowering the Humanchild in others. *It is not enough to free people from the Powers. They must still become the persons that the Powers have prevented them from becoming.* For Jesus to identify himself as the Messiah would be to localize all that power in himself and block its access to others. We can see from Jesus' sending the twelve disciples to heal and cast out demons (Mark 6:7) that he wanted them to discover the same powers within themselves that they were busy projecting onto him. Nevertheless, had the messianic hope not been alive in Israel, it would not have been available to galvanize expectations. Only Israel could have given birth to Jesus.

D. Rejection at Nazareth (Mark 6:1-6 // Matt. 13:53-58)

> He left that place and came to his hometown, and his disciples followed him. On the sabbath he began to teach in the synagogue, and many who heard him were astounded. They said, "Where did this man get all this?

What is this wisdom that has been given to him? What deeds of power are being done by his hands! Is not this the carpenter, the son of Mary and brother of James and Joses and Judas and Simon, and are not his sisters here with us?" And they took offense at him. Then Jesus said to them, "Prophets are not without honor, except in their hometown, and among their own kin, and in their own house." And he could do no deed of power there, except that he laid his hands on a few sick people and cured them. And he was amazed at their unbelief.

The people of Nazareth are also "scandalized" (NRSV "offended") by his wisdom and works. For our purposes a single comment is in order: Jesus makes no appeal to "messianic" authority here, but describes himself simply as a "prophet."

E. Plucking Grain on the Sabbath [Mark 2:23-28 par.]

And he said to them, "Have you never read what David did when he and his companions were hungry and in need of food? He entered the house of God, when Abiathar was high priest, and ate the bread of the Presence, which it is not lawful for any but the priests to eat, and he gave some to his companions." (2:25-26)

As we saw earlier, it is the disciples who break the sabbath by plucking standing grain. Jesus is depicted as defending his disciples' actions by appealing to what David did when he and his disciples ate the bread of the Presence on the altar. Striking here is what Jesus fails to do: arguing from the lesser to the greater, he should have appealed to his authority as the Messiah. If *David* acted thus, how much more *the son of David!* As in Peter's "confession," however, Jesus switches from Messiah/Christ to the son of the man, suggesting a genuine shift from one archetype to the other.

F. About David's Son [Mark 12:35-37]

While Jesus was teaching in the temple, he said, "How can the scribes say that the Messiah is the son of David? David himself, by the Holy Spirit, declared, 'The Lord said to my Lord, "Sit at my right hand, until I put your enemies under your feet." ' David himself calls him Lord; so how can he be his son?"

It is hard to comprehend why the evangelists preserved this passage. The clear tendency, as we have seen repeatedly, is to augment the messianic claims for Jesus. This passage aside, the New Testament universally regarded Jesus as the son of David.[9] Yet, comments Eduard Schweizer with representative bafflement, "Jesus' question might lead us to suppose that he is disputing the Davidic origin of the messiah. Certainly that would be the easiest interpretation of the statement."[10] In the face of a tradition that was to outdo itself in making increasingly lofty claims for Jesus, Jesus himself seems to be denying the foundation of these claims.

Why? Is he asserting that he is the Messiah despite not being of the Davidic line? There are good reasons, however, for believing that he might have been a descendent of David, though he himself made nothing of it.[11] Or, apart from his own genealogy, is Jesus insisting that the Messiah is of a higher order than the Davidic king? Or is he (or the church) amalgamating Psalm 110, quoted in this passage, with Dan. 7:13, and rejecting the messianic figure for the son of man seated at God's right hand? In the words of Herman Waetjen, "David's lord is none other than the New Human Being [son of man] whom Jesus embodies and manifests . . . who, because he is David's lord, cannot be David's son."[12]

G. The Rich Fool [Luke 12:13-14; Gos. Thom. 72]

> Someone in the crowd said to him, "Teacher, tell my brother to divide the family inheritance with me." But he said to him, "Friend, who set me to be a judge or arbitrator over you?"

Jesus is not just refusing to become involved in a family feud. He is rejecting the role of the king in the gate who provides justice: "Give the king your justice, O God, and your righteousness to a king's son. May he judge your people with righteousness, and your poor with justice" (Ps. 72:1-2). One of the acts of the Davidic king would be to restore the thrones of judgment set up in the "house of David" (Ps. 122:5). Normally a local court would have handled such a case. Presumably this man has tried that route and failed to get satisfaction. He is going over the court's head to Jesus, appealing to him to act as king.

Jesus refuses to play the role of judge. Yet the church would later deck him out in royal robes and declare him judge of "the quick and the dead."

Thomas's version depicts Jesus as baffled by the man's request. "A man said to him: Speak to my brothers that they divide my father's possessions with me. He said to him: O man, who made me a divider? He turned to his disciples and said to them: I am not a divider, am I?" How odd—he does not seem to know!

Sometimes what is not said is as important as what is said. When a woman anoints Jesus, he does not interpret her act as an investiture to kingship, but as an anointing of his body beforehand for burial (Mark 14:8; Matt. 26:12).

H. Jesus' Temptation [Matt. 4:1-11 // Luke 4:1-13]

Inexplicably, this Q narrative depicts Jesus as rejecting the three leading messianic roles of Jewish hope: the prophet like Moses, the priestly messiah, and the kingly messiah. The church was later to ascribe all three roles to him: prophet, priest, and king. Who, then, in the early church could have written this account? We know of Jewish Christians who rejected the titles of priest and king, but they stoutly believed that Jesus was the Mosaic prophet.[13] Was there a branch of the earliest community that rejected all ascriptions of majesty to Jesus? Yes, there was: the communities that produced Q and *Thomas* (though the latter lacks this narrative). However this narrative may have been produced—and it is one of the most profound in all literature—only Jesus seems capable of having been its source, or someone else who had a very accurate and equally profound grasp of Jesus' self-understanding. Once more, the category of historicity yields to the question of truth: this story is true, whether it happened or not, whether Jesus told it or not.

I. Jesus before the Sanhedrin [Mark 14:61-62 par.]

Asked if he is the Messiah, Jesus' silence before the Sanhedrin and Pilate seals his fate. The Romans regarded the refusal to answer the charge as a confession of guilt. It was seditious to claim to be Messiah, but it was not blasphemy. In the war against the Romans of 132–135 C.E., Rabbi Akiba declared that the Jewish military commander, Bar Kokhba, was the Messiah, and he was not charged with blasphemy. None of the charges brought against Jesus by the Jewish authorities and their accomplices accuses him of claiming to be the Messiah. To its credit, the Sanhedrin is depicted here as rejecting the trumped-up charges that false witnesses have brought against Jesus. Finally the high priest asks Jesus directly, "Are you the Christ, the Son of the Blessed?" That was a charge the Romans could understand: treason.

Mark has Jesus answer, "I am" (*ego eimi*), followed by a saying about the son of man seated at the right hand of Power and coming with the clouds of heaven. Matthew and Luke, curiously, lack this straightforward "I am." Matthew has *su eipas*, an ambiguous phrase that can mean either "That's what *you* say," or "You said it!" The first is a refusal to answer that implies a "no," the second implies "yes." Elsewhere Matthew uses the same expression with the implication that it means yes (Matt. 26:25). But here, judging from Pilate's response later, *su eipas* must mean "you have said so," implying no.

Luke has two answers, the first from Luke's special source of passion traditions, the second drawn from Mark. In the first Lukan answer, Jesus replies to the high priest's question with a riddle: "If I tell you, you will not believe; and if I question you, you will not answer." He then speaks about the son of man being seated at the right hand of the power of God. This statement does not evoke a charge of blasphemy; whatever the historicity of the account, Luke clearly does not regard Jesus' reference to the Humanchild as blasphemous.[14] It is the next line that seals his fate. When they ask, "Are you, then, the Son of God?" he responds, *humeis legete hoti ego eimi* — "You say that I am." They take this as "You said it," and consider the charge sealed.

The anomaly is that most scholars subscribe to the Two Document hypothesis, which conjectures that Mark and a lost "Q" document were the basic sources for Matthew and Luke, who used them independently of each other. In this narrative, however, both Matthew and Luke agree *against* Mark by having Jesus answer the high priest equivocally. There are also a few Greek manuscripts of Mark that do *not* read "I am," but rather "You say that" (*su eipas hoti*).[15] Matthew and Luke must have had texts of Mark that had the ambiguous answer (which Luke also has in a different form in his special source), and some scribe subsequently changed Mark to the open declaration, "I am."

The judgment before Pilate supports this reasoning. (What took place before the Sanhedrin was not a trial, but something more akin to a grand jury hearing in which the authorities sought to find a charge that they could take to Pilate for trial.) The charge they bring to Pilate is that Jesus claimed to be the Christ, the "king of the Jews." In all three of the Synoptic Gospels, Jesus answers: *su legeis*. Pilate hears this as "That's what you say," and responds in Mark's version, *"Have you no answer to make?"* The implication is clearly that Jesus did *not* incriminate himself, leaving Pilate wondering how to dispose of a man he regarded as innocent.

Most scholars are highly skeptical about the trustworthiness of these narratives. For our purposes, however, what is significant is the depiction of Jesus' ambivalence, his refusal to embrace the messianic role, and, at the same time, his inability to deny that God was working messianically through him. Whatever the source of the account, it shows Jesus unable either to accept or to reject the messianic title. In the trial scene, as in Peter's confession and the plucking on the sabbath, Jesus is depicted as replacing the Messiah with the son of the man ("from now on the son of the man will be seated at the right hand of the power of God"—Luke 22:69). What might be the source of this memory in the community?

The early believers fairly quickly declared Jesus to be the Messiah, and in doing so adorned him with the mythic power of Israel's messianic hope. "Jesus Christ" expressed the ambivalence—or perhaps ambipotency—of the Human Being Jesus and the mythological/archetypal Christ. Paul was content solely with the latter; for him, the archetypal power of the messianic hope was all that was necessary to trigger transformation in his hearers. Others wisely concluded, however, that they needed more than simply the divine Christ and produced Gospels that focused on the life and teaching of Jesus. This made possible a different kind of conversion: not simply rebirth (as in Rom. 6:1-11), but conforming to the life and ministry of Jesus, insofar as one was able. Now followers saw their task as continuing the mission of Jesus in exposing and overcoming the Powers That Be.

The title "Jesus Christ," however, took on a life of its own, while the Human Being all but disappeared. "Christ" came to represent the Self in its entirety: perfect, sinless, flawless, and divine almost to the point of losing humanity altogether. Some of us may want to set aside, or at least de-emphasize, the Christ-image as too perfect, lacking the trial and error necessary for all growth toward wholeness; too sinless, omitting the shadow; too flawless, breaking the spirit of those whom Jesus most cultivated—prostitutes, tax collectors, and those who shrugged off the requirements of the law; too divine, since we are all broken, lost, addicted, estranged, criminal, cruel, corrupted, or, lacking these, self-righteous.

For many, the Christ-image may still possess numinous power. For others, however, the humanness of the son of the man may offer a powerful alternative. For them it may be necessary to hold fast to that image and to see what happens to the Christ-image and the Self, as John Petroni has suggested to me.

The son of the man was not just Jesus, but any and all who were in touch with Jesus' "Abba" ("Daddy" in Aramaic). Because it is still evolving, incomplete, imperfect, unknown, and virtual, the Human Being straddles consciousness and unconsciousness. It is a partial revelation, partly hidden, partly disclosed, and still emerging. Because it is not a symbol of perfection, Sophia's Child embraces all previously excluded from the Beloved Community.

The Human Being, like the Christ, is an archetypal reality. But as an archetype of humanness, the Human Being makes people whole, not perfect. It exercises power, not through compulsion, but by nonviolence. It defines as human, not prowess in battle or beauty of body or achievement of high office, but that which is left when the desire for these has been crucified. It offers us the secret of our individuality.

Discussions of the ethics of cloning human beings have raised the question: who would we want cloned? Historically, the answer has been simple: someone who, in Nietzsche's adulatory phrase, is "haughty, manly, conquering, domineering . . . the highest and best-turned-out type of 'man'" (no doubt matched with a submissive, beautiful woman!) [16] We get the same answer from the emperor Julian (d. 363): "The nobler of the cynics, for their part, say that great Heracles . . . left to mankind the greatest exemplar of their way of life"—whose twelve labors involved acts of violence, sagacity, and seduction.[17]

The issue is the definition of the truly human: what is the anthropic revelation? What does it mean to be human, now that we have the technology to decide? Will we select athletically powerful bodies, brilliant minds, Barbie doll–like women, and soulless tyrants capable of correcting society's ills, or mystics, peacemakers, and spiritual virtuosi? How will we judge success? In the capacity to dominate others, to amass wealth, to achieve fame, to escape poverty, to rise in the organization? Will success be the willingness to offer oneself freely and sacrificially for others? Will we outlaw human cloning altogether? At stake are the entrenched values of the Domination System and its gospel corrective. The goal is not to transcend or surpass the human, but simply to become the human beings we were created to be.

I referred earlier to the positive and negative sides of the messianic image. If the messianic image is ambivalent, then the Human Being must be ambivalent as well. What then are the positive and negative aspects of Jesus' favored expression, the Human Being?

POSITIVE ASPECTS OF THE HUMAN BEING
It is proactive, nonviolent, courageous.
It sees conflict as necessary.
It is willing to sacrifice for others.
It fosters individuation.
It subordinates the ego to the Self.
It is a wanderer, a quester.
It lives by the power of the Holy Spirit.
It rejects the Domination System.

It has discipline.
It is childlike.
It shares power.
It knows itself forgiven.
It seeks wholeness.
It empowers healing and exorcism.
It blesses the poor, mourners, the hungry, and the persecuted.
It loves its enemies.
It is ruthless.
It is compassionate.

Negative Aspects of the Human Being

It is passive, nonresistant, cowardly.
It fears conflict.
It sacrifices itself, mutilates itself.
It fosters individualism.
It identifies the ego with the Self.
It is a spiritual nomad.
It lives out of the power of animal instinct.
It rejects the created world.
It is ascetic.
It is childish.
It fears power.
It feels guilty and can be scrupulous.
It is perfectionistic.
It masochistically embraces suffering.
It is sentimental.
It is judgmental.

We recognize the negative side of the Human Being archetype in a kind of spiritual rigidity, a fear of risk and exploration, a censorious attitude toward others who sin, and a fragile hold on the faith that is threatened by those who deviate from some norm. It is manifest in those who, mistaking nonviolence as nonresistance, acquiesce in evil rather than risk controversy. It rejects the body, sex, and pleasure. This false notion of the Human Being tolerates sentimental pictures of Jesus in church and second-class hymnody. It is a highly personal form of pietism that lacks connection with the needs of the social world, and that represses the shadow rather than attempting to integrate it. It fosters theological vigilantes who act as watchdogs for what they believe to be heresy, and who are, as I write, tearing denominations apart over their rejection of homosexuals.

The texts reviewed in this chapter are all the more amazing because they resist the tendency of the early church to exalt Jesus as the Messiah/Christ. Some scholars have ascribed Jesus' reticence to be called Messiah to his having redefined it in a nonmilitary, nonviolent way. Some believe that Jesus rejected the messianic role altogether, and that Mark invented the "messianic secret" in order to explain why people did not recognize Jesus as Messiah during his lifetime. Others believe that Jesus simply spiritualized the idea of messiah. There is no doubt some truth in all these views.

However, I prefer this explanation: Jesus *could not* tell others he was the Messiah. For if he told them, they would not have to discover the Messiah within themselves. And if they did not discover the Messiah within themselves, they would not learn that they had such powers of discovery within themselves. And if Jesus did not enable them to discover such powers within themselves, he was not the Messiah.

Which is to say that Jesus used the messianic idea as a way to break the disciples' projections onto him—a theme we explore in the next chapter.

7.　Projection and the Messianic Hope

If we are to build an authentic Christology from below based on the Human Being, then we must attempt to avoid the pitfalls of traditional messianism. That means, practically speaking, working with our projections onto persons of attractive or repelling power. We need to give special attention to how we project our own desires for power onto Jesus. This is what Feuerbach criticized as surrendering our own power to God, and it is the chief source of powerlessness in our churches. But projection is not all bad. It is, in fact, one of the best means we have for spiritual illumination.

Here is a very simple way to surface our projections onto Jesus (whether positive or negative). At the beginning of workshops on Jesus that my wife, June Keener Wink, and I lead, I ask the participants to write a one-paragraph description of the kind of person he was. Then I ask them to go back through the paragraph and to note everything that is also true of them, or that represents something to which they aspire. Students are astonished at the degree to which their picture of Jesus is a projected image of themselves and what they would like to be. Jesus is, to that degree, their own idealized self-image.

This, in miniature, is what Albert Schweitzer exposed on a grand scale in his *Quest of the Historical Jesus*.[1] Schweitzer demonstrated that the "biographies" of Jesus produced by nineteenth-century scholars were selective portraits reflecting the piety and prejudices of extremely learned writers. Schweitzer himself proceeded to depict a Jesus ostensibly rendered immune from modernization. Schweitzer's Jesus was enveloped in a web of apocalypticism so foreign to current sensibilities as to appear beyond possibility of projection. Then Schweitzer renounced prestigious positions as a theologian, organist, and musicologist to become a medical missionary in Africa.

He had not made Jesus over into his own image, after all; he had made himself over into his image of Jesus.

What Schweitzer did was instructive. He did not despair of historical reconstruction. He simply sought to ensure that the reconstruction was not pure projection, but that authenticity from the Gospels emerged with sufficient power to remake life. If it could not remake Europe's life, it would remake his own.

Projection[2] has been much misunderstood as a falsification of objective reality by the superimposition of subjective values and images on the data. Projection does involve such falsification, but it is more: a means to discover self and others. As Hal Childs puts it, "We are not only working on texts, but deeply on ourselves," whether we are conscious of that fact or not.[3]

My students realize not just that they make Jesus into their own images of who they are and wish to be, but that Jesus offers them a mirror for discovering their essential selfhood. Projection is not something we do. It happens to us. It is an involuntary, unconscious process. The image of the Jesus onto which we project functions within the psyche as an archetype of wholeness. Hence we who revere him unconsciously project onto him willy-nilly our intuitions of wholeness.[4] What we project onto Jesus is what we *need* in ourselves; our projection arises out of a longing to become more, *a longing that has itself been awakened in part by the figure of Jesus in the Gospels.* To a high degree, the longing for a messiah is a person's or a people's projection of the desire for fulfilled humanity. (It is also, to a remarkable degree, what drives contemporary Jesus scholarship.) Jesus acts as a pulley around which the unconscious can throw a rope in its desire to rise to consciousness. I always do the exercise along with the class, and each time my picture of Jesus is different, reflecting the growing edge of my desire to transcend what I am, to become what I can be. But my Jesus picture is itself subject to check; it must be coherent with the biblical data.

George Tyrrell complained that the nineteenth-century authors of "lives of Jesus" succeeded only in seeing the reflection of their own faces at the bottom of a deep well.[5] He intended his remark critically, and it is valid insofar as scholars failed to recognize their own faces. But if the mirror at the bottom of the well is held by Jesus (bizarre image!), then it can be a positive source of insight about the next stages of our own personal and social development. Or, as Hal Childs puts it, "The reflection at the bottom of the well reveals previously unknown aspects of the 'face of God' that desire incarnation."[6]

Jesus, of course, remains more and other than we can integrate into this picture. Sensing this, we continually seek a broader canvas, truer pigments, excluded options, new information. But even those expanded, more mature pictures of Jesus will contain a large measure of projection. This is not a violation of the text. That is why the text exists in the first place: not to provide historical information, but to foster our transformation. Schweitzer himself said that there is no historical task that reveals a person's true self as much as writing a life of Jesus, and this is true if we write only a paragraph.

We find a remarkable example of projection in the *Acts of John,* in which each disciple sees Jesus as physically different. To James, Jesus first appears as a child, while John sees him as "handsome, fair and cheerful-looking" man. Moments later, Jesus seems to John as "rather bald(-headed) but with a thick flowing beard, but to James as a young man whose beard was just beginning." Each sees the Jesus he needs to see. The reason appears in the hymn that follows: "I am a mirror to you who know me . . . see yourself in Me who am speaking. . . . You who dance, consider what I do, for yours is this passion of Man [= the son of the man] which I am to suffer."[7]

Because we recognize that our own depictions of Jesus may be narrow, nonsensical, unjust, naive, or overly conventional, we read depictions by others. They, too, project onto Jesus their own selfhood and struggles. However, in so doing they may highlight an aspect of his life or teaching—and therefore of our own human possibilities—that we have overlooked, neglected, or repressed. The task of scholarship is thus not to uncover an "objective" picture of Jesus, since that cannot be done. Rather, it is continually to enlarge our admittedly subjective pictures to include more of life and more of the data in our struggle for individuation.[8]

If what I have said about projection is true, however, then is the picture of Jesus that I am painting in this book simply one more subjective, idealized self-image foisted off on Jesus? Is this Jesus as I would have liked him to be? Have I chopped away repugnant elements in the gospel in order to present a politically correct, liberal-minded Jesus masquerading as a first-century Jewish teacher? As John Dominic Crossan writes, "[H]istorical Jesus research is a very safe place to do theology and call it history, to do autobiography and call it biography."[9]

No doubt this is true. There is no way I can avoid projecting onto Jesus my own dreams of wholeness, nor would I want to. But that picture of Jesus is also, I would like to believe, supported somewhat by the data. In this case the hermeneutical spiral proves helpful by providing a feedback mechanism that helps keep us honest to God and to the texts. I have tried to be truthful. But repeatedly, on rereading what I have written, I discover ways that I have twisted the material to fit my own predilections. I acknowledge that I am no doubt blind to realms of Jesus' reality of which I am unaware. Therefore I must listen very carefully to my critics, and not just in order to refute them (though that may be necessary, too). For I need them to help heal my blindness and to open me to more of Jesus' truth than I have yet been able to comprehend.

This preoccupation with projection is not a modern concern that we are retrojecting into the first century. Jesus shows his grasp of the phenomenon when he says, "Why do you see the speck in your neighbor's eye, but do not notice the log in your own eye? Or how can you say to your neighbor, 'Let me take the speck out of your eye,' while the log is in your own eye? You hypocrite, first take the log out of your own eye, and then you will see clearly to take the speck out of your neighbor's eye" (Matt. 7:3-5 // Luke 6:41-42). The spiritual masters of other traditions also understood the problem of projection, and sought to use it in spiritual direction. Thus the great Sufi mystic Rumi is instructed by his spiritual guide (the guide's words are in quotation marks):

> "You are the sheikh, the guide."
> But I'm not a teacher. I have no power.
> He said, "You already have wings.
> I cannot give you wings."
> But I wanted his wings.
> I felt like some flightless chicken.[10]

And Aristides, a pupil of Socrates, could philosophize very well as long as he had a corner of Socrates' toga in his hand, but when he was away from the master his gift for philosophical argument disappeared completely.[11] So also, a rabbi reportedly said, "When we stand in the presence of Rabbi Shim'on, the springs of the heart open to every side and all is revealed. When we are separated from him, we know nothing, and all the springs are stopped up."[12] When a great Jewish Zaddik was asked why he did not follow the example of his teacher by living as the teacher did, he replied, "On the contrary, I do follow his example, for I leave him as he left his teacher."[13] Popular Buddhism reflects the same insight when it teaches, "If you meet the Buddha on the road, kill him."

Franz Kafka revealed profound insight into this understanding of projection when he formulated one of his paradoxical sayings: "The Messiah will come only when he is no longer necessary; he will come only on the day after his arrival."[14] For the Messiah to come one moment earlier would be to impose divine dictatorship on the world. Thus the Hasidic mystic, the Baal-Shem Tov, commented on the passage "Noah walked with God" by saying,

"And so, when the Father departed from him, Noah knew: It is in order that I may learn to walk."[15]

We now look at some of the ways the early church dealt with the projections people placed on Jesus.

A. Breaking Messianic Projections

Jesus is repeatedly depicted dealing with the projections of his disciples. But he does not simply attempt to destroy their projections. To do so would be to sacrifice the heuristic* value of the projections themselves. So he had to carry their projections until the disciples could at last lift the projections to consciousness. Whether this teaching comes from Jesus or from the early makers of tradition and evangelists is not important. What matters is that *we* learn from the master teacher how to work with this incomparable source of buried insight.

1. No One Is Good (Mark 10:17-18 par.)

> As he was setting out on a journey, a man ran up and knelt before him, and asked him, "Good Teacher, what must I do to inherit eternal life?" Jesus said to him, "Why do you call me good? No one is good but God alone."

Several New Testament writers espoused the sinlessness of Jesus (2 Cor. 5:21; Matt. 3:14-15; Heb. 2:10). Jesus' sinlessness is not a datum of history, but a requirement of the myth of his divinity. Conversely, the modern myth of the human Jesus requires that he *not* be perfect.[16] To support the idea of Jesus' sinlessness, Matthew changed Jesus' reply to the rich man from "Why do you call me good?" to, "Why do you ask me about what is good?" (19:17). Matthew could not tolerate Jesus saying that he is not good. How remarkable, then, is Jesus' retort in Mark. "No one is good" must include Jesus himself. It is scarcely likely that anyone would have uttered such words but Jesus himself.

The rich man's class status determines his odd request. One normally does nothing in order to receive an inheritance. He most likely inherited his wealth, especially if he is young.[17] He expects God to behave like his own father and to offer an eternal inheritance. Heirs are eager to please their benefactors, so he has kept all the commandments. Yet he sees in Jesus something he lacks. He runs and kneels before Jesus, in an eagerness unbecoming his station. He addresses Jesus as his own idealized self-image: "Good teacher." He sees himself as good and Jesus as better, someone to whom he can aspire.

Jesus' response is crushing. He is not interested in people becoming better; they must become new.[18] "Why do you call me good" rings like Jesus' challenge to the "confession" of Peter: "Don't call me that!" (Mark 8:30). Jesus refuses to be idealized, set on a pedestal, and worshiped. Such adulation would be indispensable if he intended to launch a messianic career. He manifests the same reluctance when the authorities ask him to confirm the divine mandate for his work by doing signs (Mark 8:11-13 par.; Luke 11:29-32 // Matt. 12:38-42).

In fact, a number of passages render Jesus' sinlessness questionable. He submits to John's baptism for the forgiveness of sins. He petulantly withers the fig tree (Mark 11:12-14); he loses his temper at the disciples (Mark 9:19) and his opponents (Mark 3:5); he is depicted as treating the Pharisees uncharitably (Matthew 23); and he seems to get caught occasionally in visions of revenge that are at odds with his own best insights. The doctrine of Jesus' sinlessness has led exegetes to downplay these instances, rather than take Jesus at his word and concede that no one is good, himself included. The results have been christologically devastating. Jesus was declared to be like us in every way, except without sin—in other words, not like us at all.

My first professor of New Testament, J. Christiaan Beker, shocked me to my pious roots when he said, "Our dreams of perfection are our greatest sin." The very attempt to appear good grounds our lives in a lie (we know we are not as good as we pretend to be.) Worse, it makes us cautious, incapable of creativity, risk, and failure. As Jung remarked, "We all must do just what Christ did. We must make *our* experiment. We must make mistakes . . . and there will be error. If you avoid error you do not live, in a sense even it may be said that every life is a mistake, for no one has found the truth. When we live like this, we know Christ as a brother, and God indeed becomes [a human being]. This sounds like a terrible blasphemy, but not so . . . for then only does God become [human] in ourselves."[19]

2. Your Faith Has Made You Whole

Jesus apparently senses that he is becoming a power in his followers' psyches, and the discovery upsets him. Aspiring messiahs might mark this moment as the first flush of success. Jesus, however, is portrayed struggling to break the disciples' projections onto him and to relocate the Truly Human Being within them.

First and most obvious are the repeated instances in which Jesus ascribes healing to the faith of those who need healing. A woman with a hemorrhage elbows her way through a crowd, rendering everyone that she touches unclean. When she touches Jesus' garment, she feels herself instantly healed. Jesus senses power leaving him, discovers who touched him, and says to her, "Daughter, your faith has made you well; go in peace, and be healed of your disease" (Mark 5:34). It is not Jesus' word or act that heals her, as Matthew changes it to read (Matt. 9:20-22). It is her own faith. Why does Jesus say it that way? Why not say, "Your faith *in me* has healed you?" Faith in Jesus seems to have been the reason for healing. If she could have healed herself, she would have done so years before, prior to exhausting her funds on physicians. Jesus surely has been the catalytic agent of her healing, even if his role, on this occasion, was passive. Why then does he insist on ascribing the healing to the woman's faith?

Jesus follows the same pattern in the story of Blind Bartimaeus, a beggar in Jericho, whose bellowings for mercy cause Jesus to stop, call him over, and heal him, commenting, "Your faith has made you well" (Mark 10:52). Why does Jesus refuse the credit and ascribe healing to the supplicants?

Apparently because he really believes that the healing power already exists in these people, and that his presence simply triggers latent powers. When the sick are not able to exercise such faith, Jesus is satisfied to work with the faith of their friends (Mark 2:1-12 par.), a mother (Mark 7:24-30 // Matt. 15:21-28), a slave's master (Matt. 8:10 // Luke 7:9). When no one else has faith, Jesus depends on the disciples (Mark 5:27; 9:18) or his faith alone (Mark 7:31-37; 8:22-26). Sometimes even that is not enough (Mark 6:1-6).

That is why Jesus is adamant about the importance of faith. Faith is not just something on which he has a monopoly, or a consequence of his special connection to healing powers. Faith is something the disciples, in fact, anyone, can exercise, and it can move mountains (the reference may be specifically to Mount Zion—the Temple Mount—the center of religious practice in Judaism [Mark 11:22-24]). Even the tiniest amount of faith is enough, because it is not faith in our faith that creates the miracle, but faith in God (Luke 17:5-6).

3. Mark's Teaching on Projection

As long as the disciples were enthralled by Jesus' powers, however, they would not be able to find those powers in themselves. Mark contains a fascinating series of stories that address that problem.

In the first narrative, the Stilling of the Storm (Mark 4:35-41 par.), Jesus sleeps in the stern of a fishing boat as he and his disciples cross the Sea of Galilee. When a sudden storm threatens to swamp the boat, the disciples wake him, shouting, "Teacher, do you not care that we are perishing?"[20] Jesus condescends; he bears their projections and rebukes the wind: "Be silent! Be muzzled!" as if it were a demon. The wind was a demon, but not meteorologically. It was demonic only in the disciples. They had no doubt exercised heroism countless times before in storms—the Sea of Galilee was notorious for such. Where had their courage fled this time? Jesus had stolen it. More accurately, they had given up their courage by entering into dependency on Jesus. So they experienced the storm not as a challenge, but as an evil threat, and they even accuse Jesus of unconcern for their survival.

Jesus chastises them: "Why are you such cowards (*deiloi*)? Have you still no faith?" Faith in what? What had he expected of them? They are the sailors; they know this lake like the palm of their hand and have weathered innumerable storms. Waking him to bail would have made sense; why do they wake him just to accuse him of indifference? And what did Jesus want from them? What difference would faith have made?

Apparently Jesus thinks (as the story has it) that the disciples should have been able to deal with this crisis themselves. But they had never seen a storm stilled before, much less stilled a storm themselves. So he rebukes the wind and sea. "Have you no faith?" must mean something like, "Next time, take care of it yourselves and let me sleep!" In perfect accord with Feuerbach's critique of religion, the disciples are unable to locate power in themselves sufficient for the challenge. When they see Jesus exercising that power, they assume that the power is localized in him: It is *Jesus'* power. By chastising them for lacking faith, Jesus is trying to throw the issue back on them: the power is within you; use your faith! But he gets the opposite result. The disciples are swept off their feet in adulation: "And they were filled with great awe and said to one another, 'Who then is this, that even the wind and the sea obey him?' "

Such a response requires the impatient patience of the spiritual guide. The disciples cannot know that the messianic powers dwell in themselves as well as in Jesus. They have been taught that a powerful charismatic leader, soon to come, will possess these powers. Their job is to conform, to assent, to follow. That these powers might be theirs as well has never dawned on them. They have, in fact, been trained *not* to believe that such abilities lay within their reach. They have been taught *not* to seek power in themselves. The Powers want people pliant. The religious authorities tend to want their devotees passive. Leaders do not want empowered people; they want trust-worthy followers. How interesting that Jesus has chosen disciples from the margins of society, people not caught up in the power game. He wants to be the torch to their tinder, to set them on fire for God: "I came to bring fire to the earth, and how I wish it were already kindled!" (Luke 12:49). But this kindling is soggy and will require drying out. Irritation jostles with compassion as the teacher struggles to awaken the disciples to the Divine Wisdom within.

How can Jesus proceed? By sending *them* out to preach, heal, and cast out demons (Mark 6:6-13). As long as they are in his presence, they will locate the healing source in him. Without him around, they will be thrown back on their own resources. They will find the Human Being within, or fail.

The attempt is a splendid success. The disciples discover that they have the resources within themselves. In a Lukan version of one of these healing missions, the disciples—Jesus with them—are ecstatic. Their capacity to expand his mission exponentially was a major defeat for the Spirit of Domination: "I watched Satan fall from heaven like a flash of lightning" (Luke 10:18).

No sooner are the disciples back in the company of Jesus than they re-project their power back onto him. They can heal *if he orders them to*, as above. However, when a boy subject to convulsions is brought to them in Jesus' absence, they are powerless to do anything (Mark 9:14-29). But then, they had never dealt with such a case before. How were they to know what to do? Apparently they were still lacking an inner principle of discrimination, the capacity to know what God wants in the particulars of human life. They are still waiting for instructions from outside, not realizing that they had access to an inner guide, the Human Being.

The impatient patience of the teacher is again put to the test when five thousand people crowd to hear him in a deserted place. When it grows late, the disciples urge him to dismiss the crowd so people can find something to eat. Jesus answers, "You give them something to eat." The disciples are incredulous. "Are we to go and buy two hundred denarii worth of bread and give it to them to eat?" It is highly unlikely that Jesus' entire band could cough up a fraction of that money, two-thirds of a working man's annual wages. Or, if they had enough money, it is unlikely that they could find that much bread for sale in the region. John 6:5-6 underscores the teacher's ruse. Jesus himself asks Philip, " 'Where are we to buy bread for these people to eat?' *He* [*Jesus*] *said this to test him*, for he himself knew what he was going to do."

Again, Jesus condescends and feeds the people. Everyone eats to the fill, leaving twelve baskets full of bread scraps and fish. Whether the "miracle" is

Jesus getting people to share their brown-bag lunches (that the women allegedly would have packed and hidden under their skirts), or whether each person got just a crumb in an inaugural eucharistic celebration of the dawning of God's new order, or whether the food actually multiplied, I leave to the reader's discretion. I am interested only in one thing: Why did Jesus say, "You give them something to eat"?

The question was something the disciples had never anticipated. How could Jesus keep expecting them to deal with new situations for which they had no precedent? To be sure, Moses fed the people with manna in the wilderness—or rather, God did so through Moses. But surely Jesus could not expect them to act with the faith of Moses! It was one thing to assert that Jesus was a greater-than-Moses (as the Fourth Gospel does). It was different to expect the *disciples* to do the mighty deeds that Moses did. They were not up to that. So again, Jesus does it for them.

What happens after the feeding may not be historical, but it certainly is hysterical. As soon as the feeding is over, Jesus orders his disciples to get into their boat and to cross to the other side while he dismisses the crowd (Mark 6:45). Then he goes into the hills to pray. (Please note that the disciples never are caught in the act of prayer. They let Jesus do all their praying for them—another sign that they are letting Jesus carry the relationship to the numinous for them. Consequently, when the crunch comes in Gethsemane and Jesus entreats their prayers, they fall fast asleep [Mark 14:32-42]. But back to our story.) "When evening came, the boat was out on the sea, and he was alone on the land." The preceding paragraph mentions "green" grass. That reference would place this narrative in the spring (Mark 6:39), suggesting a sunset around 7 P.M. Since Jesus dispatched the disciples in late afternoon, they would have left, say, around 5 P.M. "He saw that they were straining at the oars against an adverse wind." There is no danger of foundering; they are just not making headway. At about the fourth watch of the night—between 3 and 6 A.M.—Jesus comes toward them, walking on the sea. That means the disciples have been rowing fruitlessly for between ten to thirteen hours! "He meant to pass by them." What?! Well, of course, they are getting nowhere, and he can get there quicker on foot. He has already taught them how to still storms, and if they want to waste their energy they are welcome to it.

But the worst thing possible happens. The disciples see Jesus. With that, the rope of courage snaps. They take him for a ghost, and they panic. They are too terrified even to do the one thing of which they are capable: rowing. Once more the impatient patience of the teacher condescends: "But immediately he spoke to them and said, 'Take heart, it is I; do not be afraid.' Then he got into the boat with them and the wind ceased. And they were utterly astounded, for they did not understand about the loaves, but their hearts were hardened." The loaves? What do the loaves have to do with this story? Why does the meaning of this episode hang on the loaves of the preceding story?

Perhaps the clue lies in the remarkable frequency of the present tense in connection with Jesus in this scene on the lake. Literally, "he *comes* towards them, *walking* (present participle) on the sea . . . he *says* to them, "Take heart, *I AM (ego eimi)*; do not be afraid." The disciples, by contrast, are living in the past tense ("they saw him . . . they thought it was a ghost [*phantasma*] . . . cried out . . . saw . . . were terrified"). Mark seems to be saying to beleaguered Christians in Rome (or wherever): if you truly understood the mystery of the loaves, and of the Risen One in your midst (who is not a ghost), you would not be afraid, for the Bread of Heaven is here, now, in your midst, in the celebration of the breaking of the bread.

Matthew adds Peter's attempt to walk on the water. Peter is right in trying to do what Jesus does. He steps on the water—and does not sink! "But when he noticed the strong wind, he became frightened, and beginning to sink, he cried out, 'Lord, save me!' " (Matt. 14:30). Perhaps Peter's mistake was to try the unknown before he accomplished the known: he should have stilled the storm *first*, before he left the boat, and then tried walking on the water! This story takes the theme of projection another step. Here is a disciple no longer content to be bedazzled by Jesus' divine powers. He is ready to claim them for himself. He steps out into the deep. And he is successful! Jesus reproaches Peter for taking his eyes off him and turning toward the storm. Ah, the sermons that statement has spawned! The disciples' capacity to continue Jesus' mission will depend on their staying related to the Source.

Now, dear reader, I realize that I have pushed your indulgence to the limit. It is conceivable that Jesus stilled storms, multiplied bread, and walked on water; unlike Jesus' healings and exorcisms, however, the disciples seem to have been unable to replicate these "miracles." I prefer to treat them as spiritual stories that teach a remarkable truth. And that truth is no deeper if these stories happened or not. Historical or not, these stories are true, and what they require of us is a new way of relating to Jesus.

B. Incarnating God

These narratives about projection answer one of the most pressing questions in the spiritual formation of the fledgling Christian: how to relate to Jesus in a way that will not infantilize, miniaturize, and stifle the growth of the Human Being within. Jesus' intent seems to be that we incarnate the Truly

Human Being. How we deal with Jesus has everything to do with that incarnation. In traditional Christian dogma, Jesus usually has been regarded as the *sole* incarnation of God, rather than the one who shows us how to incarnate God. The traditional doctrine of the incarnation is itself mythological; the initiative is God's, and God incarnates in Jesus, rather than Jesus incarnating God. When we make Jesus the sole incarnate Son of God, Feuerbach's critique of religion is fully confirmed. We empty ourselves into transcendence. All healing power, all authority, all ecstatic union with God is focused in this one exemplary person (and perhaps in Mary and a few exemplary saints). But such a move is intrinsically "docetic"; Jesus is made a divine being who merely appears to be human (*dokoō*, "to seem, to appear"). *I* cannot be expected to be like him! So I diminish myself by projecting all the divine powers within me onto Jesus. As the great Eastern Gnostic Mani observed, "He who sees himself only on the outside, not within, becomes small himself and makes others small."[21]

The implications of these reflections are profound. It means we are free to go on the journey that Jesus charted rather than to worship the journey of Jesus. That means we are to be cocreators with God. It means that we can, if we have the courage, recover the healing ministry of Jesus and his very Jewish kind of persistent prayer. It liberates Jesus from the cloying baggage of christological beliefs added by the church. It strips away the heavy accretion of dogma that installed Jesus as the second person of the Trinity, and instead makes him as available to Jews or Muslims as to Christians, indeed, available to anyone seeking the Human Being within. It takes Jesus out of the ghetto of the churches and offers him to anyone looking for a guide to true humanity. As the philosopher Paul Ricoeur saw clearly, it frees us to see the theme of "the son of the man" as the clue to the first Christology.[22] It restores Jesus' humanity. It delivers us from the notion that God came down to earth masquerading as a man, his every step predetermined from eternity. Instead, we can picture Jesus as a human being seeking the will of God in the everyday decisions that shaped his life, living, as the temptation narrative puts it, by every word that comes from the mouth of God (Matt. 4:4).

Most important, perhaps, Jesus shows us something of what it means to become human, but not enough to keep us from having to discover our own humanity. We must weave the story, and for each of us the story will be unique.

Ascribing titles of greatness to Jesus, regardless of how elevated, diminishes Jesus, because it forces him into preexisting categories that cannot take in his uniqueness and creativity. If we insist that Jesus Christ is the only begotten Son of God, we place him on a pedestal so high that no one else can or *ought* to aspire to his stature. We worship his "arrived" humanity rather than letting him guide us into our own. We let ourselves off the hook and settle for an attenuated, shriveled, and puny humanity for ourselves.

Wait a minute, says John Starkey in a letter following a lecture I gave in Oklahoma City.

> It seems to me that there can be a dialectical relation between recognizing that another person is *both* more HUMAN than oneself *and* equally human with oneself. Albert Schweitzer, Jane Austen, my past great Jesuit spiritual advisor—all of these attained to higher levels of HUMANITY over the course of their lives than I have so far attained in mine. But they were all humans. Now, I "look up" to all of them. Should I remain in an archetypal relation of child to parent, or even adolescent to mentor? Not exactly. However, to me, so long as any of these remain in fact more HUMAN than I, when I see them as taller I may not be *pedestalizing*, but *recognizing*.

No doubt he is right. When we withdraw the projections, we can see the other as she really is. This makes possible a mature relationship in which one who is more authentic than ourselves can continue to draw us toward our fuller humanity.

Much as the Protestant Reformation stripped away accretions and superstitions that had adhered to the gospel message, so we today are stripping away the clutter that has placed Jesus under ecclesiastical house arrest and made him alien and inaccessible. That means that we are freed to learn from other traditions the teachings that are consistent with the revelation Christians have in Jesus.

A teacher's admirers may give away their power, to be sure, but they also can be parasites that suck life and energy from the teacher. They achieve a sense of self by identifying with a leader. Rather than doing the kinds of things the teacher does, students admire the teacher for doing them. This adulation is poison to the teacher, *yet the teacher must carry the burden of the disciple's selfhood until the disciple can assume it voluntarily*. It usually requires a shock, a break, or a death to shatter the projections—and even that may not be enough.[23]

C. Death: Shatterer of Projections

To a certain extent, death did shatter the disciples' projections. The presence of the Human Being within Jesus had activated their longing to find the same reality within themselves. That presence in him had drawn them to Jesus in the first place. But as long as Jesus was with them, they inevitably would identify that power as *his* power. In the stilling of the storm, Jesus' challenge to faith falls on deaf ears. All the disciples see is a miraculous calm, which merely heightens their awe: "Who then is this, that even the wind and the sea obey him!" Even if they began to realize that Jesus was a channel for the power and not the power itself, that merely would relocate the projection from him to something *in him*. So it was not just a matter of reinterpreting messiahship, because no matter how Jesus reinterpreted it, the disciples would still be frozen in fascination with its numinous power in him. No matter what Jesus did to break the messianic projection he carried for them, the disciples would readjust their expectation, because the locus of the power was Jesus himself. All Jesus could do was continually throw the question back at them: "Have you still no faith?" It is curious that this question has evoked in Christendom the response, "We believe that you are the Christ, the Son of the living God," rather than the reaction, Does he really believe that I am capable of doing the works he did, and greater works than these, because he has gone to the Father? (John 14:12).

Dead, Jesus was no longer there to carry the disciples' projections. His disciples would have to abandon him entirely (as Judas did), or find Jesus' powers within themselves. What apparently happened was that, shortly after his death, they discovered they had the same miracle-working power (Acts 3:1-10). What had occurred in the dark interval between Jesus' death and the birth of this new power and authority within? We can only speculate, and our speculations will seem reductionistic unless we concede from the outset that the mystery that now confronts us is beyond solution.

For some, Jesus' crucifixion was the death of at least some of their projections. "We *had hoped* that he was the one to redeem Israel," his disciples lament after his crucifixion (Luke 24:21). But this also means that whatever messianic longings they had attached to him were crucified as well. Paul saw this most clearly. When he says, "We proclaim Christ crucified, a stumbling block to Jews and foolishness to Gentiles" (1 Cor. 1:23), he articulates in a blistering paradox the transformation in consciousness required of the earliest Christians. The last thing one would expect of a messiah is death. Death could only spell failure. A false messiah was, by definition, one whom the Powers had seized and killed (for example, Theudas, the Egyptian, and other "messianic pretenders" whom the Romans had crushed). Jesus would seem to have been another failed messiah. One would have thought that Paul therefore would preach Christ resurrected instead. But Paul saw the need to rub people's noses in the paradox, in order to put to death their negative messianic longings and to free them for the new thing God had done in Jesus. And to a remarkable degree it worked. The longing for a military messiah was obliterated from the image of Jesus as Messiah.

With that move, however, the positive aspects of the messianic longing were re-projected onto Jesus. He became the Christ/Messiah of Christian hope, who would save one's soul for eternal life in heaven after one dies. Life on earth became a kind of holding pen in which the main task was to screen souls for eternal life or damnation after death.

And what happens to Christians today, for whom the scandalous paradox of a crucified Messiah scarcely exists? Jesus for us is the *Christian* Messiah, who died for our sins. Nothing remains in that message that can crucify our negative messianic longings. And so we take on, not just the positive messianic hopes, but the negative ones as well. We do need someone who can transform the intolerable, who can galvanize resistance to oppression. But we also long for an authority figure who will tell us what to do and take responsibility for the mess we have made. So the lowly Jesus, born in a manger and having no place to lay his head, would assume the negative messianic roles at his coming again in power and glory. In short, the roles that Jesus gave up to be Messiah the first time around would be reassumed when he came again to judge the world.

I stated earlier that projection is not "wrong." It is a perfectly normal and necessary psychic function. When we project our own inmost soul, we do so because we are unconscious of its real existence. The teacher's function is to activate that soul, and the teacher does that by manifesting his or her own soul to the learner. Those who follow Jesus need Jesus on whom to project. That is one of his gifts. Jesus carries our souls until we recognize them in him and claim them for our own. We need never stop projecting onto him. We are in a permanent feedback spiral in which we may continue to see in Jesus the next stages of our human development. He serves as an impetus for our ongoing transformation. But Jesus is not himself that transformation. Jesus puts us in touch with the Human Being within, and helps us learn to incarnate its qualities in our lives. We need the incarnation projected onto Jesus in order to discover the meaning of incarnating true humanity in ourselves. This is not pure projection either, because Jesus really did incarnate God. I mean that not in the mythical sense of God coming to earth and having been born a man. I mean it in the ordinary sense: through the power and guidance of the Holy Spirit, Jesus actualized God in his own being. He brought the potential of myth into the fabric of his human life. The sheer attraction of his being draws others to him, that they might find, mirrored in him, their own true selves.

John the Baptist apparently played the role of mentor for Jesus. Something in John drew Jesus to the Jordan River to undergo baptism. Those who believe that Jesus was sinless have a problem explaining why Jesus submitted to John's baptism for the forgiveness of sins. Apparently Jesus needed to die/drown to the world of the Domination System and be reborn to the new world of God as much as we do. Through what was symbolized by his baptism and temptation, Jesus apparently experienced the birth of something divine within. We will probably never know why he chose to call this inner being "the son of the man," though I am convinced it was prompted at least in part by meditation on God's having addressed Ezekiel in this way. Later, Jesus broke with John and developed a unique message that built on John's but that radically transformed it. That break marks Jesus' own maturation beyond his mentor and entry into his own selfhood. It may have been John's execution that shattered Jesus' projections onto John and that forced him to find the teacher within, which his tradition taught him to call the Holy Spirit (Luke 12:12). If that is the case, then Jesus himself models for us the process of making and breaking projections.

But the early theologians had already begun to historicize the mythological reality to which Jesus was related, and to mythologize the historical life that he had lived. As Elizabeth Howes writes:

> The deep interior truths leading to individual consciousness that Jesus manifested have been turned into seemingly historical events which became dogma that had to be believed. Also the history that Jesus lived was made into a myth, thus depriving his life of its own truth and substance. He has thus been made the carrier of our inner myth, and his history has become mythological. This confusion of myth and history is the very foundation of the Christian religion. . . .[24]

The early theologians historicized and literalized Jesus' insight about dying to one's ego and to the Powers (Mark 8:34-35 par.). As a result, the process of dying and rising that is at the heart of world mythology was seen as the historical event of Jesus' crucifixion and resurrection. This interpretation mythicized his experience of birthing the divine child within. This inner process was projected out as a miraculous biological event, the virgin birth. In place of the myth of the human Jesus there grew up the myth about the divine Christ. The mythic archetypal pattern of the hero's journey was historicized into the literal events of Jesus' annunciation, flight into Egypt, crucifixion, and resurrection.

Thus two stories survive, like one painting painted right over another. The first story was the mundane life of a human being seeking to embody God. This story later was overlaid by the exalted life of a divine being who descended from heaven and, dressed in human flesh, suffered rejection, and was apparently killed; but who escaped death and ascended back to heaven, leading a host of liberated captives into everlasting life. This local Jew (story number one) became the universal Logos, the creative Word that was in the beginning before the world was made (story number two). This singularly authentic individual became the second person of the Holy Trinity, of such unsurpassable divinity that it took the churches' best minds centuries to formulate language that could do justice to Jesus' divine nature without altogether eclipsing his humanity.

Please note, however, that *both stories are mythic*. One is the story of a person who consciously chose his path, living the pattern of dying and rising through execution by the Powers That Be. The other is a story imposed on his life, a story that reverts to the collective unconscious and the images gathered there.

I will not think badly of anyone who prefers that second story. But more and more people no longer find it credible. The mythic overlay that made it irresistible in the first-century Mediterranean world makes it unbelievable to many today. But that mythological story was the only story that could move people at the core of their selves in an age in which few understood projection. The theological liberalism of the past two centuries, in its turn, could reject the mythological overlay, but it could not tap the deep unconscious that had infused the second story with life. Without that archetypal depth, theology became rationalistic. The quest for the historical Jesus contributed to that rationalism, but it also began to discover, beneath the second layer of paint, another Jesus. And *that* Jesus was profoundly related to the archetypal dimension, by virtue of actually living, from the background provided by his Jewish heritage, his own myth. *One can only live one's own myth in relationship with the deeper reaches of the collective unconscious.* Only the Human One knows the secret of our true identities. The Human Being mediates that identity to us, not in a single act, but by our consciously relating to it on a day-to-day basis.

It is beyond our reach to say what Jesus experienced in his struggle to shoulder God into history. But we can draw upon the best historical research as the basis for constructing an *alternative myth*, one that we hope may speak more directly to people today. Because it is a *historical* myth, it depends on historical research. That task is not futile, but one that is required of us if we are to speak new/ancient words to those who still hunger to know Jesus' God. That our pictures fail to agree is not fatal, for what holds all our efforts together is a common commitment to work as honestly and accurately as we can.

But how do we access that deep unconscious reality that alone can give numinosity and power to our pictures of Jesus? Unless we can answer that question—and do so, not just intellectually, but in a way that transforms our entire beings—the enterprise will have been futile.

D. Projection and Inflation

The phenomenon of projection is, in religion, equivalent in importance to the general theory of relativity or Bell's theorem in physics. Today, people in all world religions have reached the stage of individuation at which divine/human wholeness can be withdrawn from its projection onto the screen of the cosmos and discovered within persons, groups, or the created order.

Paul provides an example of this process of withdrawing the projections onto holy things and places. Fifteen years before the destruction of the temple in Jerusalem, Paul had ceased to regard it as the primary locus of divine presence and atonement, and found that locus instead in individuals ("Do you not know your body is a temple of the Holy Spirit within you?" 1 Cor. 6:19) and the community ("you [plural] are God's temple," 1 Cor. 3:16). But that locus would, within several centuries, be re-projected onto cathedrals and sanctuaries, which were considered more holy than the world outside. As A. J. Levine notes, Judaism would never have survived the destruction of the temple in Jerusalem had it not also discovered that the presence of God was not restricted to the temple or to sacrifice.

Projection, quite simply, is seeing in others unconscious aspects of ourselves. It can be positive (falling in love) or negative (hating in another what is in oneself). Working with projections can be seen, then, not as correcting a falsehood, or as disabusing someone of an illusion, but as completing the process in which we find within ourselves that which corresponds to what we have perceived without. The goal is to identify the projection, to trace it back to its source in ourselves, and then to free its bearer so that she can truly be herself without bearing the burden of our superhuman (or negative) expectations. The mentor becomes a partner, the teacher a colleague, the parent a friend: "I do not call you servants any longer, because the servant does not know what the master is doing; but I have called you friends" (John 15:15).

The power of Jesus' person apparently stirred undeveloped possibilities in those who encountered him. Staying with him (the theme of "abiding" stressed in the Fourth Gospel) was important because only thus could Jesus continue to hold before the disciples the mirror that revealed to them their own powers. This is the lasting power of the Gospel stories today: the figure of Jesus, in whom Christians see the life of God visibly manifest, is able to activate the longing for God in our own depths. Jesus is God's Lorelei, luring the ego to blessed shipwreck on the rocks of the Self.

Small wonder that Christianity built a hedge around the Self to prevent the unwary from identifying with it. The danger was real; believers who experienced elements of the unconscious activated by myth or liturgy (or drugs) sometimes identified the conscious center they had discovered in themselves as the center of the universe. This is the danger of inflation: being "puffed up," as Col. 2:18 puts it, like a helium balloon drifting into the stratosphere. Harold Bloom, a contemporary Gnostic, dryly comments:

> Gilbert Keith Chesterton, shrewdest of modern Catholic writers, warned, "[T]hat Jones shall worship the god within him turns out ultimately to mean that Jones shall worship Jones." Mere Gnosticism badly needs to be distinguished from such large self-worship; Bloom does not wish to worship Bloom, that after all not being much of a religious experience.[25]

When the ego thus identifies with the inner Human Being, it believes itself to be the Self. As Jung put it:

> In order to exorcise this danger, the Church has not made too much of the "Christ within," but has made all it possibly could of the Christ whom we "have seen, heard, and touched with hands," in other words, with the historical event "below in Jerusalem." This is a wise attitude, which takes realistic account of the primitiveness of man's consciousness, then as now. For the less mindful it is of the unconscious, the greater becomes the danger of its identification with the latter, and the greater, therefore, the danger of inflation, which, as we have experienced to our cost, can seize upon whole nations like a psychic epidemic. . . . The ego is dissolved in the self; unbeknown to itself, and with all its inadequacy and darkness, it has become a god and deems itself superior to its unenlightened fellows. *It has identified with its own conception of the "higher man"* [or, in the case of a woman, the "higher woman"].[26]

When we identify with our own light and confuse the ego with the Self, we feel superior to the darkness within ourselves and other people. Our enlightenment is of no value unless it helps us recognize our own darkness. Individuation results, not from getting rid of the dark side, but from recognizing how much darkness is within, owning it, and integrating both light and darkness into a new synthesis that is more realistic, honest, and humble. But, continues Jung, this is precisely what one cannot do for oneself. "He cannot conquer the tremendous polarity of his nature on his own resources; he can only do so through the terrifying experience of a psychic process that is independent of him, that works *him* rather than he *it*."[27]

Simply knowing about the dangers of inflation does not make us immune to inflation. Nor can we ignore the implication that the Human Being also contains much darkness, not only suffering, but moral ambivalence and harshness as well: "That which you do not have within you will kill you if you do not have it within you" (*Cos. Thom.* 70). To paraphrase Jung, God wants to become incarnate in humans, even if God rends them asunder.[28] It can be terrible to fall into the hands of the living God. But that seems to be the price that must be paid for authentic life.

Part Four

The Human Being:
Post-Easter Sayings

In the pre-Easter sayings about the son of the man, it seemed important to isolate sayings ascribed to Jesus that might serve as a basis for the myth of the human Jesus. I have tried, as far as possible, to construct a picture within the range of historical accuracy. I want the myth of the human Jesus to be as honestly derived as possible. To that end I have attempted to engage in an "extremely verbatim reading," in Daniel Matt's phrase, so that I can know as much as possible about what was meant by the son of the man. No matter that we scholars cannot agree. We are mapping the spread of possible interpretations so that those on individual quests can explore the myth of the human Jesus for themselves.

In the post-Easter sayings, however, the historical issue recedes. Now we are dealing with sayings that reflect the situation after Jesus' death. As we saw earlier, these post-Easter sayings can be divided between those that deal with the ascension and those that are apocalyptic. In the ascension, Jesus enters the world of symbol and myth, attracting to himself the longings of the ages and the myths of the world's peoples. This is the imaginal dimension, the realm of vision and dream, in which meaning is woven around the commonplace, and the hidden significance of things is displayed for the wise to see.

By contrast, apocalyptic thinking tends to literalize myth. Sometimes this entails cryptic messages, such as the "666" in Rev. 13:18, or "Babylon" in Revelation 18. Often there is an "us/them" dichotomy between good and evil people, powers, and nations. History seems on the verge of ending. Time is foreshortened. There is no longer a chance to repent, to reform, or to remake the future. Fate rules. The "up" of ascension is replaced by the "down" of Christ's "second coming" on clouds of heaven. Then the sheep will be separated from the goats and the latter hurled into the lake of fire that burns forever. We return to this apocalyptic motif in chapter 9. But first we must attempt to comprehend the archetypal transformation that gripped Jesus' disciples with such power.

8. The Human Being: Catalyst of Human Transformation

Jesus incarnated the Human Being and taught his disciples to do the same. We cannot enter Jesus' mind to examine his experience, from the baptism forward, of this numinous reality. But we do know what he called it: the son of the man, which I have paraphrased by such ascriptions as child of the Human One, Sophia's Child, the New Being, or, as the Ethiopic Similitudes of Enoch put it, "son of the offspring of the Mother of the Living." Jesus apparently drew from Ezekiel's experience of having been addressed as the offspring of the Truly Human Being seated on the throne of glory. The Humanchild did not, then, take on numinous qualities only after the death of Jesus. It had them from the moment Ezekiel saw his vision, or when Daniel dreamed of one like a Human Being assuming ultimate authority over the bestial kingdoms. As Jung writes, Jesus

> would never have made the impression he did on his followers if he had not expressed something that was alive and at work in their unconscious. Christianity itself would never have spread through the pagan world with such astonishing rapidity had its ideas not found an analogous psychic readiness to receive them.[1]

It is not enough, however, to speak of preparedness in that age's collective psyche. Why did Jesus become the one who activated such powerful projections in his followers and the larger public? In some ways, John the Baptist would have been a better candidate, had his life not been cut off so suddenly.[2] Surely there must have been something about Jesus' personality, his outlook, his *character*, that people found compelling (or repugnant). The legends spun around him after his death are what people do when they cannot account for someone unfathomable. After his execution, that same numinous

quality that had adhered to his predecessors reached unprecedented proportions. His disciples called what they experienced Jesus' "ascension" and "resurrection"—terms that, through literalism and debasement and modern
skepticism, communicate little of the explosive power of the fundamental experience they denote.

A. Ascension . . .

Considering the weight the early church attached to the resurrection, it is
curious that, subsequent to the empty-tomb stories, no two resurrection accounts in the four Gospels are alike. All of these narratives seem to be very
late additions to the tradition. They answer a host of questions raised by the
gospel of the resurrection. At the core of all these accounts is the simple testimony: we experienced Jesus as alive.[3]

A later generation that had not had these visions of a living Jesus needed
more; for them the resurrection narratives answered that need. But what had
those early disciples experienced? What does it mean to say that they experienced Jesus alive? The resurrection appearances did not, after all, take
place in the temple, before thousands, but in the privacy of homes or ceme-
teries. They did not occur before the religious authorities, but only to the
disciples hiding from those authorities. The resurrection was not a worldwide historic event that could have been filmed, but a privileged revelation
reserved for the few.

Nevertheless, something "objective" did happen to God, to Jesus, and to
the disciples. What happened was every bit as real as any other event, only it
was not historically observable. It was an event in the history of the psyche.
The ascension was the entry of Jesus into the archetypal realm. Skeptics
might interpret what the disciples experienced as a mass hallucination, but
the experience itself cannot be denied.

This is what may have happened: the very image of God was altered by
the sheer force of Jesus' being. God would never be the same. Jesus had in-
delibly imprinted the divine; God had everlastingly entered the human. In
Jesus, God took on humanity, furthering the evolution revealed in Ezekiel's
vision of Yahweh on the throne in "the likeness, as it were, of a human form"
(Ezek. 1:26). Jesus, it seemed to his followers, had infiltrated Godhead.

The ascension marks, on the divine side, the entry of Jesus into the son-
of-the-man archetype; from now on, Jesus' followers would experience God
through the filter of Jesus. Incarnation means not only that Jesus is like God,
but that God is now like Jesus. It is a prejudice of modern thought that

events happen only in the outer world. What Christians regard as the most significant event in human history happened, according to the Gospels, in the psychic realm, and it altered external history irrevocably. Ascension was an *objective* event, if you will, but it took place in the imaginal realm, at the substratum of human existence, where the most fundamental changes in consciousness take place.

Something also happened to the disciples. They experienced the most essential aspect of Jesus' presence as having remained with them after his death. They had seen him heal, preach, and cast out demons, but had localized these powers in him. That power had always been in them as well, but while he was alive they tended to project these latent, God-given powers onto him. They had only known that power in him. So it was natural to interpret the unleashing of those powers in them after his resurrection as if he himself had taken residence in their hearts. And it was true: the God at the center of their beings was now indistinguishable from the Jesus who had entered the Godhead. But had they experienced Jesus alive in them, or the Human Being? Jesus, in many of the post-Easter son-of-the-man sayings, seems to speak of the Human Being as other than himself. Was Jesus stepping aside, as he seems to do in the Gospels, to let the Human Being become the inner entelechy (the regulating and directing force) of their souls? In Elizabeth Howes's words,

> So the disciples speak of the sense of the presence of Jesus, not God. The new reality of God or the image of God in them was felt as Jesus. Perhaps the steps in the evolution were like this. First, there was the experience of God or God-in-the-Self; the very reality they had experienced in Jesus they now experienced within themselves. But because they had always identified this divine Presence as being in Jesus, they called what they experienced in themselves "Jesus" *as if* he were alive. But if he was alive, then he must have been resurrected. At this point the "as if" got dropped and they identified God in the Self as the risen Jesus in a literal sense.[4]

The disciples also saw that the spirit that had worked within Jesus continued to work in and through them. In their preaching they extended his critique of domination. They continued his life by advancing his mission. They persisted in proclaiming the domination-free order of God inaugurated by Jesus.

The ascension was a *fact* on the imaginal plane, not just an assertion of faith. It irreversibly altered the nature of the disciples' consciousness. They would never again be able to think of God apart from Jesus. They sensed themselves accompanied by Jesus (Luke 24:13-35). They found in themselves the New Being that they had hitherto only experienced in Jesus. They knew themselves endowed with a spirit-power they had known only occasionally, such as when he had sent them out to perform healings (Mark 6:7-13). In their struggles with the Powers That Be, they knew that whatever their doubts, losses, or sufferings, the final victory was God's, because Jesus had conquered death and the fear of death and led these former captives out of captivity.

Jesus the man, Jesus the sage, the itinerant teacher, the prophet, even the lowly Human Being, while unique and profound, was not able to turn the world upside down. His attempt to do so was a decided failure. It was his ascension, his metamorphosis into the archetype of humanness, that turned the world upside down. The Human Being constituted a remaking of the values that had undergirded the Domination System for some three thousand years before Jesus. The critique of domination continued to build on the Exodus and the prophets of Israel, to be sure. But Jesus' ascension to the right hand of the Power of God was a supernova in the archetypal sky. As the image of the truly Human One, Jesus became an exemplar of the utmost possibilities for living.[5]

Could the son-of-the-man material have been lore that grew up to induce visions of the Human Being? Could it have been a way to activate altered states of consciousness based on meditation on the ascended Human Being enthroned upon the heart? As we shall see, both the Jewish mystical tradition and the Gnostics used their own traditions similarly. It was not enough simply to *know about* the mystical path. One needed to take it. And the paths were remarkably alike.

The ascension was real. Something happened to God, to Jesus, and to the disciples. I am not suggesting that the ascension is nonhistorical, but that the historical is the wrong category for understanding ascension. The ascension is not a historical fact to be believed, but an imaginal experience to be undergone. It is not a datum of public record, but divine transformative power overcoming the powers of death. The religious task for us today is not to cling to dogma but to seek a personal experience of the living God in whatever mode is meaningful.

B. . . . Into an Archetypal Image

If Jesus' ascension marked the transformation of the disciples' image of Jesus, that would explain why this world-historical event went unobserved by all but believers. Only the latter had access to this event, because it had hap-

pened *in* them. Yet the event was not merely subjective, because it entered
the collective unconscious to become spiritually available to all. More
specifically, it entered the collective consciousness of the Christian community, where it overflowed into architecture, art, theological treatises, new
communities, new thoughts and experiences—and, unfortunately, into new
forms of domination hierarchies, political machinations, power struggles,
inquisitions, and the rest.

Visions of the Human Being continued in the early church (Acts 7:56;
Rev. 1:9-20). They did not cease after Paul's "concluding" vision (as he
seems to imply in 1 Cor. 15:8). The Human Being is a visionary reality *now*,
and it will become a world-historic event in the fullness of time, when the
mystery of humanity, the anthropic revelation, will be fully revealed.

In the statement, "From now on Sophia's Child [the son of the man]
will be seated at the right hand of the power of God" (Luke 22:69), the imagery is of ascension, not second coming (as Mark and Matthew have it).[6] To
say that the Human Being is at God's right hand is to say to his accusers, in
effect, "The new reality has already been installed beside the very center of
being. You can kill Jesus. You cannot kill this new reality. Everything has
changed irreversibly." I had originally written, "installed *at the very center* of
being." Then I noticed the care with which the evangelists note that the
Human Being is not God, not the Self, not the core of reality. The Human
Being is only near to God, "at the right hand of the Power of God," serving
to mediate the experience of God to those who desire it.[7]

This motif of ascension burrowed deeply into the psyche of the early
church. The ascension seems to have been the primordial experience of the
early community. Resurrection may then have been a secondary inference:
if he is ascended, then he must have been raised from the dead. The resurrection, then, may reflect the tendency to literalize the ascension as an outer
act of history, and to lose the experiential immediacy. The more the event
was historicized (as in the Gospels' resurrection stories), the more mythological it became. Ephesians 4:8-10 illustrates this development, epitomiz-
ing the gospel as the descent of the preexistent Christ from heaven to earth
(and/or Hades) and his ascension back to heaven, leading a column of liberated captives. The Gospel of John also develops the theme of ascension
(3:13; 6:62; 20:17), as does Paul (Rom. 10:6-7), Acts (1:9-11; 2:34-35), and
Hebrews (4:14). Other texts speak of Jesus' exaltation (Acts 7:56, etc.). But
the idea of ascension is difficult to grasp today, when we no longer literally
(or sometimes even figuratively) think of heaven as somewhere in the sky.

The issue is further complicated by the fact that Jesus was not the first or
the last person, according to various claims, to have undergone ascension.

Already the Jews numbered Enoch, Moses, Elijah, Isaiah, and others among those who had ascended to heaven. Ascensions were also common in the literature of antiquity. In Mesopotamia, Utuabzu was said to have been taken up to heaven. Ganymede, a youth of striking beauty, was taken up in order to become Zeus's cupbearer. The Greek hero Herakles underwent divinization and was exalted to dwell among the gods on Mount Olympus. In *Oedipus at Colonus* by Sophocles, Oedipus dies and is taken up to heaven. Romulus, the founder of Rome, was snatched up to heaven during a storm. Emperors underwent apotheosis, ascending usually on a chariot or on the back of an eagle. Numerius, an ambitious senator and ex-praetor, was rewarded because he swore that he had seen the emperor Augustus ascending to heaven.[8] In each case, apotheosis reflects the admission of a singular human being into the archetypal realm.

What if we were to translate the language of ascension from the vertical transcendence of the ancient worldview into a more integral worldview that conceives such visionary statements as referring to the depths of the psyche (both personal and collective)? Then we could understand the ascension as the astonishing discovery that the Humanchild was alive and regnant in the disciples' hearts. As Paul Ricoeur writes, the ascension confirms the belief that what is highest above human beings is what is most inward.[9] That inner presence is the Human One, who is both Jesus and all others like him, taken as a single emergent reality. That is what the disciples claimed happened, and we have no reason to doubt their experience.[10]

As Edward Edinger notes, archetypal images are both objects and subjects. "That means that when we experience an archetypal image we can study it as an object—we can describe it, we can classify it. But at the same time it remains a subject. That means that the archetypal image is [like] a separate personality. It's an interior personality that has something of its own subjective will and intention—which is what we would expect when we encounter an outer personality, an outer subject."[11]

And because Jesus is virtually indistinguishable from the Human Being, an appropriate piety can address him as intercessor, friend, lover, savior, liberator, exemplar, companion, forgiver, healer. Or, in Delores Williams's words, reflecting the black experience, Jesus is our mother, our father, our sister, and our brother.[12] He is not God, but is seated on the right hand of God. He is therefore not to be worshiped ("*Jesuolatry*"—the error of mistaking the man for the power operative in him), but that does not preclude a *Jesuology* (focus on Jesus as revealer of God).

We have seen repeatedly, from Psalm 8 and 80 and Dan. 7:13, that the New Being is both personal and collective. The New Being is Jesus himself, but it is also his disciples (Matt. 9:8; 19:28; Mark 2:23-28 par.; Luke 9:58 // Matt. 8:20). And it is anyone who grasps the reality of the Human Being (Mark 2:10 par.; Matt. 9:8), who lives from that reality, whether it is Israel as a people or the human species as a whole. Although Jesus stands alone and abandoned before Caiaphas, says James W. Douglass, "He still says in faith that a collective nonviolent transformation is already taking place through God's action in his life and work." The Human Being is a divinely transformed humanity, "the communal coming, 'from now on,' of a suffering, faithful people empowered by God in their history to break through to a nonviolent Humanity, the kingdom of God. Abandoned by his followers, alone before his judge, anticipating execution, Jesus still saw that total divine revolution coming from within Humanity. He knew that God would somehow make it happen, and he was determined to embody it by his own death."[13]

In Dan. 7:13, the Human Being was brought *to* the throne of God and given authority, power, and dominion over the nations and kingship over the people of Israel. Daniel's depiction of God clearly draws directly on Ezekiel's vision of the divine Human seated on a throne of fiery flames with wheels of burning fire. Daniel's vision intuited the movement of the concretely human being toward the truly Human. The archetype of humanness was beginning to take form. But in Daniel the archetype remained at the level of pure longing. It awaited a human being willing to accept the challenge of becoming human. It wanted incarnation. What Jesus added, then, was the down-to-earth daily business of living the human into flesh.

People are not moved simply by the teachings and acts of Jesus. This has been the rationalist delusion of nineteenth- and twentieth-century scholarship: that all we need to do is strip Jesus of the theological garments that weighed him down and he would appear, charming, untrammeled, and self-evidently persuasive. Incarnation became a doctrine about Jesus, not a task for all of us to accomplish. Without a numinous dimension, the story remained two-dimensional, flat on the page. Only when the archetypal stratum—here, the ascension—is recovered does the story take on substance, dimensionality, life. Twentieth-century scholarship on the son of the man ended in a cul-de-sac, in which the expression was declared devoid of all theological meaning. Only as we recover that dimension of depth will we grasp something of what Jesus himself might have understood when he characterized himself by this expression and no other.

9. The Human Being: Apocalyptic versus Eschatology

We now encounter a seismic shift: the myth of the human Jesus is swallowed by apocalyptic fantasies. Jesus takes on a cosmic cast. He no longer lacks a place to rest his head, having become Lord of the Universe. Heaven and earth tremble at his coming, for his face is crimson with wrath. Woe to sinners on his day! The Human Being who ate with tax collectors and sinners now hates them roundly. Why is his judgment no longer tempered by mercy? He was so compassionate; what made his forehead flint? It is as if a reverse image of Jesus had erased much of what he had formerly been. How could such a inversion happen to the Human Being, who had inverted everything?

In order to answer these questions, we need first to understand apocalyptic and its significant differences from eschatology. I apologize for retaining these gargantuan theological terms, but I cannot find other words that do the job. Consoled by your forgiveness, I proceed.

A. Eschatology versus Apocalyptic

Both eschatology and apocalyptic deal with the end of things. "Eschatology" (which means the study of the last things) regards the future as open, undetermined, and capable of being changed if people alter their behavior. The urgency of the great prophets of the Old Testament came from their conviction that catastrophe need not happen, that even a small deviation from the course toward doom might avert it. By contrast, "apocalyptic" (which means "unveiling," specifically visions of things to come) judges the future to be closed, inevitable, and inescapable. Since the future cannot be averted, apocalyptic can only call people to personal repentance, so that after the catastrophe they might survive to enjoy heaven or a transfigured earth.[1] Eschatology is concerned about the goal of humanity and the world; apocalyptic is consumed with the end of the planet Earth as presently constituted. Prophetic eschatology is ruthlessly realistic, yet incurably hopeful. Apocalyptic has abandoned hope and looks for divine, miraculous intervention.[2]

Perhaps it would help to think of apocalyptic as characterized by two powers, God and Satan, and two eras, this aeon and the aeon to come. Apocalyptic has a foreshortened sense of time; it sees the final contest by these great powers as a convulsion about to take place. The present moment verges on the collision between the present age and the age to come. The old age is finished; the new world is at hand. God will quickly overthrow the power of evil and establish the divine reign on earth or in heaven. There is no time left; people must choose which side they are on. God's victory ushers in the judgment of the living and the dead. The righteous will inherit eternal life; the evil, eternal damnation (or, alternatively, eternal nonbeing).[3]

But even that characterization is deceptive. For there is a positive role for apocalyptic as well as its better-known negative. The positive power of apocalyptic lies in its capacity to force humanity to face threats of unimaginable proportions in order to galvanize efforts at self- and social transcendence. Only such Herculean responses can rescue people from the threat and make possible humanity's continuation. Paradoxically, the apocalyptic warning is intended to remove the apocalyptic threat by acts of apocalyptic transcendence. As the philosopher Gunther Anders said, we move into an apocalyptic mode when we no longer find ourselves asking "*How* shall we live?" and ask instead "*Will* we live?" The normal eschatological situation gives life urgency by forcing us to face the inevitability of our own death, the hunger for meaning, and the fear of suffering and loss. It becomes apocalyptic when it appears that there is no longer time for normal urgency. Time collapses. The Time of the End becomes the End of Time. Those "not yet nonexisting" must do everything in their power to make the End Time endless. "Since we believe in the possibility of the 'End of Time,' we are Apocalyptics," Anders wrote in the midst of the nuclear terror in 1962, "but since we fight against the man-made Apocalypse, we are—and this had never existed before—'Anti-Apocalyptics.' "[4]

The apocalyptic situation dwarfs our human capacity and reduces us to powerlessness. The negative response is passivity and despair; the other response is superhuman effort and assault on the impossible. We feel that we are smaller than ourselves, incapable of the required response. "Nothing can save us that is possible," the poet W. H. Auden intoned over the madness of the nuclear crisis. "We who must die demand a miracle."[5] The miracle we received came about because people like the physician Helen Caldicott refused to accept nuclear annihilation. She forced her hearers to visualize the effects of their inaction. Imagination, says Anders, is the sole organ capable of conveying a truth so overwhelming that we cannot take it in. Hence the bizarre imagery that always accompanies apocalyptic. Optimists want to believe that reason will save us. They want to prevent us from becoming afraid. The anti-apocalypticist, on the contrary, insists that our capacity to fear is too small and does not correspond to the magnitude of the present danger. Therefore, says Anders, the anti-apocalypticist attempts to increase our capacity to fear. "Don't fear fear, have the courage to be frightened, and to frighten others too. Frighten thy neighbor as thyself." Anders does not refer, however, to an ordinary fear; it is a fearless fear, since it dares at last to face the real danger. It is a loving fear, since it embraces fear in order to save the generations to come. That is why everything the anti-apocalypticist says is said in order not to become true.

> If we do not stubbornly keep in mind how probable the disaster is and if we do not act accordingly, we will not be able to prevent the warnings from becoming true. There is nothing more frightening than to be right. And if some amongst you, paralyzed by the gloomy likelihood of the catastrophe, should already have lost their courage, they, too, still have the chance to prove their love of man by heeding the cynical maxim: "Let's go on working as though we had the right to hope. Our despair is none of our business."[6]

Anders's insight is fundamental, because it penetrates behind the apocalyptic scenario and shows that *there were biblical apocalypticists who were anti-apocalyptics, too.* What they said, they said in order for it not to become true. Jonah understood this, and for that reason fled his task. He knew God was sending him to preach doom so that it would not happen, thus making him appear a liar.

Earlier I suggested that a positive outcome might be conceivable, *if* the human race rises to its capacities and meets the future faithfully; but if it does not, then the apocalyptic nightmare may indeed descend upon us. Luke warns:

> Be on guard so that your hearts are not weighed down with dissipation and drunkenness and the worries of this life, and that day catch you unexpectedly, like a trap. For it will come upon all who live on the face of the whole earth. Be alert at all times, praying that you may have the strength to escape

all these things that will take place, and to stand before the son of the man. (21:34-36)

It is not difficult to see real perils in that warning, perils that threaten the very viability of life on earth today. Global warming, the ozone hole, over-population, starvation and malnutrition, war, unemployment, the destruction of species and the rain forests, pollution of water and air, pesticide and herbicide poisoning, errors in genetic engineering, erosion of topsoil, over-fishing, anarchy and crime, terrorism, the possibility of a nuclear mishap: together, or in some cases singly, these dangers threaten to "catch us unexpectedly, like a trap." Our inability thus far to measure ourselves against these threats is an ominous portent that apocalypse has already rendered us powerless. *We are living in an apocalyptic time disguised as normal, and that is why we have not responded appropriately.* If we are in the midst of the sixth great extinction, as some scientists tell us we are, our response has so far been scarcely commensurate to the challenge. Our globe is undergoing the greatest annihilation of species in the past sixty-five million years, and our own extinction as *Homo sapiens* may be the climax of that slide to ecocide. Can anything less than a full-scale apocalyptic mobilization be appropriate?

B. Was Jesus an Apocalypticist?

Was Jesus' teaching apocalyptic, or was it eschatological? Jesus certainly had a prophetic sense of eschatology. He predicted the destruction of Jerusalem and its temple, but he preserved the prophetic condition: unless you repent (Matt. 23:37-39 // Luke 13:34-35; 19:41-42). He called his people to change before they were destroyed by Rome. He urged them to start living God's domination-free order now, and to build a new egalitarian society within the shell of the Domination System, represented by Rome and Israel's priestly ruling caste. He saw this new reality emerging from below, among the common people. He did not anticipate legions of angels who would forcibly transform the world into the Reign of God. Nor was he a revolutionary, organizing armies of redeemers who would overthrow the Romans by violence and reestablish the Jewish state. Notably, his parables have no trace of apocalyptic motifs, though the church's explanations of them sometimes do.[7] Nor does the Sermon on the Mount derive its moral urgency from the approach of the end of history, but from the nature of God and our desire to be like God (Matt. 5:45). The poor are not promised relief in the future; they are proclaimed "blessed" now: "Blessed are you who are poor, for yours *is* the kingdom of God" (Luke 6:20). Jesus' critique of domination in all its forms was not premised on a divine intervention that would break into the world unassisted by human participation. Rather, Jesus seems to have expected people to begin behaving differently *now*, to do justice *now*, to live the life of the "Reign of God" *now*.[8] The world of God was something that people can now "enter" (twenty-five times in the Gospels). When Jesus exorcised demons, he could declare that "the kingdom of God has come upon you" (Matt. 12:28 // Luke 11:20). The healings and exorcisms performed by the disciples caused Satan to "fall from heaven like a flash of lightning" (Luke 10:18). Jesus saw the new world of God as already in some sense present: "The reign of God is not coming with things that can be observed [that is, apocalyptic signs in the heavens or wars, earthquakes, and calamities on earth]; nor will they say, 'Look, here it is!' or 'There it is!' For, in fact, the kingdom of God is among you" (or "within you"—Luke 17:20-21), and will be consummated in the future. In a passage the church could scarcely have composed, because it ascribes the inauguration of God's reign, not to Jesus, but to John the Baptist, Jesus describes the new order of God as already present but beleaguered by its opponents. In John P. Meier's translation, from the days of John the Baptist until now "the kingdom suffers violence, and its violent opponents snatch it away from those who would receive it" (Matt. 11:12).[9] Unlike apocalyptic, which looks toward a new world after the dissolution of this world, Jesus depicts God's reign beginning in the midst of the old order. The future is now.

The evidence seems unambiguous that Jesus had a prophetic sense of eschatology. Was he also an apocalypticist? Now the definition of "apocalyptic" becomes devilishly hard to pin down. Jesus certainly believed in a final judgment, when the perpetrators of evil and injustice would face the consequences of their deeds. But this need not entail an apocalyptic scenario; most Jews, of all parties except the Sadducees, would have shared that belief. Some references to divine judgment do seem to go back to Jesus,[10] but most have been added by the church, especially by Matthew.[11] Arthur Dewey points out to me that apocalyptic is a scribal activity, in which Jesus did not engage. Shall we then confine apocalyptic to passages that anticipate the end of this world and the coming of a new? Apart from the so-called apocalyptic son-of-the-man sayings, such references are surprisingly few, and almost all are confined to the "Synoptic apocalypse" (Mark 13 par.).[12]

Most if not all of Mark 13 consists of layers of speculation about the signs that portend the end of the world. This represents a calcification of Jesus' vivid expectation of God's active presence and power in the world. The future already sensed breaking into the world in Jesus' ministry is now a programmatic scorecard for reading the warning signals of the kingdom's approach. My hunch is that Jesus is not the author of much in Mark 13 and parallels.

Perhaps we should return to the distinction between negative and positive apocalyptic. Consider South Africa. When my wife, June, and I were there in the 1980s, it appeared that armed revolution was inevitable. Blacks were becoming more desperate by the day. Teenage boys, without concern for their safety, were confronting the police and army. Chaos was beginning to overtake the townships, as children, outraged by the timorousness of their parents, seized the initiative themselves. Whites were taking an increasingly hard line. It was a recipe for disaster. The scene reeked of apocalypse.

Then the most unexpected thing happened. The white government chose, under intense internal and international pressure, to relinquish power, and negotiated with its former black enemies a process that led to the election of a black president, a model constitution, and relatively low casualties, considering the alternatives. No one to my knowledge anticipated this turn of events. What had the appearance of an inevitable (negative) apocalyptic bloodbath turned out to be a (positive) apocalyptic situation instead, thanks to the "anti-apocalyptics" who rose to the occasion.

Rather than two opposed scenarios, then, negative and positive apocalyptic seem to represent two alternatives. If the current evil course is followed, despite the warnings of the prophets (and South Africa was blessed with an abundance of these), the outcome will be negative apocalypse. If the warnings of the anti-apocalyptics are heeded, the outcome can be a miracle (see Jer. 18:7-11). Perhaps, then, we might read Revelation 18–20 as the dire *negative apocalyptic* prospect for societies that refuse to do justice, and Revelation 21–22 as the propitious *positive apocalyptic* prospect for those that repent and do justice. (Not so propitious for women, says Amy-Jill Levine, since only 144,000 male virgins make it through the first cut—Rev. 14:1-5.)

As long as the archetype of the Human Being remained tied to the Jesus of history, who lived and died and lives forever in God, Christian faith maintained an orientation to the future of humanity. But when the archetype of the cosmic Anthropos again surged from the deep unconscious, constellated by the figure of Jesus, it overpowered the lowly archetype of the Human Being. The result was the doctrine of the second coming, the notion that Jesus would come again as world ruler, using all necessary force to coerce humanity into obedience to the divine purposes.[13] It appears that God's immortal patience will finally have run out, and that the Supreme Commander of the heavenly hosts will use all the weapons in the arsenal of righteousness to devastating effect. This heavenly "son of the man" is a long way from the Galilean teacher who renounced violence in the name of a nonviolent God.

The truth in the doctrine of the second coming is that Jesus' work on earth was not finished during his lifetime. The Powers have not been brought to heel behind God's purposes. Death and decay, grief and despair, poverty and starvation, war and torture, rape and abuse—all continue unabated. The promised transformation of reality, when the heavenly Jerusalem comes down to earth, has not yet happened. The new human being has not yet emerged. Evil is as powerful today as it was the day Jesus hung on the cross. It is tragically evident that negative apocalyptic has done its part to wreak havoc on the world. The easy way out, however—the one chosen by a number of scholars—would be to reject all the apocalyptic passages in the Gospels as later additions by the church. But the situation is more complex. Like all such symbols, the second coming is ambivalent. It is true/false, good/evil. These "apocalyptic" sayings are, then, both positive and negative, and we need to listen to both sides.

The question whether Jesus was himself an apocalypticist hinges on what we conclude about the authenticity of the so-called apocalyptic son-of-the-man sayings. It can be demonstrated without much controversy that the evangelists augmented their fund of apocalyptic son-of-the-man sayings, especially Matthew. But were these sayings all produced by the church, or did an original stock get expanded? This is part of the larger question of how we see apocalyptic in the early church generally.

There are two scenarios. The first notes that John the Baptist, Jesus' mentor, was apocalyptic, that Paul, especially in his earliest correspondence, was apocalyptic, that the Q source was apocalyptic,[14] that the Synoptic Gospels are all apocalyptic, and that the Book of Revelation was an apocalypse. Given that trajectory, it would appear plausible that Jesus belonged to that thought-world and was thoroughly apocalyptic himself, as the Gospels attest.

The second scenario acknowledges that John the Baptist was indeed apocalyptic, but holds that Jesus broke with John on precisely that point. In opposition to the apocalyptic tendency to split reality, Jesus perceived God as encompassing both sides of the opposites. Dualism yields to duality: thus Jesus refused to divide people into two camps, the good and the evil. Rather, he saw both good and evil in each person. Jesus sought to embrace what had been opposites (God/Devil, light/dark, us/them, in/out, wheat/chaff, friends/enemies, rich/poor) and to reconcile them at a higher level. He never ceased to honor John, but he had a different idea of vocation (Matt. 11:2-6 // Luke 7:18-23), a different lifestyle (Matt. 11:19), and, above all, a different sense of the future. Jesus had an incandescent awareness of God's presence in his life and ministry. For him the end time was already in process of realization. In his healings and exorcisms, and above all in his penetration to a dimension of existence that emanated from the center of reality itself and that included all of Abba's children, Jesus brought a new reality of overwhelming relief, joy, and truth. John could not accept this new turn, as his lack of response in Matt. 11:2-6 implies. The early church did not fully grasp Jesus' radicalism and placed it within the framework of contemporary apocalyptic beliefs. On the whole, the apocalyptic sayings seem to have been added after Easter. So the church would be the source of this apocalypticism, probably under the influence of Daniel 7. The Similitudes of Enoch also seem to have been formative in the further development of apocalyptic, especially in Matthew, in which half the apocalyptic son-of-the-man sayings appear.[15] Finally, the parables, the Sermon on the Mount,[16] the Fourth Gospel, the earliest version of Q (if such exists), the *Gospel of Thomas*, most Gnostics, Clement of Alexandria, and Origen, witness to the presence of nonapocalyptic traditions in the early church.

It is impossible to determine which of these scenarios is correct. Each can be supported by massive exegetical data.[17] The first view is far simpler. It assumes a straight line from John to Jesus to the early church. The second is far more complex. It requires us to believe that, very soon after the crucifixion, the church in Jerusalem broke with the nonapocalyptic view of Jesus. Paul would have received this apocalyptic version of the gospel, which he gradually abandoned in his preaching to the Gentiles. This scenario is plausible, since, in historiography, Occam's razor is dull and nearly useless; events are almost always more complex than we can know. In fact, both views coexisted from the beginning.

I have taken a mediating position between these two poles. I believe that Jesus perceived the Reign of God to be breaking in already, yet that it was still to come in fullness in God's own time, and that Jesus rejected the desire for revenge, yet awaited God's final judgment on sin and oppression. I see this future judgment and consummation, however, not as a historical promise, but as a mythic necessity. Whether it ever actually happens, it remains a beacon sustaining hope into the darkest future.

To summarize, I see eschatology as a line stretching to the distant, possibly infinite, future. That is the horizon of hope, possibility, and becoming. I see apocalyptic as a detour, caused by an immediate crisis threatening whole societies. Negative apocalyptic paralyzes, positive apocalyptic energizes. When the crisis passes, normal eschatology is reinstated. Our situation today is unique in that, this time, the crisis may not pass.

10. Apocalyptic 1:
The Human Being Comes

In dealing with the apocalyptic son-of-the-man sayings, I try to do justice to both positive and negative aspects. Despite the church's clear abandonment of the human Jesus for the cosmic judge and world ruler, truth can be found in the apocalyptic "son of the man," though we may have to dig deep to find it.

A. Mark 14:62 par.

"[Y]ou will see the Human Being seated at the right hand of the Power," and "coming with the clouds of heaven."

There are sixteen sayings about the "coming" son of the man in the Gospels (nine in Matthew, three in Mark, four in Luke, and none in John).[1] Matthew contains more than half of these sayings.

This is the most audacious claim of Christianity, more audacious than the resurrection or the assertion that this crucified artisan was the awaited Messiah. The Human Being had entered Godhead *as a human being.* God wanted to become human so that humans might become like God. The violence imputed to God by so many religions around the world, Christianity included—the jealousy, the blind fits of rage, the subhuman wrath and vengefulness, the incapacity to forgive, the remorseless judgment—were now categorically jettisoned from the God-image. What was left—compassion, love, tender mercy, and fidelity—became the basis of a clarified God-image. It is the greatest scandal and infamy that the church could not live with Jesus' God, and preferred the harsh judgmental God of much of Christianity. It is no secret why. A God who keeps score is much better at crowd control. A jealous God goes hand in glove with a tight hierarchy. Clerical dominance requires heavenly sanctions. A state built on unjust power relations needs a religion that blesses the status quo. To be able to dangle the sword of judgment over every Christian's head—a sword that stays in place even without clergy—was to create an incomparably efficient system of soul policing. The Jesus who changed the image of God was in turn changed into the God he had tried to change.

To say that Jesus is at the right hand of God is to make Jesus a *criterion* of humanness. In Jesus' life it becomes clear what it means to be human—and this is so even though he was not perfect. As the emergent possibility of our humanness, Jesus is not just the lure of the future or the desire to be more, but also the standard by which humanness is known. Against that standard, the ultimate question unavoidably thrusts itself upon us: What have I done with my life?—but in such a way that it takes on immediate urgency: What am I doing, right now, with my life?

Jesus did not attempt to add the gospel to an already successful religious life, as if his were a kind of spiritual finishing school. Jesus did not ask the religious authorities to acknowledge his teaching as an addendum to their own. He told them instead to die to their past and to be reborn to God's domination-free order, to take up their cross and be willing to die for their opposition to "this world."

When we turn this image of Jesus, as the criterion of humanness, into the yardstick by which we are judged, we open the door to perfectionist attempts to emulate Jesus rather than efforts to become our true selves. But we need some kind of model, exemplar, guide. We need the wisdom of one who has stalked the Powers and finally drawn them into the open, where they can no longer hide, where their death-dealing practices are exposed. The Human Being is not complete. Jesus is not a perfect model. No model can be, because characteristics of the human are still emerging.[2] Wisdom's Child is a premonition. "What we will be has not yet been revealed" (1 John 3:2). Our task is to live into that Human Being, to complete its emerging physiognomy We are, with God, the creators of our own—and God's—humanity.

B. Mark 13:24-27 par.

But in those days, after that suffering, the sun will be darkened, and the moon will not give its light, and the stars will be falling from heaven, and the powers in the heavens will be shaken. Then they will see the son of the man coming in clouds with great power and glory. Then he will send out

the angels, and gather his elect from the four winds, from the ends of the
earth to the ends of heaven.

Suddenly we leap from the plane of history to that of the cosmos (the four
winds plus heaven and earth *define* the cosmos). If we have learned anything from depth psychology, mythological depictions of the cosmos exist
not in the sky but in the psyche.[3] What Mark 13 tells a frightened and desperate humanity at the beginning of a new millennium is that things may
not get better, but worse. Elsewhere, Jesus holds out hope to his people.
Mark 13 is the picture of what happens if the vision of a new reality is rejected. Apocalypse, he warns, may overtake eschatology. The Reign of God
is not the climax of a long evolution toward goodness, but the radical negation of an inhumane, colossal, and entrenched system. Despite all attempts
to change it for the better, if that system simply proliferates blindly, heedless
of the human or environmental cost, social collapse is predicable. Thus
Jesus warned Jerusalem of its unavoidable collision with Rome unless it radically changed course (Matt. 23:37-39 // Luke 13:34-35). Any system that allows evil to become established, institutional, and habitual will inevitably
implode. As James Douglass observes, the moral logic of violence is ultimate
destruction, leading to the end of life itself.

> In a lightning insight, whose implications are still far beyond us, Jesus
> sensed the connections between the violence done to the poor, the outcast,
> and the rebellious in a colonized first-century Judea and a violent end of the
> world—his world and any world in which the logic of violence is followed.[4]

The "Little Apocalypse" (as Mark 13 is affectionately known)[5] describes
the carnage and suffering that overtake societies when human beings abandon their humanity altogether:

> For nation will rise against nation, and kingdom against kingdom; there will
> be earthquakes in various places; there will be famines. This is but the be-
> ginning of the birth pangs. As for yourselves, beware; for they will hand you
> over to councils; and you will be beaten in synagogues; and you will stand
> before governors and kings because of me, as a testimony to them. . . .
> Brother will betray brother to death, and a father his child, and children will
> rise against parents and have them put to death; and you will be hated by all
> because of my name. . . . Woe to those who are pregnant and to those who
> are nursing infants in those days! Pray that it may not be in winter. For in
> those days there will be suffering, such as has not been from the beginning

of the creation that God created until now, no, and never will be. (Mark 13:8-9, 12-13a, 17-19)

It is at such a time that "the son of the man" comes, wrapped in clouds, with great power and glory, surrounded by angels, to rescue God's own from this intolerable situation.

Is that the way the world works? Is this not the apocalyptic deus ex machina trick—presto, our troubles are over? What is wrong with this picture? The authentic vision of the Human Being installed near the heart of reality has been debased here into a power play in which the divine patience with human evil finally snaps, and supernatural intervention sets everything straight *without our having to change at all.* Mythology eclipses history. The idea of the Human Being no longer expresses a mundane historical task performed by unexceptional humans, but the more dramatic scenario of eternity exploding into time with irresistible power.

David Spangler, a profound philosopher of "New Age" sentiments, complains that the New Age milieu has often been too esoteric and otherworldly, and too given to using apocalyptic language and images.

> With an apocalyptic view . . . all one can do is hunker down and wait. It has always seemed to me a paradoxical failure of imagination on the part of many new age groups of the late fifties and early sixties that while they could weave the most fantastic scenarios of earthquakes, polar shifts, the tilting of the earth on its axis, visitations from flying saucers, and various supernatural happenings, they could not imagine transformation brought about by thousands of people learning to see themselves and their planet differently. This assumption of powerlessness and helplessness on the part of humanity has always been a failing of the apocalyptic viewpoint.[6]

We who have witnessed the fall of the Berlin Wall and Soviet Communism and the transformation of South Africa can scarcely deny the reality of miracles. But the miracle fades. Those areas are now beset by epidemic crime, corruption, and economic collapse, so that some people long for the "good old days" of tyranny, when at least it was safe to walk the streets. "Apocalyptic" periods of history have so far turned out to be, not the end of time, but short transitional crises when we can see no way through.

Mark 13 depicts "the son of the man . . . coming in clouds with great power and glory." The quotation marks in the NRSV around "the son of the man coming in clouds" point to Dan. 7:13, indicating that Daniel's prophecy has now been fulfilled.[7] But in Daniel, the Human Being comes *to* the divine throne to receive sovereignty. In Matthew and Mark, the movement has been reversed; the "son of the man" comes from heaven to earth. The number of reports in world religions about heroes and holy ones who return to earth to save their people indicates that we are dealing with a prominent archetype.[8] Not content to leave the Human Being at the right hand of God, as Luke does in 22:69 (though not in 21:27), the early church anticipated the Human Being's return. It was not enough for the Human Being to have entered the realm of the divine; it needs to be coming toward us, coming to meet us, moving in our direction. The Human Being wants to happen in and among us. It wants to be lived in our reality. There is something dynamic in that movement, but rather than see that dynamism within, the church placed it outside the Self in the historical future. Thus the "delay" of the coming of the son of the man, which after two thousand years can be considered not a delay but a failed and misplaced hope. The second coming is like a runner preserved in glass. The runner is running, but it is going nowhere.

Has not the Human Being already come? Why this "second coming"? That first coming was in obscurity. The second will be "seen" by everyone. The church identifies this figure as Jesus, but it is not the Jesus we know from the gospel story. This Jesus comes in Roman "triumph," gathering the elect, judging the wrongdoers, avenging God's honor, vindicating his execution. This figure is more like John the Baptist's "Coming One," who separates wheat from chaff and burns the latter with unquenchable fire (Matt. 3:12 // Luke 3:17). Matthew makes this judgment motif explicit: whereas Mark's "coming" of the son of the man was an occasion for rejoicing at deliverance from tribulation, Matthew has added "then all the tribes of the earth will mourn" (24:30), shifting the focus to an adverse judgment that will overtake the enemies of the son of the man.[9]

In the trenchant statement of James Douglass, "The dynamite . . . exploded after Jesus' execution, in his resurrection and in the rise of a nonviolent movement that swept through the Roman Empire. The dynamite was God. The dynamite was a revolutionary God who ratified Jesus' message by raising him from the dead." But in the course of the Jesus movement's rapid development, "the coming revolution of God's kingdom which Jesus had proclaimed was replaced by the second coming of the revolutionary. . . . The coming kingdom of God became the second coming of Jesus. The revolution became the revolutionary. The dynamite became doctrine."[10]

So also Matt. 16:27, which tightly summarizes Matthew's apocalyptic scenario: "For the son of the man is about to come with his angels in the glory of his Father, and then he will repay everyone for what has been done."[11] Matthew apparently expects the son of the man to come at any moment with the hammer of judgment—a belief that, ever since, has been the cause of great embarrassment for the church.

C. Matt. 10:23 and 16:28

When they persecute you in one town, flee to the next; for truly I tell you, you will not have gone through all the towns of Israel before the son of the man comes. (10:23)

Truly I tell you, there are some standing here who will not taste death before they see the son of the man coming in his kingdom. (16:28)

Our most apocalyptic Gospel is deadly serious about the parousia or "coming" of the son of the man; indeed, Matthew alone of the evangelists uses the term (24:3, 27, 37, 39). The two Matthean sayings quoted above show that he literally expected the risen Jesus to return as son of the man within his own lifetime. Exegetical gymnastics aimed at circumventing the clear intent of these statements are simply attempts to avoid the embarrassment of having to admit that the Bible was wrong. To be specific, *Matthew* was wrong; he was wrong because he treated the archetypal reality of the Human Being as if it were a personage of time and space, who would momentarily reenter our history and transform it in "the renewal of all things" (*palingenesia*, Matt. 19:28).[12]

Henry Burton Sharman observed that the son of the man and the kingdom of God were seldom juxtaposed, leading him to conclude that one or the other was a secondary addition. There are significant exceptions to his observation, however, one of which is the second passage above. But Sharman has a point: speech about the kingdom of God deals with systems and structures; speech about the son of the man deals with becoming human in the company of others so engaged. The one is systemic, the other personal. Consider my trilogy on the Powers, in which there is scarcely any reference to Christology, and this volume, in which systemic issues are alluded to but not central, and in which the focus is christological. Perhaps personal and social, kingdom and son of the man, will converge only in "the renewal of all things" mentioned above.[13]

Powerful symbols, however, are always ambivalent. There is a positive side to the hope for the transformation of all things. The Human Being *did* come in the lifetime of the earliest believers, and of believers ever since. A new archetype of the divine as immanent within humanity *was* inaugurated in their day. But its domain was not history. It was the imaginal plane.*

D. Luke 17:24 // Matt. 24:27

> For as the lightning flashes and lights up the sky from one side to the other, so will the son of the man be in his day. (So Luke; Matthew reads, "so will be the coming of the son of the man.")

The infancy stories are the most profound commentary ever produced on the lowliness of Wisdom's Child. "Nowhere to rest its head" becomes "no room in the inn," birth in a stable, and homage by shepherds and pagan foreigners. The obscurity and marginality of Jesus in his "first" coming is ignored in the second. No one will be able to miss the second coming. Like circling vultures wheeling in the sky, the son of the man will be clearly visible to *all* humanity in his day.[14] *This* time it will be a grandiose media event, watched by everyone. People will *have* to believe. Nothing will be left to chance.

Again, the cosmic replaces the personal, supernatural intervention replaces conversion, lightning replaces the plodding work of nonviolent persuasion and enemy-love. Here is longing for a "final solution" that will bypass human responsibility for changing the world. The only "lightning" Jesus knew was Satan falling like lightning from heaven as a result of the disciples' healing, exorcism, and teaching in the towns of Galilee. We find here the negative side of the messianic longing: the fanning of hope for an unlikely deliverance, which, from a spiritual point of view, *ought not* to happen.

E. Luke 17:26–30 // Matt. 24:37–41; see also Matt. 24:44 // Luke 12:40

> Just as it was in the days of Noah, so too it will be in the days of the son of the man. They were eating and drinking, and marrying and being given in marriage, until the day Noah entered the ark, and the flood came and destroyed all of them. Likewise, just as it was in the days of Lot: they were eating and drinking, buying and selling, planting and building, but on the day that Lot left Sodom, it rained fire and sulfur from heaven and destroyed all of them—it will be like that on the day that the son of the man is revealed.

Much here is simply mystifying. At the least we can say that there is no appeal for corporate or personal responsibility. These events overtake people like natural disasters. Nothing is to be done. There is no way to anticipate the hour. There is no call for repentance or changed behavior. It is not even clear by what criteria some are left and others "raptured." If Luke is alluding to the catastrophes associated with the Jewish War in 66 C.E., the sense of an inescapable fate overtaking everyone is appropriate. But that war did not, in fact, reveal the Human Being to the world. As usual, when violence meets violence, nothing changed.

F. Luke 18:8

> And yet, when the son of the man comes, will it find faith on earth?

Whatever its source (it seems to be a Lukan commentary on a parable of Jesus, 18:2-5), this passage ranks in importance with any saying in the New Testament. It seems possible, this saying suggests, that the Human Being might not find faith on earth. Let us divest this verse of its literalistic sense (that, at a future date, the Human Being will return to earth). This saying then raises the possibility that humanity might fail in its vocation to incarnate the Human Being. Just when the Human Being is poised to emerge in the species, humanity may have exhausted its capacity to believe in it. This would be a failure of vision too tragic to contemplate, because it would mean the end of the human experiment. The species might survive, but as a dead end awaiting extinction. It will have failed in the act of transcendence that would have ushered in the race's next unimaginable mutation: "[W]hen it is revealed, we will be like it, for we will see it as it is" (1 John 3:2).[15]

Faith here is a function of hope. We will maintain faith only if we have embraced a hope sufficient to carry us through the wilderness of shattered expectations. Eschatology is essential to an understanding of the Human Being. Jesus' sense of God's presence must not cause us to neglect the eschatological dimension of that sense of presence. The ecstatic, the mystic, and the seer are not wholly given to the present moment. They are ecstatic in part because they have seen a vision of an alternate reality in the future. The paradox of eschatological consciousness, as Berdyayev saw, is that there are two ways to eternity, one through the depth of the moment and the other through the end of time and of the world as we know it.[16] We can experience ecstasy, we can contemplate God, we can know joy, beauty, and what the physicists are now calling nonlocal and nontemporal reality (what John's

Gospel calls eternity). But the creation also groans to fulfill its potential. It is not enough that individually we find meaning in a society torn by abuse in the home and by random killing in the streets. Vertical redemption, the capacity of some to transcend a hellish situation, cannot take the place of horizontal redemption, which is transforming the hellish situation in which the rest are stuck. There is a kind of hedonistic narcissism among the spiritually elite who have "found" God and are satisfied, and who look on those who have not been so blessed much as the rich look on the poor: it's their own fault, they should try harder.

But a wholly future eschatology is inadequate as well. The far-off, transcendent possibility of becoming truly human can lead to alienation, of hope too long deferred, of incompleteness that crushes hope. Both "realized" and "future" aspects are needed. The kingdom of God is merely a way of stating that God is active among us.[17]

When we speak about the future of the Human Being, or the coming of God's reign, we are concerned about the longest-term interests of the planet or species. We know how destructive short-term goals can be. By now all but the most obtuse can see that the selfish use of resources dooms our societies to slow collapse and ultimate ecocide.

But it is not that easy to discover the planet's long-term interests. Sociobiologist George Edgin Pugh comments that evolution theoretically could have designed biological organisms to make decisions in terms of a single long-term goal—survival of the species. But such a fundamental goal would be a useful guide to behavior only if the organism were endowed with enormous information and intelligence. Any ordinary organism could only be confused. In Pugh's words:

> It would not know what activities to begin or when to begin them. If each individual decision had to be evaluated against evolution's ultimate objective (survival of the species) the organism would have to expend all its physical resources just thinking. To avoid this problem, evolution uses a much more practical design concept. Day-to-day decisions are motivated by a multiplicity of drives, or values, that are orchestrated over time to motivate behavior compatible with evolution's objectives. The ultimate evolutionary goal does not even need to be included within this value structure.[18]

Pugh's observation is remarkably parallel to the theological issue of perceiving the will of God. If God's will has been fixed and preordained from before the beginning of time, and if it is immutable and unchangeable, then the religious goal is to discern God's will and to do it. One must, that is, attempt to enter the mind of God. But our minds are too minuscule to do that. What if God's goal for the creation, like evolution's goal, is in principle unknowable, because it is still emerging? We know from evolution's advance that, at each stage of development, when evolution seemed at an impasse, improbable solutions have enabled the process to continue. New properties emerged in physical systems that could not have been predicted from their components. If the goal embedded in *physical* systems is unknown, the astronomer John Hitchcock warns, we should be extremely cautious about asserting our knowledge of the *spiritual* goal. We are reasonably knowledgeable about the spiritual qualities of a mature human adult, but we can hardly extrapolate the potentials of the species. We have been here as *Homo* for a mere two million years, and as *Homo sapiens* for a trifling hundred thousand, whereas our sun has five billion years' worth of nuclear fuel remaining. God, Hitchcock says, would fill all of that time with creative newness and with consciousness infinitely beyond present human consciousness, so it would be futile to imagine what will evolve by the end of the sun's lifetime.[19] Human beings have no doubt brought conscious teleology to bear in a limited way on evolution; we now can "steer" evolution in certain directions. But the future of the entire species and system remains a mystery.

Nevertheless, human beings need a sense of cosmic purpose, a feeling for where the cosmos is going. The eschatological myth of the coming Reign of God provides general goals within a vague but desirable hope unbound by particulars to one vision of the future. The vagueness of this hope is its greatest strength.[20] Ezekiel saw God revealed as the human future—but all he could see was the outline of a human form, surrounded by fire. He was sure only that he was unsure of his adequacy to describe what he had seen. Jesus proclaims the Reign of God, but gives little idea of its content. His is a "blank" eschatology.

Since we cannot know the goal of the cosmic system, or even the fate of the earth, we are left with the humility of Wisdom's Child, who does not know the future but holds the promise of the future. We have to live without knowing the will of God in its fullness. We have to decide for ourselves what is right (Luke 12:57). We have to take the authority of the Human Being upon ourselves (Mark 2:28 par.) to live as humanly and humanely as we can in the maw of an unjust world. We are not asked to be gods, but to try to become human. We will fail, in part because we lack information, and in part because we refuse to choose the higher good and longer-term goals available to us. We do not know the consequences of our choices in this lifetime, much less their consequences for God's ultimate purposes. But we can have faith that no act conceived in the womb of our higher selves will be orphaned. We can throw ourselves into the struggle to trans-form the Powers without the consequences making us cowards, because we trust that the future of God will outstrip our wildest imaginations.

Even though we cannot conceive of the outcome, then, we do need vi-sions, myths, and symbols to bolster our pilgrimages into an unknown fu-ture. This is the truth in the apocalyptic Human Being sayings. These visions of the future cannot be conceptually precise, agrees Herbert Richardson, for then they would be static rather than dynamic; but they must be *symbolically* precise if they are to direct the social process. Secular-ized versions of these visions of the future always turn out to be pseudoreli-gious, the way Soviet and Chinese Communism ended in virtual deification of Stalin and Mao. Richardson insists that all such visions must of necessity be religious, because they attempt to speak about the ultimate meaning of the universe. The transcendent character of religious eschatology is the con-dition of its adequacy for guiding a cybernetic society, Richardson says; transhistorical symbolism always retains the "vagueness" and conceptual openness that prevent people from expecting absolute fulfillment in time. Or, as John B. Cobb Jr. writes, we need a unifying image to guide our hope-ful openness to transformation. We need an image of an existence open to transformation and hence appropriate as an image of what human beings should be and may become.[21]

In a world of increasingly foreshortened expectations, a powerful vision of the human future is more important than increasing the food supply or ending war. It is the precondition of all other transformations. Without such a vision, people will not make the sacrifices that a more equitable system re-quires. They will not set aside the time to work for change. They will not vote, they will not pick up litter, they will not paint their homes, and they will not love their neighbors (to say nothing of their enemies).

When Socrates was describing the ideal life and society, Glaucon coun-tered: "Socrates, I do not believe that there is such a City of God anywhere on earth." Socrates countered, "Whether such a city exists in heaven or ever will exist on earth, the wise will live after the manner of that city, having nothing to do with any other, and in so looking upon it, will set his or her own house in order."[22]

While it is true that we cannot know the future, we must try to be as human as possible in our ignorance and fallenness. We live in hope that the future, when it comes, will be like the prophets and the Gospels said it would be.[23]

But everything depends on whether the Human Being, when it appears, will find faith on earth.

11.   Apocalyptic 2:
The Human Being Judges

atthew has added to his sources five references to the "son of the man" as judge.[1] Neither Mark nor Luke mentions the son of the man as judging or acquitting.[2] Matthew's use of the judgment theme is particularly vindictive: "For the son of the man is to come with his angels in the glory of his Father, and then he will *repay* everyone for what has been done" (16:27). The unconditionally loving Abba of the Sermon on the Mount (5:45) now wants to settle some scores. Matthew's heart will not be happy until "all evildoers" have been thrown "into the furnace of fire, where there will be weeping and gnashing of teeth."[3]

Matthew, however, has not invented the judgment motif. That most unapocalyptic of Gospels, John, says that God "has given him [Jesus] authority to execute judgment, because he is a son of man" (John 5:27; see also 5:22, 24, 30). Lest we think that this judgment operates only in the present, as in John 3:19, John 5:28-29 continues, "[T]he hour is coming when all who are in their graves will hear his voice and will come out—those who have done good, to the resurrection of life, and those who have done evil, to the resurrection of condemnation" (see also 3:36). That this might be an interpolation is irrelevant (it probably is). What counts is that the image of the Human Being as judge is corroborated by the Fourth Gospel, *and in a non-apocalyptic framework.*

Despite John 5:27, however, the real burden of John's Gospel is that the eschatological moment is now, and not in some remote future. And the judgment is born of love. God's wish is to save people from the "world" (the Domination System, 3:17). People judge themselves by their response to the Human Being: "Those who believe in him are not condemned; but those who do not believe are condemned already, because they have not believed in the name of the only Son of God" (3:18). So judgment is not intrinsically apocalyptic. As "son of man," Ezekiel was repeatedly commanded to judge Israel: "You, mortal [son of man], will you judge, will you judge the bloody city?" (22:2).[4]

Nor is judgment limited to the Christian and Jewish traditions. We see the motif of judgment in the Egyptian *Book of the Dead* 125, in which the heart of the dead is weighed on a pair of scales against justice. The expression "weighing of the souls" is also found in early Greek literature (e.g., *Iliad* 22:209).[5] The failure to achieve or to serve justice is not addressed adequately during this life; there must, it seems, be a reckoning at the end.

Perhaps the full-blown idea of the Human Being as judge received its impetus from Luke 12:8-9—"And I tell you, everyone who acknowledges me before others, the son of the man also will acknowledge before the angels of God; but whoever denies me before others will be denied before the angels of God."[6] Here the Human Being is not so much a judge as a witness for the defense, somewhat like the Paraclete in the Fourth Gospel. The "angels" seem to be impaneled as the court.[7] It is not necessary to see this passage as apocalyptic; it seems to be referring to the *present* activity of the Human Being as intercessor "seated at the right hand of the power of God" (Luke 22:69).[8] It is conceivable that Jesus himself articulated something like Luke 12:8-9, since he seems to differentiate himself here from the Human Being, who will be the heavenly advocate of the faithful.[9] We have seen Jesus speaking elsewhere of the Human Being as other. Since the evangelists' tendency is to identify Jesus with the son of the man, the distinction between Jesus and the Human Being would seem to be authentic. If this is the case, it means that the eschatological son-of-the-man sayings may not all be fabrications by the church, but that Luke 12:8-9, at least, might go back to Jesus himself. This would especially be the case if, as Tödt believed, Jesus was speaking of someone or something other than himself in the apocalyptic son-of-the-man passages.[10]

Jesus does not appear in the Lukan passage as the judge of the end time. But since eternal salvation seems to hang on this acknowledgment, the son of the man who is the advocate could easily slide into the role of cosmic judge. This likelihood would be augmented if the Similitudes of Enoch had recently appeared, with its identification of "that son of the man" with the eschatological judge.[11] That slide is fully apparent in Matthew.

Matthew, and many Christians with him, wants to see that all evildoers receive divine retribution. Clearly, Matthew is displacing his own anger at persecution onto God, and hoping for a reckoning inconsistent with Jesus' attitude toward enemies, which Matthew himself records (5:43-48).[12] In mitigation, we can admit that Matthew's preoccupation with judgment begins with the church (the separation of the wheat from the tares at the last judgment, Matt. 13:24-30, 36-43). But it soon expands to take in all the nations (Matt. 25:31-46).

There is something to be said for the idea of judgment. Justice seems to require that we face the evil we have done to others (and ourselves). The Bolivian peasant or miner may never obtain justice in this life. Is no one answerable for that fact? Should we not hold out hope for divine vindication of the victims of inhumanity? But how do we prevent that hope from being twisted in turn into a *justification* for perpetuating injustice, since the poor will get their reward in the world to come? Should we insist that there is no score settling in the afterlife, and that, therefore, we must work harder to attain justice for all while we live? But we will not succeed, or we will succeed only partially. What then?

Such convoluted arguments have left the idea of a last judgment in disrepair. Yet the notion is unavoidable. Belief in a last judgment may have an experiential root in the near-death experience, in which many people report seeing their lives pass instantaneously before them—not passing before them sequentially, as in a movie, but simultaneously—and having to feel all the pain they have caused others. This experience seems to be virtually universal, and is not confined to cultures that hold to a belief in an afterlife.[13] This cathartic owning-up almost always has a positive effect on those who survive to tell about it. The experience generally wipes out all fear of dying. But this rudimentary scene of judgment is a far cry from the lake of fire into which sinners are thrown to boil for eternity (Rev. 20:15).[14]

Like every great symbol, that of a judge and judgment is ambivalent. On the positive side, there is truth in the image of a "last judgment." The image has inspired some of the world's greatest music and art (the requiems of Verdi and Brahms, the paintings of Michelangelo and Bosch). Medieval and Renaissance frescoes and sculptures, the soaring arches of cathedrals and their awesome liturgies—all have depicted with tremendous power God "up there," waiting to judge us. What would it mean to take this process *inside* ourselves? Could we find the "judgment seat" within, and *now*?

We cannot, however, reduce judgment to inwardness, though that is essential. Judgment is not just an idea dreamed up by furrow-browed priests. Human beings have known from the beginning that reality has built-in constraints. There are conditions which, if violated, will result in sickness, injury, or death. A good deal that passes for religion are rules and beliefs intended to enforce conformity to the requirements of the universe. Religions employ sanctions in order to force compliance to what they perceive to be life's demands. As Gerd Theissen writes, "The myth of a punitive judgment

on the whole world which we escape only by radically changing our behaviour reflects a basic fact of our life. Like all life we are subject to a harsh
pressure of selection."[15] To take the judgment process *within* means taking
a modicum of responsibility for the direction of human evolution. Specifically, it means opposing the process of selection itself, with its preference
for the "fittest," and joining in solidarity with its victims—the poor, dis-
abled, or disadvantaged.[16]

In the Bible, these "least" are vindicated by judgment. The image of a
final accounting in part affirms the just cause of the victims of the Domination System. But even here, the emphasis lies not on God's meting out reward or punishment as recompense for people's works, but God's gracious
transformation of the world into a domination-free order.

On the negative side, however, there is a great untruth in the threat of
judgment. Reality is not punitive. Nature does not lash back at its polluters.
It simply waits until pollution becomes our food and drink. The Jesus who
warned against judging (Matt. 7:1-5 // Luke 6:37-38, 41-42), and who refused to be made a judge himself (Luke 12:13-14), has metamorphosed into
the Judge of all, supplanting God. Judgment has now been made final,
rather than the first step toward reform. The forgiveness that seemed infinite
(Luke 17:3-4 // Matt. 18:21-22) no longer plays any role in apocalyptic
Christianity. Jesus has lost contact with the earth; he now rides the clouds of
heaven. Symbols intended to evoke spiritual growth in the imaginal realm
are transferred to external history and made the object of endless speculations about the coming of an end that keeps not coming. Religion is reduced
to terror that we might come up short. No mitigating circumstances are allowed to soften the blow, no compassion melts the Judge's heart.[17] Sensitive
persons, who know themselves to be a mix of good and evil, are left to pon-
der what degree of good is needed to counter their evil. The freedom of
Wisdom's Child to judge good and evil is abandoned for the safety of a conventional Christian life, in which we are coerced into other people's notions
of good and evil. The salutary need to answer for one's life is replaced by an
overscrupulous calculation of merits and demerits. The gospel is debased to
legalism.

Worst of all, the searchlight of justice turns from ourselves to others; we
cease to find both good and evil in ourselves, or to see ourselves in solidarity
with the sins of everyone, and begin to think of some people as good and
others as evil. Fear of condemnation in the fires of hell—or simply the fear
of divine rejection—can lead to spiritual despair, or to a frantic attempt to
prove oneself worthy of God's love. God is made into an abusive parent
whose love is measured out in dribbles, and whose delicate sense of honor
is so precarious that the merest infraction of the moral code (itself largely

the decrees of the Powers) leads to a massive overreaction of divine wrath, making life imprisonment seem like a slap on the wrist.

The early church theologian Tertullian scoffed at the Roman entertainments of feeding Christians to lions and of gladiatorial combats. Such diversions were nothing, he mused, compared to the delights afforded the saints in heaven, who will watch as Roman poets, tragedians, philosophers, charioteers, and wrestlers are enveloped in flames. "What quaestor or priest in his munificence will bestow on you the favor of seeing and exulting in such things as these?"[18] Centuries later, Jonathan Edwards echoed similar sentiments from his New England pulpit: "The sight of hell-torments will exalt the happiness of the saints forever."[19]

Robert Jewett and John Shelton Lawrence rightly identify this lust for punishment as sadism, a kind of ecstasy that works toward climactic visceral gratification through inverted foreplay. "Whereas sexual love begins with attraction, the preparation for retributive ecstasy requires revulsion triggered by negative stereotypes." The audience is cued to recognize targets of retribution through evil behavior and exclusion from the community. This disidentification and inversion of attraction blocks any sympathetic response that the audience might have when the wicked suffer their punishment. "At the moment the evil of the marked ones becomes unbearable, and the desire for punishment reaches its climax, the moralized forces of catastrophe provide a kind of retributive coitus with an ecstatic release."[20] The irony is that religious sadists can indulge their fantasies with complete confidence in their righteousness.

A. Acknowledging the Human Being

> And I tell you, everyone who acknowledges me before others, the son of the man also will acknowledge before the angels of God; but whoever denies me before others will be denied before the angels of God. (Luke 12:8-9; see Matt. 10:32-33)

Conceivably, Jesus might have told people that their response to him had eternal and fateful consequences, and that to deny him before others (or to be ashamed of him, as Mark 8:38 puts it) would deny what God was doing openly before them. As Tödt puts it, Jesus "demands with supreme authority that allegiance which detaches the disciple from this generation. In demanding this, Jesus utters an unsurpassable claim. No prophet in Israel ever claimed that [people] should confess him."[21] Seen in that light, Jesus is depicted calling people into a new social and spiritual reality. In calling his followers into the new divine order dawning in their midst, Jesus may have been trying to wean them from peer pressure and social conformity by attaching their hopes and values to the transcendent realm. To "acknowledge" means staking one's life on the gospel as articulated by Jesus.[22]

Hare notes that nothing in Jesus' cultural world would have inhibited his belief that he might play a heavenly role as witness at the judgment. Jesus himself ascribes this role to others: "The queen of the South will rise up at the judgment with this generation and condemn it" (Matt. 12:42 // Luke 11:31); similarly, in the same passage, "the people of Nineveh" will judge.[23] Lindars concurs: "Naturally, insofar as he thought of the divine judgment in realistic terms, he would expect to be there, and, as God's spokesman, to have an important position in the proceedings."[24] This saying, concludes Hare,

> betrays Jesus' profound, yet modest, conviction concerning his central importance in God's evolving eschatological drama. To deny him, Jesus informed his followers, was to deny oneself a place in the kingdom God was inaugurating through him. To shrink from confessing him among those who were rejecting him was equivalent to denying that God had chosen to act in and through him. It was not so much loyalty to his person that Jesus demanded of his followers as loyalty to his vision of God's activity. In the imminent denouement of the great drama, he would witness for and against the disciples who had witnessed for and against him.[25]

In the Markan version (Mark 8:38; Luke 9:26), however, the positive side of acknowledgment is deleted; only the threat of shame remains. These things will happen not in heaven but on earth, when the son of the man "*comes* in the glory of his Father with the holy angels." What appears in its Lukan form to have referred to the ascended Human Being on high (12:8-9) has been incorporated into the burgeoning doctrine of the "second coming" in Mark 8:38. The impact of Dan. 7:13-14 is unmistakable in Mark. By associating this saying with other apocalyptic "son-of-the-man" sayings, however, the tradition links shaming to the larger context of the last judgment. Threat now hovers heavily over the Markan form of the saying. Fear is made the motivation for championing the Human Being, rather than a deep conviction of the Human Being's truth. But the son of the man has not yet taken on the role of divine judge, as we find it in Matt. 25:31-46; he is here more a witness/intercessor (Luke) or savior (Mark).

On the other hand, to fail to live up to one's potential as a child of the Human is not a damnable crime as much as a towering misfortune. To condemn such people is itself worthy of condemnation. The Markan form of this saying clearly reflects a spirit other than that of Jesus. The Lukan saying apparently stands at the fountainhead of traditions about witnessing and judging. That all versions of the saying presuppose a context of persecution suggests that they are post-Easter reactions to duress.

B. Judging the Twelve Tribes

Both the positive and negative aspects of judgment are also present in Matt. 19:28 (see Luke 22:28-30):

> Truly I tell you, at the renewal of all things, when the son of the man is seated on the throne of his glory, you who have followed me will also sit on twelve thrones, judging the twelve tribes of Israel.

On the positive side, Jesus not only assumes the role of judge here, but passes it on to his disciples. This is a consistent extension of the Human Being's authority and preserves the corporate dimension of that authority. Jesus was not just a teacher of timeless ideals, but intended to reconstitute Israel as the locus of divine presence on earth. This passage need not be seen at odds with Jesus' hesitation to meet requests for top spots in his coming administration (Mark 10.35-45 par.), because Jesus takes the initiative here. Jesus seems to be promising the twelve seats in a kind of counter-Sanhedrin or king's cabinet that will hold Israel answerable to God.

But on the negative side, reference to "thrones" sounds uncomfortably like the values cherished by the Domination System. The "Twelve" receive the kind of esteem reserved for founding heroes. Whatever became of Jesus' teaching that those who aspired to be leaders should make themselves slaves of all? The passage can certainly be understood as a fantasy of revenge, in which the persecuted church will in the last judgment turn the tables on its persecutors and judge its judges.

C. The Human Being Is in the Least of These

> When the son of the man comes in his glory, and all the angels with him, then he will sit on the throne of his glory. . . . and he will separate people one from another as a shepherd separates the sheep from the goats. . . . (Matt. 25:31-32)

Matthew 25:32 represents the apogee of judgment's ambivalence. On the negative side, the Human Being has been thoroughly contaminated by the doctrine of the second coming of Christ. He comes in glory, his titles are King and Lord, he sits on a glorious throne (any kitchen stool would have done), he judges all the nations, and people are divided into "good" and "bad" rather than being a mix of both. The "least of these" who are the object of this king's concern are, in Matthew's eyes, not the powerless and poor in general, but the embattled and impoverished missionaries of the church (see 10:42; 18:6, 10, 14). The narrative is rife with Matthean vocabulary.[26] This parable, the heart and soul of social-justice struggles in the churches, treats the goats unjustly, since they were already goats before the judgment began. There should have been good goats and bad goats, not rejection by category. Conventional "sheep" who obey their leaders and flock together are preferred to gutsy goats, who go their own way and eat virtually anything. William Blake preferred goats: "The lust of the goat is the bounty of God."[27]

In this parable, Christian believers unfortunately claim for themselves the ancient notion of a chosen people, substituting themselves for Israel, and consigning Jews and others ("goats") to the fires of hell. This pattern divides people and justifies crusades, inquisitions, heresy hunts, and so forth. These outbursts of violence toward the "unchosen" are not accidents. They are rooted in the apocalyptic split that Jesus sought to heal.

None of that, however, touches the positive heart of the parable—arguably one of the most remarkable parables. The "sheep" are surprised that they are the elect; they were compassionate, not to earn a reward, but because they were in solidarity with the sufferers. Note that the judgment is not between believers and unbelievers, or Christians and non-Christians, or between church members and non–church members. The judgment is not based on the desire for salvation, doing good works, or the quality of one's character. It is contingent on whether one has responded humanely and compassionately to the needs of the marginalized, the nameless, the criminal element, the homeless, and the disreputable.[28] Again, the personal interpretation of the Human Being coincides with the collective; the Human Being comprehends all humanity, especially the derelict and downtrodden.[29] So great is humanity's solidarity that when we do acts of compassion for the very least, we do them for all humanity.

But that compassion begins to alter the parable itself, for when those who showed compassion see the tortures of the damned (which Matthew has added liberally in vv. 41-46) will they not renounce heaven in order to minister to those writhing in eternal fire? If the Human Being is included in the "least of these" (*not* church members, as Matthew has it, but the really down-and-out), does not the Human Being also belong among the "goats"? How can bad people be sent to hell if Wisdom's Child exists inside them? If any are lost, is not the Human Being lost inside them as well? How can this be squared with Jesus' own words: "For the son of the man came to seek out and to save *the lost*" (Luke 19:10)?

Besides, the compassionate people in the parable *did not know* that they were serving Sophia's Child, the Human Being, in their needy neighbors. But we, having read the parable, *do* know that the Human Being exists in the poor, and we have contrived to stand the parable on its head and make it the manifesto for social-action works righteousness. How much clergy burnout arises from this remarkable but double edged parable? As one workshop participant said of this passage, "But I tried that for seven years and ignored my wife and family trying to get European and U.S. money to the starving of India and Africa. I totally ignored the 'least' within myself and my family, till I lost them through divorce. Only then did I wake up to the ignored 'least' within me. It's both outer and inner: we have to respond to the 'least' on both fronts."

A woman responded immediately. "But I didn't discover something in myself first and then become compassionate. I found it through a next-door neighbor with delirium tremens whom I had to pick up in a gutter and carry home, or drag out of his burning house. He was almost always drunk and slobbering, but he was our friend. I had to get over my loathing. I had to find the part of myself that was as loathsome and helpless as he was in order to love him. But it began by just doing it."

These two reactions show us how the parable is supposed to work, not as commandment, but as provocation, needler, raiser of questions. Both responses, though opposite, are true. When the parable is twisted into a threat of punishment or a promise of reward, its versatility shatters.

It is impossible to reconstruct the original version of this parable. It is generally agreed that Matthew has added the introduction, and that the son of the man has been imported. By so doing, Matthew has made Jesus' compassion for the outcast the criterion of universal judgment. But the son of the man has taken on qualities at odds with the compassion of Jesus. In this parable we have a virtual citation from the Similitudes of Enoch:

> Open your eyes and lift up your eyebrows—if you are able to recognize the Elect One [possibly developed by Matthew into the elect not knowing they were doing kindness to the son of the man]. The Lord of the Spirits has sat down on the throne of his glory, and the spirit of righteousness has been poured out upon him. The word of his mouth will do the sinners in; and all

> the oppressors shall be eliminated from before his face. . . . pain will seize
> them when they see that son of the man sitting on the throne of his glory. . . .
> So he will deliver them to the angels for punishments in order that
> vengeance shall be executed on them—oppressors of his children and his
> elect ones. (62:1, 2, 5, 11)[30]

Again it appears that the Similitudes have played a central role in further
apocalypticizing the son-of-the-man tradition in Matthew.

One of the surprises of the parable, however, appears in v. 32—"All the
nations (*ta ethne*, neuter) will be gathered before him, and he will separate
people (*autous*, masculine) one from another . . ." A pronoun must agree
with its antecedent in gender and number. The pronoun here does not. For
us, this might mean that the nations as such are not judged, but the individuals (*autous*) among the nations; they will be judged by how their *nations*
have treated the needy—by, in effect, their nations' systems of welfare, judi-
ciary, prisons, and health care. The ultimate principle of humanness is depicted as judging all people based on how their nations have treated the
marginalized of society. Each must take individual responsibility, insofar as
they are able, for the behavior of the corporate systems to which they belong.

Judgment cannot be avoided. But to leave it to a far-off recompense allows judgment to revert to myth. We can learn from the Fourth Evangelist,
who depicts Jesus wrenching the archetype of judgment out of mythic time
and incorporating it in the present: "And this is the judgment, that the light
has come into the world, and people loved darkness rather than light because their deeds were evil" (3:19). We should continually be measuring
what our nations do to those who, like the Human Being, have nowhere decent to rest their heads. We need to see ourselves at one with those on death
row, on heating grates, and in back wards of inadequate hospitals (if they can
get in at all). "When did we see you" in these situations? Truth is, I don't
very often. I stand before the judgment seat *right now* while reading this passage, and I am squirming in the fire.

D. The Parable of the Wheat and the Weeds

We look at one final judgment scene, Matthew's explanation of the parable
of the wheat and the weeds (13:36-43). In the parable itself (Matt. 13:24-
30), which already shows signs of possible additions (v. 28a), the "harvest
time" is the only hint of an apocalyptic context. But Matthew's interpreta-

tion pulls out all the stops. The sower who sows the *good* seed (a moralizing and unparabolic comment)

> is the son of the man; the field is the world, and the good seed are the children of the kingdom; the weeds are the children of the evil one, and the enemy . . . is the devil; the harvest is the end of the age, and the reapers are angels. Just as the weeds are collected and burned up with fire, so will it be at the end of the age. The son of the man will send his angels, and they will collect out of his kingdom all causes of sin and all evildoers, and they will throw them into the furnace of fire, where there will be weeping and gnashing of teeth. (13:37-42)

This interpretation is rife with Matthew's language and interests. People are divided into good and bad; dualism appears throughout. Yet the passage teaches the church to *tolerate* the mix of good and bad people and to leave the judgment to God in the indefinite future.

Matthew's view of the son of the man here is unique. Matthew 13:37 explicitly identifies the son of the man with Jesus (use of the copula here is only matched by John 5:27). As the son of the man, Jesus teaches on earth with full authority and already reigns in his kingdom (the church) prior to the last judgment.[31] In the meantime, true and false people coexist in the church. Only after the judgment will the son of the man and his own bask in the glory of "the kingdom of their Father." For the rest, Matthew's familiar business about torture in fire and gnashing of teeth. This window into Matthew's vindictiveness is not flattering, and it speaks poorly of his community that it allowed Matthew to deviate so far from the standards of humaneness that Jesus articulates elsewhere in this very Gospel. Matthew's theology of vengeance is a throwback to the message of John the Baptist and lends support to the second scenario discussed earlier, in which Jesus is seen as de-apocalypticizing and the church later re-apocalypticizing on the basis of the Similitudes of Enoch. The interpretation of the parable is clearly Matthean redaction.

12.   Apocalyptic 3:
The Future of the Human Being

The apocalyptic son-of-the-man sayings in their negative form reflect a situation in which present urgency has been replaced by the threat of future judgment. Freeing people from domination is seen less as our current task than as what the coming son of the man will accomplish. The power of the powerless, exercised by nonviolent resistance, is replaced by the fantasy of an all-powerful redeemer who will come at the end of time and rectify all injustices by necessary force. The peaceable kingdom is replaced by the violence of an absolute dictator who will coerce people into the kingdom (the Book of Revelation).

The human Jesus was an itinerant preacher with no place to lay his head. He suffered and was treated with contempt, but nevertheless had authority on earth to forgive sins and to decide what is right. On his death, however, he became the exalted Lord of all, who reigns with God in heaven, and who will come again to judge the quick and the dead. It appears that the public was not ready for the Human Being that Jesus knew and to which he called others to relate. Soon after Jesus' death, says Hal Childs, these aspects fell again into the unconscious and were projected onto the divine Christ. But the apocalypticization of the gospel nevertheless served an important purpose. It held the urgency of the Human Being's "coming," as it were, in suspension, preserving the potential of the Human Being for future generations. The apocalyptic gospel has permanently preserved the unconscious contents of the psyche in dormant form, ready at any time to irrupt into consciousness. When these unconscious elements are related to consciously, as emerging aspects of the Self in transformation, they yield unexpected riches. Consequently, all through the history of the church we see outbreaks of creative energy and vision, as seers and prophets made the virtual possibilities concrete and actual. When the archetypal contents are allowed to remain unconscious, however, violent explosions of chiliastic zeal follow: crusades, pogroms, inquisitions, holy wars, persecutions, anti-Semitism, and millenarian delusions.

A. The Eclipse of the Human Being

The image of Jesus Christ seated at the right hand of Power and coming on the clouds of heaven, however, quickly reverted to the negative side of the messianic archetype. Now he was the conquering king who will subdue all things under his feet. The Christ who comes again will not come as Jesus came, as a marginalized Jew of the working class, who preached in obscurity and died ignominiously. Rather, he will come endowed with all the power of the omnipotent God. Something has slipped here. The God made over into the image of Jesus has recoiled to his royal throne. Jesus now appears in the image of the omnipotent God and even possesses a throne of his own (Matt. 25:31). On his return, therefore, *Jesus will do all the things he himself resolutely refused to do during his actual ministry.* The God of unconditional love proclaimed by Jesus has become extremely touchy; even the slightest misstep can lead to endless torment. Jesus had brought the nonviolent God to conscious religious awareness. The returning heavenly Christ, however, "judges and makes war" on all the enemy nations, slaying them with the sword of his mouth and treading them in the "wine press of the fury of the wrath of God the Almighty" (Rev. 19:11-15). Commentators have frequently attempted to dodge the clear intent of these texts. Christ the king, they argue, does not really kill these opponents. The sword in his mouth is the Word of God and therefore represents a spiritual victory. But that reading wrecks on the verses that follow, in which the carrion birds are summoned to "eat the flesh of kings, the flesh of captains, the flesh of the mighty, the flesh of horses and their riders" (Rev. 19:17-18). Jesus has not yet been able to transform the God depicted in the Book of Revelation and in the torture scenes of Matthew and in other Christian sources. God still seems as content to bully, curse, and kill as any pagan tribal deity, even to this day.

Moral discrimination is inherent in the Self. As we saw earlier, the Human Being is capable of that discrimination, in violation, if need be, of the conventions of society. The Human Being has authority on earth to decide what furthers and what undermines human transformation. But,

Childs suggests, when moral discrimination is unrelated to Sophia's Child, the son of the man, it is projected onto authority figures and external collective images, and becomes equivalent to Freud's superego. This element of projected judgment can be damaging in preaching about God's anger at sin and the fires of hell prepared for sinners. However, if we remove the apocalyptic framework, with its residue of power-lust, judgment can be seen as a perpetual feedback loop aimed, not at condemnation, but at correction.

Jesus himself condemned condemnation. If we judge, we must submit to the same judgment ("Do not judge, and you will not be judged . . . for the measure you give will be the measure you get back," Luke 6:37-38 // Matt. 7:1-2). He refused to play the role of judge in a case of inheritance ("Who set me to be a judge or arbitrator over you?" Luke 12:14), and he welcomed known sinners to his table (Mark 2:15-17 par.). There is an interesting commentary on this matter in a variant reading of Luke 9:51-56 (found in the marginal notes of the NRSV and set in italics):

> When the days drew near for him to be taken up, he set his face to go to Jerusalem. And he sent messengers ahead of him. On their way they entered a village of the Samaritans to make ready for him; but they did not receive him, because his face was set toward Jerusalem. When his disciples James and John saw it, they said, "Lord, do you want us to command fire to come down from heaven and consume them?" But he turned and rebuked them, *and said, "You do not know what spirit you are of, for the Human Being has not come to destroy the lives of human beings but to save them."* Then they went on to another village.[1]

It is not that Jesus repudiated the necessity of moral discrimination or judgment; indeed, his life was an accusation against all blocked or unlived potential. Thus in his saying about the folly of building one's house (= self) on sand (Matt. 7:26) or without adequate foundation (Luke 6:49), Jesus speaks impersonally about the inevitable debacle. Life itself will bring a flood that sweeps the house away. There is no hint here of divine judgment. This is just the way life is. The flood is not allegorized to refer to the messianic tribulations. There is time to build the house right. One can see how easy it would be to moralize this passage, making God the sender of the flood as punishment for sin. That is what begins to happen to the Human Being, who is turned into a terrifying Judge who will examine the secrets of every heart and consign sinners to everlasting fire.

B. The Recovery of the Human Being

When I speak of the "son-of-the-man" sayings as apocalyptic, however, I am not saying that they are without historical value. I believe that Jesus did look for the final (but undatable) triumph of God in history, that he did await a realm of justice and peace, that he felt the urgency of this new reality pressing into the world, and that he lived "as if" that new order already was dawning. This attitude constituted a flaming rebuke to everything and everyone who stood in the new world's way.

A striking image of the future human mutation appears in *4 Ezra* 13:52: "Just as no one can search out or perceive what may be in the depths of the sea, so no one on earth will be able to see my son or those who are with him except in the time of his day." The son of the man emerges from the unconscious (out of the sea) and is hidden until the moment of manifestation. In evolutionary terms that could be hundreds or thousands of years in the future, or tomorrow. The perpetual coming of the Human Being is not an artifact of a prophecy that failed, but a permanent state of readiness to be part of that unimaginable transformation. The human species as we know it has not stopped evolving. We trivialize these mythic images of the future when they are made the basis of temporal predictions. As pointers toward a real but undatable mutation, however, they are necessary as checks on the human arrogance that thinks humanity has arrived. We are as yet fractions of our potential, mere apprehensions and approximations of humanness; what we will be has not yet been revealed.

Perhaps it would help if we thought of the intrapsychic impact of apocalyptic in psychodynamic terms. According to Childs, when the ego's hubris shatters in the ego's encounter with the Self, the Self stretches the ego to a new breaking point. In this encounter is a drive for wholeness that entails a radical change (*metanoia*) in the ego. The ego could easily experience this demand for wholeness as judgment. One conceivably could sense that urgency as the threat of final judgment, depending on how the demand is mediated. The Self's drive for individuation is ruthless and brooks no delay; therefore, the ego must decide to go with it or against it.[2] The Self demands that we let go of old ego boundaries and our socialization into domination. One must suffer death to that old order, so as to encounter the Self in the immediacy of the present. The Self wants to incarnate at any price. Once the urge to individuation has been stirred in the person's depths, woe to that person who tries to abort it. "No one who puts a hand to the plow and looks back is fit for the kingdom of God" (Luke 9:62). One must yield to the internal demand to end the old ego definitions and become alive to the Self breaking into consciousness and history.³ Childs continues:

> From the point of view of consciousness on the ego's side, this demand of the Self, when it is not mediated through consciousness, is experienced as the Final End-Time; indeed, the Last Judgment of the ego. From the Self's point of view, however, it is only another step in the eternally on-going process of becoming conscious.⁴

Likewise, we have to acknowledge that apocalyptic motifs are almost universal among all cultures and religions. One can find belief in a return-ing hero, ancestor, savior, or saint in religions and cults all over the world. The Iranian First Man, Yima, would return at the commencement of each new age or reign, and the sun god Mithra was expected to reappear soon as well. Shi'ite Muslims expect a "return" or parousia of the awaited imam as a signal for the resurrection of resurrections. The Druze of Lebanon and Palestine believe that their early leaders, al-Hakim and Hamza, will return to establish justice on earth.⁵ The Jon Frum cargo cult in the South Pacific awaits Jon Frum's return laden with modern appliances.⁶ One day, the Maya of Central America believe, a Maya king will reign again; when that hap-pens, the umbilical cord at the navel of the world will emerge again and re-unite the Maya to the original source of sustenance.⁷ Thoho-ya-Ndou, the culture-hero of the Bavendas who had ruled a great empire, disappeared during a hunt and was never seen again. But he did not die and will return to bring back the ancient greatness of his people. Oirot Khan, the leader of Altaic Turks, was said to be returning soon to restore the ancient Khanate of Oirot and to set the people free from czarist domination. Alexander Bed-ward, founder of Bedwardism in Jamaica, announced his coming ascension into heaven and his subsequent return as savior of his people.⁸ A modern Swiss cult is led by a man named Raël who claims to have been contacted in 1973 by almond-eyed aliens who created human beings in laboratories and who will one day return to our earth.⁹ And fans of Elvis Presley, esti-mated at about one million worldwide, claim that he will return in 2001. Examples could be multiplied. A valid human hunger for a transformed re-ality crops up in cultures around the world, and these returning-savior fig-ures are proof of its persistence.

In short, I regard the passages that speak of Jesus' ascension as registering a psychic fact. I believe that the sayings that speak of his "second coming" are literalizations of these psychic events. I find them true insofar as they anticipate the coming into human beings of the New Being prophesied in

1 John 3:2. The passages are, I believe, true also when they affirm the final victory of God over evil, sin, and death. In that sense I regard the future manifestation of the truly human in a truly humane society to be an authentic expression of eschatological hope. However, that eschatological vision is falsified when treated as the datable appearance of a cosmic dictator ruling an autocratic regime.

Tödt registers surprise at what he calls the restraint of the church, which realized that none other than Jesus is the son of the man to come, yet did not transfer the heavenly attributes of that figure to the person of Jesus on earth.[10] But that is because the direction of development was just the reverse: from the Jesus who was incarnating the Human Being in its mundane, everyday reality, to the glorious son of the man who validates the earthly Jesus by a dazzling display of almighty power on his second coming. The church was not acting with restraint at all, but rather was progressively pulling out all the christological stops until Jesus had been thoroughly divinized and even was called God.

Likewise, Tödt argues that Jesus did not identify with the coming son of the man, whereas I see the situation as a bit more complicated. Just as he did with the messianic hope, Jesus could neither identify himself totally with the son of the man, nor deny that he was living out the son of the man in history. So he could speak of the Human Being as indistinguishable from himself (Matt. 11:19 // Luke 7:34), and at other times treat it as a corporate entity in which not only he but the disciples (Mark 2:23-28 par.) and even outsiders could participate (Mark 9:38-41 // Luke 9:49-50). The Human Being is more than simply Jesus; it represents the future of all humanity, indeed, the world, in the purposes of God (Rom. 8:18-25). Thus, during his Galilean mission, Jesus could at times virtually identify with the Human Being (while occasionally including his disciples as well), because it was Jesus who was primarily incarnating the Human Being and using it as an image of transformation. After his ascension, the Human Being "seated at the right hand of the power of God" became universal—what Ernst Bloch called "*the founders' increasing self-injection into the religious mystery.*"[11] As an archetype, as noted earlier, the Human Being now mediates the possibility of becoming more human in the image and likeness of God, the Humane One. The Human Being is a catalytic agent for transformation, providing the form, lure, and hunger to become who we were meant to be. In that transformative process, the Holy Spirit is the active agent that *effects* the change into who we are meant to be.

Why then did the expression "the son of the man" go so quickly into eclipse? We can now attempt an answer. The community that produced Q saw its task as teaching what Jesus taught about the Human Being. Thus they continued the ministry of Jesus, perpetuating in their own teaching, healing, and exorcism the same sovereign authority that Jesus had exercised and had extended to his disciples during his earthly ministry.[12] Without ever abandoning that task and teaching, the church at large increasingly regarded Jesus' passion and resurrection as central—themes that Q never mentions. The focus was not so much carrying forward Jesus' critique of domination. Rather, the focus became the worship of Jesus as divine bearer of salvation. The Proclaimer became the Proclaimed.

As Tödt explains, a community that calls on the risen Christ needs a title suitable for the language of worship. The name "the son of the man" could not be employed in that way. In a Greek-speaking context the term was semantically grotesque, as I have no doubt drummed into your ears by my insistence on a literal translation of that inelegant phrase. There is no evidence that "the son of the man" was ever prayed to or made an object of worship in the early church.[13] However, the name *Kyrios*, or Lord, was a name that might be invoked in worship. Kyrios already was well-known from the Greek version of the Hebrew Scriptures (the Septuagint) and from pagan religions. The name was ready-made to expand into the space being created by the church's growing Christology. So the church edged out of its worship and piety the name that Jesus had given himself. Thus "the son of the man" virtually disappeared; it is almost completely absent from the rest of the New Testament, the church's creeds, doctrines, liturgies, prayer life, and reflections on what Jesus accomplished.[14] In time it disappeared like a stone in a lake.

In addition, a burgeoning church hierarchy found the sovereign freedom of the Human Being, shall we say . . . inconvenient—as did the Roman Empire once it had nosed into church affairs.

Some of us have become convinced that we do not need to worship Jesus; not only that, but it is necessary *not* to worship him. Worshiping Jesus lies at the core of what Feuerbach fingered as "emptying ourselves into transcendence." What many people today sense as the imperative of the gospel is to continue Jesus' mission. We can unmask the Domination System and liberate those being crushed by it. We can help open people's lives to the living presence of God. We can foster individuation and build nurturing communities as we seek to become the people we were made to be. In that process, the human Jesus will continue to be a living representation of the Human Being, without being completely identified with it. Jesus' refusal to identify completely with the Human Being frees us from having to be like him. Otherwise we would be robbed of our own uniqueness. As Sheila Davaney points out, there is no universal human being. Human being is wrought out of particularity, historicity, and novel cultural practices. Human identity is always dependent on local communities. We are traditioned beings with multiple traditions. Everywhere people improvise local rituals. There are diverse ways of being human, and people name themselves in a variety of ways. The archetypal must not lose sight of the local.[15]

I have attempted to honor the eschatological element in the "future" son-of-the-man sayings, while at the same time showing how their apocalypticization led to their being literalized and projected onto the cosmos as a future, calendrical event. When that event failed to transpire, many Christians must have experienced some cognitive dissonance. But the literalized "second coming" was not an original part of the gospel message in the first place. That is why the New Testament shows little evidence of a spiritual crisis over its delay. The early Christians were already experiencing the firstfruits of God's reign in their own lives and communities. Even during Jesus' life, his followers were learning to incarnate the "possible human." Nevertheless, that new order needs to happen, not just in the depths of the soul, but in time, in history—in ghettos and townships and slums and boardrooms and brothels and sports complexes and condominiums. As Paul Tillich put it, the criterion of a revelation's finality is whether it has the power of negating itself without losing itself; and that the gospel was eminently able to do.[16]

In practical terms, the early church found itself heir to the authority and power of the Human Being that it had experienced in Jesus. Thus Jesus' followers did not just speak *in the name of* the Human Being, but *as* the Human Being. They could speak with the full authority of the Human Being because they *were* the Human Being speaking. They could heal and cast out demons, not because they had been authorized to do so by the Human Being, but because they *were* the Human Being healing and exorcising. They could declare sins forgiven without the necessity of sacrifice and temple, not because they had been commissioned to do so by the Human Being, but because they *were* the Human Being forgiving. Like Jesus, they too had no place to lay their heads; as such they were living the unsettled life of the Human Being. Like Jesus, they early on had discovered their sovereign freedom to decide what is right (Luke 12:57); as such, they were exercising the divine authority of the Human Being.

Despite our best efforts, however, the Human Being will forever remain shrouded in mystery. We cannot say definitively what the Human Being is or means, for the nature of a powerful, living symbol is that we *cannot* reduce it to words, as if our explanations were more meaningful than the symbol itself. When what we say about a symbol becomes more important than the symbol, the symbol has ceased to live. So the inability to define the Human Being is due not just to our inadequacies, which are obvious, but to the nature of archetypes, which are by definition unknowable, except by their effects.[17] Therefore, everything said in this book must of necessity have "as it were" inscribed beside it.

Nor does wishing the Human Being to manifest itself as a "powerful, living symbol" make it happen. For this reason I must warn against turning the real experience of the darkness surrounding God into a mere idea. God *is* "in the likeness, as it were, of a human being." But God is much more: nonhuman, totally other, incomprehensible, incalculable, unfathomable, all of these, none of these—yet capable of being experienced, at least fractionally, by everyone. Are we not all children of the Human One, and therefore made for communion with the Mystery and each other?

> As it ever was and will be—
> As a thief in the night, silently and where you least expect,
> Unlearned perhaps, without words, without arguments, without influential
>   friends or money—leaning on himself alone—
> Without accomplishments and graces, without any liniments for your old
>   doubts, or recipes for constructing new theological or philosophical
>   systems—
> With just the whole look of himself in his eyes—
> The Son of Man shall—yes, shall—appear in your midst.
> O beating heart, your lover and your judge shall appear.

> He will not bring a new revelation; he will not at first make any reply to the
>   eager questions about death and immortality; he will present no stainless perfection;
> But he will do better: he will present something absolute, primal—the living rock—something necessary and at first hand, and men will cling to
>   him therefor;
> He will restore the true balance; he will not condemn, but he will be absolute in himself;
> He will be the terrible judge to whom every one will run;
> He will be the lover and the judge in one.

> The Son of Man—
> Ponder well these words.
> After all I cannot explain them: it is impossible to explain that which is itself initial and elementary.

You will look a thousand times before you see that which you are looking
    for—it is so simple—
Not science, O beating heart, nor theology, nor rappings, nor philanthropy,
    nor high acrobatic philosophy,
But the Son—and so equally the Daughter—of Man.[18]

13.   The Human Being in John

The Fourth Gospel shows how deeply the Human Being archetype burned into the consciousness of the early church. It is striking that no son-of-the-man sayings in the Fourth Gospel parallel those in the Synoptics. Yet the expression continues to appear only on the lips of Jesus as a form of third-person self-reference, as in the pre-Easter son-of-the-man sayings in the Synoptics. Likewise, John preserves the barbaric Greek expression *ho huios tou anthrōpou* with the double articles (with a single exception in 5:27), when he could have translated the expression into good idiomatic Greek, as does Paul. John's son-of-the-man sayings show no trace of the apocalyptic "second coming" motif; by his exaltation to the Father, Jesus had completed the work he came to do.

A. The Leader Is a Ladder

John 1:51 provides a window into John's understanding of the Human Being. Jesus has just astonished Nathanael with his extrasensory perception. Nathanael responds with the kind of acclamation usually reserved until we know someone better: "Rabbi, you are the Son of God! You are the King of Israel!" But Jesus shatters this messianic projection. He tells Nathanael, in effect, to forget about psychic powers: "Do you [singular] believe because I told you that I saw you under the fig tree? You [singular] will see greater things than these." To which Jesus adds, "Very truly, I tell you [plural], you [plural] will see heaven opened and the angels of God ascending and descending upon the Human Being."[1] You too, and others like you (the plurals), will be able to see angels. You too will open to the transcendent, which so astonishes you when you see it manifested in others. When Nathanael learns to "see" (in the shamanic way),[2] as Jesus sees, he will see that the Human Being lives at the center of the world. There one finds the axis of the ladder, or world pole, with angels ascending and descending. These angels are the messengers of the imaginal realm, the eternal now, nonlocal reality. Jesus' task as Human Being is to unite heaven and earth. He causes us to "see" with the eye of the imagination. He transforms us, as Blake grasped, by cleansing our sight so that we can see ecstatically, see the world as it is, infinite.[3]

The imagery is from Jacob's dream of a ladder extending from earth to heaven, with angels ascending and descending on it (Gen. 28:10-17). In Hebrew the word "on it" (*bo*) is ambiguous. It could also mean "on him." Rabbinic exegetes were divided. *Bereshith Rabba* 70:12 contains this revealing discussion between Rabbi Ḥiyya and Rabbi Jannai (first half of the third century C.E.):

> R. Ḥiyya the Elder and R. Jannai disagreed. One maintained: They were *Ascending and descending* the ladder; while the other said: they were *Ascending and descending* on Jacob. The statement that they were *ascending and descending* the ladder presents no difficulty. The statement that they were ascending and descending on Jacob we must take to mean that some were exalting him and others degrading him, dancing, leaping, and maligning him. Thus it says, *Israel in whom I will be glorified* (Isa. XLIX, 3); it is thou, [said the angels,] whose features are engraved on high; they ascended on high and saw his [Jacob's] features and they descended below and found him sleeping.[4]

Elsewhere we read that the Merkabah mystic is like a person "who has a ladder in his home that he ascends and descends, and nobody can interfere with what he does." Again, mention is made of a "heavenly ladder which stands on earth and reaches up to the right leg of the Throne of Glory."[5] The idea here is popular Platonism and is common in the literature of that period, especially in the Hermetic literature and Philo. As the ancestor of Israel, Jacob summarizes in his person the ideal, archetypal Israel. Jacob *is* Israel.

John has taken over this mode of thought in his depiction of Jesus as the Human Being. According to C. H. Dodd, "He [Jesus] is archetypal at least in the sense that His relation to the Father is the archetype of the true and ultimate relation" of human beings to God. Moreover, the Human Being is represented symbolically by light, bread, and the vine. In relation to these, he is *alēthinos*, the true or ultimate reality lying behind phenomenal existence, or that to which these symbols point. It is not a long step to say that,

for John, the Human Being is the *alēthinos anthrōpos,* the real or archetypal
Human Being, or the Platonic idea of humanity.[6] As the heavenly Human
Being dwelling in everyone, but waiting for awakening or new birth, this figure sums up humanity as such. For John, then, the Human Being, Wisdom's Child, is the inclusive representative of ideal or redeemed humanity.
It is the vine, human followers are the branches (John 15:1-11). As the incarnate Humanchild, Jesus dies and ascends to God, that where he is believers may be also (14:3). In his death, the son of the man thus draws all
peoples into union with himself (with the exception of his own Jewish flesh
and blood!), and thus affirms his character as inclusive representative of the
redeemed race.[7]

Revelation therefore becomes crucial: you are saved by what you see.
Dodd continues, "As the 'looking' at the serpent caused Israel to 'live,' so the
'contemplation' of the Son of Man in His exaltation brings life eternal."[8] As
the ladder to an open heaven, the Human Being is not simply the revealer.
He is "the inclusive representative of true humanity," who "incorporates in
Himself the people of God, or humanity in its ideal aspect." But what had
previously been an abstraction has now become flesh. What languished as
pure potential has become manifest. As "the true self of the human race,
standing in that perfect union with God to which others can attain only as
they are incorporate in Him,"[9] Wisdom's Child is both corporate and individual. She is the Truly Human Being who gathers those who aspire to true
humanity within herself. That is why Nathanael is overwhelmed; in Bultmann's words, Jesus is the Revealer who knows his "own" (10:14), "and
[who] in his word reveals to them what they are and what they will be. . . .
Thus faith in him is grounded in the fact that in the encounter with him the
believer's own existence is uncovered."[10]

The leader has become the ladder. Wisdom incarnate has become the
way. But what is at the top of that ladder, and what is the goal of the way? Angelic communications will, from that time forward, travel the trunk line that
is none other than the Human Being. This is a symbolically clothed manner
of saying that the Human Being is "the way, and the truth, and the life" (John
14:6). The ladder is the way. The way is incarnation. The ladder is a two-way
link. Christianity is not the way. Religion is not the way. The way is not ascending to heaven, for "No one has ascended into heaven except the one
who descended from heaven, the Human Being" (John 3:13).[11] Incarnation
does not mean spiritual ascent to the ineffable. The ineffable has become ef-
fable and dwelt among us (John 1:14). The Way is not something we seek,
but seeks us; an a priori or archetypal truth calls from within and is shared by
all.[12] We do not need, therefore, to empty ourselves into transcendence;

rather, we are invited to live with the Human Being in the most mundane and secular ways, to take it within ourselves, to digest it, to assimilate it into our beings: "Very truly, I tell you, unless you eat the flesh of the Human Being and drink his blood, you have no life in you" (John 6:53).[13] We become human as we "eat" the Human Being, who has become the "bread of life" (6:35), "the bread that came down from heaven" (6:41). "For the bread that I will give for the life of the world is my flesh" (6:51).

Contrary to a dogma tenaciously held, Jesus does not exhaust the possibilities of incarnating God. As Tom F. Driver notes, Jesus is neither the sole incarnation of God nor the perfect incarnation. As a male, he does not provide a definitive picture of what incarnation might look like for a woman. But neither does he provide a definitive picture for a man. Jesus did not experience marriage, child rearing, long life, debilitating illnesses, and a host of other things commonly experienced by human beings. Jesus' incarnation is complete from the point of view of his own life, but not from the point of view of others' lives.[14] Put more positively, Jesus is not the incarnate God, but a human being who incarnated God and who taught us how to do the same, through the working of the divine Spirit within us. That is what it means to incarnate God.

If Jesus is divine, how can we be like him? But even if he is "just" a religious genius, how can we be like him? The two alternatives are false. He is only divine if, by that, we mean fully human. Nor are we asked to be geniuses like Jesus. His genius has already done its work, and we are the beneficiaries. Nor are we expected to be revealers as he was. For what God gave him, he has revealed, and our path is lit by his light. No, we are asked to become ourselves, aided by what Jesus revealed and by the genius of his life and teaching.

The son of the man in John is not an apocalyptic figure who will come on the clouds of heaven at the end of time. Yet the Human Being is invested with all the archetypal significance with which faith could imbue it. When the blind man whom Jesus healed shows himself ignorant of who the Human Being might be, Jesus asks him, "Do you believe in the son of the man?" The man answers, " 'And who is he, sir? Tell me, so that I may believe in him.' Jesus said to him, 'You have seen him, and the one speaking with you is he.' He said, 'Lord, I believe.' And he worshiped him" (John 9:35-38).[15]

The meaning of the man's response is ambiguous. It could imply that the man has no idea what "the son of the man" means. Or it could mean that he knew of the expectation but wanted to know who would fill the role. We find the same ambiguity in John 12:34. John apparently intends to leave the reader confused as to who the son of the man really is.

In John 3:14-15, Jesus says, "And just as Moses lifted up the serpent in the wilderness, so must the son of the man be lifted up, that whoever believes *in him* may have eternal life."[16] "Believe" appears ninety-eight times in the Fourth Gospel. Believe what? Sometimes John asks the reader to believe Jesus' words. Yet John also uses the word to mean "believe in," where the idea seems to be committing oneself to him, placing one's trust, hope, or salvation in him.

As Delbert Burkett notes, for John, "the son of the man" has become a christological confession, equivalent to "the Son of God," "Son of the Father," and "the Son." These expressions are all fundamentally relational: they express Jesus' sonship, his relation to the Father. They do not represent different Christologies, but a single Christology of the Son. "This filial relationship to God is the central aspect of Jesus' identity in John. All other facets of his identity are subordinate to this central feature."[17] But while "Son of God" expresses Jesus' sonship explicitly, "the son of the man" does so cryptically. According to John, Jesus understood this riddle, but apparently others did not unless he explained it to them. Hence the peculiar usage of the term only on the lips of Jesus.[18] Clearly, the son of the man was not just a name for the earthly Jesus. In Margaret Pamment's words, "the son of the man" in John's Gospel, "while referring to Jesus, draws particular attention to his representative humanity, that is, Jesus is pictured as representing not what every [one] is, but what [one] could and should be."[19] The epiphany that Jesus' hearers expect in the future is already present in Jesus. Bultmann can conclude, "Thus everything that he is, can be referred to by the mysterious title 'Son of Man.' "[20] In addition, Pilate's declaration in the heart of the passion narrative—"Behold the Man"—may signify the Human Being, the epitome of humanity (uttered ironically, of course; this flogged, broken figure hardly appears a threat to Roman hegemony).[21]

The absence of the apocalyptic scenario in John's Gospel means that there is no split between pre-Easter and post-Easter Human Being sayings. In John's Gospel, the earthly Jesus has, so to speak, been engulfed by the archetypal. He is not so much related to the Human Being as identical with it. But his disciples will also be identical to the Human Being. John's Jesus is not the son of the man seated at the right hand of God and coming with the clouds of heaven, as in the Synoptics. Instead, Jesus is identified with the Human Being for eternity. *He is the past, present, and future of humanity in its destiny before God.*

The son of the man is God's ultimate statement about the goal of the human enterprise. Yet Jesus' followers are not excluded from the reality that the Human Being represents. In ways that go far beyond the Synoptic Gospels, Jesus the Human Being incorporates his disciples into union with himself in God. He gives them "power to become children of God," as he is (1:12). They are not just born of earthly parents, but of God, as he is (1:13). Jesus ascends to heaven (3:13); so, in apparent contradiction, will his disciples (14:2). Jesus testifies to what he has seen and heard from God (3:32); the disciples do likewise (12:17). Jesus judges and forgives (3:17-21); the disciples will also (20:23). Jesus does the works of God; his followers do as well (6:28-29; 9:4), and greater works (14:12). Jesus is God's son; his followers are "gods" and "children of the Most High" (Ps. 82:6; John 10:34-35). Where Jesus is, his disciples will be also (14:3). Jesus alone sees and knows the Father, but the disciples do as well (14:6-7, 9). He is the vine, they are the branches, and the Father is the vinedresser (15:1-11). Nothing could express more completely the collective, corporate nature of the Johannine Human Being than 14:20—"you will know that I am in my Father, and you in me, and I in you." John has, in short, not only preserved the collective aspect of the Human Being, but raises it to its apogee.[22]

The supreme revelation that the Human Being provides is not a trip into the heavenly spheres, as we see in many first- and second-century documents.[23] The ladder is not for people but for angels, not for mystics but for heavenly messengers. The Gospel according to John does not disclose heavenly secrets. For John, the gospel reveals "this world" (*kosmos*) as the Domination System.[24] The gospel inaugurates an alternate reality, the Reign of God. John likes to call it "eternal life"—life in a new dimension, which begins the moment one encounters the son of the man. To "believe in the Human Being" (John 9:35) is to affirm that this new reality that Jesus incarnates and reveals is from God. To "believe" is to join the struggle against the authorities and powers that seek to extinguish this new revelation (like the religious leaders in the healing of the blind man, John 9:13-41). That the Powers will crush the Human Being is certain; that their victory will prove empty is God's great secret: "And I, when I am lifted up from the earth, will draw all people to myself" (12:32).

B. Exaltation through Execution

"And just as Moses lifted up the serpent in the wilderness, so must the Human Being be lifted up, that whoever believes in him may have eternal life" (3:14-15). The comparison seems to be between a death-dealing power (the serpent, possibly suggesting Satan)—neutralized by being "lifted up" on a pole—and a death-dealing pole (the cross) on which the crucified Human Being neutralizes death.[25] His "lifting up" is not to the divine throne room in heaven, but onto the timber on which he was executed: "When you have lifted up [onto the cross] the Human Being, then you will realize that I AM, and that I do nothing on my own, but I speak these things as the Father instructed me" (8:28). The Human Being is "glorified" by his crucifixion (12:23, 32; 13:31) because his death exposes this world's deceit. As Liberator, he frees those held hostage, in bondage to the System (in Hebrew, "lifting up" can refer both to hanging and to honoring—Gen. 40:13, 19).[26]

James W. Douglass, who has consistently lived the way of the cross, writes in a personal letter, "The transformation of humanity into the Human Being becomes possible to the extent that we are willing to accept as a necessary consequence the same bloody ascension that the Powers rewarded Jesus with—a public execution, with the loss of every kind of security by a total commitment to our doing God's will of love, justice, and peace right now on earth. If we don't choose the way of (the willingness of) the cross, we choose or submit to a way of death to our brothers and sisters, whom we kill now on a global scale. But the way of the cross—or as Gandhi put it, experimenting in that truth—opens up the way to the Human Being."

Here is the pathos of this Gospel, according to E. A. Abbott: that the promise of angels ascending and descending upon the son of the man was not fulfilled. John provides nothing, not even a corresponding event to the transfiguration in the Synoptic Gospels, nothing but a succession of misunderstandings. These culminate in a voice from heaven that some identify as thunder, others as an angel, but that no one comprehends. Even at the close of Jesus' public ministry, people still ask, with no perception, "How can you say that the son of the man must be lifted up? Who is this son of the man?" (12:34).[27] Well they might ask. For the "one like a son of man" in Daniel appeared in heaven, coming to the throne of God, not as a little-known charismatic healer and preacher, a nobody among the nobodies of Palestine. How could the people know? The Human Being had never been revealed before. John places before them, in plain sight, this revelation—blinding, by virtue of its ordinariness, a secret displayed before their eyes, incomprehensible due to the totality of its demand.

But John does tell us who this Human Being is. In 5:26-27, Jesus declares: "For just as the Father has life in himself, so he has granted the Son also to have life in himself; and he has given him authority to execute judgment, because he is 'a son of man.'" John 5:27 is the only case among the phrase's more than eighty appearances in the New Testament in which "the son of the man" appears without definite articles. Why do we not find more examples of this usage? If John can do without the articles here, why not elsewhere? Does John mean that any human being can execute judgment? Besides, as noted previously, the articles produce a grotesque Greek expression. One answer might be that the definite articles emphasize that "the son of the man" is neither Adam ("the son of *the Adam*"!) nor humanity generally ("the son of *the* humanity"!), but "the son of the Human or Humane One" whom Ezekiel encountered at the fountainhead of Jewish mysticism (Ezekiel 1). In Ezekiel, "son of man" is consistently used in the vocative, in direct address ("O mortal"—*ben 'adam*); hence the absence of the articles there. In Jesus' use of the phrase, now become Aramaic (*bar enasha*), however, the expression was no longer vocative. Some way was needed, when the tradition was translated into Greek, to make clear that the phrase was *not* a way of referring to all of humanity or to Adam, but in an utterly unique way to Jesus and to others whose lives are transparent to God. This supposition would account for the remarkable consistency in all our sources—Matthew, Mark, Luke, John, Q, L (Special Luke), M (Special Matthew), *Thomas*, and the Nag Hammadi texts generally—in reproducing the expression with both articles when the articles could easily have been dropped.

In 5:27, and only there, the verb "to be" is used: Jesus *is* "son of man." Yet this saying expresses not only equation but difference: he is also "the Human Being." Schematically, A = B, but B > A: Jesus is the Human Being, but the Human Being includes others as well—his followers, kindred spirits, and saints of all times and places. (See Diagram 2.) To paraphrase John, we could have Jesus say, "The Human Being and I are one," but also "the Human Being is greater than I" (10:30; 14:28). So Jesus is fully the Human Being without exhausting what the Human Being is. Followers of Jesus engaged in individuation are also children of the Human. They are "born again/from above" (John 3:3) and invested with the power of God. Such a person actualizes the divine-child archetype, which is the child born from the maturity of the adult.[28]

In John 8:28-29, Jesus again takes on the role of exalted Human Being.

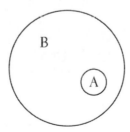

DIAGRAM 2: The Human Being and Jesus

"When you have lifted up the son of the man, then you will realize that I am he, and that I do nothing on my own, but I speak these things as the Father instructed me. And the one who sent me is with me; he has not left me alone, for I always do what is pleasing to [God]." "The son of the man" here refers to a transcendent heavenly reality that Jesus has become as a result of his incarnation and glorification through suffering. The double meaning of "lifted up" refers not just to his crucifixion, but to the crucifixion as the means by which he is exalted to heaven.

In order to communicate this exaltation through crucifixion, John has invented an altogether new way of writing, in which the heavenly being of Jesus shines through the earthly. This creates a portrayal of Jesus that to many has seemed "docetic," making Jesus only "appear" (*dokeo*) to be a real human being. But the evangelist is trying to guide us, by means of Jesus, into the imaginal realm, into what John himself calls the "eternal" dimension of life lived in the "now." Consequently, "seeing" becomes an act of vision, not sight. To see the Human Being ascended is thus to set our perception on what it means to become a human being. Wisdom's Child, "lifted up," "ascending to where he was before," represents the future of the species. "Seeing" this truth is to recognize that the Human Being as lived by Jesus has entered the collective consciousness of humanity. It is now an archetypal image capable of spurring unlived life and of mobilizing untapped resistance to the institutions and structures that grind the life out of people.

Picturing heaven as "up" is, of course, merely a convention of thought. But it well captures the sense that this figure, exalted from ignominious execution, shame, and abandonment, has lifted up the Human Being as the "highest" value in the universe. He has become the criterion by which we decide what is of value. He is the revelation of humanity's evolutionary goal, as Teilhard de Chardin saw clairvoyantly.

I spoke earlier of the statement in John's Gospel that "no one has ascended into heaven except the one who descended from heaven, the Human Being" (John 3:13). This is spiritual relief. We do not have to scale the ramparts of heaven to find God. Spirituality is not the monopoly of a few religious athletes who have mastered their bodies and tethered their souls. God has found us where we are. This does not mean that one is in constant communion with God. One still must live by faith. Hence the repeated use of "to believe" in John. But John introduces us to a world in which God is immediate to our souls.

John, more than anyone, fathomed the archetypal meaning of the ascended Jesus. If his Jesus sometimes appears more divine than human, it is because John is intent on showing him in his eternal, archetypal mode of being. Now all can know God through Jesus and as well as any mystic. We are all now, in a sense, mystics. The Jesus of John's Gospel establishes a democracy of mystics: common folk who have experienced, in their own selves, the presence of God.

14. The Human Being in Letters Ascribed to Paul

Paul never mentions "the son of the man."[1] And for good reason: few of his Gentile readers would have comprehended that enigmatic phrase. Not only would they have regarded the expression as awkward translation Greek, but they would not have been familiar with its meaning in the Palestinian context. Yet Paul was surely aware of the archetypal reality that the Human Being constituted. This is clear from his use of the term *anthrōpos*, which, as he used it, was tantamount to Human Being. As Kirsopp Lake and Foakes Jackson comment, Paul "was too good a Grecian to translate *Barnasha* [Aramaic for "son of man"] by so impossible a phrase as *ho huios tou anthrōpou* [Greek for "the son of the man"], and rendered it idiomatically by *ho anthrōpos*."[2] That Paul and the later writers of the New Testament were aware of the semantic field that "the son of the man" occupied is shown by the number of son-of-the-man parallels in the epistles:

> Luke 12:8 — "everyone who acknowledges me before others, the son of the man also will acknowledge before the angels of God"; compare Rom. 10:9 — "if you confess . . . that Jesus is Lord . . . you will be saved."

> Luke 6:22 — "Blessed are you when people hate you, and when they exclude you, revile you, and defame you on account of the son of the man"; compare 1 Peter 4:14 — "If you are reviled for the name of Christ, you are blessed."

> Mark 2:10 — ". . . that you may know that the son of the man has authority on earth to forgive sins"; compare Eph. 1:7 — "In [Christ] we have redemption through his blood, the forgiveness of our trespasses."

Mark 10:45—"[T]he Son of Man came . . . to give his life as a ransom for
many"; compare four passages: in Eph. 5:2 and Titus 2:13-14 "the son of the
man" is replaced by "Christ"; in Gal. 2:20 by "Son of God"; and at 1 Tim.
2:5-6 there is an exact equivalent: "the *anthrōpos* Christ Jesus, who gave
himself a ransom for all."[3]

In addition, Paul developed a new set of images that embraced the collective dimension of the Human Being: the expressions "the body of Christ"
and life "in Christ Jesus."

A. The Inner Anthropos

Paul and his lieutenants used *anthrōpos* eight or so times in a way that not
only was continuous with the Gospels' use of "the son of the man," but that
also created a vocabulary on which the Gnostics later would seize. "Clothe
yourselves with the new self [literally, 'new anthropos'—*kainon anthrōpon*],
created according to the likeness of God in true righteousness and holiness"
(Eph. 4:24). This sense of a radical new inwardness at the core of a person's
being—a being lived forward into history—is one of the most significant in-
novations of that era. The idea was fully articulated by Augustine in his new
notion of the individual personality. In the New Testament, however, the
idea is still an emergent intuition. "We know that our old self [literally, "old
anthropos"] was crucified with him [Christ] so that . . . we might no longer
be enslaved to sin" (Rom. 6:6). "Our outer nature [literally, "outer anthropos"] is wasting away, our inner nature ["anthropos" implied] is being renewed day by day" (2 Cor. 4:16). "You have stripped off the old self
["anthropos"] with its practices and have clothed yourselves with the new
self ["anthropos" implied] . . . according to the image of its creator" (Col.
3:9-10). "Be strengthened in your inner being ["inner anthropos"] with
power through his Spirit . . . that Christ may dwell in your hearts through
faith, as you are being rooted and grounded in love" (Eph. 3:16-17). This
last text indicates that this inner self—what 1 Peter 3:4 calls "the hidden anthropos at the center of your being"—is in development; it is not yet complete. The same idea is expressed by Eph. 4:13—"until all of us come to the
unity of the faith and of the knowledge of the Son of God, to maturity [*eis
andra teleion*, lit., "into the finished/completed/perfect Human Being"], to
the measure of the full stature of Christ."

Further evidence that Paul equates the son of the man with the inner *anthropos* is provided in reverse by Matt. 9:8, in which Matthew concludes the healing of the paralytic story with the words, "and they glorified God, who had given such authority to human beings (*anthropois*)." The Syriac here is "the sons of man."[4]

But this radical inwardness is even more radically social. Psalm 80 and Daniel 7 had spoken of Israel as the collective Human Being. Ephesians now extends it to encompass all peoples. Thus Eph. 2:15-16 can speak of Christ creating "in himself *one new anthropos* in place of the two [Jew and Gentile]" and of reconciling "both groups to God in one body through the cross." First Corinthians 15:47-49 compares the first and second Adams: "The first *anthropos* was from the earth, a man of dust; the second *anthropos* is from heaven. As was the *anthropos* of dust, so are those who are of the dust; and as is the *anthropos* of heaven, so are those who are of heaven. Just as we have borne the image of the *anthropos* of dust, we will also bear the image of the *anthropos* of heaven"—the latter an unmistakable allusion to the ascended Human Being of the Gospels. Second Adam ("second man"), of course, is a pun on "the son of the man."

The new Adam = second Adam = son of Adam = son of the Man typology is set forth in greatest detail in Rom. 5:12-21, in which all humanity is incorporated into the first Adam and his fallen estate, or into the second Adam and the fellowship of those being redeemed. No one grasped more profoundly the corporate dimension of the "inner *anthropos*" than Paul, who saw it embracing humanity as a single Human Being.[5]

B. The Body of Christ

These few references to an inner, new, heavenly, or spiritual Anthropos or Human Being are supplemented by numerous references to the "body of Christ."[6] In these sayings, the corporate dimension of the Human Being again is underscored. "Now you are the body of Christ and individually members of it" (1 Cor. 12:27). First John 3:2 is echoed by Eph. 4:12-13—"to equip the saints for the work of ministry, for building up the body of Christ, until all of us come to the unity of the faith and the knowledge of the Son of God, to maturity [literally, "into a mature person"—*eis andra teleion*], to the measure of the full stature of Christ." Again, "Just as we have borne the image of the man of dust, we will also bear the image of the man of heaven" (1 Cor. 15:49).

But the body of Christ is not simply a conglomerate of individuals. It is an organic entity, a realm, a dimension of present existence, a quality of becoming. It enables people to terminate complicity with dehumanizing systems, such as legal arrangements subverted by the Domination System: "You have died to the law through the body of Christ, so that you may belong to another, to him who has been raised from the dead in order that we may bear fruit for God" (Rom. 7:4). Gentiles, once excluded from the promises of God, "have become fellow heirs, members of the same body, and sharers in the promises in Christ Jesus through the gospel" (Eph. 3:6). Believers fit together organically: "For as in one body we have many members, and not all the members have the same function, so we, who are many, are one body in Christ, and individually we are members of one another" (Rom. 12:4-5). Membership in the one body has ethical and organizational consequences: "For in the one Spirit we were all baptized into one body—Jews or Greeks, slaves or free—and we were all made to drink of one Spirit" (1 Cor. 12:13). Thus different members are called to different tasks to build up the total body (12:27-31). The Human Being must be corporate to further the human project, because we cannot become human by ourselves. (Recent research on the Berlin Jews saved from deportation by non-Jewish neighbors in the 1940s indicates that, for every Jew saved, an average of twelve Gentile Berliners had to help.)[7] We are inescapably social. Individuation is not individualism. We are one body, not just as a church, but as a species.

Where, asks Eduard Schweizer, did the body-of-Christ imagery first arise? John develops the collective imagery of the vine and the branches (John 15:1-11) and the notion of Jesus' body as the replacement for the temple (2:21), and he does so independently of Paul. Thus the Pauline idea of Christ incorporating believers into his own existence was known in other parts of the early church, using other imagery. But the vine motif can be traced to Ps. 80:16, in which Israel is represented collectively as the son of man. So the corporate dimension of the son of man has a deep prehistory that both John and Paul augmented.[8]

C. In Christ

This same corporeal relationship can be alluded to by the simple expression "in Christ Jesus." Redemption is "in Christ Jesus" (Rom. 3:24), believers are baptized into Christ Jesus (6:3), they live to God in Christ Jesus (6:11), they have eternal life in Christ Jesus (6:23). Believers now live by the grace of

God that has been given in Christ Jesus (1 Cor. 1:4), who is the source of our life in Christ Jesus (1:30). As all die in Adam, so all will be made alive in Christ (15:22). And so on, dozens of times. Incorporation into Christ is so vital that believers already have entered the other dimension: "[God] raised us up with him and seated us with him in the heavenly places in Christ Jesus" (Eph. 2:6). Believers already partake of the reality of the Human Being.

We in the individualistic West have virtually no categories for taking seriously, or for comprehending, such an organismic understanding of being in Christ. One is "saved" by incorporation into this living being, Christ. One lives by participation in the life of Christ. In short, *Christ became the Self of the early Christians, without remainder.*

At the same time, the individual experienced this corporate participation in Christ as an indwelling of Christ within one's person. "Christ is speaking in me" (2 Cor. 13:3). "Do you not realize that Jesus Christ is in you?" (2 Cor. 13:5; here "you" is plural but includes both the community and the individual member). Believers are a temple of the Holy Spirit, both corporately and individually (1 Cor. 3:16; 6:19; 2 Cor. 6:16). Paul could scarcely do more justice to the personal/corporate aspect of the Human Being than in his use of the term *anthrōpos*, his exposition of the body of Christ, his image of dwelling in Christ, and his statements about the body as the new, inner temple that replaces the old, exterior edifice. And this personal/corporate reality is not reserved for heaven or an afterlife, but it has already begun.

Part Five

The Human Being in Jewish Mysticism and Gnosticism

While the following two chapters are not essential for understanding the son of the man in the New Testament, they are indispensable for comprehending the way in which the son-of-the-man archetype was developing in the Mediterranean basin and beyond during the first centuries of the common era. Jewish mysticism developed further the notion of God as Human that had been inaugurated by Ezekiel. It also flirted with the dangerous notion of a human being ascending to heaven and being vested with incomprehensible authority and power. Here the Gospel writers and the Jewish mystics plowed parallel furrows, apparently without being aware of how close they were. To be sure, the *content* of their reflections was different, but the *structure* was strikingly similar. Failure to respect these family resemblances has led to sibling rivalry and even fratricide, with Jews suffering by far the greater devastation. Once we recognize the ubiquity of the archetype of the Human Being, we can move beyond the provincialism that declares Jesus the world's sole savior and lord. Instead, we can begin to appreciate that Jews who do "the will of God" are "my brother and sister and mother" (Mark 3:35). Perhaps we might recognize that Jewish insights about ultimate reality may be as good as our own, and in some cases better. After all, all the earliest Christians—Jesus included—were Jews (it is necessary to remind people!).

Chapter 16, on Gnosticism, also tells us nothing about the son of the man in the New Testament, since Gnosticism rose well after the Gospels were written. But again, if our concern is to comprehend the son-of-the-man archetype, then it is important to learn about the extravagant speculations of these wild metaphysicians. Secondary reports of the Gnostics' writings were largely unintelligible until the discovery of the Nag Hammadi texts and the advent of depth psychology, both in the twentieth century. In the Nag Hammadi texts, the Gnostics used the son-of-the-man title well over fifty times, virtually always of a heavenly being or a hierarchy of beings. If we wish to learn what it means to become more fully human, we can scarcely ignore the Gnostics' mythological psychology. Jung called them, with justice, the first depth psychologists.

There is another reason that we need to learn about these ancient myth spinners. Gnostics have been the heretics of choice for Christian vilification. To dismiss someone's thought, however carefully crafted, one only needs to tar it as "Gnostic." In a period in which we are beginning to appreciate and to learn from Native Americans, Zen Buddhists, Hindus, Jews, and others, "Gnostic" is still a dirty word. Thanks to the scholars who have brought the Nag Hammadi texts to light, we can see how badly the early-church theologians caricatured the Gnostics. Today we are in a position to appreciate the depths of gnostic wisdom and to benefit from it.

15. The Human Being in Jewish Mysticism

Jewish Merkabah ("throne chariot") mysticism descended directly from the visions of God in Isaiah 6, Ezekiel 1, and Daniel 7. Early traces appear in pre-Christian apocalypses and the Dead Sea Scrolls, Paul (2 Cor. 12:1-10), and Revelation 1 and 4–5. It then proliferated in Palestine between 200 and 700 C.E. in what is called the *Hekhalot* ("Divine Palaces") literature. My interest in this remarkable mystical tradition centers on its striking parallels to what was happening in Christian psyches of that same period. These Jewish mystics developed further the revelation in Ezekiel 1 that God is ultimate humanness. They also told of the ascension of human beings into heaven, where they, too, like the ascended Jesus, received divine authority to judge and save the world. These Jewish mystics were experiencing at a profound level something of the same archetypal reality that the Gospels identified as "the son of the man." From those experiences, these mystics spun an esoteric tradition that continues to be vital right up to the present. This chapter on Jewish mysticism, and the following chapter on Gnosticism, reveal the breadth and depth of the psychic disturbance and transformation that Ezekiel's vision inaugurated—and that caused Ezekiel's vision.

I am not competent to give a rounded picture of the spirituality that Jewish mysticism produced.[1] Fortunately, for a nonspecialist like me, there has been in the last decade or so a small rivulet of excellent studies. These books can help us enter, imaginatively, some of the mysteries of Merkabah, or divine-throne-chariot mysticism.[2] The date of the Jewish sources appearing in this chapter is of no relevance for this study, since we are not reconstructing historical development so much as attempting to identify the emergence of an archetypal image. Thus even late-medieval speculations and modern Hasidism may be relevant to our inquiry.

We focus on just two issues in this chapter: anthropomorphisms in the mystics' descriptions of God, and the phenomenon of human beings ascending to heaven. Other traditions besides the Christian depicted God as Human. The persistence and ubiquity of this motif indicate that something powerful was at work in the collective unconscious of that period to birth the Human Being.

A. God as Human in Jewish Mysticism

In the early stories of Genesis, God frequently appears as an angel ("messenger") who looks like a human being but who, in fact, is God. We can allay this apparent confusion, however, by recognizing that God *is* Human. This equation is recorded as early as the story of Jacob at the River Jabbok, wrestling with an *ish* ("man") later identified as God (Gen. 32:22-32).

Many such encounters with God occur in the Hebrew Bible. The living heart of postbiblical Jewish mysticism, however, was the ascent to the heavenly throne room to see God (or that face of God or of God's Glory that the mystic could survive seeing). Curiously, around 500 c.e., Jewish mystics began to speak, not of an *ascent* (though they continued to use the symbolism of "up" to speak of heaven), but of a *descent* to the *merkabah*, or divine throne chariot.[3] One familiar with depth psychology will find it irresistible to regard this shift as the mystics' conscious recognition that the cosmological journey through the seven heavens does not take place in space, but in the depth of the psyche. In the "Visions of Ezekiel" (fourth or fifth century c.e.), Ezekiel sees the seven heavens with their seven *merkabot* (chariots) reflected in the waters of the River Chebar.[4] This vision suggests that, symbolically speaking, one looks into the waters of the unconscious to see the mysteries of heaven. Again, "God opened to Ezekiel the seven *subterranean* chambers, and Ezekiel looked into them and saw all the *celestial* entities."[5] This element of introspection made Jewish mysticism not only more psychological than some traditions, but in historical fact the progenitor of psychoanalysis.[6] We might with justice pause in amazement, then, at the statement of the Maggid Dov Baer of Miedzyrzecz in 1770: "The righteous make God, if one may phrase it thus, their unconscious."[7]

Why did the Jewish mystics storm heaven's gates with such tenacity and spiritual daring, confronting hostile angels determined to keep heaven's secrets out of the hands of untrustworthy mortals? Unlike the Christian mystics, with their Neoplatonic craving for union with God, the Jewish Merkabah mystics wanted only to *see* and *hear* God. Why were they content with a respectful distance, rather than pressing into the very being of God, as they were to do later in medieval Kabbalah?[8] Part of the answer, one suspects, is a healthy sense of mortality and finitude. The seekers after the *merkabah*'s mysteries were all too aware of their frailty before the awesome majesty of the divine. They were fully content simply to see, on the principle that you become what your desire beholds.

There was perhaps another reason, however, why Jewish mystics persevered after the vision of God: *because they had been told no one could do so and live.* As the children of Adam and Eve, the Israelites tended to desire what had been forbidden. But this desire was not a transgression as much as a thirst for transcendence. God did not forbid so much as forewarn Israel not to attempt to look on God's face. (Here again, God is very Human.) God is so much more than human beings can comprehend or encompass that they might be annihilated by God's numinous splendor. It is as if a king leaves his newlywed wife in his castle with the freedom of the keep, *except for one room,* which it is forbidden to open. (And, of course, the key is hanging on a nail beside the door.) Jewish mystics ascended (later, descended) through the seven heavens to the seven concentric palaces (*hekhalot*). There they risked destruction due to their ignorance of heavenly geography and protocol. Finally, with the help of friendly angels, they penetrated to the divine throne in the seventh palace of the seventh heaven and saw what no mortal could see and live: the Glory seated on the throne. They did not see God in God's totality, but the degree of divine Light that the seer could endure.

> It is said: For human beings shall not see Me and live [Exodus 33:20]; and secondly it is said: That God speaks to human beings and they live [Deuteronomy 5:21]; and thirdly it is said: I saw the Lord sitting upon a Throne, etc. [Isaiah 6:11].[9]

Far more fundamentally, however, the Jewish mystics sought the face of God because God invited them to do so. God yearns for the companionship of human beings made in God's image. Thus, in Exodus 24, God commanded Moses to bring Aaron, Nadab, Abihu, and seventy of the elders of Israel, and to "worship at a distance" (v. 1). They ascended the mountain, "and they saw the God of Israel. Under his feet there was something like a pavement of sapphire stone, like the very heaven for clearness. God did not lay his hand on [i.e., kill] the chief leaders of the people of Israel; also they beheld God, and they ate and drank" in God's presence (vv. 10-11). Again there is an intuition that heaven is not above but below, that is, within: the "pavement of sapphire" is a double of heavenly blue, "like the very heaven for clearness."

God's longing for human companionship is so intense that, according to *Hekhalot Rabbati*, whenever Israel recites the "Holy, holy, holy" on earth, God bends over the image of Jacob/Israel that is inscribed on the divine throne chariot, hugs it and kisses it and embraces it.[10] This means, says Dan Merkur, that God animates the imaginal image, which suggests that the human search for God is initiated by the One searched for. This poignant passage underscores the *liturgical* context of these visions. The aim of the heavenly journey is not just to see God on the throne, but to participate in the cosmic liturgy of praise. Entry to heaven incorporates the earthly community into the heavenly liturgy, thereby turning the liturgy into a truly cosmic event encompassing heaven and earth.[11]

Pesiqta Rabbati, a midrash from the ninth century C.E., shows God not only allowing a few fearless mystics to realize the vision of God, but democratizing the vision at Sinai. Now all Israel can have the vision, though each person must be protected by ministering angels so as not to be overcome by the effulgence of divine light:

> God opened the doors of the seven firmaments and revealed Godself to the Israelites' sight, in God's beauty and glory and splendor, God's crown and the appearance of God's glory. When they heard, *I am the Lord your God* [Exodus 20:2], their souls left them. God sent down the dew with which God is going to bring the souls of the saints to life, and brought them back to life. . . . What did God do? God sent twelve hundred thousand ministering angels down to earth to them. Two angels laid hold of each Israelite: one put a hand over their hearts so that their souls would not leave them, while the other lifted up their necks so that they could see God face to face. Why did God reveal Godself to them face to face? God said to them: "See that I have revealed myself to you in my glory and my splendor. Should there be a generation that leads you astray and says, "Let us go worship other gods," then say to them: "We have a Lord whom we serve. When we abandon God, God sends us down to hell. And God will establish God's reign over all Israel."[12]

In *Deuteronomy Rabbah* (900 C.E.), we again find God actively engaged in revealing to Israel all the secrets of heaven: "On the day the Torah was given, God tore open the heavens and showed the Israelites everything that was above."[13] Yet, much as Yahweh loves Israel, says the great scholar of Jewish mysticism, Gershom Scholem, there is little talk of loving God, such as one finds in later Hasidism. God is overwhelmingly other. Yet here, too, God is distinctly Human, and the mystic sees Humanness in all its brilliance and mystery. Scholem's observation about sixteenth-century Lurianic Kabbalism is no less apt for the early Merkabah mystics: "Ecstasy is possible here only within the limits imposed . . . ; it is an ecstasy of silent meditation, of a descent of the human will to meet that of God, prayer serving as a kind of balustrade on which the mystic leans, so as not to be plunged suddenly or unprepared into an ecstasy in which the holy waters might drown his consciousness."[14]

These mystics spoke a spiritual language. What they bequeathed to their followers were a set of conventions and practices, couched in the form of travelogues, dialogues, droll tales, fantastic narratives, dreams, measurements of God's body, magic, adjurations, and endless lists of divine names that the initiate could use as guidelines for the mystical descent to the *merkabah*.[15] These are exercises of the imagination capable of positioning the seeker to experience the vision of God. They are similar to the Ignatian Exercises and Jungian active imagination. Most religious traditions have instructions for inducing visions and other experiences of the divine, from the Pentecostal who wants to speak in tongues to the shaman on a vision quest. *Hekhalot Rabbati*, for example, starts with the inquiry, "Which are the hymns that are said by the one who wishes to behold the vision of the *merkabah* and to descend and ascend unharmed?"[16]

People who fall in love go through a series of experiences that vary wildly, but that are remarkably repetitious. It is the same with seeing God. Each experience is unique, yet most are similar. None of these mystics undertook the vision quest frivolously. The rigors of the journey were so harrowing, dangerous, and demanding that dabblers quickly exited. Only those who had mastered Bible, Mishnah, halakah (the oral law), and haggadah (oral tradition), and had observed all the laws revealed to Moses on Sinai, were allowed to descend to the *merkabah*.[17] Various means were used, in addition to those listed above: prayers, prolonged fasts, vigils, meditative exercises, rhythmic chants (especially the repetition of the Qedusha or Trisagion — "Holy, Holy, Holy," etc.), special diets, magical names and amulets, weeping, baths, postures, silences, consultations, all of which can contribute to "the heavens opening" in an encounter with the ground of reality itself.[18] When that happens, God alone matters. The framework slips away. One now no longer "believes"; one *knows* the living God.

The use of such meditative techniques for inducing visions and other forms of religious experience is ubiquitous in human societies. That one tends to get the god one seeks does not invalidate the seeking or the finding.

The "local archetypes," the archetypal images that cluster around a received tradition, determine the shape, color, and texture of the religious experience. These localizations of the fundamental archetypes are inevitable, and account for the tremendous variety of religious experiences. But they all bear witness to the human desire for knowledge and transformation, a desire, the mystic insists, planted in our beings as the image of God. So the mystic is not "inducing hallucinations," or engaging in self-delusion, or simply manipulating neural circuitry. Obviously every experience we have has psychological and physiological concomitants. It is impossible to experience anything apart from the psyche and the body. However, the psychophysical components do not create the experience so much as enable it. No doubt there are pseudoreligious experiences and bogus religious guides. People do hallucinate. Distinguishing between true and false visions (or good and evil spirits) has always been the role of the spiritual mentor. Jesus himself struggled to discern whether his vision at his baptism was from God or the devil; that is the point of the temptation narrative (Matt. 4:1-11 // Luke 4:1-13). But to dismiss the long history of humanity's search for God as the excitation of electrochemical responses is a particularly sad form of materialistic reductionism. God has wired us so that we can communicate with God. One does not experience the wiring. One experiences God.

By allowing the mystics to dismantle the borders between heaven and earth, says Peter Schäfer, "God himself, in the end, has succumbed to their power. In a hardly surpassable manner, the 'distant cosmocrator' has surrendered his fate to man."[19] David Halperin speaks similarly: "Human nature has infiltrated heaven. Human invasion is now thinkable."[20] This assertion should come as no surprise to the student of religion. Intercessory prayer, magical adjurations, ascetic self-abasement, and heroic self-denial are all ways, not just for bringing oneself under the rule of God, but for getting God to do what we want. Jewish prayer in all ages has reflected this sense of wrestling with God over the fate of the individual and the nation. That is also the way Jesus prayed and taught about prayer.[21] God, according to this tradition, *wants* to be at our disposal, insofar as we are at God's disposal. God is eager to be "used" by the mystic to accomplish God's will in the world. That is why the literature is replete with warnings about the hazards of approaching the divine throne without first being covered, as it were, with the protective robe of compliance with the law. Thus, even those incapable of or unsuited for the mystical journey are enjoined to find God through the Torah, in the limited ways that we can know anything.[22]

Those who descend to the *merkabah* can thus be said to acquire "this world, the world to come and worlds upon worlds." Not just life in the hereafter is granted, but the present world is transformed; the seekers' lives take on new meaning.[23]

> When my ears heard this great mystery,
> the world was transformed over me in purity
> and my heart was,
> as if I had arrived in a new world;
> Every day it appeared to my soul,
> as if I was standing in front of the throne of glory.[24]

Such texts signify, according to Dan Merkur, that it was possible for a mortal human being such as Enoch, *or any Merkabah mystic*, to have immediate access to God.[25]

When one sees the resplendent garment of God, "whirling gyrations grip the balls of his eyes. And the balls of his eyes cast out and sent forth torches of fire and these enkindled him and these burn him. For the fire that *comes out* from the man who beholds, this enkindles him and this burns him."[26] This burning, Scholem notes, does not describe the dangers that frequently confront the mystic; this is, rather, the language of mystical transformation taking place in the "descender to the *merkabah*."[27] The fire comes *out* of the mystic, symbolizing the release of creative energies within the self. It is the flame of individuation burning off the dross of egoism.

In a mysticism of vision, anthropomorphism is inevitable. One must somehow *see* all the elements in the vision. Hence vision presents even the ineffable in imaginal form. Many of the more sober rabbis resisted anthropomorphism in reference to God, and did all they could to weed it out of the tradition.[28] But the mystics stubbornly and provocatively augmented the God-Human likeness. How could they avoid anthropomorphism, when, countless times in Jewish lore, God called the Israelites God's "children"? That language guaranteed that the divine-human likeness and parental imagery would be hammered into Israel's awareness. The Merkabah mystics were taking the metaphor with utmost seriousness.[29]

At the same time, their way of doing so was almost playful. According to the midrash on Solomon's proverbs, for example, on the day of judgment, God chastises rabbis who studied Talmud but neglected the *merkabah*, which could have provided them a direct experience of God's splendor. They should have pondered "how I [God] stand from the nails of My feet to the parting of My hair; how great is the measure of My palm, and what is the measure of My toes. . . . And is this not My greatness, is not this My glory and My beauty that My children know My splendor through these measurements?"[30]

The more rationalistic rabbis answered no. They regarded this fascination with God's body, dimensions, and human likeness as the degeneration of Merkabah mysticism. They saw it as a debasement to superstition after mysticism had lost its immediacy in experience. But Scholem concludes that these speculations about God's body were already present in the earliest *Hekhalot* texts.[31] They are collectively known as the *Shi'ur Qomah*, the "measure of the body" of God. These traditions represent the apotheosis of anthropomorphism—the divine form is envisaged as a colossal *human* figure that reaches to the ends of the universe. The units of measurement are cosmic: the height of the Creator is 236,000 parasangs, and "the measure of a parasang of God is three miles, and a mile has 10,000 yards, and a yard three spans of His span, and a span fills the whole world, as it is written: Who hath meted out heaven with the span" (Isa. 40:12).[32] "The soles of his feet fill the whole universe in its entirety, as is said: 'Heaven is My throne, and the earth My footstool' (Isa. 66:1). The height of his soles is three thousand myriad parasangs. . . . From the soles of His feet to His ankles is one thousand myriad and five hundred parasangs." Or again, God's neck is "thirteen thousand times ten thousand, plus eight hundred parasangs." Joseph Dan remarks that this parasang is closer to our modern astrophysical parsec, a distance of 2,012 miles, for God's neck, according to the mystical text, is 11,700,072,000,000 parasangs, that is, nearly twelve trillion times the circumference of the earth.[33]

These measurements go on and on, until virtually the entire body of God has been covered. As Scholem notes, it is impossible to visualize such a figure; apparently the idea was to reduce every attempt at rational comprehension to absurdity.[34] But the flagrant anthropomorphism cannot simply be dismissed. As Joseph Dan notes, "One cannot claim here that this is all a metaphor, that it doesn't mean exactly what it says. For the measurements are precise, and the details about the different organs and their structures make it clear that the author means them to be taken literally."[35] Had the *Shi'ur Qomah* mystics wanted to defeat all attempts to visualize God, they could have done so using the well-known negative theology popularized by Neoplatonism. The Jewish exegete Maimonides (d. 1204) is a model of that response. What is at stake is the difference between the totally other God of Neoplatonism and the quantitatively greater God of Aristotelianism. That the mystics chose to make God infinitely large indicates that they did think of God as humanlike, only incomparably greater. Such a God can be known directly, as opposed to the unknowable God of the Neoplatonists (and later the Kabbalists). God's measurability means that, though God remains incomprehensible, *God's body is everywhere.*[36]

As Daniel Matt observes, the gross physiological speculations of the *Shi'ur Qomah* depict the experience of the limitless Self and of connectedness to everything by *being* everything. These speculations mark a recovery or recapitulation of the child's original boundaryless experience, and a transcendence of the separateness instilled in us by the necessity of living in the world. By seeing through the apparent solidity of the ego, Matt says, we shed the illusion of being separate from what surrounds us. Awe at God's vastness leads to the recognition that "there is no place empty of It" (Dov Baer, eighteenth-century Jewish mystic). One no longer has an independent self, but one is contained in the limitless body of the Creator. Humility is the fruit of recognizing that all our physical and mental powers and our essential being depend on the divine elements within.[37]

Third Enoch 48A:9 (fifth to sixth century C.E.) avers that when God finally reveals God's great arm to the Gentiles (that is, when God rescues the Jews), God's arm "shall be as long as the world and as broad as the world."[38] This deliberately hyperbolic description of God as a human being of infinite proportions is a clever way of renouncing the so-called qualitative distinction between God and human beings. It asserts instead that human beings are only quantitatively distinct from God, since they are made in the form, image, and likeness of God, only infinitely smaller, weaker, and less wise. Human beings are *micanthrōpoi*, or lesser human beings, and God is the *macanthrōpos*, or greater Human Being, according to this way of thinking.[39] As a saying ascribed to Rabbi Akiba puts it, "[God] is like us, as it were, but greater than everything; and that is God's glory which is hidden from us."[40]

Astonishingly, the *Shi'ur Qomah* concludes its description of God's immense face with this statement: "And this is also the size of every human being." Gruenwald stresses that God shares these gigantic proportions with human beings, since God created them in the divine image. Since people are clearly not of these proportions, one must assume that human beings, before the fall, had these dimensions. These hyperbolical measurements represent our essential likeness to God, before we obscured it by idolatry and sin; sin led to the shrinkage that accounts for our present diminutive state.[41] These observations are tightly parallel to my earlier assertion that God alone is truly Human, while we are but intimations, approximations, or glimpses of what it means to be human.

B. Enoch/Metatron and the Human Being in Jewish Mysticism

The mystics did not confine their speculations, however, to the Humanity of God. The man Enoch was caught up to heaven and became the angel Metatron. He confides to the mystical journeyer that he "was enlarged and increased in size till I matched the world in length and breadth"; he was given seventy-two wings and 365,000 eyes. "There was no sort of splendor, brilliance, brightness, or beauty in the luminaries of the world that [God] failed to fix in me" (3 *Enoch* 9:2-5).[42] Thus Metatron's dimensions do not represent mimetic rivalry with God, but suggest, a bit grotesquely, that the human future is a future with God the Human One. Metatron is already what we shall be, but to an incomparable degree. One cannot help comparing 1 John 3:2, substituting Metatron for Jesus: "Beloved, we are God's children now; what we will be has not yet been revealed. What we do know is this: when he is revealed, we will be like him, for we will see him as he is."

It is astonishing nevertheless that Metatron should have a body the size of the world, just like God. It seems as if God's every attribute were showered, without discrimination, on this transcendent human figure, so that one begins to wonder what function God retains.[43] We find this same tendency elsewhere. The "one like a Human Being" in Rev. 1:9-20, identified later as the risen Christ, has taken on the features and functions of Yahweh described in Dan. 7:9 ("his head and his hair were white as white wool"); in Ezek. 1:7, 27 ("his feet were like burnished bronze, refined as in a furnace"); and in Ezek. 1:26 ("one like a human being"). In the *Apocalypse of Abraham*, a first-century Jewish work with at least one Christian revision, the angel Iaoel also has attributes that elsewhere are ascribed to God: his body of sapphire recalls the sapphire pavement of Exod. 24:10 and the sapphire throne of Ezek. 1:26, and his head is like snow, as is God's in Dan. 7:9.[44] God seems to be promiscuously sharing God's attributes in order to equip these human/angelic surrogates. There is no holy hoarding; God wants those who have glimpsed God's essence to have every divine quality—which means, apparently, to be truly human.[45]

Jesus was a mystic, but apparently not of the Merkabah type. The account of his baptism is the cryptic report, not of an ascent to heaven, but of heaven opening out to him, in him, while he was still on earth (Mark 1:9-11).[46] This experience implied that God's kingdom had begun to manifest itself, "on earth as it is in heaven." Thus, instead of finding heaven through the ascent to the divine throne chariot, Jesus found it in marginalized people, sinners, rejects, compromisers; in the power to heal and exorcise; in parables of divine reality that teased their hearers into a primary encounter with the reality to which the parables pointed. The Merkabah mystics stormed heaven, where they were given great authority and witnessed mysteries. When Jesus is exalted to heaven after his crucifixion, he does nothing, is taught nothing, is shown nothing. He does not exercise authority over the angels. He merely sits on the right hand of God. That is, revelation takes place, in Jewish mysticism, *in heaven*, whereas, in the Gospels, it takes place *on earth*, before Jesus' death. I do not mean to imply that Jesus' way was better, only different. His way was more mundane, "down to earth," available to the masses. But it was authentic Jewish mysticism all the same. Some rabbis' resistance to Merkabah mysticism stemmed precisely from its elitism and unavailability to the rank-and-file believer (Merkur).

Paul definitely was a mystic, probably of the Merkabah type (2 Cor. 12:1-10). He entered the third heaven ("Paradise") and learned inexpressible mysteries. But neither Jesus nor Paul required others to replicate the experiences they had had. In Paul's case, the Corinthians wrenched the story out of him by the extremity of their disagreements. Otherwise he never alluded to it in any of his letters. Even the baptism of Jesus, a practice later made into an entry rite for the church, is told with stunning economy, as if skirting a mystery beyond comprehension. Baptism surely had significance beyond the rebirth of the individual. It seems to have been a symbol for psychological descent into the waters of the unconscious, into primordial archetypal depths, signaling a psychic upheaval at the core of humanity. Both Jesus and Paul seem to have experienced the living God of Isaiah, Ezekiel, and Daniel, a God who wants to be seen, heard, known, and incarnated as the Human Being who bears the secret of our becoming—of our becoming human, like God.

C. Ascended Humans in Jewish Mysticism

In Jewish tradition, a number of persons ascended to God upon their deaths: Enoch (Gen. 5:24), Elijah (2 Kings 2:11), and, according to later tradition, Levi, Phinehas, and Moses.[47] Moses had ascended into heaven, according to later midrash, in order to receive the Torah and to return with it to earth.[48] Obviously the Fourth Gospel is engaged in polemic with those developing in the Gospel's time a lore of heavenly ascents. When John categorically insists that "no one has ascended into heaven except the one who descended from heaven, the son of the man" (3:13) and that "no one has ever seen

God" (1:18), he immediately creates a problem: what to do with Old Testament worthies whose ascensions to heaven were recorded in Scripture, and with others, mostly prophets, who had had visions of God (Isaiah 6; Ezekiel 1; 1 Kings 22:19-23)? John solves the latter problem by asserting that the prophets did not see God in their visions, but God's Son. The "Glory" that Ezekiel saw on the throne was the preexistent Christ, who was with God from all eternity. Thus the book of Revelation could picture the "one like a human being" (Jesus as the risen Christ) using the descriptions of God in Ezekiel 1 and Daniel 7.

What to do about earlier ascensions required a different solution. After all, the ascensions of Elijah and Enoch were not particularly invested in Scripture with archetypal significance. Elijah was expected to return in the last days (Mal. 4:5-6), and Enoch, beginning with the Similitudes of Enoch, took on divine attributes, but these individuals did not modify the way human beings see God. Ascension signified consolation (in Enoch's case) and vindication (in Elijah's); exaltation to heaven introduced nothing new into heaven, but closed a chapter on earth.

With Jesus' ascension, the situation was different. Here was a figure who changed the way his followers knew God, and the God they knew. Jesus entered the divine archetype and so transformed the God-image that a new metaphysics crystallized around him: the doctrine of the Holy Trinity, which the philosopher A. N. Whitehead said was the only metaphysical doctrine to have improved on Plato.[49]

Christians have treated Jesus' ascension as unique. They are little aware that Judaism developed, in independence from Christianity, a similar notion: the exaltation of "that son of the man," Enoch, and his fusion with the heavenly figure Metatron (1 Enoch 70-71). Both developments attest to the movement of the collective unconscious toward the revelation of the Human Being.

In the early centuries of the common era, Merkabah mystics began to report the presence in heaven of a mysterious "youth" (na'ar) whose "splendor is like his king's splendor, his glory like his creator's glory." This was Metatron. So impressive is he, texts said, that the visitor must take care not to treat him as divine.[50] Christian Trinitarianism, a Jew might argue, illustrates what could happen when one did not take sufficient care.

Two out of the three references to Metatron in the Talmud are critical of him, for fear that he might usurp the role of God.[51] Metatron's title in 3 Enoch 12:5, "The lesser YHWH," and his rise to the title of God, "the Great Glory,"[52] only exacerbated this anxiety.[53] Third Enoch 16 attempts to mitigate this problem by knocking Metatron down a notch. Metatron is seated on the throne that God had made specifically for him, a duplicate of the throne of Glory (10:1), judging all the denizens of the heights and assigning greatness and rank to the angels. But when 'Aher, a mystic, enters the heavenly realms and sees Metatron thus seated and surrounded by ministering angels, 'Aher is discomfited, and cries out, "There are indeed two powers in heaven!" Metatron had permission from God to sit, but he should have stood when the rabbi approached. As punishment, one of the eight angels higher than Metatron strikes him with sixty lashes of fire.[54]

There is a longer version of this tale.[55] The text advises: "If a youth (na'ar) comes out to meet you from behind the throne of glory, do not bow down to him—for his crown is as the crown of his King, and the sandals on his feet are as the sandals of his King, and the robe upon him is as the robe of his King. . . . his eyes blaze like torches, his eyeballs burn like lamps; his brilliance is as the brilliance of his King, his glory is as the glory of his Maker—Zehobadyah is his name"—a name apparently equivalent to Metatron. This is shockingly similar to the Christian description of the heavenly Christ, except that the Jews resisted worshiping any powers of heaven but Yahweh.

There were, to be sure, differences between the ascended Jesus and the ascended Enoch. Enoch was never identified as the Messiah (though Metatron was). Metatron, however, never becomes God, only an angel. Metatron was not expected to return to earth to establish God's reign, but remained in heaven ready to judge humanity in the last judgment. In short, Metatron, though usually the chief angel in heaven, was only a functionary. "The Holy One, blessed be He, decrees and Metatron executes."[56] By this means, Jewish mystics could maintain the exalted role of Metatron/Enoch while distancing themselves from Christian worship of a heavenly earthling.[57]

This phenomenon of a human being elevated to heavenly status is not confined to the Enoch literature. According to the Dead Sea Scrolls, the human priest Melchizedek who has been gathered up to heaven, exalted above all angels, presides over a heavenly assize, and exacts punishment (11QMelch). Here again we find independent development in Jewish thought of a divine "lieutenant" who assumes many of the functions previously ascribed strictly to God.

At about the same time, or perhaps a bit later, Philo (20 B.C.E.–50 C.E.) also was describing, in effusive terms, a similar "lieutenant" of God whom he called the Logos, God's Man, God's firstborn, the elder and ruler of the angels, the issue of a divine birth, the Beginning (or First Principle), the archetypal idea, the pre-measurer of all things, the Name of God, the Man after His image, "he that sees," heavenly wisdom, the vision of God, the Son, the Son of God, the second God, and, even at times, God.[58] Such intemperate language is astonishing in a context of belief in one God.

Why did Jewish mystics deliberately skirt so close to the Christian worship of a "second power" in heaven? If these stalkers of the divine throne chariot were anxious to prevent the worship of angels, why introduce Metatron as a "youth" turned out in the garb, eyes, brilliance, and names of Yahweh? Why, for instance, does the Holy One take the seventy names inscribed on the divine throne chariot and bestow them on Metatron—"seventy names by which the ministering angels address the King of the kings of kings in heaven above" (3 Enoch 48D:5)?[59] How could this reference be anything but confusing? There must have been an overwhelming necessity forcing them to take such enormous risks.

I believe that necessity was the imperative of individuation, breaking free and surfacing from the collective unconscious. Clearly, many of the mystics' fellow rabbis already eyed them with suspicion. There was nothing to be gained and much to be lost by introducing this "youth." This imperative of individuation cries out for explanation. Only an overwhelmingly compelling reason could account for such a risk: a mutating archetype of the human, with its demand for actualization. The "youth" in symbolic terms is something new, emergent, demanding awareness. *This emergence is essentially the same phenomenon that we have been calling the Humanchild throughout this study.* This "youth" is an archetype of transformation in Jewish mysticism, representing the breakthrough of the adept into nonlocal reality, the eternal Now, where one experiences God directly, without mediation.

It is significant that some Merkabah mystics seem far more fascinated with the "youth" (Metatron/Enoch) than with God. We learn very little about God from these "revelations," apart from God's names and measurements. It almost appears that the mystical journey has been diverted from the vision of God to the activities of this "lesser Yahweh." Revelation in these writings is a humanly initiated but divinely given vision of God and of the celestial realms.[60] As Dan Merkur observes, revelation has become self-knowledge.[61] If we hear that statement in individualistic terms, however, we falsify Merkur's meaning. The Jewish writings present the anthropic revelation: the Christology of humanity, the manifestation of the Human in humans. Human invasion of the divine realm seems in that era to have gripped people from all sorts of traditions. Ezekiel's vision was bearing late fruit. The "youth"—the Humanchild, what else?—was not the exclusive property of Christians, after all. The revelation was popping up everywhere.

The same archetypal dynamism that was forcing its way to consciousness in Jewish lore was also coloring the Christian understanding of the ascended Jesus. Deep spirits of the age sensed a new drive toward the humanization of God. This revelation had steadily been asserting itself from the time of Ezekiel forward, and was now affecting everything in its path. It not only dominated Christian and Jewish theology and mystical practice, but manifested itself in a novel way in Gnosticism, and within the bosom of Islam, in Sufism.[62]

D. Conclusion

Mystics create a metaphor for the Ineffable that provides a bridge for others to experience the same unspeakable reality. Later, others come who have not experienced the reality and who turn the metaphor into a pale reflection, fact, or dogma. Having literalized the metaphor, religious proponents tend to emphasize what separates them from others. But the mystics, who live out of a primary experience of the reality of God, often see through the differences to a unitary reality. *Knowing* God relativizes all doctrines, creeds, dogmas, liturgies, and practices, while one still remains grounded in a particular tradition.[63] How tragic, then, that Christianity and Judaism focused on their differences rather than affirming their commonalities. How tragic, in other words, that more Jews and Christians do not live out of a primary experience of the reality of God. We humans are only a blip on the evolutionary scale. We are like the "youth," Metatron: late arrivals, barely begun, almost pure possibility. Perhaps one way to understand the imperative toward individuation is in the "youth" or "child" archetype. Metatron's vast extension toward God is as good a way as any to highlight this human potentiality. That potential is parabolically depicted by the image of God as Human.

If the Human Being is an archetype, it participates in the universal Self. Therefore Jesus does not exhaust what the Human Being can mean. According to an earlier expression, Christ is *totus Deus sed non totum Dei*: wholly God yet not the whole of God. Put in terms of this study, Jesus is the Human Being, but not the only Human Being. In our Father/Mother's house there are many mansions, with rooms for Moses, Elijah, Enoch, Metatron, Melchizedek, and—why not blurt it out—everyone who has served to reveal the Humanchild since history began. Any number of traditions can nurture this archetype of human transformation. The archetype can embrace a variety of parents. What wants to be born, nurtured, and matured in us is not religion, dogma, or certainty, but the Human Being.

Nevertheless, Jesus remains, for me, indispensable as an epitome of humanness. I believe he is a treasure intended for the whole human race. He is the property of the world. He was a Jew, not a Christian, and Christians do not own him. From Jesus, everyone can learn something of what it means to live faithfully in the teeth of the Powers That Be. They do not have to join the club first in order get Jesus. They do not have to believe that Jesus is divine. Nothing is required in advance. If our task is to learn to be humane, Jesus the Jew can teach us. We can love him for it, honor him for it, and be grateful to him for it without having to worship him or to regard him as a god.

16. The Human Being in Gnosticism

There is no agreed definition of Gnosticism. "Gnosis" ("knowledge") must be distinguished from "Gnosticism" and "Gnostics." The latter represented a second- to fourth-century kind of theosophy characterized by an intuitive grasp of the collective unconscious and wild metaphysical speculations. Some Gnostics referred to a demiurge (creator god) who made this evil earth. In some cases a radical dualism between flesh and spirit led them to practice asceticism. The term "gnosis," on the other hand, was used by Paul and all the early church writers, and simply refers to an inner or spiritual kind of knowing. In Henry Corbin's words, gnosis is a "salvational, redemptive knowledge," because it has the virtue of bringing about inner transformation. That definition of gnosis would apply to virtually any person on a spiritual path.[1]

Michael A. Williams has argued that "Gnosticism" was the invention of nineteenth- and twentieth-century scholars.[2] Defining a broad and inchoate phenomenon like Gnosticism, however, is no different than defining apocalypticism, mysticism, Christianity, Judaism, or any number of general categories that lack specificity or consistency. All of these categories bleed into each other, forming a penumbra that becomes fuzzy at the fringes, and that often overlaps with other general categories. Thus Gnosticism would have a large overlap with Christianity, but an almost equally large overlap with Judaism and, to a lesser extent, with paganism. Within that penumbra there would be room for a variety of definitions, with the differences shading almost into identity at the edges. I will limit my remarks to what the "Gnostics" had to say about God as the Human One and the identity of the "Son of the Man."[3]

The fascination with God as Human that is manifested in Jewish mysticism burned to brilliance among the Gnostics of the second through fourth centuries. The Gnostics penetrated as deeply as anyone into the enigma of "the son of the man." These fearless theosophists elaborated lavishly on the implications of Ezekiel's vision of God as "something that seemed like a human form" (1:26). Turning their imaginations loose in a field of dazzling images, they distilled intriguing and often bewildering reflections about God as the Human Being, and about "the son of the Man" as the child of that Human One. Small wonder, then, that the Gnostics used the term "the son of the Man" so often. The Gnostics offered an interpretation of "the son of the Man" that makes sense of the double articles in the expression's Greek form; their interpretation makes clear their assumption that the last term, "the Man," indicates God.[4]

One branch of Gnostics, the Valentinians (followers of Valentinus, second century) ably summed up the unique features of their belief:

> [T]here are others who assert that the Forefather of all things himself, the Pre-beginning and the Pre-unthinkable, is called "the Human One," and that *this is the great and hidden mystery*, namely, that the power which is above all and which embraces all is termed the Man. And because of this the Savior designates himself the Son of the Man.[5]

While the "mainline" church was maintaining a virtual silence regarding the Human Being, the Gnostics featured it as one of the preeminent designations of the savior figure. Apparently the expression was avoided by the "orthodox" Christians because the Gnostics had co-opted it. The Gnostics also used such titles as Father, Christ, Son of God, Logos (Word), Sophia (Wisdom), and the like. But the Gnostics elevated the Man and the Son of the Man to incomparable heights, and created a new *language* for the divine. No doubt the Gnostics enjoyed the endless possibilities for punning (son of Adam = son of man = humanity = son of the Man = Son of God). The son of the man could thus be at once the human Adam's son and the son of the Human Being on the heavenly throne. Here, again, the incomprehensible and ineffable God is nevertheless regarded as "Human."[6]

I make no attempt to discuss Gnosticism as a whole. I have made a stab at deciphering it in a little book, *Cracking the Gnostic Code*,[7] and I refer you to that work for a broader perspective. I am indebted to Carl Jung for his comprehension of gnostic texts. He has frequently been misunderstood as *being* a Gnostic when he simply was trying to understand them, just as he attempted to grasp the meaning of the Roman Catholic Mass and the doctrine of the Trinity. His goal was to provide a nonreductionistic psychological interpretation of the religious experiences that gnostic traditions evoked.

We begin by exploring the Nag Hammadi Library of gnostic texts, in which "the son of the Man" appears more than fifty times. Then we examine secondhand reports about the Gnostics in the early church fathers before concluding with the *Poimandres* in the *Corpus Hermeticum*.

A. The Human Being in the Nag Hammadi Library

The manuscripts that comprise the Nag Hammadi Library were discovered in Egypt in 1945.[8] They are the richest source of information about the gnostic movement ever found.

As is often the case in gnostic works, "son of man" in the Nag Hammadi tractate *Eugnostos* is linked to a divinity named "Man." This is to be expected; if there is a "son of Man," then there must be a Father-God named Man and vice versa: "For whenever there is a 'father,' it follows that there is a 'son' " (*Tripartite Tractate* 51:14-15, NHL1). The issue of capitalization is relevant. Virtually all English versions of the Bible read "the Son of man," not only omitting the second definite article, but suggesting by capitalization that "Son" is the more significant noun. If we shift the capital letter to the last term, as in "son of Man" or "the son of the Man," the emphasis changes. The Gnostics tended toward this sense and pondered who this Man was, whose son was the world's savior.

Douglas M. Parrott lists five principal divine beings in *Eugnostos*: (1) the unknowable and unbegotten Forefather; (2) his reflection, called Self-Father; (3) Self-Father's hypostatized power, Immortal Man, who is androgynous; (4) Immortal Man's androgynous son, Son of Man; and (5) the Son of the Son of Man, the androgynous Savior. The female aspects of the Godhead include Begettress Sophia, Great Sophia, and "First-begotten Sophia, Mother of the Universe, whom some call Love." The Forefather is "Father of the universe" (73:2-3); there is as yet no hostility to the created order in *Eugnostos*, though that theme is added by *Pistis Sophia*, a later document that incorporates virtually all of *Eugnostos*.[9]

Psychologically speaking, we might treat all these human images of the divine as re-presentations of the Self. However, they are not mere projections of the individual personality onto the heavens, but intimations of the suprapersonal cosmic Self, which has no boundaries and is coextensive with the universe. Thus the Gnostics reflect the same preoccupation with emergent humanness as others whose writings we have been examining. Something mighty and irresistible was churning up from the psychic depths of people from Rome to Persia and, ultimately, via Manichaeism, from as far as China, beckoning humanity to its highest potential.

On the Origin of the World features "an immortal Man of light" who appears to be the high God, or at least a high god.[10] Likewise *Melchizedek*, which also knows of a divine "Man-of-light."[11] There are many other references in gnostic sources to divine beings that are described as human.[12] The heresiologist Hippolytus alone lists:

The Man (Anthropos)	The Upper Man	Adamas
Protoanthropos	The Inner Man	The Great Man
Archanthropos	The Son of the Man	The True Man
Preexistent Man	Adam	Heavenly Man
The Man according to the Image	Perfect Man	The Great and Beautiful Man[13]

Behind most of these references to God as Human lies Ezekiel 1, elaborated in all sorts of directions. Philo employed the language of Platonic archetypes (see appendix 2). Others wove mythical speculations about a heavenly "Man" who was in various ways employed in delivering humanity from a fallen world through "the Son of the Man." It was a logical step to take: if there is a heavenly archetype of humanity, then it is a heavenly human being, and it could be amalgamated with other heavenly figures, from the highest God on down.

The Apocryphon of James presses beyond philosophical speculation to experiential exercises. Its deliberate contradictions apparently are intended to throw the reader or hearer into an alternate state of consciousness by humiliating rational control and thereby reducing the initiate to helplessness. Thus: blessed are you if you have seen the Son of the Man; woe to you who have seen the Son of the Man (3:11-25). "Become full, that you may not be in want. They who are in want, however, will not be saved. For it is good to be full, and bad to be in want. Hence, just as it is good that you be in want and, conversely, bad that you be full, so he who is full is in want, and he who has been filled, in turn, attains due perfection. Therefore, you must be in want while it is possible to fill you, and be full while it is possible for you to be in want" (4:4-16).

Paradox functions here as a way to convey the *unknowable*. What Werner Kelber says of Jesus' parables applies as well: "[T]he 'oddness' of the [parabolic] narrative serves to disconfirm conventional expectations and encourages experimentation with a new logic in defiance of common sense."[14] Paul Ricoeur calls this "reorientation by disorientation." The purpose, says Stevan Davies, is to produce confusion, unstructuring, restructuring, and receptivity, in short, to evoke an *experience* of a state called the Reign of God, not to communicate certain beliefs *about* that state.[15]

Earlier I suggested that the inducement of altered states of consciousness is common to most religions. Here, as in more orthodox circles, the son of the man seems to have become an avenue to such states. The author insists that there is no advantage for those who have seen the actual person Jesus; all must find the truth for themselves. "He [the risen Jesus] said, 'Verily I say unto you, no one will ever enter the kingdom of heaven at my bidding, but only because you yourselves are full' " (2:28-33). "Become better than I; make yourselves like the son of the Holy Spirit!" (6:19-20). "If possible, arrive even before me" (7:14).

The *Treatise on the Resurrection* states, "Now the Son of God . . . was Son of Man . . . , possessing the humanity and the divinity, so that on the one hand he might vanquish death through his being Son of God, and that on the other through the Son of the Man the restoration to the Pleroma ["Fullness"] might occur; because he was originally from above . . ." (44:21-34). "For we have known the Son of the Man, and we have believed that he rose from among the dead. This is he of whom we say, 'He became the destruction of death. . . .'" The "Son of the Man" here does not designate the human nature of Jesus, as in the mainstream Christian theologians (when they refer to the son of the man at all). If anything, the roles are reversed, and the Son of the Man is the highest accolade that can be bestowed on the Redeemer.[16]

The *Testimony of Truth* polemicizes against the vain hope of some orthodox Christians that their martyrdom will guarantee a carnal resurrection. In this text, true spiritual resurrection consists of knowledge of the Son of the Man, which is self-knowledge: "He has come to know the Son of the Man, that is, he has come to know himself. This is the perfect life, that one knows oneself by means of the All."[17] But the Human Being here is a transpersonal reality, the *imago Dei*, the divine within. It is that which is brought from death (or pure potential) to life, through what the *Testimony of Truth* calls "resurrection," but which might more properly be dubbed "rebirth," as in 40:6-7. The selfhood gained from this rebirth is not personal, but cosmic. It is participation in the human reality coming to birth through the midwifery of the Human Being.

In short, the Human Being is something like the true Self within a person, the lost essence restored, the residue of being left after all roles, images, identities, and accomplishments are scoured away. This essence is known, not by introspection, but by an interior opening to the revelation of the real nature of spiritual reality, brought by a transcendent Revealer, the Human Being.[18]

The star of the *Apocalypse of Adam* is Seth, the third son of Adam. Adam says to Seth, "I too called you by the name of that Human Being (*'adam*) who is the seed of the great race" (65:7-9). The "name" here is Seth, who is at the same time the "son of Adam" by lineage and "Son of the Man" by divine nature. This same Seth, the son of Adam/Humanity, will appear in a final advent to "ransom souls from the day of death" and will become incarnate in the form of a mortal human being who is superior to the Powers. "And he will perform signs and wonders, in order to heap scorn upon the powers and their ruler." In response, the god of this world "will raise up great wrath against That Human Being, the son of the man. And the glory shall go elsewhere" (77:4-10). This is apparently a reference to the docetic ("merely seeming") notion of Jesus' crucifixion, in which the human form is left to suffer ("they will punish the flesh of the man," 77:16-17), while the divine aspect returns to the spiritual world from which it came.[19]

In the *Apocryphon of John*, Ezekiel's seminal vision of God as Human has been developed into a profuse metaphysics with a string of heavenly emanations. The emanations include Adamas, the perfect human being, and his son Seth, the son of the Man. The ultimate mystery revealed is that the "First Human" who bears and mediates the divine image is not the Adam of the biblical story, but rather a much earlier, transcendent, androgynous First Thought and self-image of the true God.[20]

> And a voice emanated from above the exalted aeons: "The Human Being [Adamas, "Man"] exists, and the Child of the Human Being [the "Son of the Man/Adamas," Seth]. But Ialtabaoth the first ruler listened and thought that this voice came from its mother, and it did not know where it had come from. (14:13-18)

God is envisioned here as Human in very essence, and is revealed as such. But the Father of the All only *appears* as the Logos "in their tents" (in conscious opposition to John 1:14); that is, he appeared in the "likeness of their shape" but did not become flesh as the "orthodox" believe.[21]

Why, asks the Gnosticism expert Hans-Martin Schenke, is God called the first Human? It is, he answers, because God is the archetype of humanity.[22] Such archetypal thinking already had been developed by Philo (see appendix 2) and by the author of the Epistle to the Hebrews, to say nothing of Gen. 1:26 and Plato. Even if we accept an early-second-century C.E. date for this apocryphon, as Schenke suggests, this mode of thinking already was widespread.

Thus, according to Hippolytus, the Gnostic Monoimos could make the breathtaking assertion that "Humanity (anthrōpos) is the All (to pan)."[23] Read as a statement about the ego, this is a towering inflation, precisely the kind of arrogance that has led to anthropocentrism, ecological devastation, and the worst forms of unrestrained capitalism. Humanity is thus answerable to no one and nothing. Read as a statement about God, however, the saying asserts that the ultimate Mystery who permeates the universe and who is manifest in every granule is, in reality, characterized by attributes that we regard as most humane, raised to the superlative degree. In short, the "Human Being" that Ezekiel saw on the divine throne chariot is a truth about the mystery we call God, however shocking to "orthodox" sensibilities. At last the definite articles ("the Son of the Man") make complete sense as a reference to the Glory of God beheld by Ezekiel.

As the offspring of the Human, the Human Being again "does" almost nothing; nevertheless, its existence is revelatory. The knowledge that these two heavenly human powers exist is devastating to Ialtabaoth, the demiurge, who had thought himself the highest power, and who now knows the shattering truth. Again we see the Human Being as a revealed archetypal image, a transformative truth that heals by simple sight.

The Nag Hammadi *Gospel of the Egyptians* (not to be confused with the apocryphal Gospel by the same name) is a revisionist history of the creation, again featuring Seth, the son of the heavenly and incorruptible Adamas, who incarnates in Jesus by putting on Jesus like a garment (64:1-3).

Seth was the preexistent savior and the father of the incorruptible race, the Gnostics. Thus we again encounter the saying, "The Man exists, and the Son of the Man" (59:3), which we saw in the *Apocryphon of John.* "The Man" is the heavenly Adamas, while "the Son of the Man" is the heavenly Seth. But, as seen in *The Apocalypse of Adam*, as son of Adam, Seth is the "Son of Man," so that the paucity of references to the Son of Man in this text is misleading; in fact, every reference to Seth is about the Son of Adam/Humanity/Human Being.

"Son of Man" appears eight times in the *Gospel of Philip*, where it is used as a synonym for "Christ" and "the perfect human being" (55:16-17).[24]

The "offspring of the perfect human being," "the sons of Adam/Humanity," are those who "do not die but are being born at every moment" (58:17-22). Verses 76:1-2 speak of " 'the true man' and 'the son of man' and 'the seed of the son of man.' " God is "the true human being." All these titles are archetypes of transformation, or what Jung called the transcendent function. The same lineage of begetting is reflected in 81:14-24:

> There is the son of man and there is the son of the son of man. The lord is the son of man, and the son of the son of man is he who creates through the son of man. The son of man received from God the capacity to create. He also has the ability to beget. He who has received the ability to create is a creature. He who has received the ability to beget is an offspring. He who creates cannot beget. He who begets also has power to create.

The Human Being has the capacity to beget offspring, the imperishable race. This is not accomplished the way children are begotten.

> People cannot see anything in the real realm unless they become it. In the realm of truth, it is not as human beings in the world, who see the sun without being the sun, and see the sky and the earth and so forth without being them. Rather, if you have seen any things there [in the realm of truth], you have become those things: if you have seen the spirit, you have become the spirit; if you have seen the anointed (Christ), you have become the anointed (Christ); if you have seen the father, you will become the father. Thus here in the world, you see everything and do not see your own self. But there, you see yourself; *for you shall become what you see.* (61:20-35, emphasis mine)

Earlier, I posited that we tend to become what our desire beholds. Here that idea is reversed with startling perception: we behold what we become. "People cannot see anything in the real realm unless they become it." The distance between subject and object collapses. Beholding ceases to be a means of gaining distance, perspective, noninvolvement. Instead, beholding converges into being, independence is absorbed into identity, and uniqueness yields to union. William Blake understood this when he wrote, "As a man is, So he Sees."[25] Yet the opposite still holds: "For you shall become what you see." To see, then, is to be begotten as "the child of the child of the Human Being." The Human Being begets simply by being and being beheld. Van Harvey summarizes, "We humans only seem to decide concerning the truth about life in general when confronted by a life in particular."[26] To see the Human Being is to be freed from the delusions of the Domination System. To behold the Human Being is to become a Human Being: "If you have seen the anointed (Christ), you have become the anointed (Christ)." This is not magic; it is the power of truth, which needs no defenders, only light, in order to drive back the night of ignorance, corruption, and deceit.

The "gnosticism" of the *Gospel of Philip* is scarcely more radical than any genuinely God-conscious "orthodox" Christian might espouse.[27] But the *Gospel of Philip* also contains a statement shockingly similar to Feuerbach: "In the beginning, God created humanity. But now humanity creates God. This is the way it is in the world—human beings invent gods and worship their creation. It would be more fitting for the gods to worship human beings."[28]

At first glance, this seems to be typical Jewish or Christian ridicule of pagan idolatry. But rather than saying that humanity creates "gods," *Philip*'s opening statement has "God." This turns the sentence (but not the one that follows, in which the text does have "gods") into the assertion that human beings create their own god-images. *Philip* differs from Feuerbach, of course, in the confidence that God initially created human beings. But one almost senses in *Philip*'s comment the opening of an abyss that everyone had tried to keep hidden: that the anthropic revelation is an act of reciprocal cocreation between human beings (supposed to be sinners that could not possess such power) and God.

The "perfect human being" that *Philip* mentions can also be seen as an eschatological possibility, as in *Hypostasis of the Archons:*

> Then I said, "Sir, how much longer?"
>
> He said to me, "Until the moment when the True Man, within a modelled form, reveals the existence (?) of the spirit of truth, which the father has sent. Then he will teach them about everything: And he will anoint them with the unction of life eternal . . . and they will trample under foot death, which is of the authorities." (96:31–97:7)

This statement is so similar to 1 John 3:2 that one wonders if it is not inspired by it. In any case, both texts reflect the longing for the consummation of the human enterprise in the Humanity of God.

The Gospel of Mary has a memorable son-of-the-man saying:

> "Beware that no one lead you astray, saying, 'Lo here!' or 'Lo here!' For the Son of the Man is within you. Follow after him! Those who seek him will find him. Go then and preach the gospel of the kingdom. Do not lay down

any rules beyond what I appointed for you, and do not give a law like the law-giver lest you be constrained by it."

But they were grieved. They wept greatly, saying, "How shall we go to the gentiles and preach the gospel of the kingdom of the son of the man? If they did not spare him, how will they spare us?" (8:15—9:12)

It is striking that the Human Being has taken the place of the kingdom of God in Luke's parallel saying ("Nor will they say, 'Look, here it is!' or 'There it is!' For, in fact, the kingdom of God is within you"—17:21). More exactly, the son of the man has *become* the kingdom. The gospel of the kingdom that followers preach is that the Son of the Man is the goal and content of the term "kingdom." So in both Gnosticism and the orthodox churches, the proclaimer has become the proclaimed. The religious task is not so much to continue what Jesus did, but to unite with the divinized Jesus as the Savior and Son of the Man.

That Son of the Man, we are told, is "within you." The author tells us how she knows. Mary asks Jesus, " 'Lord, now does she who sees the vision see it through the soul or through the spirit?' The Savior answered and said, 'She does not see through the soul nor through the spirit, but the mind which is between the two—that is what sees the vision' " (10:17-23). This sounds much like what Henry Corbin has taught us to call the "imaginal realm."[29] The Human Being is experienced "within," but not by sensation or logic, but by an imagination initiated into the kingdom of heaven. Or the reverse can be true: the imagination is that by which *we* are initiated into realizing our oneness with the kingdom of heaven/Human Being.

This focus on radical inwardness and imagination is one of Gnosticism's great gifts to world religions. It is tragic that the Great Church was so threatened by Gnosticism that it tried to liquidate it rather than reap its profound insights. We might wish to urge the Gnostics to avoid "intrapsychic reductionism" (the tendency to regard the inner world of the psyche as of greater significance than the outer world). For the Human Being is also seen in the "least of these, my brothers and sisters" (Matt. 25:31-46). As the earliest commentary on Luke 17:21 puts it: "the kingdom of God is inside of you, and it is outside of you" (*Gospel of Thomas* 3).[30] As a mystic, the believer has direct access to heavenly reality and no longer needs the dictates of dogma or the moralisms of codes. "Do not lay down any rules beyond what I appointed for you, and do not give a law like the lawgiver lest you be constrained by it." This sovereign freedom from the law is the direct corollary of Jesus' teaching about the authority of the Human Being in Mark 2:23-28 and of the love commandment in the Gospel of John. So far as we can tell from the Nag

Hammadi documents, this kind of advice did not lead to licentiousness and lawlessness, but to asceticism and sometimes abstinence from sexual activity.

For the Gnostics, the Human Being is within, in the imaginal realm. Archetypally. The Human Being is, as it were, the "perfect one" (18:16), the magnetic lodestone drawing the self toward its fullest realization.

We can safely pass over a number of other son-of-the-man sayings in the Nag Hammadi Library. But now we turn to the same Man/Son of the Man pattern in the reports of the early Christian theologians.

B. The "Orthodox" Theologians' Reports about the Gnostics

Irenaeus (d. 200 c.e.) is our chief external source for early Gnosticism. The Nag Hammadi documents tell us virtually nothing about the names of the gnostic sects; for that we must depend on the Christian heresiologists.

We learn of the Ophites through Irenaeus and Origen.[31] In the beginning, according to this sect, there were three divine beings: the First Light = First Man; the Son of the Man = Second Man; and the Holy Spirit, the female principle. Father and Son have intercourse with the female principle and beget a son, the Third Man, Christ. As the result of a tragic devolution caused by the female, the world is created, along with the demons and every evil. At last the Holy Spirit, at the request of her emanation, Sophia, asks the First Man to send Christ (the Third Man) as helper. He descends through seven heavens and "puts on" Sophia like a groom with a bride. United with her, they descend upon Jesus at his baptism. Jesus then begins to confess himself openly as son of the First Man. Jesus is left to suffer on the cross while Christ and Sophia remove themselves to the Imperishable Aeon.[32]

Irenaeus is also our source for assorted teachings of the Valentinian school. Some Valentinians argued that the Savior derived from the pair "Man and Church, and on this account he designates himself Son of Man, being, as it were, a descendant of Man. . . . And there are others who assert that the Forefather of all things himself, the Pre-beginning and the Pre-unthinkable, is called 'Man,' and that *this is the great and hidden mystery*, namely, that the power which is above all and which embraces all is termed Man. And because of this the Savior designates himself Son of Man."[33] The ultimate mystery for this school is the humanity of God. Perhaps they were right.

Epiphanius (d. 403 c.e.) had a slightly different take on the Valentinians. They spoke, he says, of a self-engendered one who copulated with Sige

("Silence") to produce "the Father of Truth whom the perfect ones rightly call 'Man' because he is an antitype of the pre-existent unbegotten one."[34] Humanity is not an emergent quality, but is of the essence of the Godhead. One continues to see the vast influence of Ezekiel in all these systems. Curiously, we find none of this focus on copulation in the Nag Hammadi Library. It appears that the "orthodox" theologians were engaged either in voyeuristic fantasies, or were trying to frighten believers away from the gnostic option by defaming them.

Epiphanius also quotes the Gnostic Basilides to the effect that the human race will be saved. But not all living creatures called human beings will be saved. Those who are without spirit, who feel thoroughly at home in the immanent world and have no longing for the higher realm—can these, Basilides asks, really be called human? By no means. "We are human," Basilides declares, "all the others are pigs and dogs."[35] Again, how likely is this to be true, when the saying appears nowhere at Nag Hammadi? Basilides applies the notion of evolution to humanity: Let us, he says, observe the development of a human being. The teeth appear several months after birth; the sexual organs develop during puberty; the intelligence develops after a certain number of years—in short, the growing person gradually becomes what he was not before. Yet all his faculties were virtually present in the newborn babe. The aim of history and the universe is to "manifest human beings and to restore them" to their true, spiritual home. In Quispel's words, the aim is to "regain the place which was appointed to them by nature but which they never occupied before."[36]

This is similar to the assertion when considering Ezekiel 1 that human beings are an emergent reality, far from human, far from finished—but with this huge difference: Basilides seems to have believed that only spiritual people would be saved, those who have reached gnosis. I would argue that those who have been robbed of their humanity, whose higher self has been eclipsed by dehumanizing labor, or by a brutal or perverse upbringing, or by seductive delusions, most need and deserve to be restored to their higher or fuller selves in the "restitution of all things" (Acts 3:21).

With Monoimus the Arabian we encounter a different strain of Gnosticism: the Naassenes. Yet here, too, we find similar reflections on Genesis 1 and Ezekiel 1, developed into an extravagant cosmogony. The Human One ("Man") is the All, the beginning of all things, without origin, incorruptible, eternal. His son, the Offspring of the Human One (the son of the man), came into being quicker than thought or will. The Human One and its Offspring came into being the way fire and light come into being together, without lapse of time, without will, without forethought. This Human One is a *coniunctio oppositorum,* a single unity, incomposite and indivisible, composite and divisible; wholly friendly, wholly peaceable, wholly hostile, wholly at enmity with itself, dissimilar and similar, producing all things, generating all things. This unity is Mother and Father. From this perfect Human One has come the Offspring of the Human One, "for the whole fullness was pleased to reside in the Humanchild in bodily form" (see Col. 2:9, which lacks reference to the son of the man). "The Offspring of the Human One is that single Iota, the single stroke, which runs down from above, which is full and which fills all things, having in itself everything that belongs to the Human One, that is, the Father of the Offspring of the Human One."[37]

Then, in one of the most pregnant passages in all gnostic literature, Monoimus advises:

> Cease to seek after God and creation and things like these, and seek after yourself of yourself, and learn who it is who appropriates all things within you without exception and says, "*My* God, *my* mind, *my* thoughts, *my* soul, *my* body," and learn whence comes grief and rejoicing and love and hatred, and waking without intention, and sleeping without intention, and anger without intention, and love without intention. And if you carefully consider these things . . . you will find yourself within yourself, being both one and many like that stroke [of the letter iota], and will find the outcome of yourself.[38]

It appears that the human task is the integration of opposites in a higher synthesis, for, without that higher synthesis, the opposites are merely contraries, and nothing creative is possible. The Son of the Man—the Human Being—is that synthesis, or, better, that synthesizer. Jung called that process the "transcendent function," and comments, "The transcendent function does not proceed without aim and purpose, but leads to the revelation of the essential man."[39]

That Iota, initially identified as the "image of the perfect Man," has passed to the Son of the Man ("the Son of the Man is that single Iota, the single stroke"), and thence, mysteriously, to the believer. "You will find yourself within yourself, being both one and many *like that stroke,* and will find the outcome of yourself." The children of the Human Being thus participate in the Human Being from whom all things come. Who then says, "*My* God, *my* mind," and so on? With that question, still unanswered, depth psychology was born. Perhaps the question is not meant to be answered. Perhaps to think one knows the answer is fatal to all thought and becoming.

The "Naassene Sermon" also speaks of the heavenly Adamas, the Primal Man, self-originating, who makes everything, but who is not identical with anything that he makes. According to our source, Hippolytus, the Naassenes "reverence beyond all others Man and the Son of the Man."[40] This Son of Man is also called the Great Man and is identified with Jesus and the Christ. As usual in Gnosticism, the Human Being is a heavenly figure who incarnates in Jesus. Indeed, I can recall only a couple of instances in gnostic sources in which "the son of the man" is used for the human nature or being of Jesus.[41] The rather consistent way gnostic texts treat the Son of the Man as a heavenly being indicates their recognition that the Son of the Man belongs to the realm of the archetypes. Surprisingly, "Man or Primal Man or Adamas" is also "the inner human," who exists in everyone as the redeemable spiritual element in humanity.

The Peratae bear a family resemblance to the Naassenes, for both built on John 3:14, in which the Son of Man is compared to the serpent that Moses lifted in the wilderness to protect the people from snakebite. In an inversion of Genesis 3, the Peratae interpreted the serpent as a savior figure. Thus the brazen serpent that Moses lifted in the wilderness, the "perfect serpent," was made in the image of the son of the Man.

C. The Human Being in Poimandres

While apparently innocent of any knowledge of Christianity, the second-century *Poimandres* (*Corpus Hermeticum*, vol. 1) shows how widespread the mythology behind Gnosticism was. Again we encounter God as the parent of the entirety, a heavenly archetypal human being, from whose form human beings were made. Betraying some knowledge of Gen. 1:27, *Poimandres* depicts the "archetypal human being" as reflecting "God's beautiful form," which must also be human. "The Father of all, the Nous, who is life and light, bore a man who was like him, whom he loved as his own child. For he was exceedingly beautiful, and wore his father's image. Even God actually loved his own form and handed over to him all his creatures" (1.12). The "primal man" has intercourse with Nature: "So Nature produced bodies [human beings] in the shape of the Man" (17). As a result, human beings are divided, mortal because of the body, immortal because of the "essential Man" (15). Salvation, as usual, requires knowledge of the "essential Man" within, divestment from the body, and return to the spiritual world.[42]

A fourth-century Egyptian alchemist named Zosimus linked the Hermetic teaching of *Poimandres* with medieval and Renaissance alchemy, especially speculations on the god "Man." Zosimus speaks of the first human being, whom he calls the "inner Adam," "pneumatic man," or "light" (Adam of Light), who is persuaded by the archons in paradise to put on, and so bring to life, the "external (bodily) Adam" the archons created. The primordial human being in heaven is the soul of the primordial human being on earth; each person has a piece, as it were, of the heavenly primordial man. But Zosimus does not touch on the relation of this Primal Man to God, or to the image of God.[43]

Like the other myths emerging in that time, there is here no direct communion between God and earthly people, but always these mediators, heavenly but human, the promise of an emergent race. It would appear that the archetype of the human was like a field of wildflowers, bursting and scattering seeds in the most unlikely and hidden places.

D. Conclusion

As we look back over the ensemble of references to the Human Being in Gnosticism, we notice at once a major difference from the "orthodox" Christian theologians: the latter almost never use the expression "the son of the Man." When they do, it usually refers simply to the human nature or existence of the Christ. It is significant that, of the Nag Hammadi texts in which the son of the Man appears, all but one (*Eugnostos*) are Christian forms of gnosis. These Gnostics somehow succeeded in preserving the sense of the Human Being as the archetype of wholeness imaged by Jesus.

The "Great Church" and the Gnostics met in their almost total mythologization of Jesus, to the point that his life recedes entirely, and only the mythic outline survives. In the Nag Hammadi texts, the mythological motifs proliferate luxuriantly. But the same thing happens, if more soberly, in the Nicene Creed, to mention only one of many such creeds: ". . . born of the virgin Mary, suffered under Pontius Pilate, was crucified, dead and buried; on the third day he rose again, and is seated at the right hand of God. From thence he shall come to judge the quick and the dead." Nothing is left of Jesus' proclamation of the presence of God and the coming of God's domination-free order; of his healings, exorcisms, polemic against domination and inequality; of his critique of the family, gender relations, and violence; of his unmasking of the Powers; of his parables and other teachings; of his life as a whole; of his character or personality; of his hopes and pains and disappointments: in short, of everything that makes a person human.

I have not tried to make a brief for the Gnostics, but rather to comprehend their intense fascination with the Human Being in their theological context. They were clearly interested, not in the human Jesus, but in the transformation of Jesus into a new archetypal image. By contrast, I am interested in recovering enough of Jesus' life and teachings to enable us to envision anew his being and message in a way that can repristinate Christianity for a new millennium. In that quest, we have observed, around the beginning of the first millennium, the explosion of a massive archetypal mutation: an inner Anthropos, a divine child, born of the divine Human—a homing device orienting us toward our true selves. Call it what we may, describe it however inadequately, this new spiritual understanding burst on the scene with incomparable power. Drawing on Ezekiel's seminal vision, Jewish, gnostic, and Christian mystics discovered—in the depths of their psyches— God, as it were, in the likeness of a Human Being. A second figure, related to the first as parent to child, was revealed to them: call it the divine or inner child, Metatron, the son of the Man, or any of the scores of names in Gnosticism. It was an archetype capable of transforming human consciousness. The trick was to maintain the archetypal function of this "lieutenant" without abandoning its human dimension. None of these traditions succeeded in that trick. In Jewish mysticism, the human Enoch became the angelic Metatron, losing his humanity. In Christianity, the human Jesus became the divine Christ, though the doctrine of the two natures asserted the simultaneity of the human and divine. In fact, the human Jesus was virtually eclipsed. In Gnosticism, the human was devoured by divinity. But the Gospels kept something of the human Jesus alive, and they are what enable us to seek a new God-image and picture of Jesus that might empower a spiritual awakening in our time.

Jesus' humanness was an unadorned robe that could be stripped from his flesh, as he was reclothed in the garments of royalty (Messiah, Christ), of ultimacy (Logos), and of divinity (Son of God, God). Later, in Gnosticism, Jesus could be the garment put on by the preexistent heavenly Son of the Man, by Christ, by the Savior, by Seth, or by whatever mythological figure anyone might conjure. "Orthodox" Christians insisted on their kind of myth to the exclusion of all others, unaware that their mythmaking activities were no different in kind, only in content, from those they labeled gnostic. Had not Paul and his followers already spoken of "putting on Christ," as if Christ were a garment by means of which to "clothe yourselves with the new self" (*anthrōpos*, Gal. 3:27)? (See also Eph. 4:22; Col. 3:9-10.)

The genius of the Merkabah mystics and the Gnostics lay in their attending to what was deep in the heart. Their elaborate scaffolding was not just to help them access the truth, but to prevent them from falling head-long into mysteries too great to endure. But they glimpsed, from the vantage provided by their own tradition and reflections, the inauguration of the an-thropic revelation, and they preserved it, against the hostility of heresy hunters and inquisitors, for future generations to redeem.

As is often the case, those closest ideologically are often most violent in their mutual opposition. It is sad that Christians and Gnostics became arch-enemies, for they had more in common than not. Rather than gathering in silence around the Mystery, honoring each other as bearers of the most sa-cred realities, these fraternal twins fell on each other with a virulence that negated either party's right to speak for God. But the Christians had the sup-port of the empire, which needed the church to cement its crumbling arches, and "orthodox" Christianity won, won totally, thanks in part to the imperial legions.[44] Even when the coals of Gnosticism, long thought dead, burst to new flame in the medieval Albigensians and the Cathari, they were quickly and brutally snuffed out; more than a million of these "heretics" were killed to protect the "truth." So far are we from repentance that, to this day, to smear something as "gnostic" makes it instantly and unanimously suspect.

Today, Gnosticism is making a small comeback. I have had remarkable dialogues with Gnostics. I find them very open and very well informed, and I am eager to see Christians as willing to learn from our gnostic sisters and brothers as we have begun to be from Jews, Buddhists, Hindus, Muslims, Native Americans, and others.

Truth is manifold. But it is also one. Christians unable to appreciate gnostic truths may miss out on some of their own.

Part Six

Results and Conclusions

A. Once More, Seeing

"What if you were to see the Human Being ascending to where he was before?" (John 6:62). What, indeed? It is surely not an empty-handed return trip. Something has been accomplished on this mission of descending and ascending. To what has the Human Being ascended? Certainly to visibility. In passage after passage, the stress is on "seeing" the Human Being, either coming or going, ascending or descending. Mark 14:62 depicts Jesus himself prophesying that "you will see Wisdom's Child [the son of the man] seated at the right hand of the Power."[1] We need not read this literally, as if Jesus rode a sunbeam back to God's throne room in the sky. Rather, we can take it as the accurate report of an archetypal mutation. According to Edward Edinger, it appears that once someone has seen and recognized the unconscious for what it is, that creates a need for the unconscious to change.[2] Something that had been gestating for centuries, since Ezekiel and Daniel, had come to birth in the psyches of the disciples. The Human Being whose divine power and authority they had seen incarnate in Jesus, and occasionally in themselves, had now entered the heart of reality as a catalyst in human transformation. Like a bell that reverberates to the core of our being, the Human Being is, as it were, an invitation to become the fullness of who we are. And with the invitation comes the power to do it.

The ascension of the Human Being does not represent a mutation in humanity, but in the archetype of humanity. It is not a question of some people having new "genes" (Nietzsche's "superman"), and others who do not, but of a new possibility available to all, that each must consciously *choose*.

The motif of ascension, then, is not grist for a discussion of miracles, because it was not miraculous. Rather, the motif marks a change in the way some people experience the divine. That means that the transformation that Jesus triggered is not exclusively Christian. Anyone can be drawn by the attractive power of Jesus. Similarly, non-Jews can experience the visionary incandescence of Jewish mysticism, and a Christian can penetrate the depths of Gnostic wisdom. That means that, at the center of reality, there is more than one religious way. There are many ways to the center, many traditions, many truths. Jesus does not belong to Christians. He is the property of the world. How would Gandhi have been improved by joining a Christian church? He himself regretted that Christians had tried to hoard Jesus for themselves.[3]

The world that Jesus entered was seething with human longings that showed in messianic dreams, millennial fantasies, apocalyptic desperation, mystical revelations, suicidal nationalism, religious critique and reform, reactionary rigidity, and a sense that time was collapsing, that the future was foreshortened, that the mystery of reality was about to be revealed. In such a milieu, the authenticity of Jesus was like a beacon that drew all mythological motifs to itself. Incubating in the womb of that period was God's rash gamble that humanity might become more humane.

Frederick Borsch concludes his book *The Son of Man in Myth and History* with the observation that God had given Jesus a myth to live out.

> Jesus, however, was not content to preach about a myth; he had to discover how that myth related to the actualities of his own life and those of his disciples. In everyday situations as well as in his entire ministry he was engaged in the process of forcing the myth up against the hard facts of life, making what truths it held to become real and alive. . . . Without the myth, Jesus might not have been able to accept the cross; without the cross we would never have known how much truth lay beyond even the revelatory powers of this myth.[4]

In that struggle, Jesus could draw on the experience of Ezekiel, who also had known what it meant to suffer and to be treated with contempt.[5] But Ezekiel was not killed. At that point, events overtook Jesus' comprehension, and his personal myth was shattered on a rock larger than he. The cry of abandonment from the cross, whatever its source, is Jesus' entry into unfathomable darkness. In that cry we hear the chorus of all whose lives have been ripped from them without meaning or effect. At that point, two tendencies emerged. One tendency attached to Jesus the mythologies of the world and the projections of his followers. The result was the God-Man, whose might, power, authority, and dominion the Book of Revelation celebrates most lavishly. The other tendency has not yet fully emerged. It is what I have been calling, following Berdyayev, the anthropic revelation. It is the myth of the human Jesus, who rose from the dead into the archetype of the Human Being. If we claim that Jesus lived authentically, that he is exemplary, and that he is the human face of God; if we see in him the son of the man, and that he is the firstborn of many sisters and brothers; if we assert that he was like us in every way, including being an imperfect, wounded, sinning human being—historiography can prove none of it. The myth of the human Jesus simply *requires* it.

B. Will the Real Human Being Please Stand Up?

Now that we are reaching the end of our inquiry it is time to weigh in on theories about the Human Being. This concluding summary is immensely aided by Delbert Burkett's masterful survey, *The Son of Man Debate: A History and Evaluation*,[6] in which he succinctly reviews hundreds of studies. I make no attempt to summarize his work, but simply comment on some of his findings.

Some scholars conclude, Burkett notes, that the "son of the man" might refer to a person of the lower classes, a "nobody."[7] Others see the expression as an allusion to Jesus' solidarity with all people as a kind of "Everyman." Or Jesus could be the exemplary human being, the ideal or archetype of the race. These statements all lack the eschatological dimension. That deficiency, Burkett continues, is redressed somewhat by views that see the son of the man as the goal of human history.

We might also play with the possibility that Jesus used "the son of the man" to critique, lampoon, ridicule, or negate the dominant messianic beliefs. As Kathlene Peterson Nicol observes, the church did not build a son-of-the-man Christology, because it could not: use of the title was Jesus' way of eschewing *all* titles.[8] Similarly, as William L. Dols Jr. notes, "*ho huios tou anthrōpou* is the one description of Jesus that the church from the very beginning has been unable to define and thus own. It thereby retains an element of the numinous. It bears witness to the mysterious transforming power of God enfleshed in Jesus and longing to be born in each of us."[9]

My own choice of the archetypal explanation of the son of the man is not, as some might suspect, a modernism. Plato and Philo show how thoroughly conversant the first century was with archetypal thought (see appendix 2 on the archetypes in Philo). No one needed to have read Plato, any more than they need do so today, to pick up the cultural significance of his ideas. Archetypes were in the air. They were, among other things, the basis of the allegorical interpretation of Scripture that was to play a central role in Jewish and Christian theology.

But that archetypal interpretation must not focus solely on Jesus. From Psalm 80 and Daniel 7 to the Gospels and the post-Christian Similitudes of Enoch and *4 Ezra* 13:52, there is a collective dimension that we neglect to our great loss. If Jesus alone is Sophia's Child, if he alone assumes archetypal dimensionality, if he alone is at the heart of reality, then Christianity does indeed possess a monopoly on truth. But if he is an elder brother within a large family (Rom. 8:29), then we can interpret Jesus' ascension as a mutation in the archetype of wholeness. The Human Being has the capacity to make humans humane, whatever their religion or lack thereof.[10]

How shall we respond to the philologists who believe that "the son of the man" was merely a form of self-reference with no theological content? Geza Vermes argued that *bar enasha*, like *hahu gabra*, could be used in Aramaic as a circumlocution for "I." These occasions arose when (*a*) a speaker wished to avoid undue or immodest emphasis on himself, or (*b*) when he was prompted by fear or by a dislike of openly asserting something disagreeable in relation to himself. Aramaic scholars are generally agreed that the examples Vermes produced do not show a circumlocutional use of *bar enasha*. They reflect instead a generic use (meaning "humanity" in general) or an indefinite use (meaning "a person," "someone"), in which a person might include himself or herself with others. Here are some characteristic attempts at generic explanations of "the son of the man":

> Casey: "a man" spoken generically but indicating the speaker[11]
> Lindars: "a man in my position"[12]
> Bauckham: "a man" or "someone" as a deliberately ambiguous
>   self-reference[13]

In each case, those who understood the speaker would recognize that she referred to herself.

Burkett's critique is cogent. First, he notes that such usage would require a demonstrative pronoun ("this son of man") or a gesture pointing to oneself.[14] In addition, he observes that while the Aramaic *bar enasha* could be translated as "a man," the Greek *ho huios tou anthrōpou* could not. Depending on whether the first article is individualizing or generic, the Greek expression could mean "the son of (the) man," referring to an individual, or "the human being" ("man" in a generic sense), but not "a man." Thus, says Burkett, these scholars base their theories on neither of the two meanings of *bar enasha* that the Greek could express, but on the one meaning that it could not. Consequently, they must assume that the Aramaic has been mistranslated. While this is possible, it is more likely that the translators knew their business and gave *ho huios tou anthrōpou* as the best equivalent of the underlying Aramaic.[15] The most serious objection to all such theories, says Burkett, is that they produce such implausible results when applied to actual sayings. "A fellow (*ho huios tou anthrōpou*) has nowhere to lay his head" (Casey) is so unremarkable and untrue as a generalization that one is unable to explain why it would have been remembered—and this the only saying about the son of the man attested in more than a single source (*Gos. Thom.* 86 = Luke 9:57-58 // Matt. 8:19-20). Nor is Lindars's explanation of Matt. 11:19 any better. He translates "the son of the man came eating and drinking" as "a man has come eating and drinking," when clearly the phrase means Jesus, not a class of people to whom Jesus belongs. Having rejected all these options, Burkett himself opts for a titular sense, prompted by Dan. 7:13. But this cannot account for the collective sense implied in such texts as Matt. 9:6-8. I conclude that none of the generic or indefinite translations works in more than a few cases. Vermes' original suggestion, "I," which in some cases is used in place of the son of the man in the Gospels, fails as well.[16] We still have no answer to why the evangelists did not use "I" in every case instead of "the son of the man." Any third-person singular term used as a means of self-reference would be equivalent to "I" or "me." But "the son of the man" does not *mean* "I"; it can simply be used occasionally as a substitute for "I." As an example, if a celebrity enters a party announcing, of himself, "His Excellency has arrived," it is clear that "I" could replace this form of self-address. But "I" does not convey the self-mockery or perhaps arrogance that "His Excellency" carries. Similarly, in the Gospels, "the son of the man" is not coextensive in semantic content with "I." Therefore the phrase is not a true equivalent, although it could occasionally be enlisted for that task.[17]

We are now in a position to see why the expression "son of the man" could strike some as lacking content. The reason is that they treated the expression in isolation from everything else Jesus did and said. But if "the son of the man" is the name Jesus gave to the dawning reality he was incarnating in his life, work, and being, then the entire gospel is the content of the son of the man. As Oscar Cullmann put it, "The idea of the Son of Man . . . embraces the total work of Jesus as does almost no other idea."[18] *The Human Being means what Jesus was, and how he was, and what his process of individuation was.*

Furthermore, the translation "son of Adam," preferred by the Jesus Seminar, is excluded by the second definite article: "the son of *the* Adam" makes no sense. Perhaps the articles were added specifically to block that translation. As Joseph Fitzmyer writes, since New Testament writers use "Adam" as a name, it seems that they would have written *ho huios tou Adam* if they had meant that.[19] Jews and Christians regularly translated *bar (e)nas* literally into Greek as *huios anthrōpou* ("son of man") without articles, or simply as *anthrōpos.* Again, it is the awkward neologism with two definite articles that we must explain.[20]

If the church had wanted to address Jesus as "the son of the man" in a titular sense, it would have done so in the usual way: it would have made Jesus speak about himself using the normal "I." Or the evangelists would have spoken *about* the son of the man in the third person rather than have Jesus speak thus about himself. When the press reports that "Bob Dole reiterated that he would not raise taxes," we assume that he said, "I won't raise your taxes." We would not have expected him to say, "Bob Dole won't raise your taxes." That is a peculiar way of speaking in any age. But Bob Dole at least used his own name, rather than an enigmatic puzzler.

Whatever the case, the evangelists continued to place this idiosyncratic form of self-address solely on the lips of Jesus. This does not indicate that the church has invented all such instances. Rather, Jesus' unparalleled usage has constrained additions by the church that would conform to his singular mode of address. Even when the church invented son-of-the-man sayings, as in the case of the Fourth Gospel or apocalyptic scenarios in the Synoptic Gospels, it did so consistent with Jesus' own linguistic practice.[21]

Randall Buth notes that bi- and trilingualism were widespread in both Galilee (where Aramaic, Hebrew, and Greek, in descending order, were spoken) and Judean villages (where people knew Hebrew and Aramaic). Upper classes knew Greek, Aramaic, and Hebrew, in that order, and the urban lower classes knew Aramaic, Hebrew, and Greek.[22] Many Jewish copies of the Greek Old Testament did not use the title "the Lord," as Christians did, but instead retained the Hebrew letters of the divine name. Similarly, some Qumran scrolls reproduce, within an Aramaic document, the divine name in the old Hebrew script.[23] So, continues Buth, if Jesus had wanted to signal to his hearers that he stood in the same line of descent as Daniel's "one like a son of man," how better to accomplish this than *to put the Aramaic term* bar enasha *in the middle of a Hebrew sentence?* "The brief language switch would let the audience know that some other sense than the basic one was intended. It would have the effect of putting the phrase in quotation marks."[24] When the expression was translated into Greek, and neither Aramaic nor Hebrew could be used, the same effect could be achieved by using definite articles. The result is a Greek phrase that is simultaneously inelegant and mysterious, flagging the reader that something extraordinary is here. This would also explain the all but complete agreement of the Gospel writers in using the double articles.

One may support this hunch by comparing the Syriac versions and quotations of the Gospels. In order to represent the Gospel term, they sometimes resort to a form that "does not occur in Syriac except as a rendering of the Gospel phrase."[25] This indicates either that the title perplexed the Syriac translators or that they understood perfectly well its cryptic meaning.

Norman Perrin regarded all the son-of-the-man sayings as church creations. He saw two levels of this Christian exegetical activity. First, believers thought Jesus had ascended to God, on the basis of Dan. 7:13 and Ps. 110:1. Second, they believed that Jesus would return to earth (the "second coming").[26] Perrin's thesis explains the post-Easter son-of-the-man sayings. But it does not explain adequately the origin of the pre-Easter son-of-the-man passages. Once believers had identified Jesus as the transcendent judge of the world and heavenly redeemer, seated at the right hand of the Power of God, there would have been no compelling reason to create those sayings that I have identified as pre-Easter. Paul had already received and developed the Son of God Christology prior to the writing of the Gospels. There was no incentive for the evangelists to abandon that line of development in order to create a different Christology of the son of the man. Nor does Perrin's theory explain why the son-of-the-man phrase appears only on the lips of Jesus. "Son" and "Son of God" also appear on the lips of Jesus, notes Burkett. However, they also appear as christological confessions on the lips of others, while "the son of the man" does not.[27] Surely, Burkett continues, at least one of the Gospel writers would have sensed that the son of the man had no future in Hellenistic circles. They would then have abandoned the effort for the already well-established and far more familiar Son of God Christology, as Paul did. Later New Testament writings and subsequent theological texts, liturgies, and creeds developed "Son" and "Son of God" further. But the son of the man virtually disappeared from Christian parlance.[28] Surely, had Jesus not been the source of this unusual expression, the translators would have rendered it in a variety of different ways.

Jesus may have used the term "man" in the phrase "son of the man" as a way of referring to God rather than humanity (e.g., "Man"). The Gnostics certainly understood it that way, building from Ezekiel's use of the expression. Yet the phrase still harks back to its use in Psalm 8, which stresses the lowliness and exaltation of human beings. In this light, Son of God is not the higher honorific. It is arguably a paraphrastic commentary on what the "the son of the man" means as the ascended archetype of human becoming,

seated at the right hand of God the Human One (Luke 22:69). And if the
"son of the man" has God as his Father, then Jesus is, by inference, the Son
of God.[29] This line of christological development might have gone something like this:

> God as the Human One
> Ezekiel as the son of that Human One
> Jesus as the son of that Human One
> Hence Jesus as the Son of God, the Human One.

"Son of God" would then be derivative of "son of the man" and flow naturally from Jesus' self-designation, without his having taken that step in his
lifetime. Might he have taken that step during his lifetime? Perhaps, if he
meant "son" in a relational sense rather than as an ascription of deity. But as
the gospel moved into a Gentile environment, people heard "Son of God"
in a different way, as a divine being.

It is this study's judgment that Jesus did indeed utter a number of the
pre-Easter son-of-the-man sayings in the Gospels; that he expressed the core
of the suffering sayings, in that he did anticipate his execution; and that he
looked forward to the transformation of human beings into the fuller humanity exemplified and made possible by Jesus as the Human Being. That
churches developed additional sayings is only to be expected. That they
were not always true to his meaning goes without saying. Scholars have
erred, however, by applying exclusively rational categories to what are essentially archetypal images. These images were precipitated involuntarily
from the unconscious, as indications from the psychic depths about the significance of Jesus' life. Their truth lies not in their historicity but in their
faithful rendering of the intrapsychic transformations taking place in believers after the ascension, that is, after Jesus entered the archetype of the
Human Being. That is the real miracle of Easter.

Put another way: As bearer of the archetype of the Human Being, Jesus
activates the numinous power that is capable of healing, transforming, or re-
birthing those who surrender themselves to it. As such, Jesus knew himself
to be in the grip of a power greater than he. A problem arises at just this
point, however, When Jesus is worshiped as the sole bearer of the archetype
of humanness, he is made a supernatural being. As such, he loses his connection to the struggle to be human, and becomes a cult figure in a religion
focused on his person rather than on the reality that he bore.

"Language is inside seeing," wrote the poet Rumi.[30] Ezekiel's vision,
which stands at the fountainhead of the Human Being tradition, is language

inside seeing. Ezekiel's language cracks and sags under the impact of a seeing so overwhelming. What language seeks inside seeing is genuine vision, truth, correspondence. Language divorced from seeing is hollow, opinionated, vapid. The renewal of language comes from those who actually see, and, seeing, wrestle language until it blesses them. When the church attempted to express what God had revealed, and continued to reveal through direct experience, through apostles and prophets and the tradition and finally the Gospels, it sometimes transposed "inside seeing" with "outside seeing," vision with mere sight. The son of the man who comes on the clouds of heaven to judge and destroy is the result. Ever since, not just the church's persecutors, but also its leaders and members, have too often tried to prevent an outbreak of serious Christianity.

We may attempt to reverse that process and seek in the imaginal realm a vision, audition, or intimation of Wisdom's Child, who, as a present archetypal reality, is even now creating the future humanity. We do not surrender the final victory of God, but we acknowledge that this victory is prepared in nonlocal reality long before it bursts into history. As the poet Rilke put it, "The future enters into us in this way in order to transform itself in us long before it happens."[31]

C. The Human Being

Lo, I tell you a mystery:
God is Human,
and we are to become
like God.

Our spiraling itinerary brings us back to Nicolas Berdyayev, one of the true prophets of the twentieth century and the herald of the anthropological revelation. He believed that the future coming of the Human Being "with great power and glory" (Mark 13:26) will reveal humanity's christological nature. "The Coming Christ will come only to a humanity which courageously accomplishes a christological self-revelation, that is, reveals in its own nature divine power and glory." Berdyayev bemoaned the false humility and passivity of much Christianity, which withers the people's creative capacities and renders them merely obedient. Christ, he said, will never come in power and glory to people who are not active creatively; for it is the creative act that reveals human nature.[32] But Christianity has often crushed the creative spirit. Believers are made to feel guilty of hubris for reaching too high or risking too much. Authorities punish people for failure, so they learn to defend themselves against possibilities too lofty. Against this tendency, Berdyayev announces the anthropic revelation, which John's Gospel had already declared: "The one who believes in me will also do the works that I do and, in fact, will do greater works than these, because I am going to the Father" (14:12). The same sentiment is expressed in an apocryphal saying about the Human Being: "When you make the two one, you will become Truly Human Beings ["sons of men"], and when you say, 'Mountain, move away,' it will move away" (*Gos. Thom.* 106).

The task of humanity's religious consciousness, Berdyayev thought, is to reveal its christological consciousness. Only the mystics, transcending all times and seasons, have glimpsed the Christology of humanity. Only the Christology of humanity, the reverse side of the anthropology of Christ, will reveal in the humanity of Christians the genuine image and likeness of God.[33] The great insight of Joachim de Fiore (d. 1202), an insight trivialized if treated literally, was that the era of the Father and the era of the Son were soon to inaugurate the era of the Holy Spirit. For us today that means that, for some situations, there is no explicit guidance from Scripture or tradition. In cases dealing with modern science, politics, technology, genetics, abortion, sexual orientation, and even situations in which the injunctions of Scripture are unambiguous, we must still, according to a saying ascribed to Jesus, "judge for yourselves what is right" (Luke 12:57). (And we must even decide whether *that* saying is right. Apparently most Christians have decided that it is not, since they do not live that way.) Our attempts to find guidance by prooftexting is born of religious anxiety bordering on despair. Our purpose can no longer be revealed from above. We are left without external authority, forced to find it within ourselves, like Jesus' disciples in the story of plucking on the sabbath. The God who commands, withdraws. That absence of aid from on high shows the great wisdom of God. The attempt to limit our purpose to keeping the commandments turns creativity into submission, which is to say that there is no creativity. Only human beings in touch with the Human Being can reveal the truth about the daring now required of us. There can be no divine revelation of this secret, Berdyayev insists. God does not wish to know what the anthropological revelation will be, since to do so would violate the freedom God has given us. More fundamentally, God *cannot* know, because our creative responses, in principle, cannot be known in advance, even by God.[34]

So humanity is called to create a new and hitherto unknown world through creativity. The psychic bearer of that Christology of humanity is the Human Being, the son of the man. For two thousand years this powerful

image has languished, unused and ignored, though individuals and movements have kept this archetype very much alive. Many have risked everything, persisting against incredible odds, because something was at work
within them—the same archetype that gave birth to the image of the son of
the man. Can it be that God within us, hungering to become human,
prompts our quest to become human? Theologians have exploited to the
limit every conceivable title of Jesus, while ignoring the Human Being. I believe that the time for the anthropological revelation has come, and that the
stone the builders rejected will become the head of the corner.

The christological revelation, centered in Jesus, was that God desired to
become incarnate in humanity. The anthropological revelation, not yet
consummated, is that God has destined humanity, or at least has called it, to
become human as God is Human. We can redefine divinity, not as superhuman, posthuman, or godlike, but more fully as what we already are:
human beings. As I said earlier, we are not called to become what we are
not—divine—but to become what we are: human. Accomplishing these
tasks—God incarnating in human beings and human beings incarnating
God—will require great maturity, even heroism. Some will, like Feuerbach,
decide that we create God by the powers of imagination, rather than the
imagination enabling us to experience God. It is true that the God-arche-
type evolves in interaction with us, but it is nevertheless transcendent and
Other, as all who have encountered the living God attest.

The gist of this book is, simply, that Jesus as the son of the man is
enough. What a lean and pared-back Christianity has to give to the world is
not its creeds, dogmas, doctrines, liturgies, and devotions, though some of
these traditions still hold great validity for many. It offers, simply—Jesus.
And the Jesus it has to give is not the Jesus of the two natures, or the second
person of the Trinity, or the one who is of one being (*homoousios*) with the
Father, though people within certain belief traditions may value all these
concepts. If the Human Being archetype is to carry out its transformative
task, we will need to develop new theologies, liturgies, prayer forms, and devotional practices that can help people tap that numinosity. But I want to
worship the God Jesus worshiped, not worship Jesus as God.

All Christianity has to give, and all it needs to give, is the myth of the
human Jesus. It is the story of Jesus the Jew, a human being, the incarnate
son of the man: imperfect but still exemplary, a victim of the Powers yet still
victorious, crushed only to rise again, in solidarity with all who are ground
to dust under the jackboots of the mighty, healer of those under the power
of death, lover of all who are rejected and marginalized, forgiver, liberator,
exposer of the regnant cancer called "civilization"—that Jesus, the one the

Powers killed and whom death could not vanquish. Jesus' is the simple story of a person who gambled his last drop of devotion on the reality of God and the coming of God's new world. In the process, he lived out, in his flesh and blood, the archetype of the son of the man, the Child of the Human One, Sophia's Child, the New Being, the Sisterchild—call it what you will—as the intimation of what that new humanity might entail. In so doing, he not only incarnated God, he changed the way people *experienced* God. In short, the gift of Christianity to the world, as the Hindu Gandhi saw with such lucidity, is not Christianity, but Jesus, revealer and catalyst of our true humanity.

Appendix 1:
Was There a Primal Man Myth?

rthur J. Ferch argues that the "history of religions" interpretations of
Daniel 7 "have suffered considerable setbacks because they were too synthetic and unsupported by evidence."[1] The "one like a human being" in
Dan. 7:13 is not derived from the Babylonian chaos myth, nor was Adapa or
Marduk an antecedent for the Daniel figure. Adapa is designated "the seed
[shoot] of mankind" or "human offspring," but he refuses to imbibe the
bread and water of life that would have given him immortality; thus, he is
closer to Adam than Ben Adam. He has no eschatological or judicial function. Marduk is once "the man," but never *ben 'adam*. Daniel is more interested in history and the future than in creation mythology. While it is not
impossible that the apocalypticist used Babylonian or Canaanite traditions,
he would have had to transform these so that the pagan antecedents were
hardly recognizable and consequently of little value for reconstructing the
origin of the son-of-the-man figure.[2]

Ferch believes that the Iranian Primal Man (*Urmensch*) speculations are
a pastiche created by Wilhelm Bousset and Richard Reizenstein from the
Naassene sermon (from Hippolytus, after 200 C.E.); the Gnostic *Omega*
(fourth century C.E.); the Neoplatonist Jamblichus (died around 330 C.E.);
and *Poimandres* (first or second century C.E.). Carl Kraeling thinks the Anthropos motif migrated from Iranian sources to Babylonian Marduk mythology to gnostic texts. The Prototypical Man became the Great Man, who
prepared the victory of the heavenly powers over those of the lower world.
We have no evidence that there was such a myth or that it had earlier forms.
When Kraeling finally introduces his reconstructed myth late in his book,
he admits that the traditions he draws upon do not antedate the Muslim era.[3]
For his part, Sigmund Mowinckel bases his reconstruction of the son-of-
man belief on the Similitudes of Enoch, now generally dated after the

ministry of Jesus, and on gnostic texts authored in the second century and later.[4] The Primal Man is not eschatological, and Daniel's eschatological "one like a son of man" is not protological. Salvation for the pagans is cyclical, a return to the golden age and the Perfect Person.[5] By contrast, in the New Testament, Christ as the Second Adam has already inaugurated a new age, now, which will be consummated in the future. When Gayomart finally appears in Manichaean texts in an eschatological role, it is in the Middle Persian period (third to seventh centuries C.E.), and his task is to pioneer a resurrection and not to exercise dominion over all peoples.[6] The descent into the lower regions and subsequent conquest or death of the primal figure, by which the salvific process is precipitated in both Iranian and Hellenistic or gnostic sources, is completely foreign to Daniel 7.[7] Nor does Daniel "eschatologize" an enthronement festival (A. Bentzen), draw on a myth of a solar, heavenly Man (H. Gressmann), develop an Iranian rite of enthronement (E. Herzfeld), or adapt an ancient solar ritual like Tyre's (J. Morgenstern) or like Canaan's (J. A. Emerton).[8] All these theories ignore the "like" before "son of man" in Daniel 7, and treat this humanlike figure as if it had been called "man" or "son of man." We know too little about the date, content, or actuality of Urmensch speculations for us to assert that Daniel drew upon them.

As for the Ras Shamra texts from Ugarit, they are badly mutilated and fragmentary. Scholars are not in agreement about the meaning or even details of the mythic materials. That in the Canaanite pantheon the father, El, has a son, Baal, has numerous parallels, but none is close enough to be regarded as formative of biblical texts. A chaos monster such as the fourth beast (Lotan, mentioned only once in Ugaritic texts) is irrelevant, since Leviathan is nowhere mentioned in Daniel. None of the features of the fourth beast in Daniel fits Lotan. Nor does the son of man subdue any of these beasts; God does. Daniel's four beasts represent kings or kingdoms, not chaos. Daniel's beasts are not divine, the sea is inanimate, and Daniel's creatures are winged, whereas winged deities are almost nonexistent in Ugarit. Yahweh has some of the attributes of both El and Baal, but the son of man does not. There is so little real parallel material that one must posit a creativity in Daniel's use of the material that is nothing less than the creativity required for him to have invented the entire narrative (though with elements drawn from Ezekiel).[9] Even if Daniel could be shown to be based on Canaanite motifs, what would we gain? The Jews always transformed their borrowings; establishing parallels proves nothing. More important, why, in a work dedicated to resisting Hellenistic religion that pagans were forcing on Jews, would a Jew draw on pagan myths?

Granted all that, what is striking is that a variety of cultures all lit on a similar archetypal image—a human being charged with numinous significance. The differences among the conceptions invalidate the comparative approach, but they confirm the archetypal, because they show that there was not, in fact, a simple linear borrowing, but that each culture developed the archetype of "the human being" in its own way, consistent with its own myths, rituals, and traditions, and possibly drawing at times on motifs from other religions.[10] The prodigality of such images, in all their variety, shows them to be the outworking of psychic contents. It is not that people thought up this new archetype, or borrowed it from other cultures, but that the archetype imposed itself on people's minds. As Jung put it, "[T]he symbols represent the prototypes of the Christ-figure that were slumbering in man's unconscious and were then called awake by his actual appearance in history and, so to speak, magnetically attracted."[11]

In any case, whether borrowed or original, the result is the same: we find a number of cultures and religions in the first century reflecting on the symbolic meaning of a divine Human Being, the forebear and/or fulfillment of the human race.

Both sides err—the history-of-religions school by seeking the lineal descent of symbols and ideas, and their critics by failing to see the archetypal commonality of motifs in the religions of other peoples. In principle, the documented diffusion of myths predisposes us to expect some forms of borrowing or adaptation. But we can easily fall into what Samuel Sandmel called parallelomania, the fallacy of thinking that establishing a source throws light on a text's meaning. Once we understand what lies behind the archetype of the Human Being, we can learn from other religions that are in touch with something comparable. In the process, we can develop an appreciation for other religious visions without having to stress the uniqueness of biblical religion, as if it held an exclusive claim to truth.

Appendix 2:
Philo on the Archetypes

Philo is explicit about the archetypal framework of his thought.

> For God, being God, assumed that a beautiful copy would never be produced apart from a beautiful pattern [*paradeigmatos*, "paradigm"], and that no object of perception would be faultless which was not made in the likeness of an original [*arxetypon*, "archetype"] discerned only by the intellect. So when He willed to create this visible world He first fully formed the intelligible world [the world of ideas or archetypes], in order that He might have the use of a pattern (*paradeigmati*) wholly God-like and incorporeal in producing the material world, as a later creation, the very image of an earlier, to embrace in itself objects of perception of as many kinds as the other contained objects of intelligence.[1]

Philo makes a clear distinction between the archetypes, which are invisible, and what Jung called archetypal images, which are visible "objects of perception" patterned after the invisible archetypes. This distinction between archetype and archetypal image (the first representing only the possibility of certain types of perception or action, the second shaped by our own personal, cultural, and spiritual history) enabled Jung to abandon Lamarckism (the belief that experience can become genetically encoded).[2]

First, says Philo, an invisible light (the archetype), for example, becomes perceptible to the mind; then it comes into being "as an image of the Divine Word Who brought it within our ken." The archetype is like "a supercelestial constellation, fount of the constellations obvious to sense."[3] Yet God "is not only light, but the archetype of every other light, nay, prior to and high above every archetype, holding the position of the model of a model. For the model or pattern was the Word which contained all His fullness. . . ."[4]

If human beings have been made in God's likeness (Gen. 1:26), that likeness cannot refer to the body, Philo asserts, because God is incorporeal, but only to the mind; "for after the pattern of a single Mind, even the Mind of the Universe as an archetype, the mind in each of those who successively came into being was moulded."[5] Human beings are an example of failure to live up to the divine image. This leads Philo to his famous distinction between the two creation accounts in Genesis. In the first (Genesis 1), God created the divine image as "an idea or type or seal, an object of thought only, incorporeal, neither male nor female, by nature incorruptible." Thus the souls of human beings have been "made after the image of the Archetype, the Word (*logos*) of the First Cause."[6] In Genesis 2, on the other hand, God formed human beings from the clay of the earth and breathed life into them. Thus people are a mix of created clay and uncreated soul.[7] "For this reason he says that the heavenly man was not moulded, but was stamped with the image of God; while the earthly is a moulded work of the Artificer, but not his offspring."[8] Thus Philo can speak of the Logos as the true man in the world, who is "the greatest and most perfect Man."[9]

The Creator made both the pattern (*paradeigma*) and the copy (*mimema*) of all. Now "the archetypal seal is an incorporeal idea, but the copy which is made by the impression is something else—a material something, naturally perceptible by the senses, yet not actually coming into relation with them."[10] This brings in a new aspect of the archetypes: they are not wholly passive, as the image of a seal and its copy might suggest, but are, through the power of the Logos (the Mind of the Universe), capable of activating change without themselves being altered or changing their nature in the process—"naturally perceptible by the senses, yet not actually coming into relation with them." In short, they are comparable to a catalyst. Archetypal images act catalytically to transform; that is their function. In language that sounds almost as if the Fourth Gospel drew it directly from Philo, the latter states, "For that man [the Logos] is the eldest son, whom the Father of all raised up, and elsewhere calls him His first-born, and indeed the Son thus begotten followed the ways of his Father, and shaped the different kinds, looking to the archetypal patterns which that Father supplied."[11]

Those made after the divine image yearn after that image, "For the image of God is a pattern (*arxetypos*) of which copies are made, and every copy longs for that of which it is a copy, and its station is at its side."[12] We long to become what we were created to be: the image of God in us. And that image is revealed to us by the Human Being. By longing to become like the Human Being, we are oriented toward it, we are attracted to it, we desire it, we hunger for it, perhaps we leave everything behind to search for it, we may even give our lives for it.

Not all the initiative, however, comes from the archetypes. People who live exemplary lives are gathered in the archetype of the self as models for others to emulate. "These are such men as lived good and blameless lives, whose virtues stand permanently recorded in the most holy scriptures, not merely to sound their praises but for the instruction of the reader and as an inducement to him to aspire to the same."[13] The veneration of saints, the apotheosis of great historic figures, the divinization of those whose lives reflected the divine—all are examples of "an inducement . . . to aspire to the same." An exemplary life becomes archetypal, and the more powerful the life, the more the effect. Those who dwell in the light of eternity glow with its light, and in their light others see light.

Thus, when Jung gave new vigor to the notion of the archetypes, he was not coining a new idea but reviving one that goes back to Plato, Philo, and much of the ancient world. If we want to understand archetypal meanings in the first century, we have to understand the use of archetypes by first-century thinkers like Philo.

Likewise, we today can grasp the meaning of archetypes by analogy with neurophysiology. The cognitive operators "shape all our thoughts and feelings, but they are not themselves ideas. They are, instead, the organizing principles of the mind."[14]

For us to say that, by his ascension, Jesus entered the realm of the archetypes, is no different from an early Christian saying that Jesus was raised from the dead and seated at the right hand of God. Where the Gospel writers differed from Philo was their emphasis on the future of the Human Being. Philo was preoccupied with the Logos/Sophia/Anthropos that was the firstborn of all creation, the archetype of rationality in the world's creation. Philo's glance was back, to the beginning. The Prologue to the Gospel of John, Col. 1:15-20, and other passages in the New Testament also look back, but their real concern is with the future of humanity, our becoming what God intended. Again, 1 John 3:2 is the watchword: "what we will be has not yet been revealed." That idea required an open archetype, its content only partially revealed, luring us forward through opacity toward a new world whose guarantor is the same one whose life was already a prefigurement.

Appendix 3:
Ezekiel's Influence on Jesus

It is striking how little attention scholars have paid to the son of man in Ezekiel and its possible influence on Jesus. They generally dismiss it with a sentence, or ignore it altogether.[1] Yet I believe that Ezekiel is the best clue for understanding Jesus' use of the term. Ezekiel's use prefigured Jesus' in significant ways, and Jesus apparently learned from Ezekiel, as follows:

- Other prophets were rejected, but only in the case of Ezekiel and Jesus is it written that they were rejected and treated with contempt in their roles *as son of man.*
- In the case of both Ezekiel and Jesus, God gives judgment over the people *to the son of man* (Ezek. 20:4; 22:2; 23:36; Matt. 19:28 // Luke 22:28-30; Matt. 25:31-46; John 5:27).
- God says to Ezekiel, "*Son of man . . . you shall bear their punishment*" (4:4). So also Jesus says *"The son of the man* came . . . to give his life as a ransom for many" (Mark 10:45). Other prophets spoke of an individual bearing the peoples' iniquities (e.g., Isa. 53:4-6), *but not in the role of the son of man.* These first three examples are alone so weighty as to make the case virtually by themselves for Jesus' dependence on Ezekiel. But there are other parallels:
  - Ezekiel alone of all the prophets is depicted as experiencing the Holy Spirit "entering" him; so also Jesus (Ezek. 2:2; Mark 1:9-11 par.). Heaven is not recorded to have been "opened" for any Hebrew prophet except Ezekiel; so also Jesus (Ezek. 1:1; Mark 1:10).
  - God will be Israel's shepherd who will "seek the lost," according to Ezekiel, just as Jesus spoke of a good shepherd who

"came to seek out and to save the lost" (Ezek. 34:16; Mark 6:34; Luke 15:3-7; 19:10).

- Like Ezekiel, Jesus spoke in parables, figures, and riddles. No other prophet is commanded to speak a parable to rebellious Israel (Ezek. 17:2; 24:3). Ezekiel does so expressly as the son of man. In Abbott's words, "We can hardly fail to recognize that, in teaching thus through parables, Jesus would have in view the prophet who was expressly bidden to teach in parables."[2]

- Jesus used Ezek. 17:22-24 as a foil for his parable of the mustard seed. The "lofty cedar" to which Ezekiel refers becomes the lowly mustard plant in Jesus' reversed values. Jesus may also have taken up Ezekiel's "I bring low the high tree, I make high the low tree" (17:24) in his otherwise unparalleled statement, "All who exalt themselves will be humbled, and all who humble themselves will be exalted" (Matt. 23:12; Luke 14:11). This adage would have come directly out of their joint experience of the lowliness of the "son of man." Also, Matt. 25:31-33 seems to echo Ezek. 34:17.

- Ezekiel censures those who "trust in their righteousness" (33:12-13), a theme Jesus takes up in his parable of the Pharisee and the publican, in which he explicitly challenges those like the Pharisee "who trusted in themselves that they were righteous" (Luke 18:9).

- Jesus often ended his parables with the warning, "Let anyone with ears to hear listen!" a phrase he may have taken from the other great parabler in Scripture, Ezekiel: "Let those who will hear, hear" (Ezek. 3:27; Matt. 13:9, 43; Mark 4:9, 23; Luke 8:8; 14:35; *Gos. Thom.* 8:4; 21:10; 24:2; 63:4; 65:8; 96:3). According to Abbott, no prophet but Ezekiel used these words.

- Jesus also seems to have found the basis of his saying about Sodom (Matt. 11:22-23 // Luke 10:14) in Ezek. 16:48.

- Ezekiel, notes Abbott, is the only prophet to predict in clear terms the construction of a new temple as well as the destruction of the old one. Jesus does the same, though metaphorically.[3]

Most striking is Jesus' high degree of familiarity with the book of Ezekiel, without any sign of the early church's predilection for prooftexting. The Gospel accounts show no sign of the formative influence of Ezekiel in the construction of proofs from prophecy, or in the prophetic development of "new" sayings of Jesus shaped by material in Ezekiel. Jesus seems to have fully heard and digested Ezekiel much as Ezekiel himself had done: he ate the scroll entire. Hence Jesus' sovereign freedom is not only in following Ezekiel but, in at least one case, in rejecting Ezekiel's narrowness (Ezek. 22:26). The evidence that Jesus knew and used Ezekiel in developing his own parables and teachings makes it more probable that Jesus took from Ezekiel at least aspects of Ezekiel's understanding of *ben 'adam* as well. I suggest that Ezekiel served as the immediate inspiration for Jesus' use of that idiom as a self-reference—virtually, as with Ezekiel, as a personal nickname that nevertheless still possessed its prophetic and collective resonances. But there was this difference: unlike Ezekiel, Jesus never spoke in the name of God, or claimed that God spoke to or through him. Thus there was no one to call Jesus "son of man"—*except Jesus himself.*

Glossary

archetype: an inherited pattern or mode of thought that is derived from the experience of the species and that is present in the individual's unconscious. Because such patterns or modes are in the collective unconscious, they cannot be known except by their effects. *Archetypal images,* on the other hand, are the "local" images that draw on contemporary cultural symbols and that point beyond themselves to unconscious archetypes. Carl Jung has elaborated on this idea, which derives from Plato and Philo (a first-century Jewish philosopher). See appendix 2, "Philo on the Archetypes."

Domination System: a world-encompassing system characterized by unjust economic relations, oppressive political relations, patriarchal gender relations, prejudiced racial or ethnic relations, hierarchical power relations, and the use of violence to maintain them; in short, "civilization." See my *Engaging the Powers: Discernment and Resistance in a World of Domination* (Minneapolis: Fortress Press, 1992), chaps. 1–5.

ego: the conscious aspect of the self, subordinate to the self, and related to the self like a part to the whole (Carl Jung, *Aion,* CW 9.2 [1959], 51).

God-image: depictions of God, drawing on cultural, religious, and personal imagery. Not to be confused with God, who is beyond representation. The God-image is not something *invented* but *experienced,* and it comes upon a person spontaneously. It can be altered once it has been raised to consciousness (Carl Jung, *Aion,* CW 9.2, 194).

heuristic: something that serves as an aid to discovery or to problem solving by experimental or trial-and-error methods.

Holy Spirit: the power of transformation. More specifically, "The Spirit is that impulse in the psyche that is capable of opposing the unconscious surge of instinct, in order to transform nature into a conscious human experience." (John Perkins, *The Forbidden Self* [Boston: Shambhala, 1992], 39.)

imaginal plane: produces a third kind of knowing, intermediate between the world of ideas, on the one hand, and the object world of sense perception on the other. The imaginal possesses extension and dimension, figures and colors, but lacks full materiality and hence cannot be perceived by the senses. In dreams and visions, for example, we perceive the action *as if* it were staged on the physical plane, but it is not. We may falsely assume that these images are subjective creations of our psyches, or pseudo-objective delusions, like hallucinations. But we do not make all of them up. We imagine them, to be sure, but often something real evokes our imagination.

individuation: the process of becoming oneself, integrating the various aspects of ourselves, conscious and unconscious, negative and positive, strengths and weaknesses, to bring about the unification of body-mind-spirit.

myth: not a made-up story, fiction, or false idea. Rather, it refers to those founding narratives that provide whole societies with orientation to the world.

numinous: something filled with a sense or experience of the holy, the transcendent, or the Other.

projection: seeing in others unconscious aspects of ourselves.

self: at a personal level, one's self is the totality of one's being. But because one's own self is related to everything that is, the personal self participates in the totality of selves, and, by extension, with the total Self, which, from a psychological point of view, is indistinguishable from God. Hence, Carl Jung capitalizes the term *Self* when it refers to this transpersonal level.

Notes

The volume epigraph comes from Albert Schweitzer, *The Quest of the Historical Jesus* (Baltimore: Johns Hopkins University Press, in association with the Albert Schweitzer Institute, 1998), 399.

Preface

1. The Powers trilogy consists of *Naming the Powers: The Language of Power in the New Testament* (Philadelphia: Fortress Press, 1984); *Unmasking the Powers: The Invisible Forces That Determine Human Existence* (Philadelphia: Fortress Press, 1986); and *Engaging the Powers: Discernment and Resistance in a World of Domination* (Minneapolis: Fortress Press, 1992). There is a summary of the trilogy, focusing on the third volume, entitled *The Powers That Be: Theology for a New Millennium* (New York: Doubleday, 1998). I have, in addition, written books that apply the Powers analysis to practical issues: *Violence and Nonviolence in South Africa* (Philadelphia: New Society, 1987); and *When the Powers Fall: Reconciliation in the Healing of Nations* (Minneapolis: Fortress Press, 1998). I also served as editor for *Peace Is the Way: Writings on Nonviolence from the Fellowship of Reconciliation* (Maryknoll, N.Y.: Orbis Books, 2000).

2. An M.Div. thesis by a Union Theological Seminary student, Kathleen Peterson Nicol, first introduced me to interpretations of the son of man akin to those discussed in this book. Her arguments were cogent, but so at odds with my own indoctrination that I was unable to grasp their importance until I was introduced to the thought of Elizabeth Boyden Howes.

Introduction

1. To use Carl Jung's terms, the son of the man may be considered an image of the archetype of wholeness, which mediates between the transcendent Self and the individual ego.

Part 1
The Original Impulse of Jesus

1. Daniel C. Matt, "'New-Ancient Words': The Aura of Secrecy in the Zohar," in *Gershom Scholem's Major Trends in Jewish Mysticism Fifty Years After*, ed. P. Schäfer and J. Dan (Tübingen: Mohr/Siebeck, 1993), 201.

2. Ibid.

Chapter 1
The Human Being in the Quest for the Historical Jesus

1. Brian Stock, *Listening for the Text: On the Uses of the Past* (Baltimore: Johns Hopkins University Press, 1990), 80–81.

2. Lynn M. Poland, "The New Criticism, Neoorthodoxy, and the New Testament," *Journal of Religion* 65 (1985): 473. The bankruptcy of objectivism has been pointed out redundantly, but a surprising number of scholars still embrace it. Against that view, Theodor Adorno writes: "The detached observer is as much entangled as the active participant." So also Sheila Rowbotham: "All revolutionary movements create their own way of seeing" (cited in Catherine A. MacKinnon, *Toward a Feminist Theory of the State* [Cambridge: Harvard University Press, 1989], 106, 115).

3. Wendy Doniger O'Flaherty, "The Uses and Misuses of Other Peoples' Myths," *JAAR* 54 (1986): 219–39.

4. Walter Kasper, cited in Hal Childs, *The Myth of the Historical Jesus and the Evolution of Consciousness*, SBL Dissertation Series 179 (Atlanta: Scholars Press, 2000), 85.

5. Childs, *Myth of the Historical Jesus*, 227–28.

6. It is also true that others study the past in order to prevent change.

7. I use "son of man" when referring to the expression in the Hebrew Bible or intertestamental writings, since there the expression lacks definite articles. I use "the son of the man" when dealing with the New Testament and later writings, since that is what the Greek says.

8. Bruce J. Malina, *The Social Gospel of Jesus: The Kingdom of God in Mediterranean Perspective* (Minneapolis: Fortress Press, 2001), 7.

9. Richard Rohr, "Let Us Be Up and Building," *Radical Grace* 6 (1993): 1.

10. "Missa Campesina," from Songs from the Batahola Cultural Center in Nicaragua, includes lines such as these:

> You are the God of the poor,
> the human and simple God,
> the God who sweats in the street,
> the God with the weather-beaten face.
> That's why I can talk to you
> the way I talk with my people,
> Because you are God the worker
> and Christ is a worker, too.

11. Gerald O'Collins, *Interpreting Jesus* (London: G. Chapman, 1983), x.

12. W. Taylor Stevenson, *History as Myth* (New York: Seabury Press, 1969), 6.

13. Bruce Chilton, *Rabbi Jesus* (New York: Doubleday, 2000); Betty Sue Flowers, "Practicing Politics in the Economic Myth," *The Salt Journal* 2 (2000): 53.

14. Walter Wink, *Engaging the Powers: Discernment and Resistance in a World of Domination* (Minneapolis: Fortress Press, 1992); idem, *The Powers That Be: Theology for a New Millennium* (New York: Doubleday, 1998).

15. Poland, "New Criticism," 468.

16. Eugen Rosenstock-Huessy, "Farewell to Descartes," *Out of Revolution* (New York: William Morrow, 1969), 751.

Part 2
The Anthropic Revelation: The Human Being

1. This count includes Matt. 18:11 and Luke 9:56, both of which are poorly attested and probably on loan from the story of Zacchaeus. Not included in the total number of son-of-the-man sayings is the quotation of Ps. 8:4 in Heb. 2:6, which most commentators read as referring to humanity in general.

2. Mark 2:10, 28; 8:31, 38; 9:9, 12, 31; 10:33, 45; 13:26; 14:21, 21, 41, 62; Matt. 8:20; 9:6; 10:23; 11:19; 12:8, 32, 40; 13:37, 41; 16:13, 27, 28; 17:9, 12, 22; [18:11]; 19:28; 20:18, 28; 24:27, 30, 30, 37, 39, 44; 25:31; 26:2, 24, 24, 45, 64; Luke 5:24; 6:5, 22; 7:34; 9:22, 26, 44, [56,] 58; 11:30; 12:8, 10, 40; 17:22, 24, 26, 30; 18:8, 31; 19:10; 21:27, 36; 22:22, 48, 69; 24:7; John 1:51; 3:13, 14; 5:27 (the only instance in the Gospels lacking both definite articles); 6:27, 53, 62; 8:28; 9:35; 12:23, 34, 34; 13:31.

3. Joachim Jeremias thought that in cases where one version of a saying had "I" and the other "the son of the man," the simple "I" was to be preferred to the solemn son-of-man expression (*New Testament Theology* [New York: Charles Scribner's Sons, 1971], 259–60). But an analysis of each case shows that the earliest form is sometimes one and sometimes the other. In Matt. 5:11, "my" is secondary and "son of man" primary in the Lukan parallel, 6:22. In Luke's version, Jesus does not fully identify himself with the son of man, whereas Matthew does so identify him, consistent with his tendency to elevate the Christology of his sources. "Son of man" is also primary in Luke 12:10 (where Mark 3:28 changes "son of man" in Q to "sons of men" to avoid saying that it is all right to blaspheme the son of the man), and in Luke 12:8 (for the same reasons as in Luke 6:22). On the other hand, "I" seems to be the earlier tradition in Luke 22:29 (compare "the son of the man" in Matt. 19:28). It seems impossible to decide whether Mark 10:45 (with "the son of the man") or Luke 22:27 (without) is the more authentic. Clearly, "I" and "the son of the man" were treated on occasion as if they were interchangeable, though they served different semantic fields.

4. With a few exceptions (John 12:34 twice; Luke 24:7), "the son of the man" appears in the Gospels only on the lips of Jesus (and none of these are real exceptions, since in each case Jesus is being quoted by someone else). Outside the Gospels, the expression is used in the New Testament only in Acts 7:56 and in Rev. 1:13 and 14:14. The latter two references lack the definite articles and should be translated "one like a human being," but this figure is identified with the risen Christ in 1:1, so

these verses also belong in the database. Matthew also adds a number of son-of-the-man references (10:23; 13:37, 41; 16:28; [18:11]; 24:30; 25:31; 26:2). Luke adds 17:22; 18:8; 19:10; 21:36; 22:48; and 24:7.

Chapter 2
The Enigma of the Son of the Man

1. Jeremias, *New Testament Theology* (New York: Charles Scribner's Sons, 1971), 258–59. Alan F. Segal suggests that there is no need to posit a pre-Christian savior model who came equipped with a fixed title and job description. Rather, the debate between Judaism and Christianity proceeded partially along midrashic or exegetical lines. There was no "son of man" redeemer figure with whom Jesus might have identified. Christology built up through exegesis rather than through hypothetical, pre-existent titles. "Christians, believing in his translation to heaven, could have applied to Jesus a number of passages describing either God's principal angel or some other divine but anthropomorphic manifestation described in Israel's scriptures." The titles for Jesus emerged after Jesus' life, as a result of exegesis. "Insistence on divine perquisites for God's principal assistant was apparently not unique to Christianity and became exactly the detail which put Christianity in the category of heresy from the rabbinic perspective" (Alan F. Segal, *Two Powers in Heaven: Early Rabbinic Reports about Christianity and Gnosticism*, Studies in Judaism in Late Antiquity 25 [Leiden: E. J. Brill, 1977], x–xi).

2. Mark 6:4 par.; Luke 13:33. But the first is a well-known proverb and the second appears to be a proverb as well. In John 1:21, Jesus is depicted *rejecting* the title "the prophet." So "the son of the man" appears to be virtually the *only* way Jesus referred to himself.

3. The exceptions are Acts 7:56, Rev. 1:13, and 14:14. Cyril of Jerusalem, *Catechesis* 10.4 and Hegesippus, cited by Eusebius, *Ecclesiastical History* 2.23.13, are rare cases in which "the son of the man" is found on the lips of someone other than Jesus.

4. Barnabas 12:10; Justin *Dialogues* 31.1; 76.1; Ignatius, *Ephesians* 20:2; Irenaeus, *Against Heresy* 3.16.7; 17.1

5. Edwin A. Abbott examines the data. See his *Son of Man, or Contributions to the Study of the Thoughts of Jesus* (Cambridge: Cambridge University Press, 1910), 69–71.

6. Geza Vermes, "Appendix E: The Use of *bar nash/bar nasha* in Jewish Aramaic," in *An Aramaic Approach to the Gospels and Acts*, by Matthew Black, 3d ed. (Oxford: Clarendon Press, 1967). Vermes cites eleven texts, but two are merely variants of the same story.

7. Arthur Dewey reminds me that President Richard Nixon was fond of this form of third-person self-address, as was the athlete Bo Jackson.

8. Douglas R. A. Hare, *The Son of Man Tradition* (Minneapolis: Fortress Press, 1990), 23.

9. Morna Hooker, "Is the Son of Man Problem Really Insoluble?" in *Text and Interpretation: Studies in the New Testament Presented to Matthew Black*, ed. Ernest Best and R. McL. Wilson (Cambridge: Cambridge University Press, 1979), 157.

10. Ulrich Luz, "The Son of Man in Matthew: Heavenly Judge or Human Christ?" *JSNT* 48 (1992): 7–8.

11. Hebrews 2:6 confirms this. In quoting Ps. 8:4, which refers to humanity in general, the author reverts to the anarthrous form (lacking definite articles). This shows that the translators knew just what they were doing when, in reference to Jesus, they used the definite articles.

12. Vermes, "Appendix E"; Maurice Casey, *Son of Man* (London: SPCK, 1979); Barnabas Lindars, *Jesus Son of Man* (London: SPCK, 1983); and, omitting the mistranslation theory, Hare, *Son of Man Tradition*. Bruce Chilton counters: "Why should the article appear consistently, if an occasional mistranslation is at issue?" ("The Son of Man: Human and Heavenly," in *The Four Gospels*, ed. F. van Segbroek et al. [Louvain: Louvain University Press, 1992], 217).

13. Philipp Vielhauer, "Jesus und der Menschensohn: Zur Diskussion mit Heinz Eduard Tödt und Eduard Schweizer," *ZTK* 60 (1963): 133–77.

14. The exception is John 5:27.

15. Hare notes that the "messianic secret" in Mark is kept from the public until the end of the story, yet Jesus is represented referring to himself publicly as "the son of the man" in early chapters (2:10, 28). This suggests that the expression "the son of the man" is not understood by Mark as a messianic title (*Son of Man Tradition*, 181–82).

16. Ibid.

17. Georg Fohrer, "son of," *TDNT* 8:345–47. "Sons of the prophets," however, are not the offspring of prophets, but simply "prophets" (1 Kings 20:35), just as "your sons" in Matt. 12:27 are members of the same faction (Joachim Jeremias, *Jerusalem in the Time of Jesus* [Philadelphia: Fortress Press, 1969], 177).

18. Herman Waetjen (*The Origin and Destiny of Humanness* [Corte Madera, Calif.: Omega Books, 1976]).

19. See, for example, Walther Zimmerli, *Ezekiel*, ET *Ezekiel*, 2 vols., trans. R.E. Clements and J. D. Martin, Hermeneia (Philadelphia: Fortress Press, 1979–83). The scholars who atomize the Ezekiel text show no awareness of the numinosity of the material they are carving up so rationalistically. For our purposes it does not matter if Ezekiel is the source for this entire vision. It is all the same whether we are asking what the vision meant to Ezekiel or what it meant to his "school" or to his contemporaries or to the successors whose own religious visions were modeled on it. The remark of V. Herntrich is typical of the hypercritical approach: "Chapter 1 is clearly a production," he writes, concluding that no true prophetic experience is reflected in the text ("Ezechielprobleme," *ZAW* 61 [1933]: 79). David Halperin, who accepts Ezekiel 1 as essentially a unity, nevertheless regards whatever goes back to Ezekiel as hallucinatory, and all else as fabrication (*The Faces of the Chariot: Early Jesish Responses to Ezekiel's Vision*, Texte und Studien zum autiken Judentum 16 [Tübingen: Mohr/Siebeck, 1988]). There is no recognition by these writers of the nature of religious experience, no appreciation for the reality of the visions, and no sense that the visions might have anything to do with the living God. For the more recent consensus that Ezekiel is more or less a unity, see John F. Kutsko, *Between Heaven and Earth: Divine Presence and Absence in the Book of Ezekiel* (Winona Lake, Ind.: Eisenbrauns, 2000), 5.

20. Ithamar Gruenwald, *From Apocalypticism to Gnosticism* (Frankfurt: Peter Lang, 1988), ii. Jung's research into the "hallucinations" of schizophrenics revealed that the "madness" acted out by the patient, and the symbols that appeared sponta-

neously in their dreams, visions, and auditions, were in fact meaningful within the person's pathology. Thus "hallucinations" can no longer be treated reductionistically, as pure psychic "noise." Unfortunately, many people still operate with the old assumptions.

21. 4QSongs of the Sabbath Sacrifice (4QShirShabb); 4QPseudo-Ezekiel (4Q386 [4QpsEzek]).

22. This list only loosely approximates chronological order. It is not possible to date some of these documents within four to six centuries of their actual writing. Ithamar Gruenwald demonstrates that Jewish mysticism starts (contra Gershom Scholem) in Hebrew Scripture ("Reflections on the Nature and Origins of Jewish Mysticism," in *Gershom Scholem's Major Trends in Jewish Mysticism, Fifty Years After: Proceedings of the Sixth International Conference on the History of Jewish Mysticism*, ed. P. Schäfer and J. Dan [Tübingen: Mohr/Siebeck, 1993], 25–48). Gruenwald comments, "We have to assume that a straight line leads from the scriptural forms of theophany and angelophany to the visions of the apocalyptics and Merkavah mystics, and beyond that to the medieval Qabbalah-mystics" (27). Michael Fishbane expands the field even more, to include the ecstatic states ordinary rabbis experienced studying Scripture. Citing several convincing examples, he concludes, "The midrashic exposition leaves no doubt that for the sages the meditative linking of the words of Scripture could induce some sort of mystical trance" ("Response" to Gruenwald, ibid., 49–57, at 54).

23. Jerome said that Jews could not read Ezekiel until they were thirty. His source, Origen, was right not to specify an age; no fixed age was set (Halperin, *Faces of the Chariot*, 26 n. 17). A student who expounded the *merkabah* (the throne chariot vision of Ezekiel 1) without his teacher's permission, it was believed, became leprous (*y. Hag.* 77b; cited by Christopher C. Rowland, "The Influence of the First Chapter of Ezekiel on Jewish and Early Christian Literature" [Ph.D. diss., Christ's College, Cambridge, 1974], 207). *M. Hag.* 2:1 forbids anyone to expound "the Chariot before one alone, unless he is a Sage that understands of his own knowledge"; see also *T. Hag.* 2.1. The Jewish exegetes Rabbi and R. Isaac (ca. 160 C.E.) permitted Ezekiel 1 to be expounded, but they excluded the description of the figure on the throne (1:26-27) and the Glory (1.28) (ibid., 157).

24. *b. Hag.* 14b.

25. Bruce Chilton, *Rabbi Jesus* (New York: Doubleday, 2000), 50–51. Chilton also sees Ezekiel as formative for Jesus: "Jesus learned to become Ezekiel's text" (52; see also 53, 57, and 158).

26. In each religion, "the minds of the members are filled, from childhood onwards, with a certain set of images and symbols that structure their imaginative world. . . . When those rare persons who were gifted and trained for esoteric practices embarked on their meditations, it was within the same consensus. They saw, heard, felt, and smelt an environment that may have been novel and full of wonders and surprises, but was still controlled by their faith and expectations. Only when the mystic passed beyond the inner senses was he or she liberated from what had been learned through the outer ones. Then, as all students of mysticism know, the descriptions become halting: the mystic cannot find words for the experience. It is all light and unity, and paradoxical categories where the rational mind has no foothold" (Joscelyn Godwin, "Annals of the Invisible College," *Lapis* 10 [n.d.]: 73–74).

So also Dan Merkur: "The very fact that Catholic, Sufi, and Jewish mystics have apologized for experiences that they did not wish to experience proves that the experiences were real" ("Unitive Experience and the State of Trance," in *Mystical Union in Judaism, Christianity, and Islam,* ed. M. Idel and B. McGinn [New York: Continuum, 1996], 143).

27. We might distinguish between anthropomorphism as simile or metaphor and anthropomorphism as theophany. In the first, one speaks poetically, likening God to some aspect of human beings, as in Exod. 6:6—"I will redeem you with an outstretched arm." Here most readers would not think to ask whether God really has an arm. But when prophets and seers "saw" God, as it were, in human form, they really thought that God had human form. The Jewish scholar of mysticism Elliot R. Wolfson notes that the text of Ezek. 1:26 depicts God as actually human, not figuratively. This is not merely a linguistic representation of God, Wolfson insists. One must be careful to distinguish between rhetoric and religious experience. The prophets, according to the sages, not only spoke of God in figurative language; they heard and saw God in the shape of a "Man." "At least some of the rabbis understood full well that biblical faith demanded a view of God who appeared to human beings in various physical [human] forms" (Elliott R. Wolfson, *Through a Speculum That Shines: Vision and Imagination in Medieval Jewish Mysticism* [Princeton: Princeton University Press, 1994], 49). Wolfson gives a host of examples from Jewish sources (37–49). So also Roelof van den Broek: "[T]he prophet Ezekiel . . . saw the Glory of God in the shape of a man: the first manifestation of the transcendent God appears in human form. This and a specific interpretation of the creation of man in Genesis eventually led to the myth of the heavenly Man" (*Studies in Gnosticism and Alexandrian Christianity,* Nag Hammadi and Manichaean Studies 39 [Leiden: E. J. Brill, 1996], 19). Speaking of the *imago Dei,* Jarl Fossum notes, "[I]t is a thoroughly Jewish idea that it is the *body* of man which was made on the model of the Man [God], who is now present in all men as the spiritual element. . . . If Adam is an image of God, there must be a way in which God or a certain aspect of [God] is human-like . . ." ("Jewish-Christian Christology and Jewish Mysticism," *VC* 37 [1983]: 268–69). Edwin. A. Abbott was among the first modern scholars (1910) to understand that Ezekiel's vision implied the humanity of God, suggesting that *ben 'adam* be translated "son of the human or humane God," or "son of the divine Man" (*Son of Man,* 651).

28. Jewish Merkabah mysticism reached the same insight. As Gilles Quispel notes, the *morphē or* "form" of God is identical with *kabōd* or "glory" in Ezekiel 1, and both are equivalent to *eikōn* or "image," for human beings are made after the image of God and thus are faint copies of the divine form ("Ezekiel 1:26 in Jewish Mysticism and Gnosis," *VC* 34 [1980]: 9). E. A. Abbott puts it more simply: "Thus the Man on the throne in heaven addresses the prophet as 'son of man' on earth, as much as to say, 'Thou, made in my image, art destined to be superior to the Beasts on earth, as I am superior to them in heaven; and thou art to go as my messenger to deliver Israel from the Beasts [the Domination System]' " (*Son of Man,* 113). The scientist/mystic Emanuel Swedenborg (1688–1772) received visions of angels who "are accustomed to say that the Lord alone is man, and that it is from Him that they are men, and that each one is a man in the measure of his reception of the Lord." Hence "all heaven in the aggregate reflects a single man" (*Heaven and Its Wonders*

and Hell [New York: American Swedenborgian Printing and Publication Society, 1900], 49–50). All we have to do to make Swedenborg's insight correspond to the son of the man is to add an eschatological element. Another great clairvoyant, William Blake, said much the same.

29. Jürgen Moltmann, "The Category of the New in Theology," in *The Future of the Presence of Shared Hope*, ed. M. Muckenhirn (New York: Sheed & Ward, 1968), 31.

30. Gerd Theissen, *Biblical Faith: An Evolutionary Approach*, trans. J. Bowden (Philadelphia: Fortress Press, 1985), 122.

31. Seventeenth-century scientist, inventor, and philosopher Blaise Pascal hurled this challenge against the philosophers: "Learn that man is infinitely beyond the reach of man, and hear from your Master what is your true condition, so far unknown to you" (*Pascal's Pensées* [1670; New York: Pantheon, 1950], 151, no. 258). Jon Sobrino writes, "The crucial point about Christology is that it calls into question the very thing that the natural human being takes completely for granted. Natural human beings assume that they know what human nature is and what divine nature is" (*Christology at the Crossroads: A Latin American Approach*, trans. J. Drury [Maryknoll, N.Y.: Orbis Books, 1978], 330). The Greek poet Pindar (d. 438 B.C.E.) reflects Greek ontology when he says, "Become what you already are" (*Pithian Odes* II.72). But human beings are an eschatological reality, a future, emergent work in progress, still well behind our realization.

32. Ibn 'Arabi, *Book of Theophanies*, final canto, in Henry Corbin, *Creative Imagination in the Sufism of Ibn 'Arabi*, Bollingen Series 91 (Princeton: Princeton University Press, 1969), 174.

33. See Walter Wink, *Engaging the Powers: Discernment and Resistance in a World of Domination* (Minneapolis: Fortress Press, 1992), chap. 14.

34. The Christian "is no longer what he was, but he is not yet what he is, so that he is waiting for what he has" (Dan O. Via Jr., "Justification and Deliverance: Existential Dialectic," *Sci. rel.* 13 [1971]: 207).

35. Bill Wylie Kellermann, "Genesis as Resistance," *The Witness* (October 1992) 21. See also John F. Kutsko, "Will the Real *Selem 'elohim* Please Stand Up? The Image of God in the Book of Ezekiel," *SBLSP 1998* (Atlanta: Scholars Press, 1998), 55–85.

36. John F. Kutsko, "Ezekiel's Anthropology and Its Ethical Implications," in *The Book of Ezekiel: Theological and Anthropological Perspectives*, ed. M. S. Odell and J. T. Strong, SBL Symposium Series 9 (Atlanta: Scholars Press, 2000), 119–41.

37. Gerhard von Rad, *Old Testament Theology* (New York: Harper & Row, 1962), 1:146.

38. Moshe Greenberg, *Ezekiel 1–20*, Anchor Bible 22 (Garden City, N.Y.: Doubleday, 1983), 44.

39. Walther Eichrodt, *Ezekiel*, trans. C. Quin, Old Testament Library (Philadelphia: Westminster Press, 1970), 55.

40. God appears elsewhere in the Hebrew Bible in human form: God's feet (Exod. 24:10), hand, face, and backside (Exod. 33:22-23). God is called "a human being" in Gen. 32:24 (*'ish*); 18:2, 16, 22. Daniel 7:9 describes God as an old man with white hair, sitting on a throne. *Genesis Rab.* 27:1, commenting on Gen. 6:5 (Soncino edition, p. 220), declares, "Great is the power of the prophets, who liken

the image [that is, the human being] to its Creator!" The expositor then (I think correctly) interprets the "human being" (*'adam*) of Dan. 8:16 as God: "Then someone appeared standing before me, having the appearance of a man, and I heard a human voice by the Ulai, calling, 'Gabriel' " (but in 9:21 Gabriel is called "the man" [*'ish*]) (Halperin, *Faces of the Chariot*, 251). The thirteenth-century French exegete Isaac ben Judah ha-Levi makes the connection between Genesis 1 and Ezek. 1:26 explicit: "Let us make man in that very image that the Holy One, blessed be He, showed to the prophets in the form of an anthropos" (quoted in *Tosafot ha-Shalem: Commentary on the Bible*, ed. Gellis, 1:61; cited by Wolfson, *Through a Speculum That Shines*, 211).

41. Jean Burnier-Genton thinks that the image of God refers to the inner spiritual being of persons (*Ezékiel fils d'homme*, Essais bibliques 5 [Geneva: Labor et Fides, 1982], 70–73). But Ezekiel, and the whole tradition of Jewish mysticism that flowed from it, sees the *imago Dei* precisely in its bodily form (see the Shi'ur Qomah speculations below, chap. 15). David Halperin shows how the Targum to Ezekiel 1 attempted to soften or eliminate that vision's anthropomorphisms. Thus in Ezek. 1:27 the twice-repeated phrase "from the appearance of his loins" is replaced by "an appearance of glory which the eye could not look at and which it was impossible to contemplate." (So also at Ezek. 8:2.) Similarly, "the hand of the Lord" in 1:3 becomes "the spirit of prophecy from before the Lord" (so also 3:14, 22; 8:1; 33:22; 37:1; 40:1). For "visions of God" (1:1), the Targum has "the vision of the glory of the Shechinah of the Lord"; and for "from its place" in 3:12 the Targum has "from the place of the dwelling of his Shechinah." But the most drastic expedient is in one manuscript of a targumic Tosefta to Ezek. 1:26, which replaces "the appearance of a human being" with "the form of Jacob our father upon it from above." From other texts it becomes clear that Jacob is not seated on the throne; rather, his likeness is *carved* on the side of the throne, possibly as a reminder that a celestial embodiment of Israel (= Jacob) is perpetually in God's sight (Halperin, *Faces of the Chariot*, 121).

Some of the rabbis tried to play down Merkabah mysticism by minimizing Ezekiel's vision in favor of the revelation given to all Israel at Sinai. "R. Hoshaiah said: The lowliest person in the days of Moses saw what Ezekiel, the greatest of the prophets, never saw—people with whom the Shekinah spoke face to face, as it is said, 'The Lord spoke with you face to face' (Deut. 5:4)" (*Deut. Rab.* 7:8). Again, "Twenty-two thousand chariots descended with the Holy One blessed be He [at Sinai], and each and every chariot was like the chariot which Ezekiel ben Buzi saw" (Quoted from Ira Chernus, *Mysticism in Rabbinic Judaism: Studies in the History of Midrash*, Studia Judaica 11 [Berlin: de Gruyter, 1982], 21, 27). Comments such as these served as a corrective to the elitism toward which all forms of mysticism are inclined; but they also betray the condescension of rationalists toward mysticism.

42. "*The quest for what is truly human transcends the human race.* In the last resort humans cannot define what constitutes their humanity. It transcends them. . . . Judaism, Christianity, and Islam agree that the humanness of the human race is grounded in the mercy of God" (Geiko Müller-Fahrenholz, *The Art of Forgiveness: Theological Reflections on Healing and Reconciliation* [Geneva: WCC Publications, 1997], xi).

43. Edward Edinger finds a possible clue about psychic inflation in the doctrinal battle between Eastern and Western churches over the *filioque* ("and the son")

clause. The Western church believed that the Holy Spirit proceeded from both the Father and the Son; in the East, only from the Father. Psychologically, says Edinger, by allowing the Son, who brings consciousness to the Godhead, to share in generating the Holy Spirit, the ego is given a special function. "The whole Western tradition then has built into it, in its mythology, an importance to the ego that the Eastern tradition does not grant." Because the ego now has a part in the divine drama, it is unshielded from possible inflation, unlike the Eastern mystics (*The New God-Image* [Wilmette, Ill.: Chiron, 1996], 99). Divinization also holds a significant place in Islamic Sufism. Frithjof Schuon says that, for any religion, "all Revelation is a humanization of the divine for the sake of a deification of the human" (*Islam and the Perennial Philosophy* [London: World of Islam Festival, 1976], 40). Those of us who have been raised in Western church traditions are fairly defenseless in the face of such grand aspirations. Our egos all too quickly identify with the deep Self at our core—the image of God—and launch into the stratosphere of delusional self-worship and narcissism.

44. This theme of becoming human rather than divine is not foreign to the Western Christian tradition. Thus the German mystic Hildegard of Bingen (1098–1179) could utter, "Become what you are—human, realize your humanity!" (*O Vis Aeternitatis* [Freiburg: Freiburger Musik Forum, 1997], 17). The *Acts of Andrew* notes the obverse: the lack of self-knowledge. "We leave you to be what you were, although you do not know what you are" (*NTApoc* 2:422).

I sometimes use "divine" as an adjective, but not as a predicate adjective. To speak of "divine" love is simply to say "God's" love. But to say "Jesus is divine," or "I am divine," equates Jesus, or oneself, with God.

45. William Stringfellow, *A Private and Public Faith* (Grand Rapids: Eerdmans, 1965), 13.

46. Compare Cyril of Alexandria: the Son took the form of a slave, to make the slave a son (or daughter) (*In Ioannem* 9.1 [Pusey 2, 482]; in *The Image of God in Man according to Cyril of Alexandria*, by Walter Burghart [Washington, D.C.: Catholic University of America Press, 1957], 165).

47. Jung comments that we should make clear to ourselves what it means when God becomes a human being. It means nothing less than a world-shattering transformation of God ("Answer to Job," *Psychology and Religion: West and East, CW* 11:401). Edward Edinger interprets Jung's statement as referring to the humanization of the unconscious on all levels. The unconscious is not human. The personal unconscious is infantile. The collective unconscious is animal, or inorganic, or divine. In this view, God becoming human means something like the humanization of the universe, or the humanization of reality. Reality takes on a human face, has become friendly to humanity rather than being the brute, indifferent nature that we perceive it to be. At the time of the creation, God revealed Godself in Nature; now God wants to be more specific and become a human being (*Transformation of the God-Image* [Toronto: Inner City Books, 1992], 71).

48. See also Ezek. 3:23-24; Dan. 10:9-11; *1 Enoch* 14:24-25.

49. Outside Ezekiel, *ben 'adam* is used in the Hebrew Scriptures collectively of humanity in general, e.g., Num. 23:19; Isa. 51:12; 56:2; Jer. 49:18; Pss. 8:4; 80:15, 17; Job 16:21; 25:6; 35:8. Its application to a specific individual is peculiar to Ezekiel.

50. Jung: "God wants to become man. What is more, in Ezekiel we meet for the first time the title 'Son of Man,' which Yahweh significantly uses in addressing the prophet, presumably to indicate that he is a son of the 'Man' on the throne and hence a prefiguration of the much later revelation in Christ" ("Answer to Job," *CW* 11:421).

51. Jung: "The self is the Anthropos above and beyond this world," and in it is contained the freedom and dignity of the individual. "Here Ezekiel has seen the essential content of the unconscious, namely *the idea of the higher man* by whom Yahweh was morally defeated and whom he was later to become" (*Psychology and Religion: West and East*, CW 11: 292, 420).

52. Ezek. 24:2; 43:11. See Ellen F. Davis, *Swallowing the Scroll: Textuality and the Dynamics of Discourse in Ezekiel's Prophecy*, Bible and Literature Series 21 (Sheffield: Almond Press, 1989).

53. Ezek. 5:15, 17; 17:21; 21:17, 32; 23:34; 26:14; 28:10; 30:12; 34:24; 36:36; 37:14; 39:5.

54. Davis, *Swallowing the Scroll*, 82–83.

55. "Son of man" was certainly understood at Qumran as Ezekiel's prophetic role; in 4QPseudo-Ezekiel this phrase appears: "And he said, 'Son of man, prophesy over the bones' " (Florentino García Martínez, *The Dead Sea Scrolls Translated* [Leiden: E. J. Brill, 1992], 286–87). Given the frequency of God's address of Ezekiel as *ben 'adam*, one would have expected the address to become standard prophetic practice. Yet I am able to find only one similar use: Dan. 8:15b-16. "Then someone appeared standing before me, having the appearance of a man (*geber*), and I heard a human ('*adam*) voice by the Ulai, calling, 'Gabriel, help this (one) understand the vision.' " Here Gabriel has the appearance of a man, and the voice calling to him can only be that of God, and it is a *human* voice. Daniel prostrates himself, but the voice speaks again: "Understand, Humanchild (*ben 'adam*), that the vision is for the time of the end" (8:17b).

56. Margaret S. Odell speculates that Ezekiel 1–5 is a coherent unity that should be interpreted as an account of a prolonged counterinitiation in which Ezekiel relinquishes elements of his identity as a priest to take on the role of prophet. Though a priest, he is separated from the temple and unable to function as priest. He is in a "liminal state" in which he is separated from his old identity but has not yet been fully invested in a new one. Stripped of all status insignia, he utterly identifies with his people and their fate. He is not even to be known by his own name, but only as *ben 'adam*, representative human. By eating the scroll and other symbolic acts, he demonstrates that he has taken upon himself his people's fate. Depicting first exile, then siege, famine, and destruction, he is the first to suffer what is in store for all of them, yet he is powerless to avert it ("You Are What You Eat: Ezekiel and the Scroll," *JBL* 117 [1998]: 242–43).

57. Christopher Rowland notes that despite all the qualification in the language of Ezek. 1:26-28, the reader gets the impression that it was in the form of a human being that the prophet perceived the God of Israel. That the essence of the narrative is the revelation of God as Human is shown by Ezek. 8:1-4, which refers simply to "a figure that looked like a human being" (here, '*ish* rather than the usual '*adam*). Some Hebrew texts read '*esh*, "fire," with reference to the fire below the human one's loins and brightness above; and the figure, too, is identified as the "Glory of the God

of Israel." The rabbis later treated this figure as merely an aspect of the divine, but *Apoc. Ab.* 17:13 regarded it as Jaoel, the companion of the throne of glory, and Revelation 1 understood it as the risen Christ ("The Vision of the Risen Christ in Rev. 1.13ff.: The Debt of an Early Christology to an Aspect of Jewish Angelology," *JTS* 31 [1980]: 1–11).

Justin Martyr comments that the Old Testament sometimes called God an Angel, or Power, "and that [God] is called Glory (*doxa*) because he appears sometimes in a vision that is beyond the capacity of human understanding, and that he is sometimes called Man (*aner*) and *Anthropos*, because he appears arrayed in such forms if so pleaseth God" (*Dial.* 128.2). Philo also speaks of a heavenly Man, whom he identifies with the *Logos* and sometimes calls "Man after (God's) image" (*Conf.* 146) or "Man of God" (*Conf.* 41), thus combining the Hebraic and Platonic ideas of the archetypal human (Quispel, "Ezekiel 1:26 in Jewish Mysticism," 2, 4).

58. Thus Gilles Quispel can say that in Ezekiel's vision, "God, when he reveals himself, is like man. He really is Man. Or, rather, his *kabod* [glory] is" ("Ezekiel 1:26 in Jewish Mysticism," 1). Gershom Scholem concurs. The Godhead had a mystical form of manifestation, the form of Humanness upon the throne, which represented the highest archetype, in whose image humanity was created (*Von der mystischen Gestalt der Gottheit* [Zurich: Rhein, 1962], 21). Some Jewish Christians actually regarded Jesus as the Glory of God, and thus as the Human Being on the throne whom Ezekiel beheld (Fossum, "Jewish-Christian Christology," 260–87). That position was similar to the Fourth Gospel's assertion that all the Old Testament theophanies were really christophanies: what the prophets of old saw was the preexistent Christ.

59. Dan Merkur, "Unitive Experience and the State of Trance," in *Mystical Union in Judaism, Christianity, and Islam*, ed. M. Idel and B. McGinn (New York: Continuum, 1996), 141.

60. Rabbi Johanan ben Zakkai distinguished two kinds of revelations. The first, in which God's word is revealed directly and in its totality, is lethal to human beings. The second, in which God's word is mitigated ("sweetened") and tempered to fit the capabilities of each individual, offers life. The mystics chose the former, and hence underwent spiritual death and resurrection (Ira Chernus, *Mysticism in Rabbinic Judaism* [Berlin: Walter de Gruyter, 1982], 42).

61. What these mystics saw really was God, but not the whole of God. Ira Chernus cautions that if we restrict ourselves to the textual evidence, we cannot conclude that the "throne chariot" (*merkabah*) mystics distinguished between God in God's totality, and some visible manifestation of God. "If we take the texts at face value, those mystics who held it possible to see God were saying that what the seer saw was God. There is no more precise information or definition offered. . . . Many, and probably most, of the merkavah mystics did think it possible to see God; thus the vision of God was most probably the culmination (and therefore possibly the goal) of their visionary experiences." Later, in the Kabbalah, this issue was made explicit by distinguishing the incomprehensible depth of God (*Ein-Sof*) from God's manifestations in the world through the *sefirot* (Chernus, *Mysticism in Rabbinic Judaism*, 42).

62. Thus, according to the *Zohar*, a mystical document from the Middle Ages, when the four living creatures of the divine throne chariot were formed, "The [face of the] Man gazed upon them all, and all of them rose and gazed upon him. Thus all of them were formed in their engravings, in this form by the mystery of the one

name that is called Awesome, and then it is written concerning them, 'Each of them had a human face' " (19a).

Our near contemporary, Teilhard de Chardin, echoes something of the same sentiment: "[T]o see more is really to become more. . . . deeper vision is really fuller being. . . ." "From now on man willy-nilly finds his own image stamped on all he looks at" (*The Phenomenon of Man* [New York: Harper & Row, 1959], 33).

63. James R. Davila ("The Hekhalot Literature and Shamanism," *SBLSP 1994*, 767–89) suggests that shamanism provides a useful parallel to the "ascent to the *merkabah*," especially as a way of accounting for the strong admixture of magic and theurgy in Jewish sources. Davila follows Åke Hultkrantz's definition of a shaman: "A social functionary who, with the help of guardian spirits, attains ecstasy in order to create a rapport with the supernatural world on behalf of his group members" ("A Definition of Shamanism," *Temenos* 9 [1973]: 25–37).

64. The writers of the Pseudo-Clementine novels (fourth century C.E.) believed that, at the creation of the world, God appointed a prototype for each of his creatures: an angel for the angels, a spirit for the spirits, a star for the stars, a demon for the demons, an animal for the animals, and for humanity the True Prophet, who became embodied first in Adam, then through the right side of a series of paired opposites, and finally in Jesus (Oscar Cullmann, *The Christology of the New Testament*, trans. S. C. Guthrie and C. A. M. Hall [Philadelphia: Westminster Press, 1959], 148). These theologians would have had no problem with Montaigne.

65. Edmond Barbotin, *The Humanity of God*, trans. M. J. O'Connell (Maryknoll, N.Y.: Orbis Books, 1976), 9.

66. Ibid., 196.

67. Jung says that "Ezekiel witnesses the humanization and differentiation of Yahweh," and that the book speaks of "what is going to happen, through the transformation and humanization of God, not only to God's son as foreseen from all eternity, but to man as such" ("Answer to Job," CW 11:428).

Chapter 3
Feuerbach's Challenge

1. Ludwig Feuerbach, *The Essence of Christianity* (1841; Buffalo: Prometheus Books, 1989). I have focused on this work, rather than his later *Das Wesen der Religion* and the *Lectures on the Essence of Religion* (1848), since his critique of Christianity and its impact on the public interest me here. Van Harvey argues that these later works provide a far stronger basis for the critique of religion, cleansed of earlier Hegelianism and grounded in the loneliness and helplessness of the ego confronted with the world and others, in the anxiety of the psyche facing necessity and death, and in the desire for recognition and self-esteem (*Feuerbach and the Interpretation of Religion* [Cambridge: Cambridge University Press, 1995]). See also Harvey's earlier articles, "Ludwig Feuerbach and Karl Marx," in *Nineteenth-Century Religious Thought in the West*, ed. N. Smart et al. [Cambridge: Cambridge University Press, 1985], 1:291–328), and "Feuerbach on Religion as Construction," in *Theology at the End of Modernity: Essays in Honor of Gordon Kaufman*, ed. S. G. Davaney (Philadelphia: Trinity Press International, 1991), 249–68. Charley D. Hardwick provides a helpful critique of Harvey in "Harvey's Feuerbach and the Possibility of a Lib-

eral Theology," *JAAR* 66 (1998): 863–85, which includes responses by Harvey and Hardwick.

2. Harvey, *Feuerbach and the Interpretation of Religion*, 25.

3. Karl Barth, introduction to *The Essence of Christianity* (New York: Harper & Row, 1957), xix. See Van Harvey's *Feuerbach and the Interpretation of Religion* for a more complete bibliography. Frederick Engels, *Ludwig Feuerbach and the Outcome of Classical German Philosophy* (New York: International Publishers, 1941), comments on the sensation that Feuerbach's works created: "We all became at once Feuerbachians." Later, Engels jettisoned Feuerbach for a consistently materialist philosophy.

Other works include John Glasse, "Why Did Feuerbach Concern Himself with Luther?" *RIP* 26 (1972): 364–85; W. B. Chamberlain, *Heaven Wasn't His Destination: The Philosophy of Ludwig Feuerbach* (London: George Allen and Unwin, 1941)—basically an encomium, but a useful summary; Karl Löwith, *From Hegel to Nietzsche: The Revolution in Nineteenth Century Theology*, trans. D. E. Green (New York: Holt, Rinehart & Winston, 1964), 71–83; Marx W. Wartofsky, *Feuerbach* (Cambridge: Cambridge University Press, 1977). The short paragraph on Feuerbach in the *Oxford Dictionary of the Christian Church*, ed. F. L. Cross (London: Oxford University Press, 1958), dismisses him with the snide comment, "He exercised a far wider influence than the intrinsic merits of his writings deserved." See also Walter Jaeschke, "Speculative and Anthropological Criticism of Religion: A Theological Orientation to Hegel and Feuerbach," *JAAR* 48 (1980): 345–64. Eugen Schoenfeld ("Images of God and Man: An Exploratory Study," *RRR* 28 [1987]: 224–35) attempts a social-scientific survey that would disprove Feuerbach's thesis that humanity alienates itself from its own qualities by projecting them onto God. His attempt can only be judged a total failure. Feuerbach is right for those for whom he is right—many people do empty themselves into transcendence, though they can withdraw the projections and enjoy a healthy religion (contra Feuerbach).

4. Plato long since had lost confidence in the rationality of humanity, and had declared that God, not humanity, is the measure of things. "In our eyes God will be 'the measure of all things' in the highest degree—a degree much higher than any human being. Whoever wishes to become dear to God needs to become, so far as is possible, of a like character" (*Laws* 716C).

5. Barth, introduction to *The Essence of Christianity*, xxix. In *The Crucified God*, Jürgen Moltmann provides a brief rebuttal of one element of Feuerbach's thought. He sees Feuerbach's rejection of a theistic God as simply a transfer of power from God to human beings. "God is man come to himself, and man himself is God. In that case God and man are no longer separated and alienated from each other in religious terms, but are one being. This antitheistic atheism leads unavoidably to anthropotheism, to the divinization of man, of humanity and those parties who claim to be a cadre representing non-alienated, divine humanity in the realm of alienation. If for this atheism 'man is finally man's God', this may be morally fine as an ideal in face of the situation where man is man's wolf. But a century's experience has shown that even these human deities can become man's wolf. . . . the anthropotheists of modern times from Feuerbach to Rilke, from Marx to Block, have overlooked the dark side of evil in man and the problem of suffering in the world" ([London: SCM Press, 1974], 251–52).

6. Henry Mottu, "Feuerbach and Bonhoeffer: Criticism of Religion and the Last Period of Bonhoeffer's Thought," *USQR* 25 (1969): 11.

7. The atheistic Marxist philosopher Ernst Bloch advanced the idea that the "Lord God," sponsor of domination and oppressor of humanity, must be destroyed as an object held over us. In its place would be the depths of our subjective Self (*Atheism in Christianity: The Religion of the Exodus and the Kingdom*, trans. J. T. Swann [New York: Herder and Herder, 1972], 213). Is Bloch then Feuerbachian? Not quite. For Bloch looks toward the future, to the coming of the son of man. "He is to be the active principle at the end of time—active in the creation of a new heaven and a new earth—and not before" (162). From the Yahweh of the Exodus to the "breakthrough made by Jesus" (150), humanity reaches out for humanization. "We are hidden: unrealized, unachieved as no other living being, still open to what lies ahead. . . . But with a sign that our plan is good; a sign called Jesus: one that is not yet rid of restlessness and journeying; but one that is bound in unique intimacy to man, and stays by him" (123). Jesus is "the archetypal Son of Man" (162), who takes the place of "the Lord God." This is the final twist of the biblical Exodus—that it is an exodus from Yahweh, too. But, Bloch declares against Feuerbach, "man" cannot be the measure of all things, for human beings will not be human until the son of man is revealed at the end of time. Consequently, "human history to date is simply prehistory" (263).

Bloch's atheism, on the one hand, and radical biblical faith on the other, are like two lines meeting at the horizon. If God is Human, and we are to be like God, that is, human, then there is no difference whether one calls this being "God" or "the son of the man." At the point of convergence they will be one and the same.

8. Carl Jung, "Letter to Father Victor White," *Collected Letters*, 10 April 1954; cited by Edward Edinger, *The New God-Image* (Wilmette, Ill.: Chiron, 1996), 156.

9. As the Guild for Psychological Studies's John Petroni pointed out to me, however, we can withdraw our projections of our parents from God and still face the "wrath of God." When we are untrue to ourselves, or when we poison the water we drink and the air we breathe, or when a few monopolize the wealth created by the many, "God gives us over," forcing us to suffer the consequences of our own acts. Then we can only pray the rabbinic prayer that God's mercy might overcome God's wrath.

10. L. von Franz notes five stages in the withdrawal of projections: (1) identity of the subject and object; (2) separation of the subject and object through differentiation; (3) moral evaluation (is the content of the projection evil or good, healthy or pathological?); (4) acceptance of the content as a projection; and (5) reflection on the reality of the content within the psyche (*Projection and Re-collection in Jungian Psychology* [La Salle, Ill.: Open Court, 1980], 9–19).

11. According to Van Harvey, Marx rejected the belief, shared by Hegel and Feuerbach, that all objectification is alienating. But if not all human objectifications are intrinsically alienating, asks Harvey, why must one assume that all religious objectifications are alienating? "Why could there not be forms of religious expression in which human dignity, responsibility and freedom are affirmed, which is to say, religions that can be appropriated humanly?" (An example would be Fidel Castro's recognition that liberation theology was not alienating, though much of traditional Christianity continues to be.) Nor need we assume that all religious ideas are false.

Religious symbols and ideas are projections no more true or false than other human projections like, say, mathematics or scientific theories.

Marx's distinction also permits us to argue that the God–human relation can be and often is alienating, but need not be so. Marx, in effect, recognized that institutions can be good, but his philosophy allowed only a distinction between good (nonalienating) and bad (alienating) institutions, a distinction I have rejected as nondialectical in my trilogy on the Powers. I see all the Powers That Be (institutions, systems, structures, ideologies, images, and so forth) as intrinsically good, insofar as they are created to serve the humanizing purposes of God revealed in Jesus. And all Powers, without exception, are fallen, and not only become alienated, but alienate people from their essential humanness. And all can be redeemed (changed, neutralized, or destroyed)—here the utopian vision is kept alive as hope for the coming of God's reign in the world. (Van Harvey, "Ludwig Feuerbach and Karl Marx," 303–4.)

12. Teilhard de Chardin: "[S]ince the atom is naturally co-extensive with the whole of the space in which it is situated—and since, on the other hand, we have just seen that a universal space is *the only space there is*—we are bound to admit that this immensity represents the sphere of action common to all atoms. The volume of each of them is the volume of the universe" (*The Phenomenon of Man*, trans. B. Wall [New York: Harper & Row, 1959], 45).

13. Brian Swimme, *The Universe Is a Green Dragon* (Santa Fe, N.Mex.: Bear, 1985), 109.

14. John A. Wheeler, intro. to John D. Barrow and F. J. Tipler, *The Anthropic Cosmological Principle* (New York: Oxford University Press, 1986), viii: "Imagine a universe in which one or another of the fundamental dimensionless constants of physics is altered by a few percent one way or the other," says physicist John A. Wheeler in his introduction. Humanity could never come into being in such a universe. "That is the central point of the anthropic principle. According to this principle, a life-giving factor lies at the centre of the whole machinery and design of the world."

15. Gabriele Uhlein, *Meditations with Hildegard of Bingen* (Santa Fe, N.Mex.: Bear, 1983), 105.

16. Hugh T. Kerr, ed, *Calvin's "Institutes": A New Compendium*, I.1.2 (Louisville: Westminster John Knox Press, 1989), 18. The same was said by Clement of Alexandria: "Therefore, it seems, it is the greatest of all disciplines to know oneself; for when a man knows himself, he knows God" (*Paedagogus* 3.1). Compare James B. Ashbrook and Carol Rausch Albright, *The Humanizing Brain* (Cleveland: Pilgrim Press, 1997), xxi—"God-talk is really human-talk, since it is we who are conversing. . . . We cannot know or speak of God as something—a Being, even Being itself—without connection to human consciousness." The idea is widespread in the world's religions. Ibn al-'Arabi wrote, "The Prophet said, 'Who [truly] knows himself knows his Lord' " (*Bezels of Wisdom* [New York: Paulist Press, 1980], 74). To which Nicolas Berdyayev adds: any doctrine that is degrading to human beings also degrades God (*Slavery and Freedom* [New York: Charles Scribner's Sons, 1944], 39).

17. Carl Jung, *Psychological Types*, CW 6, 243. Jung quotes Meister Eckhart: "For humanity is truly God, and God is truly humanity" (245).

18. Human beings project ultimate meanings into reality, says Peter Berger, because that reality is, indeed, ultimately meaningful, and because our own beings (the

empirical ground of these projections) contain and intend these same ultimate meanings. "Such a theological procedure, if feasible, would be an interesting ploy on Feuerbach—the reduction of theology to anthropology would end in the reconstruction of anthropology in a theological mode." "The theological decision will have to be that, 'in, with, and under' the immense array of human projections, there are indicators of a reality that is truly 'other'" and that the religious imagination of humanity ultimately reflects it (*The Sacred Canopy: Elements of a Sociological Theory of Religion* [Garden City, N.Y.: Doubleday, 1967], 47).

19. See Walter Wink, *Naming the Powers: The Language of Power in the New Testament* (Philadelphia: Fortress Press, 1984), 143–45.

20. Henry Corbin, ed., *Spiritual Body and Celestial Earth: From Mazdean Iran to Shi'ite Iran*, trans. N. Pearson (Princeton: Princeton University Press, 1977), 12.

21. James Hillman, *Pan and the Nightmare* (New York: Spring Publications, 1972), xxi.

22. George Bernard Shaw, *Saint Joan*, in *The Complete Plays of Bernard Shaw* (London: Odhams Press, 1934), 967.

23. Feuerbach, *Essence of Christianity*, 214. I unknowingly seem to have replicated a theory of projection published in the Netherlands in 1956 by Fokke Sierksma (*Projection and Religion: An Anthropological and Psychological Study of the Phenomena of Projection in the Various Religions* [Ann Arbor, Mich.: UMI Books on Demand, 1990]), which created a sensation when it was published there but was virtually unknown in the United States until recently. Sierksma argues that projection need not be seen as an illusory phenomenon and, hence, regarded negatively. Rather, it should be seen as a normal and necessary part of the perceptual process by means of which animals and human beings create and stabilize their worlds. Religious projection is a special type of projection that occurs in humans by virtue of self-consciousness (Harvey's summary, "Feuerbach," 253). Van Harvey observes that Sierksma's analysis can be turned on its head: religions may serve to stabilize the world, but they are still illusions. I agree with Van Harvey that Sierksma's blanket endorsement of religions leaves no room for criticizing them; but I think Sierksma legitimately could question how Harvey knows that religions are illusions. "Illusion" depends on someone's definition of reality, and that is a matter of one's worldview. Thus one ought to be able to argue that religions are capable of being criticized without concluding that they are all, without exception, illusory.

24. Henry Corbin, "*Mundus Imaginalis* or the Imaginary and the Imaginal," *Spring* (1992): 12; and his "The *Imago Templi* and Secular Norms," *Spring* (1975): 185. See also my *Naming the Powers*, 143–45.

25. Elliott R. Wolfson, *Through a Speculum That Shines: Vision and Imagination in Medieval Jewish Mysticism* (Princeton: Princeton University Press, 1994), 107–8.

26. Hananel, *Otzar ha-Geonim*, vol. 1, tractate *Berakhot*, appendix, p. 3; cited in Wolfson, *Through a Speculum That Shines*, 147.

27. Wolfson, *Through a Speculum That Shines*, 324.

28. James Hillman, "The Thought of the Heart," *Eranos Lectures* 2 (Dallas: Spring Publications, 1981), 3, 9, 19.

29. Feuerbach, *Essence of Christianity*, 17.

30. Wolfson notes that the entire enterprise of the Merkabah mystics (see chap. 15 below) is predicated on the acceptance of an anthropomorphic representation of

God as a visible, humanlike form, and that it is based on the theophanies in Scripture (*Through a Speculum That Shines*, 105).

31. Tom F. Driver comments, "If we do not personify what we're with, we lose it. . . . It is not possible simply to *be* a person. One can only *become* a person, never finished, and the way to do it is to personify whatever we meet. 'Person' is a way of relating. . . . 'In the beginning is the relation' " (*Christ in a Changing World* [New York: Crossroad, 1981], 102).

32. Carl Jung, "Jung and Religious Belief," *CW* 18:740–41. So also elsewhere: "[A]lthough our whole world of religious ideas consists of anthropomorphic images that could never stand up to rational criticism, we should never forget that they are based on numinous archetypes, i.e., on . . . [a] foundation which is unassailable by reason. We are dealing with psychic facts which logic can overlook but not eliminate" ("Answer to Job," *CW* 11:360–62). Our God-images tend to favor human images of God because God is Human.

33. This Jewish prohibition extended to artistic portrayal of human beings. An ancient principle stated that "all pictures are permissible except those of human beings" (*b. 'Abodah Zarah* 42b). Since human beings are in the likeness of God, a depiction of humans is a depiction of the image of God (G. Kittel, "*eikōn*," *TDNT* 2:384).

34. John Polkinghorne, *The Faith of a Physicist* (Princeton: Princeton University Press, 1994), 53.

35. Ashbrook and Albright, *The Humanizing Brain*, xv–xxxiv, italics mine. Swedenborg said much the same: "God is in a human form"; "in him only is the Divine Human;" and "it is impossible to think of God except in a human form," for a person is capable of worshiping what she has some idea of, but not what she has no idea of (*Heaven and Hell* [London: Swedenborg Society, 1896], 36, 40).

36. Edward Harrison, *Masks of the Universe* (New York: Collier Books, 1985), 14.

37. Anne Harrington, foreword to Ashbrook and Albright, *The Humanizing Brain*, xiii.

38. Barrow and Tipler, *Anthropic Cosmological Principle*, passim.

39. Ashbrook and Albright, *The Humanizing Brain*, 44. This stunning insight into the humanlike nature of reality confirms, in an unexpected way, another intuition of the Jewish *Shi'ur Qomah* mystics, with their fantastical measurements of the body of God. Interpreted along the lines provided, these mystics were saying, in a mythological way, that God is Human and is coextensive with the universe—*just as we are*, though to a minuscule degree. Leland C. Wyman writes, "By themselves natural phenomena are lifeless, but an inner human form set within them functions as their life principle. This vitalizes and also personalizes each phenomenon. These inner anthropic forms are particularly crucial for human existence (*Blessingway* [Tucson: University of Arizona Press, 1970], 109, 121, 124). This "inner human form" is thus more than simply *Homo sapiens*; it appears to be the basis of all life.

40. Personal response to the manuscript of this book.

41. Karen Armstrong notes the dangers of a personal God: making it into an idol carved in our own image and a projection of our needs, fears, and desires, who loves what we love and hates what we hate. She concludes that a personal God can only be a stage in our religious development (*A History of God* [New York: Knopf, 1993], 209–10). Her proclivity is toward apophatic (imageless) mysticism; others (such as myself) may need the personal imagery of kataphatic mysticism.

42. Martin Buber, *Hasidism and the Modern Mind*, cited without page number by Ashbrook and Albright, *The Humanizing Brain*, xi.

43. William Blake, "Auguries of Innocence," in *The Complete Poetry and Prose of William Blake*, ed. David V. Erdman, commentary by Harold Bloom, rev. ed. (Berkeley: University of California Press, 1982), 493.

44. Hillman, "Thought of the Heart," 50.

45. Elsa Tamez, "How We Dream Tall," *The Other Side* (January–February 1997): 39.

46. Cited by Hillman, "Thought of the Heart," 23–24, 44.

47. The charge that humans create God in their own image was made as early as the sixth century B.C.E., when the Greek philosopher Xenophanes observed that the gods of the Ethiopians were black with flat noses while those of the Thracians were blond with blue eyes. Giambattista Vico, David Hume, Montaigne, and Voltaire made the same observation, but Feuerbach was the first to employ the concept as the basis for a systematic critique of religion (Harvey, *Feuerbach and the Interpretation of Religion*, 4).

48. Owen Barfield, *Saving the Appearances* (New York: Harcourt, Brace & World, n.d.), 127. The paleontologist and priest Teilhard de Chardin looked forward to human becoming as "an anthropogenesis which is itself the crown of a cosmogenesis" (*Phenomenon of Man*, 34).

49. Nicolas Berdyayev, *The Meaning of the Creative Act* (New York: Harper & Bros., 1954), 59.

50. Ibid., 92. Here, as was the case with Feuerbach, I have closely followed Berdyayev's actual words but avoided direct quotations because of the high density of male terms.

51. Ibid., 19. This insight was already a part of the Jewish mystical tradition.

52. Ibid., 130.

53. Berdyayev, *Slavery and Freedom*, 85.

54. Ibid, 80–81. Berdyayev wrote *The Meaning of the Creative Act* in 1914.

55. Carl Jung, "To the Rev. David Cox," 25 September 1957, CW 18, 734–35.

56. Karl Barth, *The Humanity of God*, trans. J. N. Thomas and T. Wieser (Richmond: John Knox Press, 1960), 46, 49, 51, emphasis his. Frederick Houk Borsch, with utmost circumspection, observes that if people were made in the image of God, there must also be a way in which it is true to say, however guardedly, that an aspect of the infinite and unknowable God is humanlike (*The Son of Man in Myth and History* [Philadelphia: Westminster Press, 1967], 408).

Chapter 4
Other Biblical and Extrabiblical References to the Human Being up to 100 C.E.

1. The NRSV has rendered these singular Hebrew forms as plurals in order to avoid sexist language.

2. Bruce Chilton, "The Son of Man: Who Was He?" *BR* 12 (1996): 35.

3. The expression "son of man" could also have negative connotations, as in Job 25, in which Bildad equates it with maggots and worms. The Qumran "Rule of the Community" echoes Bildad's theology: "What, indeed, is the son of man. . . . what shall one born of woman be considered in your presence? . . . maggots' food shall be

his dwelling; he is spat saliva . . ." (1QS 11:20). In *The Chapter of R. Nehuniah b. ha-Qanah*, an independent *Hekhalot* text well after the New Testament era, an angel named Yofiel castigates a young mystic for daring to disturb heaven by his presence. "What are you, son of man, that you have disturbed the great retinue? . . . Son of man, stinking drop [of semen], worm and maggot . . ." (text in David Halperin, *The Faces of the Chariot* [Tübingen: Mohr/Siebeck, 1988], 378). This view, I should add, is no more that of the *Hekhalot* author than Bildad the Shuhite's theology is that of the author of Job.

4. Elliott R. Wolfson, *Through a Speculum That Shines* (Princeton: Princeton University Press, 1994), 30. The motif of seeing God in a human form on the divine throne chariot is continued in *1 Enoch* 71:10-11; *2 Enoch* 20:3; 22:1-7 (especially text A); and 39:1-6. In *Apoc. Abr.* 18:12—19:1, a visual revelation is replaced by an auditory one; but it is still a voice "like the voice of a single man" (18.11). Why the stress on seeing God? *Mekilta de-Rabbi Ishmael*, tractate *Bahodesh* 2, vol. 2, p. 209, gives one answer: "[The Israelites] said [to Moses]: It is our desire to see our king, for the one who hears cannot be compared to one who sees."

5. Some scholars (Procksch, Feuillet, Smythe) deny that "the one like a human being" in Daniel 7 shows any dependence on Ezekiel. But literary dependence is clear in Daniel's depiction of the throne of fiery flames and wheels of burning fire. True enough, Ezekiel's "One in human form" was God. But tradition had by the time of Daniel identified the "Glory of the Lord" as a divine hypostasis, deemed identical with Daniel's "one in human form."

H. E. Tödt begins his study of the Jewish background of the "son of man" phrase with Dan. 7:13-14, mentioning Ezekiel but once, and then only in passing. Having already decided that the apocalyptic "son of man" sayings are of most significance, Tödt could dismiss Ezekiel's ninety-three references as inconsequential because they were nonapocalyptic. That is like saying that, apart from the leaves, there is no foliage on the tree. See H. E. Tödt, *The Son of Man in the Synoptic Tradition*, trans. D. M. Barton (Philadelphia: Westminster, 1963), 304; so also A. J. B. Higgins, *Jesus and the Son of Man* (Philadelphia: Fortress Press, 1964), 195.

6. The Ugaritic (Canaanite) texts depict the god 'El as the "Father of Years" (the Ancient of Days?), having gray hair (hair white as wool?). Eternal dominion and kingship is conferred upon Ba'al by 'El's official decree (E. Theodore Mullen Jr., *The Divine Council in Canaanite and Early Hebrew Literature*, Harvard Semitic Monographs 24 [Chico, Calif.: Scholars Press, 1980], 160–62). Whether that constitutes a sufficient parallel the reader must decide. Lowell K. Handy insists that "nothing suggests that El was removed from a position of authority by Baal" (*Among the Host of Heaven* [Winona Lake, Ind.: Eisenbrauns, 1994], 71, 101). Chrys C. Caragounis (*The Son of Man: Vision and Interpretation*, Wissenschaftliche Untersuchung zum Neuen Testament 38 [Tübingen:Mohr/Siebeck, 1986], 36–41) lays down stringent criteria for claiming a nonbiblical source for biblical elements. Against these criteria, all attempts to ground the son of the man in other traditions fail. According to Jarl Fossum, Ezekiel 1 was the fountainhead of "the Son of Man," "the heavenly Man," and "the Man from heaven"; but the Anthropos and Urmensch are scholarly phantoms ("The New *Religionsgeschichtliche Schule*," *SBLSP 1991*, 645). I concur; but the issue is not one of borrowing, or of establishing the genesis of an idea, but of recognizing how in a variety of cultures, and often independently of

each other, the same kind of psychic contents arise and are invested with various kinds of meaning, depending on the values, traditions, and institutions of that society. And while the full-scale Primal Man myth may never have existed, there is evidence in many Near Eastern cultures of archetypal images that picture the human as divine or the divine as human.

7. See appendix 1, "Was There a Primal Man Myth?" Carl Jung reads the mythic motif here as more positive than the Canaanite myth from Ugarit. The "one in human form" in Daniel, he says, is a son of the Ancient of Days, and his task is to rejuvenate the father. Furthermore, by drawing the human to the divine, the father indicates the desire to become the son, to reverse the aging process (by which an archetype is superseded as no longer powerful and numinous), and to be reborn in the son (*Psychology and Religion: West and East*, CW 11: 421).

8. Scholars give the following arguments for the "one like a son of man" being Israel:

1. The "holy ones" cannot be angels, since angels do not rule earthly kingdoms, nor are they to be served by "all peoples, nations, and languages" (7:14).
2. The kingship that the "one in human form" receives is not transcendent, but earthly, like the despotic empires of the four beasts.
3. The Syrian king Antiochus could not have "waged war" on angels (7:21) or prevailed over them for three and a half years (7:25).
4. The "saints" do not enjoy a heavenly existence, but are being persecuted by a pagan tyranny.
5. Angels already appear in heaven (7:10), whereas the "one like a human being" is brought into the divine presence as if this were a new thing.
6. Angels are clearly distinguished from this human figure (7:16).
7. If the saints are angels, it is hard to see how the vision consoles those victims of persecution to whom the book is addressed.

Consequently, Alexander A. DiLella concludes that "the one in human likeness" (7:13) is a corporate personification of faithful Israel, "the holy ones of the Most High" (7:18, 21, 22, 25, 27). This use echoes Psalm 80, since both "speak of Israel under the similitude of a human figure, humiliated into insignificance until visited by God and raised to glory." Later rabbis tended to read Dan. 7:13 messianically, but at the time of Jesus and the Gospel writers only the corporate interpretation was certainly present ("The One in Human Likeness and the Holy Ones of the Most High in Daniel 7," *CBQ* 39 [1977]: 1–19).

9. The angel *is* Israel in its spiritual aspect. We know that the author of Daniel believed that Michael was the guardian angel of Israel (chap. 10); it would be odd if he did not so regard the heavenly "man" in chapter 7 (Helge S. Kvanvig, *Roots of Apocalyptic: The Mesopotamian Background of the Enoch Figure and of the Son of Man*, Wissenschaftliche Monographien zum Alten und Neuen Testament 61 [Neukirchen-Vluyn: Neukirchener Verlag, 1988], 583). If this figure is only "like" a human being, then it is clearly *not* a human being, but only looks like one. The angels are frequently described as humanlike. This angelic being (possibly Michael or Gabriel) receives in heaven what the saints receive on earth. It receives dominion from God in heaven after the destruction of the fourth beast; the saints

receive dominion from God on earth after the destruction of Antiochus Epiphanes, who was to be the last king of the kingdom that the fourth beast symbolized (Maurice Casey, *Son of Man: The Interpretation and Influence of Daniel 7* [London: SPCK, 1979], 24–25). It would follow that the manlike figure is the heavenly representative of the saints of the Most High. His ascendancy to kingship means that the human values cherished by the saints in their nonviolent struggle against Antiochus will be established by God in a humane order. This archetypal motif of "as above so below" was familiar to ancients from Heraclitus to Plato to Jesus' contemporary Philo. See Martin Noth, "The Holy Ones of the Most High," in *The Laws in the Pentateuch and Other Essays* (Philadelphia: Fortress Press, 1967), 194–214; Ulrich B. Müller, *Messias und Menschensohn in jüdischen Apokalypsen und in der Offenbarung des Johannes* (Gütersloh: Mohn, 1972); John J. Collins, *The Apocalyptic Vision of the Book of Daniel*, HSM 16 (Missoula, Mont.: Scholars Press, 1977), 141–46.

10. The discovery of the Kölner part of Papyrus 967 fills the lacunae in Dan. 7:1–14, and confirms the LXX reading (Johan Lust, "Dan 7:13 and the Septuagint," *ETL* 54 [1978]: 62–69. Lust's argument is plausible: the LXX identifies the "one like a son of man" with the "Ancient of Days." He is God. Hence, as gods do, he comes with clouds. So Daniel 7 is consistent with Ezekiel 1. Margaret Barker believes that the Ancient of Days is 'Illaya (Elyon), the ancient name for the High God, and that the unnamed angel/son-of-man figure was the Holy One, Yahweh (*The Great Angel: A Study of Israel's Second God* [Louisville: Westminster John Knox Press, 1992], 38).

11. Mark 14:62 par. and all other predictions of a "second coming."

12. Paul Ricoeur, foreword to *The Book of Daniel*, by André Lacocque (Atlanta: John Knox Press, 1979), xxii–xxiii.

13. Morna Hooker, *The Son of Man in Mark* (Montreal: McGill University Press, 1967), 11–12.

14. Dan Merkur, from a course I co-taught with him at Auburn Theological Seminary, March 1998. To be sure, we are dealing here with the apocalyptic genre, which is a *literary* form. But this is the report of a new archetypal image bursting from the collective unconscious of that period. So it scarcely matters how this text was produced. A creative writer could receive this message every bit as well as a dreamer.

15. Elizabeth Boyden Howes, "The Son of Man—Expression of the Self," in *Intersection and Beyond* (San Francisco: Guild for Psychological Studies Press, 1971), 175; Edward F. Edinger, *The Transformation of the God-Image* (Toronto: Inner City Books, 1992), 84–91.

16. Robert D. Rowe, "Is Daniel's 'Son of Man' Messianic?" in *Christ the Lord: Studies in Christology Presented to Donald Guthrie*, ed. H. H. Rowdon (Downers Grove, Ill.: InterVarsity Press, 1982), 96.

17. Ezekiel the Tragedian, *The Exagoge* 70.

18. 4QAges of Creation (4Q181). "Son of man" is used in the Dead Sea Scrolls, *ben 'adam* appearing in synonymous parallelism once in 1QH IV, 30 with *'enosh*, and in 1QS 11, 20 of humanity in general; again in parallelism in 4Q418, frag. 55 (frag. 7, line 11); and *bar 'enosh* occurs in the generic sense of humanity in 1QApGen 21, 13; 11QTgJob 9, 9 and 26, 3.

19. E.g., APOT 2:171.

20. J. T. Milik, "Problèmes de la littérature Hénochique à la lumière des fragments araméens de Qumrân," *HTR* 64 (1971): 333–78. Milik's late date is untenable, since Pseudo-Philo's *Liber Antiquitatum Biblicarum* 3:10 has a clear allusion to *1 Enoch* 51:1. Since Pseudo-Philo is now being dated ca. 100 C.E., this requires a date for the Similitudes earlier in the first century. The absence of the Similitudes at Qumran may not be all that significant; only about 5 percent of the whole of Ethiopic *Enoch* appears there (Matthew Black, *The Book of Enoch* [Leiden: E. J. Brill, 1985], 1, 214.)

21. E. Isaac, *OTP* 1:7.

22. See Charles's list of parallels (*APOT* 2:180–81), to which I would add several others, notably Rev. 19:15 = *1 Enoch* 62:2; Rev. 21:1 = *1 Enoch* 45:4; Matt. 25:31 = *1 Enoch* 62:5, and from whose list I would delete a number of passages that do not appear to be genuine parallels indicating dependency. T. F. Glasson challenges Charles's parallels altogether, unsuccessfully, it seems to me (*The Second Advent* [London: Epworth Press, 1945], 41–48). David C. Sim demonstrates that the flow of borrowing was from the Similitudes to Matthew in at least one passage ("Matthew 22.13a and 1 Enoch 10.4a: A Case of Literary Dependence?" *JSNT* [1992]: 3–19).

23. Mark 14:21 = *1 Enoch* 38:2. In the early Pauline epistles, there are only two possible parallels, 1 Thess. 5:3 = *1 Enoch* 62:4; and 2 Thess. 1:7 = *1 Enoch* 61:10. Both could be apocalyptic commonplaces.

24. Kathlene Peterson Nicol argues that *1 Enoch* 70–71 is the climax toward which the whole of the Similitudes builds: the son of man is *Enoch*, not Jesus. Consequently, she believes that the Similitudes are engaged in conscious anti-Christian polemic in reaction to the use of the son of the man in the Gospels ("'Son of Man': Its Background and New Testament Usage," B.D. thesis, Union Theological Seminary, 1970).

25. Isaac (*OTP* 1:43.j), whose translation I will follow except where noted. All are translation variants for *bar 'enosh* or *ben 'adam*.

26. E. A. Abbott, *The Message of the Son of Man* (London: Adam and Charles Black, 1909), 16.

27. Hooker, *Son of Man in Mark*, 44.

28. The same messianic excitement is evident in an inscription on an altar in Priene in Asia Minor, which hails the birth of Augustus: "This day has changed the aspects of the world; it would have perished, had felicity for all men not appeared in the one born this day. To date your own life and your vital forces from this birthday shows good judgment; gone at last are the days when you had to rue being born. Providence, which so showered this man with gifts, has sent him to us and to coming generations as a savior (*sōtēr*); he will end strife and gloriously fashion all things. To the world this god's birthday brought the good news (*evangelia*) that go with him; his birth launches a new count of time" (text in Ernst Bloch, *Man on His Own: Essays in the Philosophy of Religion*, trans. E. B. Ashton[New York: Herder and Herder, 1970], 181).

29. Feuerbach saw in the species sense the source of all religion. As Van Harvey summarizes, "God is the notion of the species transformed by the imagination into a perfect exemplar of the species, a conscious being with perfect knowledge, will, and, above all, feeling" (*Feuerbach and the Interpretation of Religion*, Cambridge Studies in Religion and Critical Thought 1[Cambridge: Cambridge University Press, 1995],

39). This, I would argue, is precisely the insight at which humanity needs to arrive *but has never yet done so.* This species sense is the eschatological task of humanity. Thus, in the light of Ezekiel's vision, I can agree with Feuerbach that "*God is the idea of the species as an individual*—the idea or essence of the species, which as a species, as universal being, *as the totality of all perfections,* of all attributes or realities, freed from all the limits which exist in the consciousness and feeling of the individual, is at the same time again an individual, *personal* being" (*The Essence of Christianity,* trans. G. Eliot [Buffalo: Prometheus Books, 1989], 153). But I regard God as real rather than, as Feuerbach did, imaginary.

30. Text in *OTP*, 2:725–71.

31. Charlesworth guesses that the speaker here is the Christ. But in v. 13 there is a clear reference to the role of Wisdom/Sophia in the creation, echoing Proverbs 8 and Wisdom of Solomon 7. The reference to breasts and milk, while it could have otherwise referred to the Father, as we shall see, could not refer to the Son, who is the recipient of the milk, not its dispenser.

32. Frederick Houk Borsch, *The Son of Man in Myth and History* (Philadelphia: Westminster Press, 1967), 68. But he did not develop the idea further.

Part 3
The Human Being: Pre-Easter Sayings

1. Norman Perrin, *Rediscovering the Teaching of Jesus* (New York: Harper & Row, 1967), 175–81.

Chapter 5
Jesus and the Human Being

1. The discussion is handily summarized by Frederick Houk Borsch, *The Son of Man in Myth and History* (Philadelphia: Westminster Press, 1967). See my appendix 1 for a fuller treatment.

2. Elizabeth Boyden Howes, *Intersection and Beyond* (San Francisco: Guild for Psychological Studies, 1971); *idem, Jesus' Answer to God* (San Francisco: Guild for Psychological Studies, 1984). Howes was not the first to see the archetypal dimension of the son of the man. It was frequently appealed to in the nineteenth and early twentieth centuries. The son of the man was the person without equal, the noblest, most excellent human exemplar, the idea or archetype of humanity (J. Lutz, 1847). As the normative and model human being, he was the ideal of humanity (E. Reuss, 1852). He was the Ideal, Absolute, Heavenly Man (Beyschlag, 1866), for whom the parousia relates not so much to Jesus' own "I" as to the Ideal Man (W. Brückner, 1886). "This son of the man is the representative of the whole race . . . in whom all the potential powers of humanity were gathered . . . in whom the complete conception of manhood was absolutely attained . . . who gathers up into Himself all humanity and becomes the source of a higher life to the race" (Westcott, 1908). None of these do justice to the eschatological dimension. That element was included by Hoffmann (1886), who spoke of the son of man forming the conclusion of the history of the Adamic race in contrast to the one who began it. Zahn (1903) regarded the son of the man as "that member of the human race in whom the history of the race comes to its conclusion." A full archetypal interpretation such as Howes's, however, had to wait on

Jung's theory of the archetypes. (See Delbert Burkett, *The Son of Man Debate: A History and Evaluation* [SNTSMS 107; Cambridge: Cambridge University Press, 1999], for bibliography).

3. D. E. Nineham, *St. Mark* (Baltimore: Penguin Books, 1964), 107. See also Eduard Schweizer, *The Good News according to Mark*, trans. D. H. Madrig (Richmond: John Knox Press, 1970), ad loc.

4. Marcus Borg, *Jesus: Conflict, Holiness, and Politics in the Teaching of Jesus*, Studies in the Bible and Early Christianity 5 (Lewiston, N.Y.: Edwin Mellen Press, 1984), 153.

5. Phillip Sigal, *The Halakah of Jesus of Nazareth according to the Gospel of Matthew* (Lanham, Md.: University Press of America, 1986), 232 n. 59.

6. See the superb article by Maurice Casey, "Culture and Historicity: The Plucking of the Grain (Mark 2.23-28)," *NTS* 34 (1988): 1–23.

7. Oscar Cullmann, *The Christology of the New Testament*, trans. S. C. Guthrie and C. A. M. Hall (Philadelphia: Westminster Press, 1959), 152. Cullmann thinks that *Mark* read "the son of the man" christologically here as an exclusive reference to Jesus; but he suspects that, in the original, Jesus referred to human beings in general.

8. Alan Segal believes that all the christological designations were applied to Jesus after his ascension. These were not so much preexistent roles and titles as the result of the church's own exegetical work. Thus Jesus was invested with the authority of the "son of man" of Daniel 7, so that in Mark 2:10 and 2:28 Jesus' authority as "son of man" can be extended even to abrogating the law and forgiving sins (*Two Powers in Heaven* [Leiden: E. J. Brill, 1977], 208–9). However, neither Markan saying betrays any dependence on Daniel 7, which after all is set in heaven, not earth.

9. Gerd Theissen, *Sociology of Early Palestinian Christianity*, trans. J. Bowden (Philadelphia: Fortress Press, 1978), 26.

10. The Marcan variants at v. 27 are Codex Bezae (D) and some Italian versions. That Matthew had Mark 2:27 in his sources, and has deliberately omitted it, is shown by the *gar* in Matt. 12:8, which implies a missing antecedent. The *Gospel of Thomas* also found this saying too radical, and substituted for it the following: "If you do not keep the Sabbath as Sabbath, you will not see the Father" (27b).

11. The Mishnah does not unanimously prohibit "plucking" (*tolesh*) on the sabbath (*m. Shab.* 10:6), nor is plucking one of the thirty-nine categories of prohibited work (*m. Shab.* 7:2) (Sigal, *Halakah of Jesus of Nazareth*, 160). Perhaps the disciples did nothing more than pull some seeds from ears of grain in order to reduce hunger pangs. Fasting on the sabbath was forbidden (*Jub.* 50:11; Judg. 8:6). Sigal argues that the "Pharisees" of the Gospels were not the same as the "lawyers"; the former (*perushim*) were ultrarigorous and made no exceptions for sabbath observance, whereas the latter were proto-rabbis who were very close to Jesus' position and who were the predecessors of the circles that produced the Mishnah. Pharisees are generally *not* identified as rabbis. Jesus *is* identified as a rabbi. Jesus attacks "rabbis" only once, in a clearly Matthean composition (23:7-8). Pharisees are not listed as the founders of rabbinic Judaism in *m. 'Abot* 1:1-12. The Pharisees Josephus describes were exceptionally fastidious about ritualism, just as they are in the New Testament, says Sigal. Rabbinical literature refers to the Pharisees only in negative terms. The latter were more similar to the settlers at Qumran than to the proto-rabbis. In the period of Jesus,

these proto-rabbis were not numerous and were divided into a variety of schools (Hillel, Shammai, Johanan ben Zakkai). None of these schools was opposed to Jesus, says Sigel; no anti-Jesus or anti-Christian polemic survives from that time.

12. Hal Childs, "Son of Man: A Principle of Incarnation" (M.Div. thesis, Union Theological Seminary, New York, 1975), 107–10.

13. Notes from Henry Burton Sharman, courtesy of Elizabeth Boyden Howes. Isaiah 56:2 reads, "Happy is the man (*'enosh*) who does this, the son of man (*ben 'adam*) who holds it fast, who keeps the sabbath, not profaning it. . . ." Here Jesus' disciples, acting out of the son-of-the-man reality, brashly take on the role of the son of the man and judge for themselves what constitutes a sabbath violation.

14. *Mekilta de Rabbi Ishmael*, tractate *Shabbat I*. Even closer to Jesus' time, 2 *Baruch* 14:18 reads, "And you [God] said that you would make a man for this world as a guardian over your works that it should be known that he was not created for the world, but the world for him" (100–120 C.E.). The rabbis allowed labor such as the disciples' here if necessary for a constructive purpose (*t. Beṣah* 8a). B. *Yoma* 83a and *Deut. Rabbah* 10.1 state that where there is the least question of danger to life, the sabbath laws are suspended; even an earache can be healed if it is considered dangerous. Other passages stressed the gravity of sabbath violations, counting them as greater than adultery or murder or idolatry (*Aboth Rabbi Nathan* 38). M. *Ker.* 2:1ff. states of a sabbath breaker, "If in these things he transgressed wantonly he is liable to extirpation," which entailed stoning, strangling, burning, or forty lashes. All of these witnesses, of course, are much later than New Testament times, and may reflect a later situation.

15. Ernst Bammel, "The Cambridge Pericope: The Addition to Luke 6.4 in Codex Bezae," *NTS* 32 (1986): 408, 423.

16. Ibid., 422.

17. Mark Twain, *The Adventures of Huckleberry Finn* (1884; New York: Grosset & Dunlap, 1918), 270–72.

18. Elizabeth Boyden Howes, "The Son of Man—Expression of the Self," in *Intersection and Beyond* (San Francisco: Guild for Psychological Studies Press, 1971), 177.

19. Nicolas Berdyayev, *The Destiny of Man*, trans. N. Duddington. 4th ed. (1937; London: Geoffrey Bles, 1954), 134.

20. People understandably shy away from sentiments such as those expressed by the seventeenth-century Ranter Jacob Bauthumley, who insisted that it is a sin to perform an action authorized by the Bible if "the commanding power which is God in me" forbids it. Again, "The Bible without is but a shadow of that Bible which is within." "I do not expect to be taught by Bibles or books, but by God." In commenting on these statements, Christopher Hill says that it is a very small step, though a momentous one, from such dependence on the Holy Spirit to absolute trust in reason (*The English Bible and the Seventeenth-Century Revolution* [New York: Allen Lane and Penguin Press, 1993], 181, 234). Milton echoed the sentiment: "Precise compliance with the commandments . . . when my faith prompts me to do otherwise . . . will be counted as sin" (183).

21. José Cárdenas Pallares, *A Poor Man Called Jesus: Reflections on the Gospel of Mark*, trans. R. R. Barr (Maryknoll, N.Y.: Orbis Books, 1985), 22. Pallares makes a virtue of a mistake in the text, which reads "Abiathar" instead of "Ahimelech"

(1 Sam. 21:1-6). "Jesus' reply is scarcely a learned one. Even his reference to a high priest in the time of David is anachronistic. . . . What is important is that Jesus opposes his own reading of scripture, the reading of a poor person, to the reading of the Pharisees, the reading of the influential."

22. *y. Ber.* 1. This text, however, is considerably later than the first century.

23. Howes, "Son of Man—Expression of the Self," 174.

24. Typical is Tödt: "Thus it is by no means intended to proclaim man, i.e. the disciples, the community, as being lords of the sabbath; their behaviour is rather traced back to Jesus' *exousia*, to Jesus' lordship" (*The Son of Man in the Synoptic Tradition*, trans. D. M. Barton [Philadelphia: Westminster Press, 1965], 132). On the contrary, the disciples initiate this conflict, and the disciples take upon themselves the authority to interpret for themselves what is right.

25. Most of these views can be found in Rudolf Bultmann's *History of the Synoptic Tradition*, trans. J. Marsh (Oxford: Basil Blackwell, 1963), 14–16. A different tack is taken by Martin Dibelius, who argued that the reference to forgiveness was already in the text, and that vv. 6–10 were added by a preacher to legitimate the church's practice of forgiveness (*From Tradition to Gospel*, trans. B. L. Woolf [New York: Charles Scribner's Sons, n.d.], 66–68). C. P. Ceroke proposes yet another solution: v. 10 has been added as an editorial aside, hence the inconsistency between v. 5 and v. 10 ("Is Mk 2.10 a Saying of Jesus?" *CBQ* 22 [1960]: 369–90).

26. See Vincent Taylor, *The Gospel according to St. Mark* (London: Macmillan, 1957), 192–95.

27. Ched Myers et al., *Say to This Mountain: Mark's Story of Discipleship* (Maryknoll, N.Y.: Orbis Books, 1996), 18.

28. C. C. Caragounis, *The Son of Man* (Tübingen: Mohr/Siebeck, 1986), 187.

29. For example, Bultmann, *History of the Synoptic Tradition*, 14–16.

30. Robert Tomson Fortna, *The Fourth Gospel and Its Predecessor: From Narrative Source to Present Gospel* (Philadelphia: Fortress Press, 1988), 113–17.

31. Fortna argues that John's signs source only contained the healing story (5:2-9a), and that the references to the man's sin, the conflict, and the "son of man" are additions by the evangelist (ibid., 113–17). But it is inconceivable that the Fourth Evangelist could have added those details independently with no knowledge of the Synoptics; if he did know the latter, then he could not have been drawing on a signs source in which these details were lacking.

32. William Herzog has argued independently for the integrity of the paralytic story. He sees Jesus playing the role of a broker of God's forgiveness, and, "by simply assuming this role, challenges the brokerage house in Jerusalem called the temple." Jesus' strategy bypasses the temple and establishes another means of access to forgiveness. The paralytic cannot rise from his mat, because he is unable to make pilgrimage to the temple. So what the temple has failed to do, Jesus does.

The reaction of the scribes, Herzog continues, is to attempt to shame Jesus, murmuring against him, but leaving him outside the conversation. Jesus counters with a conundrum ("which is easier?"), neither pole of which the scribes would find palatable. Here the form-critical separation of healing from conflict becomes indefensible, says Herzog, for the healing is utterly necessary if the conflict is to have meaning. Without the healing, the conflict degenerates into a war of words, and the man remains paralyzed on his mat. More to the point, the healing indicates that

God's power is at work, confirming the identity and role of Jesus as a legitimate broker. In that context, "the son of the man" emphasizes his role as one of the common people, who were mere laity, not priests. God had rejected the temple and its priesthood and opened an alternate way. Jesus addressed the paralytic as "my child" and offered him healing while he remained on his mat. A story created by the church would surely have provided a more christological ending; instead, the people glorified God, not Jesus (William R. Herzog II, *Jesus, Justice, and the Reign of God* [Louisville: Westminster John Knox Press, 2000], 124–32). Gerd Theissen has also broken ranks with the form critics by seeing this pericope whole (*The Miracle Stories of the Early Christian Tradition* [Philadelphia: Fortress, 1983], 113).

33. Caragounis, *Son of Man*, 32. Caragounis pans the notion that exorcists/healers were a dime a dozen in first-century Palestine. We know of only two: Honi and Hanina ben Dosa, who were chiefly rainmakers. So far as we know, no one else was declaring people forgiven in first-century Palestine apart from John the Baptist and Jesus and their disciples.

34. Neither Mark nor Luke develops the collective sense of the son of the man in this story. But the fact that Jesus sends out his disciples preaching repentance (Mark 6:7-13 par.), which implies a response of forgiveness, indicates that he has authorized them to forgive.

Even if my defense of the historicity of the paralytic story fails to convince, Matthew's collective interpretation in 9:8 still gives us an open window into his understanding of the son of the man.

35. T. W. Manson, *The Teaching of Jesus*, 2d ed. (1931; Cambridge: Cambridge University Press, 1959), 227.

36. Ibid., 231.

37. Manson, "Mark ii.27f.," *Coniectanea Neotestamentica* 11 (1947): 146.

38. Ibid., 235.

39. Ibid., 214. His reasons were ideological: he believed that Jesus spoke little, if at all, of the son of the man until the decisive turning point in his ministry (Peter's confession). Hence the son-of-man references in Mark 2 come too early to fit his thesis.

40. I have not attempted a redaction-critical evaluation of the son of the man sayings because Todt has already done that (*The Son of Man in the Synoptic Tradition*). For a more recent redaction-critical study of the son-of-the-man sayings in Luke, see C. M. Tuckett, "The Lukan Son of Man," in *Luke's Literary Achievement*, ed. C. M. Tuckett, JSNT Supplement Series 116 (Sheffield: Sheffield Academic Press, 1995), 198–217—"Luke *does* reproduce his sources faithfully and he does not introduce new meanings. . . . His ideas about [the son of the man] largely coincide with those of his sources" (215). For Matthew, see Heinz Geist, *Menschensohn und Gemeinde: Eine redaktionskritische Untersuchung zur Menschensohn-pradikation in Matthausevangelium* (Würzburg: Echter, 1986); and U. Luz, "The Son of Man in Matthew: Heavenly Judge or Human Christ?" *JSNT* 48 (1992): 3–21. For Q, see C. M. Tuckett, "The Son of Man in Q," in *From Jesus to John*, ed. Martinus C. De Boer, JSNT Supplement Series 84 (Sheffield: Sheffield Academic Press, 1993), 196–215; Leif E. Vaage, "The Son of Man Sayings in Q: Stratigraphical Location and Significance," *Semeia* 55 (1991): 103–27; and Heinz Schürmann, "Observations on the Son of Man Title in the Speech Source," in *The Shape of Q*, ed. John S. Kloppenborg (Minneapolis: Fortress Press, 1994), 74–97.

Schürmann writes that in the Q son-of-the-man sayings, "[N]o uniform redactional tendency exhibits itself in any place or in any way" (94). "The Son of Man title, unintelligible as it was to Hellenists, vanished quite early from the living tradition of community preaching, even though the acquaintance of the evangelists with the Son of Man title proves that it was, after all—as a given—still usable" (93). This statement is self-contradictory. If the title had vanished, it could no longer be used.

41. This is one of only two nonapocalyptic son-of-man sayings in Q. It is the only son-of-man saying in the *Gospel of Thomas*, which is virtually identical to the Q version of this saying except for the addition of "to rest." The saying, retranslated into Aramaic, is a poetic gem, with balanced, rhythmic stitches arranged in a pair of rhymed couplets. Mahlon H. Smith comments, "As it stands, the saying about foxes' holes makes no claims about Jesus that are overtly confessional. And the fact that it (*a*) reflects a Palestinian origin, (*b*) is quite dissimilar to sayings elsewhere in Jewish tradition, (*c*) articulates a paradoxical reversal of popular wisdom typical of other Jesus sayings and (*d*) has been preserved in rather awkward contexts in two independent collections of logia, commends it as an authentic utterance of Jesus" ("No Place for a Son of Man," *FFF* 4 [1988]: 86). In *Thomas* there is no mission context; this has probably been added by Q to integrate the saying with those that follow. When we remove the introduction (v. 57), a host of problems drop away: the man's offer already accepts homelessness as a condition of discipleship; no motive is given for Jesus' unaccountable brusqueness; and Jesus seems to be discouraging discipleship in a section in which he is calling them to it (ibid.). I refer the reader to Smith for exegetical details.

42. E. A. Abbott, *The Son of Man, or Contributions to the Study of the Thoughts of Jesus* (Cambridge: Cambridge University Press, 1910), 161–62.

43. Smith, "No Place for a Son of Man," 99–100.

44. Ibid., 100.

45. Herman C. Waetjen, *The Origin and Destiny of Humanness: An Interpretation of the Gospel of Matthew* (Corte Madera, Calif.: Omega Books, 1976), 120.

46. Luke 10:4; 9:3; Matt. 10:10. Mark has them taking a staff and wearing sandals (6:9). See Richard A. Horsley, *Sociology and the Jesus Movement* (New York: Crossroad, 1989), 117. For a survey of this issue and bibliography, see Paul Rhodes Eddy, "Jesus as Diogenes? Reflections on the Cynic Jesus Thesis," *JBL* 115 (1996): 449–69.

47. Cited by R. Bracht Branham and Marie-Odile Goulet-Cazé, eds., *The Cynics* (Berkeley: University of California Press, 1996), 27.

48. Ibid., 44.

49. Ibid., passim.

50. F. Gerald Downing, *Cynics and Christian Origins* (Edinburgh: T. & T. Clark, 1992), 134–35.

51. Derek Krueger, "The Bawdy and Society: The Shamelessness of Diogenes in Roman Imperial Culture," in Branham and Goulet-Cazé, *The Cynics*, 229. Downing's attempts to play down the offensive elements in Cynicism are wholly unconvincing (*Cynics and Christian Origins*, 50–53). Diogenes found no place in a glittering mansion to spit, so he spat on the face of his host (cited by Downing, *Cynics and Christian Origins*, 289). Downing says that Chrysostom praised this behavior; I am unable to find that praise in the text he cites. I cannot imagine such a story being circulated as exemplary by Christians, but it was exemplary for Cynics.

52. A simple comparison tells the difference:

JESUS: "When you give a luncheon or a dinner, do not invite your friends or your brothers or your relatives or rich neighbors, in case they may invite you in return, and you would be repaid. But when you give a banquet, invite the poor, the crippled, the lame, and the blind" (Luke 14:12-13).

DIOGENES: Having been invited to a dinner, he declared that he wouldn't go; for, the last time he went, his host had not expressed a proper gratitude (*Diogenes Laertius* 6.34, LCL).

53. Archaeological evidence indicates that Hebrew language and literature, as well as Aramaic and Jewish culture, dominated Galilee at the time of Jesus. "Nothing suggests that Greco-Roman philosophers would have been found there" (Mark Chancey and Eric M. Meyers, "How Jewish Was Sepphoris in Jesus' Time?" *BAR* 26 [2000]: 33).

54. See the attack on the Cynic position by Paul Rhodes Eddy ("Jesus as Diogenes: Reflections on the Cynic Jesus Thesis," *JBL* 115 [1996]: 449–69); and the rejoinder by David Seeley, "Jesus and the Cynics Revisited," *JBL* 116 (1997): 704–12.

55. Bruce Chilton sees "the son of the man" here as applying "not simply to Jesus but also to the homeless disciples, and it carries with it a resonant sympathy for all homeless people. The 'son of man' here cannot mean 'me, myself, I, and no one else.' Others are included with the speaker, as in Ps. 8:4" ("The Son of Man: Who Was He?" *Bible Review* 12 [1996]: 36).

56. Howes, "Son of Man—Expression of the Self," 181.

57. Rabbi Rami M. Shapiro understands this open receptivity:

God said to Abraham, "Leave your country, your family, your father's house, and walk inward to the land I will show you." This is what true spirituality demands: to leave everything we know; to relinquish everything we are . . . simply trusting that when we get "there . . ." we will know. Buddha did that. So did Lao Tzu, Jesus, and Mohammed. They all left home.

But we do just the opposite. Worse! We take refuge in those who taught No Refuge. We imitate those who demanded No Imitation. We study each other's floor plans, and borrow each other's furniture, when what we really need is to leave home. (Rabbi Rami M. Shapiro, quoted in "Should You Design Your Own Religion?" *Utne Reader*, [July–August 1998], 47)

58. Carl Jung, *The Development of Personality*, CW 17, 174.

59. James D. G. Dunn, *The Christ and the Spirit*, vol. 2: *Pneumatology* (Grand Rapids: Eerdmans, 1998), 165.

60. Hans Dieter Betz, *The Greek Magical Papyri in Translation* (Chicago: University of Chicago Press, 1986), 4–6 (PGM 1.42–195).

61. Matt. 12:28 // Luke 11:20.

62. Douglas R. A. Hare, *The Son of Man Tradition* (Minneapolis: Fortress Press, 1990), 149.

63. *Gospel of Thomas* 44 has a surprisingly trinitarian form of the saying: "Jesus said: He who blasphemes against the Father will be forgiven, and he who blasphemes against the Son will be forgiven; but he who blasphemes against the Holy Spirit will not be forgiven, either on earth or in heaven." Luke's version of the saying is generally regarded as the most authentic, but Luke has torn it out of its Q context and added it to a string of sayings for no other reason than its catchword similarities. Matthew seems to have preserved the Q context.

64. Howes, *Jesus' Answer to God*, 72–74.

65. In the discussion that follows I have drawn heavily on a paper by Tom Goodhue, "Jesus as Wino, God as Woman" (New Testament 340, Union Theological Seminary, 1974), and on a paper I presented to the Jesus Seminar, "A Brief for Reconsidering Q 7:33-35 // Matt. 11:18-19." I have unfortunately forgotten the date.

66. Luke 7:28b // Matt. 11:11b // Gos. Thom. 46; Matt. 3:14-15; Luke 3:15; John in every reference to the Baptist. See my *John the Baptist in the Gospel Tradition* (Cambridge: Cambridge University Press, 1968).

67. Contra Richard Horsley, *Jesus and the Spiral of Violence: Popular Jewish Resistance in Roman Palestine* (San Francisco: Harper & Row, 1987), 212.

68. Phillip Sigal notes that the rabbis hedged Deut. 21:18-21 with one limitation after another to make it virtually impossible to stone a rebellious son (*Halakah of Jesus of Nazareth*, 62–63).

69. Proverbs 1:24; Bar. 3:14, 29f.; Wisd. Sol. 7:27; *1 Enoch* 42: 93:8.

70. Jeremias, *New Testament Theology*, 26.

71. Patrick J. Hartin, "'Yet Wisdom Is Justified by Her Children' (Q 7:35)," in *Conflict and Invention: Literary, Rhetorical, and Social Studies on the Sayings Gospel Q*, ed. John S. Kloppenborg (Valley Forge, Pa.: Trinity Press International, 1995), 155.

72. Bultmann, *History of the Synoptic Tradition*, 153.

73. Jeremias, *New Testament Theology*, 83. James Hope Moulton cites the English expression "I came for business, not for pleasure" as an example of a nonmythical use of "I came" (*A Grammar of New Testament Greek*, 3d ed. [Edinburgh: T. & T. Clark, 1985], 1:138). What we have in Luke 7:34 // Matt. 11:19 is a form of synonymous parallelism, inverted from the usual order in Hebrew Scriptures: "The son of man . . . eating and drinking . . . a man . . . a glutton and drunkard."

74. Robert W. Funk, *The Five Gospels: The Search for the Authentic Words of Jesus. New Translation and Commentary* (New York: Macmillan, 1993), 42, 180. Compare Mark 14:21 — "For the son of the man *goes*," which in context means "dies, is killed." So the son of the man "came" is merely an idiomatic way of speaking of one's destiny.

75. Maurice Casey crams this saying into the Procrustean bed of a generalized translation when he renders this passage as "a son of man comes eating and drinking," as if it could refer to anyone ("General, Generic, and Indefinite: The Use of the Term 'Son of Man' in Aramaic Sources and in the Teaching of Jesus," *JSNT* 29 [1987]: 39).

76. Frederick W. Danker, "Luke 16,16—An Opposition Logion," *JBL* 77 (1958): 231–43.

77. *b. Qidd.* 66d.

78. Goodhue, "Jesus as Wino, God as Woman."

79. A. J. B. Higgins, *Jesus and the Son of Man* (Philadelphia: Fortress Press, 1964), 138.

80. Matthew, on the other hand, is not content to leave it there. There *is* a sign after all: the resurrection of Jesus. So Matthew changes the Q saying to read, "For just as Jonah was three days and three nights in the belly of the sea monster, so for three days and three nights the son of the man will be in the heart of the earth" (12:40). Matthew also interprets Jesus' return on the clouds of heaven as "the sign" of the son of the man (24:30). With these two changes Matthew completely reverses Jesus' refusal of a sign.

81. Adela Yarbro Collins, "The Son of Man Sayings in Q," paper delivered at the Society of Biblical Literature Annual Meeting, Orlando, Florida, 1998, p. 7.

82. The story of Jonah is mythologically of a piece with all stories of descent into the underworld. In the words of Patrick Oliver,

> Wherever there is a death within the personality, there is the invitation to descend into the underworld and its silence. The sharp clarity of the conscious physical world is doused, and the sojourn in the land of shadows commences. The conquered conscious ego is given an opportunity to be connected and integrated with the eternal and the creative in the spiritual world, through its tumble into darkness and its abnegation of egocentricity—a sacrifice which results in disidentification with one's own preferred attitudes and functions. Jesus' reply to the Pharisees that the Son of Man's only sign will be that of Jonah (Matt. 12:38-42) can be paralleled with this same mythological motif, which is the perennial psychic movement of being swallowed and regurgitated. (Patrick Julian Oliver, "Implications of the Psychological Theories of Morton Kelsey for a Contemporary Individual Understanding of the Mythological Elements of Matthew's Gospel" [Ph.D. diss., Griffith University, Queensland, Australia, 1999], 314.)

83. The "first will be last, and the last will be first" appears in one form or another in Matt. 19:30; 20:16; Mark 10:31; Luke 13:30; P.Oxy. 654 4:2a; Gos. *Thom.* 4:2a; and *Barn.* 6:13a. Sayings about being a servant of all appear in Matt. 20:25b-28; 23:11; Mark 9:35b; 10:42b-45; Luke 9:48b; 22:25-27; and John 13:14. This paradoxical reversal of the understanding of power was fundamental to the message of Jesus. On the issue of historicity, see P. Stuhlmacher, "Existenzstellvertretung für die Vielen: Mk. 10:45 (Mt. 20:28)," in *Werden und Wirken des Alten Testament: Festschrift für Claus Westermann,* ed. Rainer Albertz (Göttingen: Vandenhoeck & Ruprecht, 1980), 412–27; Ben Witherington III, *The Christology of Jesus* (Minneapolis: Fortress Press, 1990), 251–56.

84. Fernando Belo, *A Materialist Reading of the Gospel of Mark,* trans. M. J. O-Connell (Maryknoll, N.Y.: Orbis Books, 1981), 176.

85. Tödt, *Son of Man in the Synoptic Tradition,* 207.

86. The Greek word *lutron* ("ransom") is used in the LXX especially of God's acts of deliverance in freeing Israel from bondage, both at the Exodus and in the return from exile in Babylon. It is never used of a sin-offering or guilt-offering, and is

not associated with the sacrificial cultus or blood atonement (Morna Hooker, *The Son of Man in Mark* [London: SPCK, 1967], 144; Procksch, *"lutron," TDNT* 4:328–35).

87. Ibid., 144–45. I have transliterated the Greek term.

88. Chris Rice, "Separate *and* Equal?" *Sojourners* (January/February 2000): 43.

89. Hooker, *Son of Man in Mark*, 144–45.

90. The Lukan parallel (Luke 22:27) uses "I" where Mark and Matthew read "the son of the man," which has led some scholars to conclude that Luke represents earlier tradition. Higgins objects: Luke has no theory of the efficacy of Jesus' death and would have rejected Mark's ransom theory. In addition, Higgins argues, Luke's version of the saying has been honed to fit a setting, not in the dispute over greatness, but in the Last Supper. Luke has inadequately fit the saying to the context, however, since Jesus is *not* waiting at table but presides. To Higgins, Lukan vocabulary reflects the concerns of Hellenistic churches; if Mark 10:45 were based on Luke 22:27, it would be archaizing to fabricate a son-of-the-man saying out of an I-word from the *Greek*-speaking church (Higgins, *Jesus and the Son of Man*, 39–41). Luke clearly regards the son of the man as synonymous with Jesus' "I" and may drop the son of the man in 22:27, 29–30 to prevent redundancy (he uses the son of the man in 22:22 and 48).

91. Horsley, *Jesus and the Spiral of Violence*, 244.

92. Fernando Belo thinks that the reference to James and John having to take the same cup and baptism as Jesus points directly to their murder by the authorities in the first decades after the judicial murder of Jesus (*Materialist Reading of the Gospel of Mark*, 275). This would underline the true nature of the Powers that Jesus describes in Mark 10:42 and make all the more absurd these disciples' desire to emulate the powerful.

Vincent Taylor examines the alleged Papias tradition of the murder of James and John and ends by rejecting it (*Gospel according to St. Mark*, 442). The evidence is weak either way; but this verse in Mark seems to presuppose their deaths as martyrs.

93. Niall O'Brien gives a wonderful example of baptism as a renunciation of torture, injustice, and militarism, and shows how the Eucharist can be used as a nonviolent action. See his *Revolution from the Heart* (New York: Oxford University Press, 1987), 209–15, 261, 265–66. George D. McClain has developed a number of liturgies for confronting the Powers (*Claiming All Things for God: Prayer, Discernment, and Ritual for Social Change* [Nashville: Abingdon Press, 1998]).

94. Cited by Stephen Hart, "How Grassroots Christians and Congregations Connect Faith to Local Social and Political Issues," in *SBLSP* (1992), 6.

95. There are numerous references; see "power" in a concordance.

96. Howes, "Son of Man—Expression of the Self," 182.

97. Ibid.

98. Hooker, *The Son of Man in Mark*, 140.

99. This is the title of Hugo Echegaray's book on liberation theology, *La Práctica de Jesus* (Lima: Centro de Estudios y Publicaciones, 1980).

100. Matt. 16:21-23 // Mark 8:31-33 // Luke 9:22; Matt. 17:22-23 // Mark 9:30-32 // Luke 9:43-45; Matt. 20:17-19 // Mark 10:32-34 // Luke 18:31-34; Mark 9:12; Luke 17:25; Matt. 17:12; 26:2.

101. Matt. 17:22-23 // Mark 9:30-32 // Luke 9:43-45; Matt. 20:17-19 // Mark 10:32-34 // Luke 18:31-34; Matt. 26:2.

102. Mark 8:31-33 // Luke 9:22; Luke 17:25.

103. Tödt concludes that all the suffering-son-of-man sayings have been fabricated by the church (*Son of Man in the Synoptic Tradition*, chap. 4). I would say, rather, that these sayings have been modified by the church, but that the prediction of execution is historical.

104. Mark 2:7 par.; Matt. 11:19 // Luke 7:34 = Deut. 21:20; Matt. 23:37 // Luke 13:34. John's Gospel mentions two attempts to stone him (8:59; 10:31, 39).

105. Hare, *Son of Man Tradition*, 193, 275; David R. Catchpole, "The 'Triumphal' Entry," in *Jesus and the Politics of His Day*, ed. Ernst Bammel and C. F. D. Moule (Cambridge: Cambridge University Press, 1984), 326–28. Eduard Schweizer rightly insists that the Satan passage cannot be attributed to the early church and that it makes no sense without some kind of passion prediction ("Der Menschensohn," ZNW 50 [1959]: 195).

106. Among the "will be delivered" passages is also one that says nothing about crucifixion and resurrection. Luke 9:44 says simply, "The son of the man (*bar 'enash, o huios tou anthrōpou*) is going to be delivered into the hands of sons of men (*bene 'enasha, anthrōpoi*)," which makes a nice pun in both Aramaic and in Greek.

107. It is significant that Mark 8:31, which is usually regarded as the model for Mark 9:31 and 10:33-34, is in fact quite different; the latter two emphasize Jesus being "delivered," which is not in the former. Higgins also notes that the term "rejected" in Mark 8:31 is not drawn from the passion narrative, but represents the Hebrew *hadhal* of Isa. 53:3 (*Jesus and the Son of Man*, 35).

108. Luke 22:48 ("Judas, is it with a kiss that you are betraying the son of the man?") seems to be an expansion on 22:22 ("For the son of the man is going as it has been determined, but woe to that one by whom he is betrayed!"). Neither Mark nor Matthew has the son of the man in their parallels to Luke 22:48. Luke omits the material in Mark 14:38b-42; when two verses later he adds a son-of-the-man saying in the same context and in reference to the same betrayal, it would appear that he is simply revising Mark, and not, as some argue, using a special source. (The historicity of the Judas materials is a sharply controverted issue that I cannot undertake in this study.)

109. Hare, *Son of Man Tradition*, 227. We have to assume, says Hare, that even when Christians added suffering-son-of-the-man sayings to the tradition, they did so on the assumption that "this strange idiom would be accepted as 'authentic' by their contemporaries because it was already well established in the tradition of Jesus' sayings" (228).

110. This is the truth in Mephistopheles' statement in Goethe's *Faust*: "I am a part of that power which always wills evil and always works good" (act I, scene 3), though I would change the latter part to "sometimes works good."

111. Matthew replaces Luke's "on account of the son of the man" with "on my account" (5:11). It is easy to see how "the son of the man" could be replaced by "my account." It is difficult to imagine any reason to shift from "my account" to "the son of the man." Luke 6:22 clearly appears to have been in Q, judging from the Matthean parallel.

112. Mark 8:31 par.; Luke 17:25; 24:7; John 3:14; 12:34.

113. Morna Hooker makes a strong case for understanding the "one like a human being" in Dan. 7:13 as suffering Israel, in the throes of Antiochus's attempt

to proscribe the Jewish religion. Indeed, one of the anomalies of research on the "one in human form" in Daniel is that scholars seldom place the phrase in the political context of persecution; hence, they deny that suffering plays any part in Daniel 7 (Hooker, *Son of Man in Mark*, 30). This requires that scholars overlook 7:21 (Antiochus "made war with the holy ones and was prevailing over them"), 7:23 (he shall "devour the whole earth, and trample it down, and break it to pieces"), and 7:25 (he shall "wear out the holy ones of the Most High"), to say nothing of 7:7 ("was devouring, breaking in pieces, and stamping what was left with its feet").

114. Ignatius, *To the Romans* 3:3.

115. Roger Cohen, "Big Brother Is Still Haunting Society in German's East," *New York Times*, 29 November 1999 (Internet edition).

116. They could not forget, but they could hide Judas's betrayal: Paul makes no mention of Judas.

117. *Kataphileo* is used of the woman's kissing Jesus' feet (Luke 7:38); of the jubilant father welcoming home his son (Luke 15:20); of Paul's friends' farewells (Acts 20:37). H. Liddell and R. Scott, *Greek-English Lexicon* (Oxford: Clarendon Press, 1958), 919, notes that the word is used especially of an amorous kiss, as in Lucian *Amores* 13.

118. The bankruptcy of Maurice Casey's philological approach is especially manifest in his translation of Luke 22:48. Luke reads, "Judas, do you betray the son of the man with a kiss?" Casey renders that as, "Judah, kissing a son of man and you betray him!" as if son of man here could refer to anyone in a similar situation. See his "General, Generic, and Indefinite," 21–56.

119. I am thinking of discussions I attended of the Jesus Seminar.

120. Riane Eisler woke me to this insight in her pathbreaking *The Chalice and the Blade* (San Francisco: Harper & Row, 1987), 120–24.

121. Richard McBrien, *Catholicism* (Minneapolis: Winston Press, 1980), 1:462.

122. Thelma Megill-Cobbler, "A Feminist Rethinking of Punishment Imagery in Atonement," *Dialog* 35 (winter 1996): 16.

123. Ibid., 17.

124. Peter Abelard, "Exposition of the Epistle to the Romans," quoted in ibid., 18.

125. Émile Durkheim, *The Division of Labor in Society* (New York: Macmillan, 1933), 85–86, 99–100.

126. Ernst Bloch, *Man on His Own: Essays in the Philosophy of Religion*, trans. E. B. Ashton (New York: Herder and Herder, 1970), 192.

127. Martin Luther, *Commentary on the Galatians* (1535), ed. Jaroslav Pelikan and W. A. Hansen (St. Louis: Concordia, 1963), 26:277.

128. Ibid., 278, 281; cited by Megill-Cobbler, "Feminist Rethinking," 19.

129. Bloch, *Man on His Own*, 198. J. Denny Weaver calls the Christus Victor theory *The Nonviolent Atonement Theory* (Grand Rapids: Eerdmans, 2001).

130 Jack Nelson-Pallmeyer, *Jesus against Christianity* (Harrisburg, Pa.: Trinity Press International, 2001), 221–25. Nelson-Pallmeyer objects to my saying that the cross both exposes and defeats the Powers (*Engaging the Powers*, 139–43). But I do so only paradoxically, as a matter of faith. That paradox is the very life of hope.

Second, he rejects my assertion that the Bible is the necessary precondition for the gradual perception of the meaning of violence (ibid., 147). But the problem of violence could never have arisen in a peaceful country. Nor could it have arisen in the

conquest states, where violence goes unquestioned. It could only rise to consciousness as a *problem* in a virtually constantly defeated and occupied country powerless to
use violence successfully. God (who, I assume, is real and therefore nonviolent intrinsically) could only be revealed as nonviolent in such a conflicted setting.

131. Ibid., 225. Nelson-Pallmeyer criticizes Rene Girard's theory that the scapegoat's death reunites the community. But John 11:50 makes the very point he would
deny. "You do not understand that it is better for you to have one man die for the people than to have the whole nation destroyed." To knowingly kill an innocent person
for political or religious ends fits exactly the accepted view of scapegoating. Nelson-
Pallmeyer is right, however, that any act of scapegoating has a chilling effect on a
restive populace, robbing it of hope.

132. James Killen, *Meeting the Savior* (Macon, Ga.: Smyth and Helwys, 2001),
helpfully correlates existential need and atonement imagery. Perry B. Yoder distinguishes among the variety of New Testament atonement theories, but does not cor-
relate them with individual need (*Shalom: The Bible's Word for Salvation, Justice,
and Peace* [Newton, Kans.: Faith and Life Press, 1987], 53–70). George Rupp has developed a christological grid that favors a variety of christological positions while still
rejecting what he calls a transactional type (Anselm) (*Christologies and Cultures: Toward a Typology of Religious Worldviews*, Religion and Reason 10 [The Hague: Mou-
ton, 1974]). John T. Carroll and Joel B. Green identify the atonement imagery of the
principal writers of the New Testament (*The Death of Jesus in Early Christianity*
[Peabody, Mass.: Hendrickson, 1995]).

133. See also Leanne Van Dyk, "Do Theories of Atonement Foster Abuse?" *Dialog* 35 (winter 1996): 25.

134. John G. Neihardt, *Black Elk Speaks* (New York: Washington Square Press,
1932), 4.

Chapter 6
Jesus and the Messianic Hope

1. The Davidic king: Psalm 132; Isa. 9:1-6; 55:3-4; Jer. 17:19-25; 23:1-3; 30:9;
33.15ff.; Ezek. 34:23-24; 37:24; Hosea 3:5; Amos 9:11; Micah 4:8; Zech. 9:10, to
name a few. The priestly Messiah: Mal. 3:1-4; *T. Jos.* 19:4; 18:1-11; *T. Levi* 18:1-12.
The prophet like Moses: Deut. 18:15. All three: Qumran 1QS 9,11. Some texts
combine the messiah of Aaron (priest) and the messiah of Israel (king): *T.Iss.* 5:7-8.

2. Some Jewish Christians in the early centuries rejected the identification of
Jesus as Messiah, arguing that nothing he did corresponded to current messianic belief. Consequently, they revered Jesus as the Prophet (the Pseudo-Clementine writings). According to one sect of Jewish Christians, the Qaraites, Jesus' response to
Peter's "You are the Christ" was "Do not say this" (Shlomo Pines, "The Jewish Christians of the Early Centuries of Christianity according to a New Source," *Proceedings
of the Israel Academy of Sciences and Humanities* 2, no. 13 [1966]: 45–46). This is, I
believe, the correct sense of Mark 8:30.

3. Some commentators suggest that the original story might have included only
Mark 8:27–29, 33. That would be an outright rejection of the messianic role, however, whereas v. 30 is consistent with other passages in which Jesus' response is more
ambivalent.

4. Elizabeth Boyden Howes, "Analytical Psychology and the Synoptic Gospels," in *Intersection and Beyond* (San Francisco: Guild for Psychological Studies, 1971), 164.

5. Elizabeth Boyden Howes, *Jesus' Answer to God* (San Francisco: Guild for Psychological Studies, 1984), 124.

6. See my *John the Baptist in the Gospel Tradition*, SNTMS 7 (Cambridge: Cambridge University Press, 1968), chap. 5.

7. H. E. Tödt remarks, "In the earliest material within the synoptic tradition no authentic saying of Jesus can be detected which would state, *I am* the Messiah, or the Son of Man, or the Son of God, etc. Jesus in his teaching *pointed away from himself*" (*The Son of Man in the Synoptic Tradition*, trans. D. M. Barton [Philadelphia: Westminster Press, 1965], 225).

8. A. J. Levine suggests a simpler solution: Jesus may have answered indirectly for political reasons (personal communication).

9. In the Old Testament, the Davidic descent of the Messiah is attested in Isa. 9:2-7; 11:1-9; Jer. 23:5-6; 33:14-18; Ezek. 34:23-24; 37:24; Ps. 89:20. In intertestamental writings, it is attested in *Pss. Sol.* 17–18, and in the New Testament, in Rom. 1:3; Matt. 1:1-17 // Luke 3:23-38; John 7:42; and 2 Tim. 2:8. Jesus is called son of David in Mark 10:47-48; Matt. 9:27; 12:23; 15:22; 20:30-31; 21:9, 15; Luke 1:27, 32, 69; 18:38-39.

10. Eduard Schweizer, *The Good News according to Mark*, trans. D. H. Madvig (Richmond: John Knox Press, 1970), 256. So also Joel Marcus: "The apparent claim in Mark 12:35-37 that the messiah is *not* a son of David, therefore, represents a puzzling piece of Christology that is at home neither in first-century Judaism nor in first-century Christianity. To paraphrase Mark 12:35b, how can our author say that the messiah is *not* the Son of David?" ("The Jewish War and the *Sitz im Leben* of Mark," *JBL* 111 [1992]: 457).

11. The emperor Domitian gave orders to execute everyone of the family of David, but rescinded the order when he discovered that the grandsons of Judas, the brother of Jesus, were merely poor peasants (Eusebius *Ecclesiastical History* 3.19).

12. Herman C. Waetjen, *A Reordering of Power: A Sociological Reading of Mark's Gospel* (Minneapolis: Fortress Press, 1989), 195.

13. See, for example, Jean Daniélou, *The Theology of Jewish Christianity*, trans. J. A. Baker (Philadelphia: Westminster Press, 1964); Keith Akers, *The Lost Religion of Jesus: Simple Living and Nonviolence in Early Christianity* (New York: Lantern Books, 2000).

14. In Acts 7:56, the scandal that leads to Stephen's death is not that Stephen claimed to see a vision, or that he had spoken of the son of the man standing in the presence of God—this was the son of the man's proper place, according to tradition. Did the controversy result because the authorities knew very well that by son of the man, Stephen meant no one else but Jesus? That would mean that they had murdered God's own messenger (C. C. Caragounis, *The Son of Man: Vision and Interpretation*, WUNT 38 [Tübingen: Mohr/Siebeck, 1986], 238).

15. The manuscripts are Theta, f13, 565, 700 pc, and Origen—not a weighty set of witnesses. The Aland text suggests that these represent a conflation with the text of Matthew. But this reading is not quite the same as Matthew's, though it conveys the same sense.

16. Friedrich Nietzsche, *Beyond Good and Evil: Prelude to a Philosophy of the Future*, trans. W. Kaufmann (New York: Vintage, 1966), 75.

17. Julian *Oration* 6.187c–d.

Chapter 7
Projection and the Messianic Hope

1. Albert Schweitzer, *Von Reimarus zu Wrede*, first German edition, 1906; translated by George Eliot as *The Quest of the Historical Jesus* (London: A. & C. Black, 1910; revised ed., New York: Macmillan, 1968), 4.

2. Carl Jung, *The Archetypes and the Collective Unconscious*, CW 9.1, 25. Jung defines projection as "an unconscious, automatic process whereby a content that is unconscious to the subject transfers itself to an object, so that it seems to belong to that object. The projection ceases the moment it becomes conscious, that is to say when it is seen as belonging to the subject" (60–61). The positive side of projecting is that certain unconscious components of the self can only come to consciousness indirectly, by way of projection (187).

3. Hal Childs, *The Myth of the Historical Jesus and the Evolution of Consciousness* (Atlanta: Scholars Press, 2000), 244.

4. Those who see Jesus in a negative light may also be projecting onto him an experience of a negative father or a negative religious upbringing. The point is that *everyone* projects something. Such projection is fundamental to our knowledge of any person who carries for us a charged significance.

5. George Tyrrell, cited by N. T. Wright, *The New Testament and the People of God* (Minneapolis: Fortress Press, 1992), 102.

6. Childs, *Myth of the Historical Jesus*, 98. Childs mentions Jung's comment that "projections change the world into the replica of one's own unknown face" (*Aion*, CW 9.2 [1951], 17).

7. *Acts of John* 89 (*NTApoc* 2:225); 96:25, 28–32 (*NTApoc* 2:230).

8. Majella Franzmann speaks my mind when she says: "All I can do is try to be aware constantly of the ongoing subjective play of myself as interpreter and the text which is both shaped by and shapes/reshapes my questions. . . . I have no illusions that this is not also the case with my study. In the final analysis, I am aware of the possibility that at the most fundamental level, the answers I find may be chosen for their aesthetic appeal, where the patterns of symbol and meaning find their most satisfying reflection deep within my own psyche" (*Jesus in the Nag Hammadi Writings* [Edinburgh: T. & T. Clark, 1996], 23).

9. John Dominic Crossan, *The Historical Jesus: The Life of a Mediterranean Jewish Peasant* (San Francisco: HarperSanFrancisco, 1991), xxviii.

10. Rumi, *The Essential Rumi*, trans. C. Barks with J. Moyne (San Francisco: HarperSanFrancisco, 1995), 134–35.

11. Marie-Luise von Franz, *Projection and Re-collection in Jungian Psychology* (London: Open Court, 1980), 31.

12. *Zohar* 2:86b; Daniel C. Matt, "The Aura of Secrecy in the Zohar," in *Gershom Scholem's Major Trends in Jewish Mysticism 50 Years After*, ed. P. Schäfer and J. Dan (Tübingen: Mohr/Siebeck, 1993),184.

13. Gershom G. Scholem, *Major Trends in Jewish Mysticism* (New York:

Schocken Books, 1965), 348. In Jewish mysticism, the righteous find their own way or path, and are themselves transformed into a path through which the vital strength flows from above to below. The path they open can then be taken by others (Gershom Scholem, *On the Mystical Shape of the Godhead: Basic Concepts in the Kabbalah*, trans. J. Negroschel [New York: Schocken Books, 1991], 136–37).

14. Franz Kafka, *Parables and Paradoxes*, ed. N. N. Glatzer (New York: Schocken Books, 1961), 81.

15. Cited by Erich Neumann, "The Mystical Vision," in *Man and Transformation, Papers from Eranos Yearbooks*, Bollingen Series 30.6 (1961; Princeton: Princeton University Press, 1982), 401. So also Matsuo Basko: "Do not seek to follow in the footsteps of the masters. Seek what they sought" (cited in Gabrielle Roth, *Sweat Your Prayers: Movement as Spiritual Practice* [New York: Tarcher/Putnam, 1997], 149).

16. But for Paul, Jesus' sinlessness was not moral but juridical: Jesus had done nothing for which he could be justly punished. "Innocent" carries the meaning.

17. Matthew calls him a young man (19:20, 22); Mark 10:17 features him running and kneeling, which hints at boyish impetuosity; and the statement that he has kept the commandments from his youth suggests that he cannot have left his youth very far behind. But the father of the prodigal son was not young, and he ran to greet his returning son. Matthew has no other source than Mark for this story, so the detail must be his own invention.

18. Jon Sobrino, *Christology at the Crossroads: A Latin American Approach*, trans. J. Drury (Maryknoll, N.Y.: Orbis Books, 1978), 128.

19. Carl Jung, "Is Analytical Psychology a Religion? Notes on a Talk Given by C. G. Jung," *Spring* (1972): 147–48.

20. Matthew and Luke both cannot abide the bad light this accusation casts on the disciples. Matthew changes it into a pious and expectant plea for help; Luke, to a mere statement that they are perishing (Matt. 8:2; Luke 8:24).

21. M 801, sec. 547–51, p. 34; in *NTApoc.* 1:360. The Manichaean pantheon also includes a Primal Man ("O perfect Man, haven of my trust, rise up. You are the First Man") (Simone Petrement, *A Separate God: The Christian Origins of Gnosticism*, trans. C. Harrison [San Francisco: HarperSanFrancisco, 1990], 112 n. 24). This Primal Man belongs to the Holy Trinity of Iranian Manichaeism, and is, as usual, a heavenly being: the God "Man." But he is a protological, not eschatological, figure. See Samuel N. C. Lieu, *Manichaeism: in the Later Roman Empire and Medieval China: A Historical Survey* (Manchester: Manchester University Press, 1985), 207; Hans-Martin Schenke, *Der Gott "Mensch" in der Gnosis: Ein religiongeschichtlicher Beitrag zur Diskussion über die paulinische Anschauung vonder Kirche als Lieb Christi* (Göttingen: Vandenhoeck & Ruprecht, 1962), 108–19.

22. Paul Ricoeur, *The Symbolism of Evil* (New York: Harper & Row, 1967), 269.

23. John Dominic Crossan says that Jesus preached a "brokerless kingdom," of which Jesus was the necessary broker (*The Historical Jesus*). Luke Timothy Johnson pounces on the apparent contradiction: Jesus "is precisely the 'broker' whom Christianity must reject if it is to truly live by his vision" (*The Real Jesus* [San Francisco: HarperSanFrancisco, 1996], 49). But, as we saw earlier, the "broker" has to carry the projections of the disciples until they are able to break free.

24. Elizabeth Boyden Howes, *Jesus' Answer to God* (San Francisco: Guild for Psychological Studies, 1984), iv.

25. Harold Bloom, *Omens of Millennium* (New York: Riverhead Books, 1996), 17.

26. Carl Jung, "Transformation Symbolism in the Mass," in *Psychology and Religion: West and East*, CW 11, 293. Thomas Münzer provides a harsh reminder of the cost of psychic inflation as a collective epidemic. Those who joined him in the peasants' revolt of 1524–26 would, he promised, become gods, deified by the incarnation of Christ. Instead, they were slaughtered.

27. Jung, "Transformation Symbolism in the Mass," 294.

28. Carl Jung, "To the Rev. David Cox," 25 September 1957, from Jung's *Letters*, cited in Edward Edinger, *The New God-Image* (Wilmette, Ill.: Chiron, 1996), 186.

Chapter 8
The Human Being: Catalyst of Human Transformation

1. Carl Jung, *Psychology and Religion: West and East*, CW 11:713.

2. Origen discusses an ancient tradition in which John the Baptist was indeed believed to be the incarnation of an angel who took human form in order to bear witness to the divine Logos in John 1:6-8 (*Commentary on the Gospel of John* 2.31 on 1:6).

3. Some scholars think that the earliest tradition was of Jesus' exaltation or ascension to heaven, and that the resurrection narratives are later elaborations on the immediate exaltation of Jesus after his death. See A. J. B. Higgins, *The Son of Man in the Teaching of Jesus*, SNTSMS 39 (Cambridge: Cambridge University Press, 1990), 30–31.

4. Elizabeth Boyden Howes, *Jesus' Answer to God* (San Francisco: Guild for Psychological Studies, 1984), 219.

5. What I am calling the "archetypal son of the man," Bruce Chilton calls "the angelic," using the language of traditional mysticism. Jesus' baptism, transfiguration, prayers, and meditations, says Chilton, all represent his progressive entry into the trance world of the divine throne chariot. At the transfiguration, Peter, James, and John began to see their rabbi as part of the heavenly pantheon around the throne, standing at God's side along with Moses and Elijah. "His mystical ascent began on Mount Hermon before his death." His death only "intensified his followers' experience of his angelic persona and sharpened their vision of the spirit world where they, like he, increasingly dwelled. . . . [A]s they met together, meditated, and prayed, their journey into the world of the Chariot brought them face to face with Rabbi Jesus. Their visionary trances were collective, and sometimes even on a mass scale." Chilton insists that the resurrection was an angelic, nonmaterial event, in which Jesus took on the angelic reality symbolized by the expression "the son of the man" (which Chilton infelicitously translates "the one like the person"). And not Jesus only, but every person, possessed the angelic likeness of the "one like a person" and mirrored some of the truth of the divine chariot (*Rabbi Jesus: An Intimate Biography* [New York: Doubleday, 2000], 274, 242). Allowing for the differences of language, Chilton and I see the son of the man pretty much the same.

6. The "blasphemy" with which Jesus is charged in Mark 14:62 cannot have been based on Jesus' claim to be the Christ, for this confession is not found in Matthew or Luke, and yet he is still accused of blasphemy in those Gospels. The scandal must lie in asserting that he will share a place on the divine throne chariot with God. Whether this also involves his "coming" to judge his judges is dubious; Luke has no

"coming" to earth here, and Mark and Matthew say nothing in this passage of judgment. See Craig A. Evans, "In What Sense 'Blasphemy'? Jesus before Caiaphas in Mark 14:61-64," in *SBLSP* (Atlanta: Scholars Press, 1991), 222; Joseph Plevnik, "Son of Man Seated at the Right Hand of God: Luke 22,69 in Lukan Christology," *Biblica* 72 (1991): 335.

7. Mark 13:26 par.; Matt. 13:36-43; 25:31-46.

8. Mary Dean-Otting, *Heavenly Journeys: A Study of the Motif in Hellenistic Jewish Literature*, Judentum und Umwelt 8 (New York: Peter Lang, 1984), 17.

9. Paul Ricoeur, *The Symbolism of Evil*, trans. E. Buchanan (New York: Harper & Row, 1967), 270.

10. The Merkabah mystics report a similar experience. The last three chapters of *Hekhalot Rabbati*, at the climax of the mystical ascent, consist of a long hymn uttered each day by the Throne of Glory in the presence of God, and which the mystic is instructed to recite. "It seems that the mystic is identifying himself with the Merkabah [divine throne chariot] and asking God to be *enthroned upon or within him*. In other words, he is seeking to become, like the patriarchs and righteous men of mythical history, a vehicle for the manifestation of the divine Image or Glory"— just as Paul describes it in 2 Corinthians 3 (C. R. A. Morray-Jones, "Transformational Mysticism in the Apocalyptic-Merkabah Tradition," *JJS* 43 [1992]: 26, my emphasis).

11. Edward F. Edinger, *Transformation of the God-Image: An Elucidatino of Jung's Answer to Job*, Studies in Jungian Psychology (Toronto: Inner City Books, 1992), 28.

12. Delores Williams, *Sisters in the Wilderness: The Challenge of Womanist God-Talk* (Maryknoll, N.Y.: Orbis Books, 1993), 203.

13. James W. Douglass, *The Nonviolent Coming of God* (Maryknoll, N.Y.: Orbis Books, 1991), 55.

Chapter 9
The Human Being: Apocalyptic versus Eschatology

1. These neat distinctions are only approximations. Some apocalypticists expected heaven to come down to earth, and held out the possibility of repentance to the "enemy," who, however, would be unable to accept it (Revelation 21; 2:21-22; 9:20-21; 16:9-14). Some apocalypticists were heavily involved in politics and even revolution (Thomas Münzer). Some who declare the end to be immediately at hand amass a fortune and buy mansions and fancy cars (certain televangelists). There is nothing rational or consistent about apocalyptic thought!

2. Morna Hooker, *The Son of Man in Mark* (London: SPCK, 1967), 150. Martin Buber helpfully contrasts eschatology and apocalyptic: "[T]he former allows the now aimless powers, 'evil', to find their way to God and change to good, the latter sees good and evil finally separated at the end of days, the one redeemed, the other unredeemed for ever; the former believes in the sanctification of the earth, the latter despairs of it as hopelessly ruined; the former allows the original creative will of God to be fulfilled without remainder, the latter makes the faithless creation powerful over the Creator, in that it compels him to surrender Nature. . . ." The biblical prophets "did not state something which would happen in any event, but something which

would happen, if those summoned to conversion were not converted" (*Kampf um Israel* [1933], 61–63; cited in *NTApoc.* 2:596).

3. The Society of Biblical Literature Genres Project attempted to define apocalyptic as "a genre of revelatory literature with a narrative framework, in which a revelation is mediated by an otherworldly being to a human recipient, disclosing a transcendent reality which is both temporal, insofar as it envisages eschatological salvation, and spatial insofar as it involves another, supernatural world." Several years later this definition was expanded by the following addendum: "intended to interpret present, earthly circumstances in light of the supernatural world and of the future, and to influence both the understanding and the behavior of the audience by means of divine authority" (Thomas R. Hatina, "The Focus of Mark 13:24-27: The Parousia, or the Destruction of the Temple?" *BBR* 6 [1996]: 46–47). This kind of definition by particulars can go on indefinitely, and still there will be apocalyptic-seeming texts that lack key elements. (See the discussion of "penumbras" at the start of chapter 16.)

4. Gunther Anders, "Will We Live? Thesis for the Atomic Age," *Fellowship* 28 (September 1962): 2.

5. W. H. Auden, "For the Time Being," in *The Collected Poetry of W. H. Auden* (New York: Random House, 1945), 411.

6. Anders, "Will We Live?" 9.

7. We see apocalyptic expansion of the parables, in addition to Matt. 13:36-43, in Matt. 13:49-50; Luke 18:6-8; Matt. 25:30; Matt. 22:11-14; 24:42, 51 // Luke 12:46; 25:13, 31, 41, 46. Luke is intent on decoupling the fall of Jerusalem from the end of the world, so he de-apocalypticizes the parable of the pounds by explicitly refuting those who "supposed that the kingdom of God was to appear immediately" (19:11; see also 19:12, 14-15, 27). He also moves Mark 13:8 (the beginning of the birth pangs) from its context in Luke 21:11, to v. 28, to dispel the idea that the end is at hand. He adds 21:24 to make explicit that Jerusalem's fall is an event of the past, and historicizes the "desolating sacrilege" of Mark 13:14 as the destruction of that city. Jerusalem's fate is punishment for rejecting the gospel (21:22). The end is made indeterminate: "until the times of the Gentiles are fulfilled" (21:24). But he still expects God's reign in "this" generation (21:32, 34-36; 22:16-18). So Luke might weigh in on the side of the de-apocalypticization of the gospel.

8. Mark 3:23-27 par.; Matt. 12:27-28 // Luke 11:11-20; Luke 17:20-21; Matt. 7:21-27 // Luke 6:46; Luke 13:26-27; Matt. 7:24-27 // Luke 6:47-49.

9. John P. Meier, "John the Baptist in Matthew's Gospel," *JBL* 99 (1980): 396.

10. Mark 9:42-48; 12:18-27; Luke 14:14.

11. Divine judgment in Q: Matt. 10:15 // Luke 10:12; Matt. 11:20-24 // Luke 10:13-15; Matt. 10:28 // Luke 12:4-5; Matt. 10:32-33 // Luke 12:8-9; Matt. 12:38-42 // Luke 11:29-32; Matt. 24:51 // Luke 12:46; Matt. 8:12 // Luke 13:29. In Mark: 9:43-48 par. In Luke: 12:47-48a; 16:23; 19:27. In Matthew: 5:22; 7:19; 8:12; 12:32, 36-37; 13:40, 42, 50; 15:13; 16:27; 18:34-35; 22:7, 13; 24:51b; 25:30, 41, 46.

12. Outside the Synoptic apocalypse I find non-son-of-man sayings of Jesus about the end of the world only in two Q passages: Matt. 8:12 // Luke 13:28 and Matt. 24:45-51 // Luke 12:42-46.

13. Even Tödt, who thinks that some of the apocalyptic son-of-man sayings are authentic, admits, "As the distance from Jesus' preaching increases, an increasing

number of [apocalyptic] traditional features are channelled secondarily into the Son of Man sayings of Jesus or of the community" (*The Son of Man in the Synoptic Tradition*, trans. D. M. Barton [Philadelphia: Westminster Press, 1965], 66).

14. Against John S. Kloppenborg, *The Formation of Q: Trajectories in Ancient Wisdom Collections*, Studies in Antiquity and Christianity (Philadelphia: Fortress Press, 1987), I am not persuaded that we have tools of such precision, and texts of such consistency, that we can reconstruct two (or three!) versions of Q, the first non-apocalyptic, the second thoroughly apocalypticized. No archetypal reality is consistent, for the simple reason that *archetypes are by definition ambivalent*. The apocalyptic scenario was also shared by *Didache, Barnabas, Apocalypse of Peter, Epistlula Apostolarum*, and Tertullian. See Jeffrey S. Siker, "The Parousia of Jesus in Second- and Third-Century Christianity, in *the Return of Jesus in Early Christianity*, ed. John T. Carroll et al. (Peabody, Mass.: Hendrickson Publishers, 2000), 147–67.

15. That Matthew, Jude, and Revelation are the most affected by the Similitudes supports a date for the Similitudes' publication around 50–100 C.E. Ulrich Luz thinks "that the Gospel of Matthew comes from a community which was founded by the wandering messengers and prophets of the Son of man of the Sayings Source" (*Matthew 1–7: A Commentary*, trans. W. C. Linss, Continental Commentaries [Minneapolis: Augsburg, 1989], 83).

16. Matthew 7:19 has clearly been added by Matthew; it is missing in the Q parallel.

17. The split between these two scenarios runs like a fissure within the Historical Jesus Section of the Society of Biblical Literature. The apocalyptists are represented by E. P. Sanders, Paula Fredriksen, and John P. Meier, among others. The non-apocalyptists include John Dominic Crossan, Marcus Borg, Robert W. Funk, and most members of the Jesus Seminar, to list a few. I think my work might be located somewhere between the two groups.

Chapter 10
Apocalyptic 1: The Human Being Comes

1. The Son of Man comes: Mark 13:24-27 par.; Matt. 10:23; Matt. 16:28; Matt. 24:27, 37, 39; Mark 14:62 // Matt. 26:64; Mark 8:38 par.; Matt. 24:44 // Luke 12:40; Luke 18:8.

2. Tom F. Driver, *Christ in a Changing World: Toward an Ethical Christology* (New York: Crossroad, 1981), 44.

3. In addition to the work of Sigmund Freud, Carl Jung, and Mircea Eliade, consider this statement by the philosopher Paul Ricoeur: "To manifest the 'sacred' *on* the 'cosmos' and to manifest it *in* the 'psyche' are the same thing. . . . Cosmos and Psyche are the two poles of the same 'expressivity'; I express myself in expressing the world; I explore my own sacrality in deciphering that of the world" (*Symbolism of Evil*, trans. E. Buchanan [New York: Harper & Row, 1967], 12–13). William Blake put it much more simply: "What is Above is Within."

4. James W. Douglass, *The Nonviolent Coming of God* (Maryknoll, N.Y.: Orbis Books, 1991), 15.

5. The "Little Apocalypse" lacks a number of elements usually associated with apocalyptic: no revelation from an otherworldly being or ancient worthy; no refer-

ence to the deliverance of Israel; no predetermined view of history; no mention of the righteous witnessing the punishment of the wicked; no pseudonymity; no prediction of the time of the cosmic catastrophe; omission of the fate of earthly and wicked kingdoms (Thomas R. Hatina, "The Focus of Mark 13:24-27: The Parousia or the Destruction of the Temple?" *BBR* 6 (1996): 47). But there is no reason "apocalyptic" should always contain these elements.

6. David Spangler, *Emergence: The Rebirth of the Sacred* (New York: Dell, 1984), 100.

7. All of the "coming" son-of-the-man references in the Synoptics probably are inspired by Dan. 7:13; indeed, only once is the coming Jesus called "Lord" instead of son of the man (Matt. 24:42).

8. See chap. 8.

9. H. E. Tödt, *The Son of Man in the Synoptic Tradition*, trans. D. M. Barton (Philadelphia: Westminster Press, 1965), 80.

10. James W. Douglass, cut from the final version of his manuscript *The Nonviolent Coming of God*.

11. Matthew's emphasis on recompense is not found in the Markan or Lukan parallels (Mark 8:38 // Luke 9:26), but it appears in the Similitudes of Enoch in reference to the son of the man (45:5 and 46)—still another indication of the Similitudes' impact on Matthew.

12. A. J. B. Higgins regards Matt. 19:28 as a Matthean addition. *Palingenesia* ("renewal") is Greek and untranslatable into Hebrew or Aramaic, and the expression "the son of the man shall sit on the throne of his glory" is only found elsewhere in Matt. 25:31 (*Jesus and the Son of Man*, Philadelphia: Fortress Press, 1964, 107–8). But T. W. Manson wonders why the primitive church would "have invented a saying which promises a throne, amongst others, to Judas Iscariot" (*The Sayings of Jesus* [London: SCM Press, 1957], 217).

13. Henry Burton Sharman, *Son of Man and Kingdom of God: A Critical Study* (New York: Harper, 1943). Exceptions to Sharman's views are Matt. 19:28 // Luke 22:28-30; Mark 8:38-39 par., where "the glory of the Father" is equivalent to the kingdom of God; Matt. 10:23, where the coming of the son of man is tantamount to the coming of the kingdom of God; Matt. 12:28, 32, where kingdom and son of man appear together in the same paragraph; so also 13:36-43 and 25:31-40. At the fountainhead of both son-of-man speculation and the promise of a restored kingdom is Daniel 7, where the two themes coexist. See Crispin H. T. Fletcher-Louis, *Luke-Acts: Angels, Christology, and Soteriology* (Tübingen: Mohr/Siebeck, 1997), 230; and Chrys C. Caragounis, *The Son of Man* (Tübingen: Mohr/Siebeck, 1986), 232–36.

14. Heinz O. Guenther, "When 'Eagles' Draw Together," *Forum* 5 (1989): 145.

15. Higgins thinks that the juxtaposition of "the son of the man" and "faith" indicates that the faith spoken of here is belief in Jesus as the son of the man (*Jesus Son of Man*, 92). This might be what Luke intended, though it seems more likely, in the light of the parable that Luke is commenting on, that faith refers to maintaining belief in the final triumph of God over evil and injustice. Is not belief in Jesus merely shorthand for God's final triumph anyway?

16. Nicolas Berdyayev, *The Destiny of Man*, trans. N. Duddington (London: Geoffrey Bles, 1954), 290.

17. Bruce Chilton, "Regnum Dei Deus Est," in his *Targumic Approaches to the Gospels* (Lanham, Md.: University Press of America, 1986), 105.

18. George Edgin Pugh, *The Biological Origin of Human Values* (New York: Basic Books, 1977), 73.

19. John Hitchcock, *The Web of the Universe: Jung, the "New Physics" and Human Spirituality*, Jung and Spirituality Series (New York: Paulist Press, 1991), 214–15.

20. Passages that try to sketch some details of the future Reign of God create insuperable problems for themselves. In the heavenly city of Revelation 21, for example, we can readily understand the desire to outstrip our animal past, as well as the Domination System itself, which had been symbolized by the three bestial empires of Daniel 7. Hence there are not only no women in the holy city, but no animals as well. Berdyayev was adamant: he wanted nothing to do with heaven if his cat could be with him.

21. John B. Cobb Jr., *Christ in a Pluralistic Age* (Philadelphia: Westminster Press, 1975), 182–83.

22. Rollo May, *Man's Search for Himself* (New York: W. W. Norton, 1953), 276–77, without reference.

23. Perhaps this is what Kierkegaard meant when he claimed that the person who can be said to be situated teleologically is the true apostle. (S. Kierkegaard, "Of the Difference between a Genius and an Apostle," in *The Present Age and Two Minor Ethico-Religious Treatises*, trans. A. Dru and W. Lowrie [New York: Oxford University Press, 1940], 160–61).

Chapter 11
Apocalyptic 2: The Human Being Judges

1. Matt. 13:37, 41; 16:27b; 19:28; 25:31.

2. H. E. Tödt, *The Son of Man in the Synoptic Tradition*, trans. D. M. Barton (London: SCM Press, 1965), 98.

3. "Gnashing of teeth" is characteristically Matthean (Matt. 8:12; 13:42, 50; 22:13; 24:51; 25:30; Luke only at 13:28). This "gnashing" could also involve rejection of the Jews altogether (Matt. 8:12; 23:32-36). Matthew also adds other touches that heighten the theme of divine vengeance on sinners (12:32, 36-37; 23:32-33). They will burn in everlasting fire (5:22; 7:19; 13:40, 42, 50; 18:8; 25:41, 46) and suffer eternal punishment (Matthew only, 25:46) in the "outer darkness" (Matt. 8:12; 22:13; 25:30). Mark 13:26-27 describes just the positive side of the end time; Matthew adds a negative side as well—"Then all the tribes of the earth will mourn." Likewise, Mark 8:38 merely says that the son of the man will be "ashamed" of those ashamed of him; Matt. 16:27 makes the judgment theme more explicit by substituting "and then he will repay everyone for what he or she has done." Matthew ends the parable of the unforgiving servant with, "and in anger his lord handed him over to be tortured until he would pay his entire debt." As if that were not enough, Matthew concludes, "So my heavenly Father *will also do* to every one of you, if you do not forgive your brother or sister from your heart" (18:33-35). The extraordinary number of nonparalleled judgment motifs in Matthew indicates that at least some are his additions and do not go back to Jesus.

4. See also Ezek. 20:4 and 23:36.

5. Mary Dean-Otting, *Heavenly Journeys: A Study of the Motif in Hellenistic Jewish Literature* (New York: Peter Lang, 1984), 204–5.

6. Morna Hooker notes that Mark betrays no knowledge of the son of the man as judge, and she shows how Matthew and Luke have created that role. "If a development has taken place it seems probable that it is from the understanding of the Son of Man as one who expects to be vindicated to the belief that he is the one who will exercise authority in judgment" ("Is the Son of Man Problem Really Insoluble?" in *Text and Interpretation: Studies in the New Testament Presented to Matthew Black*, ed. Ernest Best and R. McL. Wilson [Cambridge: Cambridge University Press, 1979], 164).

Norman Perrin notes the existence of an independent form of the saying in Rev. 3:5 that lacks the epithet "Son of Man," and believes that the original form of the saying read: "Every one who acknowledges me before human beings, he will be acknowledged before the angels of God" (*A Modern Pilgrimage in New Testament Christology* [Philadelphia: Fortress Press, 1974], 35–36). But the author of Revelation has already made it clear that Jesus is the son of the man (1:9-20).

7. The verb *homologein* in Luke 12:8 describes what a witness does, not a judge, and in Acts 7:56 the son of man stands (like a witness) rather than sitting (like a judge). But Robert Maddox points out that Matt. 7:23 uses *homologein* of a judge giving his verdict, and *1 Enoch* depicts the Elect One sitting in judgment in 45:3-6 and standing before the Lord of Spirits to judge in 49:3-4 ("The Function of the Son of Man according to the Synoptic Gospels," NTS 15 [1968–69]: 50 n. 1).

8. A. J. B. Higgins, *Jesus and the Son of Man* (Philadelphia: Fortress Press, 1964), 350. That we are dealing with early tradition is shown by the Aramaism, *homologein en* (Norman Perrin, *Rediscovering the Teaching of Jesus* [New York: Harper & Row, 1967], 188).

9. Rabbi Eleazar of Worms (d. 1238), drawing on an image that occurs in ancient Merkabah mysticism, may offer us a clue:

> Each person has his form above, who is his advocate . . . an angel who guides that person's "star." And when he is sent below, he has the image of that person who is beneath him. . . . And this is, "and God created man in His own image, in the image of God created He him" [Gen. 1:27]. Why twice, "in His image/in the image of"? One is the image of man, and one is the image of the angelic being, who is in the form of that man.

Both Eleazar and Luke 12:8 go beyond the idea of a guardian angel, speaking instead of a preexistent, primordial shape into which we are to live to realize our true being (cited in Gershom Scholem, *On the Mystical Shape of the Godhead: Basic Concepts in the Kabbalah*, trans. J. Neugroschel[New York: Schocken Books, 1991], 261).

10. Tödt, *Son of Man in the Synoptic Tradition*, 228.

11. According to the *Testament of Abraham* 13 (Jewish, first or second century C.E.), Abel is seated on a throne in heaven and exercises judgment over humanity. "Him Cain the wicked killed, and he sits here to judge all the creation and to examine righteous and sinners. For this reason God said, 'I do not judge you, but each

man shall be judged by a man.' " Since Abel is "the son of Adam," and "the son of Adam" is equivalent to "the son of man," it was a small step to completing the syllogism by concluding that the son of the man is the future judge of humanity (Matt. 25:31-46).

12. The vindictive passages in the New Testament (mostly contributed by Matthew and the Book of Revelation) reveal what Gerd Theissen calls "substitution of the subject of aggression," in which one who has suffered injury without reacting aggressively often punishes the aggressor in his imagination. This can safely be accomplished by visualizing the perpetrator suffering at the hands of a third party. Theissen finds evidence that this dynamic undergirds the Gospels' punitive passages. If the wandering charismatic preachers of early Christianity were rejected, they visualized eschatological judgment being visited on that place: "Truly I tell you, it will be more tolerable for the land of Sodom and Gomorrah on the day of judgment than for that town" (Matt. 10:15). They were convinced that the coming Humanchild would not forgive sins against the Holy Spirit—that is, against the prophetic spirit that spoke through them—though he would (curiously enough) forgive those who spoke against Jesus in his own lifetime (Matt. 12:32 // Luke 12:10). By thus identifying themselves with the "son of the man," they could project their aggression into an eschatological figure and delegate the performance of aggressive actions to the Human Being (Mark 8:38) (Gerd Theissen, *The Sociology of Early Palestinian Christianity*, trans. J. Bowden [Philadelphia: Fortress Press, 1978], 100–101).

13. My point holds regardless of the ontological status of these experiences. Among the hundred or so books on the subject are a critical report by Susan Blackmore, *Dying to Live: Near-Death Experiences* (Buffalo: Prometheus Books, 1993); a more sympathetic treatment by Philip L. Berman, *The Journey Home: What Near-Death Experiences and Mysticism Teach Us about the Gift of Life* (New York: Pocket Books, 1998); and the *Journal of Near-Death Studies*, in twenty-one volumes.

14. When divine judgment is coupled with divine omnipotence, God is conceived as an overwhelming, coercive power whose judgments are inescapable and whose wrath is boundless. Then, as devotees seek to imitate God, they desire to use that same power, especially in relation to enemies perceived to be enemies of God. This dynamic, says David Ray Griffin, lies behind the suicidal nuclear-weapons policies developed during the Cold War with Soviet Communism ("Liberal but Not Modern: Overcoming the Liberal-Conservative Antithesis," *Lexington Theological Quarterly* 28 [1993]: 207).

15. Gerd Theissen, *Biblical Faith: An Evolutionary Approach*, J. Bowden (Philadelphia: Fortress Press, 1985), 113.

16. Ibid., 120–21.

17. See *4 Ezra* 7:33-35—"And the Most High shall be revealed upon the seat of judgment, and compassion shall pass away, and patience shall be withdrawn, but only judgment shall remain . . . and recompense shall follow."

18. Tertullian *De Spectaculis* 1.30; *ANF* 3:91.

19. Quoted without citation by Robert Jewett and John Shelton Lawrence, *The American Monomyth* (Garden City, N.Y.: Doubleday, 1977), 159.

20. Ibid.

21. Tödt, *Son of Man in the Synoptic Tradition*, 43.

22. On the relationship between master and disciple in Judaism, see Martin S.

Gaff, "A Rabbinic Ontology of the Written and Spoken Word: On Discipleship, Transformative Knowledge, and the Living Texts of Oral Torah," *GOOIER* 65 (1997): 525–49.

23. Douglas R. A. Hare, *The Son of Man Tradition* (Minneapolis: Fortress Press, 1990), 270.

24. Barnabas Lindars, *Jesus Son of Man: A Fresh Examination of the Son of Man Sayings in the Gospels in Light of Recent Research* (London: SPCK, 1983), 57.

25. Hare, *The Son of Man Tradition*, 271. Higgins believes the twofold form of the logion (acknowledging and denying) in Q 12:8 is more likely to approximate an original utterance than the Markan form with its omission of the first part (*Jesus and the Son of Man*, 60).

26. "King" (18:23; 21:5; 22:2, 7, 11, 13); the righteous possess the kingdom (13:47, 49); "then" (ninety times); judgment as separation (13.19); the unrighteous punished in eternal fire (13:50); the party of the devil (13:39); "of my Father" (sixteen times in Matthew, none in Mark, four in Luke); "from the foundation of the world" (13:35—appears once in Matthew and nowhere else in the Gospels); the disciple as *shaliach* or stand-in for one's master (10:40-42). "All the angels with him" echoes Zech. 14:5. See Lamar Cope, "Matthew XXV:31-46: 'The Sheep and the Goats' Reinterpreted," *Nov. Test.* 11 (1969): 32–44. See also J. M. Court, "Right and Left: The Implications for Matthew 25.31-46," *NTS* 31 (1985): 223–33; and Norbert F. Lohfink, *Option for the Poor: The Basic Principle of Liberation Theology in Light of the Bible* (Berkeley, Calif.: Bibal Press, 1987), 76.

27. William Blake, "The Marriage of Heaven and Hell," in *The Complete Poetry and Prose of William Blake*, ed. David V. Erdman (Berkeley: University of California Press, 1982), 36.

28. J. A. T. Robinson notes Matthew's editorial additions to this parable, but believes that a core is still discernible in the dialogue proper, which is not only free of Matthean touches, but contains many parallels to other sayings of Jesus ("The 'Parable' of the Sheep and the Goats," *NTS* 2 [1955–56]: 225–37).

29. Oscar Cullmann, *The Christology of the New Testament*, trans. S. C. Guthrie and C. A. M. Hall (Philadelphia: Westminster Press, 1959), 158.

30. "That son of man" appears four times in this chapter of the Similitudes, "throne of glory" three times. Matthew 19:28a also reproduces 62:5 of the Similitudes: "when that son of the man is seated on the throne of his glory." Matthew 19:29 then draws on Similitudes 40:9. In addition, Matt. 26:24 // Mark 14:21 = Similitudes 38:2. David R. Catchpole ("The Poor on Earth and the Son of Man in Heaven: A Reappraisal of Mt. 25:31-46," *BJRL* 61 [1979]: 380–81) finds a trove of parallels with the Similitudes in Matthew's parable of the last judgment:

- Matt. 25:31 // Sim. 51:3; 55:4; 61:8; 62:2, 5; 69:29—the son of the man/Elect One's coming leads to his sitting on "the throne of his glory";
- Matt. 25:32 // Sim. 55:4; 61:8; 62:1—both see enthronement issuing in judgment;
- Matt. 25:32-33 // Sim. 62:1—both envisage persons from all over the world assembling for judgment;
- Matt. 25:32-33, 37 // Sim. 62:3, 8, 13—both see the assembly divided into two groups, with one group labeled "the righteous";

- Matt. 25:34, 41 // Sim. 62:13, 63:11—both see judgment issuing in ultimate and final separation of the two groups;
- Matt. 25:34, 46 // Sim. 62:14—both see the destiny of the righteous as life and as the enjoyment of the son of the man's heavenly presence;
- Matt. 25:31 // Sim. 62:5, 7, 9, 14; 63:11—most important, both see the judge as the son of the man;
- Matt. 25:34, 41 // Sim. 62:10; 63:2-10—both keep God in mind as the ultimate judge, even though the leading role is played by God's authorized agent;
- Matt. 25:31 // Sim. 62:11; 63:1—both involve angels in judicial activity;
- Matt. 25:37, 38, 39, 44 // Sim. 62:1, 3, 5-7—both scenes hinge on the idea of recognition;
- Matt. 25:25:40, 45 // Sim. 62:11—both narratives present an equivalence between those who suffer and the one who judges;
- Matt. 25:40, 45 // Sim. 62:11—the criterion of judgment is, in each case, the manner in which those being judged have treated those with whom the judge associates himself.

In addition to Catchpole's list, note that the phrase "one half portion" in Similitudes 62:5 might have suggested to Matthew the division of sheep and goats; the line in the parable about eternal fire "prepared for the devil and his angels" (Matt. 25:41) matches Similitudes 54:4-5.

These parallels do not indicate identity, but they are remarkably similar, suggesting that Matthew may have borrowed some of his "apocalyptic furniture" from the Similitudes, which may have been published shortly before he wrote. The Similitudes must have been an instant best-seller. Matthew's mining of it would have made it appear as an ancient foretelling of the exaltation of Jesus as "that Son of Man."

31. Tödt, *Son of Man in the Synoptic Tradition*, 135.

Chapter 12
Apocalyptic 3: The Future of the Human Being

1. The italicized additions in Luke 9:55-56 echo Luke 19:10 and John 3:17, but they are an excellent representation of Jesus' understanding of the Humanchild. The additions also show that the trend in the early church was not just toward apocalypticizing the son-of-the-man sayings, but also extending them in a spirit consistent with that of Jesus.

2. Henry (Hal) Childs, "Son of Man: A Principle of Incarnation" (M.Div. thesis, Union Theological Seminary, New York, 1975), 92–93.

3. Ibid.

4. Ibid., 93.

5. Henry Corbin, *Creative Imagination in the Sufism of Ibn 'Arabi*, Bollingen Series 91 (Princeton: Princeton University Press, 1981), 29.

6. Charles H. Long, "Cargo Cults as Cultural Historical Phenomena," *JAAR* 42 (1974): 403–14; Max Wyman, "Faithful Wait for God—or Prince Philip—to Bring Gifts," *Vancouver Sun* (19 June 1993), C7.

7. David Freidel, Linda Schele, and Joy Parker, *Maya Cosmos* (New York: William Morrow, 1993), 128.

8. Vittorio Lanternari, "Messianism: Its History, Origin, and Morphology," *HR* 2 (1962): 52–72.

9. *New York Times* (12 August 1997), A8.

10. H. E. Tödt, *The Son of Man in the Synoptic Tradition*, trans. D. M. Barton (Philadelphia: Westminster Press, 1965), 291.

11. Ernst Bloch, *Man on His Own* (New York: Herder and Herder, 1970), 151.

12. Robert Rhea suggests that the Jesus of the Fourth Gospel "serves as the place on earth where God is revealed to humankind. Divine revelation is thus transmitted through a human element to all humankind. After the crucifixion[,] the title Son of Man is quietly discarded by the Evangelist, since Jesus is no longer present in the earthly realm in a human body" (*The Johannine Son of Man* [Zurich: Theologischer Verlag, 1990], 70). But the son of the man in John is not simply a human being, but is preexistent, comes down from heaven, is humanly present, and ascends to where he was before.

13. With the one exception of John 9:38.

14. Tödt, *Son of Man in the Synoptic Tradition*, 289–90. See also Douglas R. A. Hare, *The Son of Man Tradition* (Minneapolis: Fortress Press, 1990), 44. Another strand can be added to that argument. Only twice in the New Testament is Jesus called "God," in John 1:1 and 20:28. But in the period after the New Testament, calling Christ "God" became commonplace. The most obvious reason is that the Gentile churches could not worship a savior who was less than God, nor could they believe that anyone not divine would have been capable of bringing salvation (James L. Kugel and Rowan A. Greer, *Early Biblical Interpretation*, Library of Early Christianity 3 [Philadelphia: Westminster Press, 1986], 165).

15. Sheila Davaney, *Pragmatic Historicism: A Theology for the Twenty-first Century* (Albany: State University of New York Press, 2000). Jung has frequently been pilloried for his ahistorical treatment of the archetypes, with little or no regard for their development in different cultures and even individuals. There is truth in the charge, especially in Jung's *Mysterium Coniunctionis* (CW 14). But Jung does distinguish between archetypes, which are fairly standard cross-culturally (people have mothers, fathers, sisters, brothers, births, weddings, funerals, etc.), and archetypal *images* (the actual shape archetypes take in cultures and individuals). So his occasional failure to maintain the distinction is a failure in practice, not in theory.

16. Paul Tillich, *Systematic Theology* (Chicago: University of Chicago Press, 1951), 1:133.

17. Carl Jung, *Psychological Types*, CW 6:1, 474–75.

18. Edward Carpenter, *Towards Democracy* (London: Swan Sonnenschein, 1907), 51–52.

Chapter 13
The Human Being in John

1. The archetypal character of the "ladder" as a symbol for communication between heaven and earth appears in the account of Horus's enthronement as the son of Osiris, in which the ladder of Osiris is raised in the coronation ceremonies (Erich Neumann, *The Origins and History of Consciousness*, trans. R. F. C. Hull, Bollingen Series 42 [Princeton: Princeton University Press, 1973], 249). The "stairway to the

sky" in Egyptian mythology provides a similar motif (James Breasted, *A History of Egypt* [New York: Charles Scribner's Sons, 1937], 64). Indeed, "ladder" in Gen. 28:12 could be better translated as "stairway" or "ramp," as in a ziggurat; so also in "The Ladder of Jacob" (*APOT* 2:401–11). The Koran speaks of "a ladder (*sullam*) into the sky" (6:35) and of "the Lord of the Stairways (*ma'arij*)" (52:38). Aristides reports how he was healed of a head ailment through a vision of Sarapis and Asclepias, who then revealed to him "ladders which mark the boundary between the upper and the nether world." Aristides ascended the ladder by means of the mystic rites and was transformed (*Oratio* 49.46-48). Philo uses the "heavenly ladder," no doubt with reference to Gen. 28:10-17, in *On Rewards and Punishments* 43–44 (LCL 8.337), but the ladder is merely an allegory for "reason." The fifth imam of Fatimid legend taught: "Strive to reach the sky gradually (by a ladder)," but he, too, meant "progress in learning" (Daniel Merkur, *Gnosis* [Albany: State University of New York Press, 1993], 210).

2. Mircea Eliade (*Shamanism*, Bollingen Series 76 [Princeton: Princeton University Press, 1964]) notes that shamans were sometimes initiated by climbing a tree or ladder. This symbolized their calling to be intermediaries between the temporal and the eternal. One thinks also of the ladder leading into the underground kiva of some Native Americans. The Dyak people of Borneo enacted ritual rebirth initiations that included an ecstatic journey to the sky on a ritual ladder (58). The South American Araucanian people's initiation ceremony for a female shaman included the ritual climbing of a tree that had been cut off, debarked, and notched to form a ladder that stayed in front of her house (122–23). Ritually ascending trees is part of the North American Pomo ceremony, Siberian shaman consecrations, and Vedic sacrifices (125), to list but a few of Eliade's examples.

3. William Blake, "The Marriage of Heaven and Hell," in *The Complete Poetry and Prose of William Blake*, ed. D. V. Erdman (Berkeley: University of California Press, 1982), 39. Physicist/theologian John Polkinghorne bridles at emphasis on Jesus as revealer. "[T]o rely on the revelatory character of his [Jesus'] life alone is to adopt a gnostic account of our redemption. Let me say again that I believe our need is for transformation, not just information. Jesus is the second Adam (the seed of a new humanity), not the second Moses (the conveyer of a new revelation)" (*The Faith of a Physicist: Reflections of a Bottom-up Thinker* [Minneapolis: Fortress Press, 1994], 140–41). But this drives apart ideas that must at all costs be held together. Jesus revealed that new humanity by incarnating it. And certainly at least one evangelist, Matthew, saw Jesus as, among other things, a new Moses.

4. *Genesis Rabbah* 27: 1 to Gen. 28:12 (Soncino edition, p. 626).

5. *Hekhalot Rabbati* 14:1. The motif of Jacob's ladder had wide influence outside Judaism. Islamic mysticism also knows a "ladder of ascension" that "causes [Divine] inspiration to reach to the pure individual souls, and on it descend [the angels] and ascend the purified spirits to the supernal world" (Ibn al-Sîd al Baṭalyawsî [1052–1127]; in Alexander Altmann, "The Ladder of Ascension," in *Studies in Mysticism and Religion Presented to Gershom Scholem* [Jerusalem: Magnes Press, 1967], 1–32).

6. C. H. Dodd, *The Interpretation of the Fourth Gospel* (Cambridge: Cambridge University Press, 1953), 243–44. Similar views appear in R. G. Hamerton-Kelly, R. H. Lightfoot, E. M. Sidebottom, P. Ricca, C. K. Barrett, Vincent Taylor, and J. O. F.

Murray (for bibliography see Francis J. Moloney, S.D.B., *The Johannine Son of Man* [Rome: LSA, 1976], 10–11).

7. Dodd, *Interpretation of the Fourth Gospel*, 247.

8. Ibid.

9. Ibid., 248–49.

10. Rudolf Bultmann, *The Gospel of John: A Commentary*, trans. G. R. Beasley-Murray et al. (Philadelphia: Westminster Press, 1971), 107.

11. See Wayne A. Meeks, "The Man from Heaven in Johannine Sectarianism," *JBL* 91 (1972): 44–72; William C. Grese, " 'Unless One Is Born Again': The Use of a Heavenly Journey in John 3," *JBL* 107 (1988): 677–93; C. H. Talbert, "The Myth of a Descending-Ascending Redeemer in Mediterranean Antiquity," *NTS* 22 (1975–76): 418–40; F. M. Sidebottom, "The Ascent and Descent of the Son of Man in the Gospel of St. John," *ATR* 39 (1957): 115–22.

12. Dag Hammarskjöld, *Markings* (New York: Knopf, 1964), 120; William L. Dols Jr., "Toward a Field Critical Hermeneutic of the Phrase *ho huios tou anthrōpou* in the Narrative World of Mark" (Ph.D. diss., Graduate Theological Union, Berkeley, California, 1987), 282.

13. Delbert Burkett, *The Son of the Man in the Gospel of John*, JSNT Supplement Series 56 (Sheffield: Sheffield Academic Press, 1991), 37, comments, "To eat the flesh and drink the blood of the Son of the Man is to assimilate the message that the Man's Son (God's Son) descended from heaven to become a flesh-and-blood human being." Burkett is one of the few who has perceived that "the Man" might refer to God in the expression *ho huios tou anthrōpou.*

14. Tom F. Driver, *Christ in a Changing World: Toward an Ethical Christology* (New York: Crossroad, 1981), 44.

15. Chrys C. Caragounis, *The Son of Man: Vision and Interpretation* (Tübingen: Mohr/Siebeck, 1986), 137–38.

16. Some manuscripts read *ep auto*, "on him," and a significant number read *eis auton*, "into him."

17. Burkett, *Son of Man in the Gospel of John*, 9, 171.

18. Ibid.

19. Margaret Pamment, "The Son of Man in the Fourth Gospel," *JTS* 36 (1985): 58.

20. Bultmann, *Gospel of John*, 349.

21. Moloney, *Johannine Son of Man*, 179.

22. The rabbis also grasped that the believer is to perform the same acts as God:

> The righteous have power over the same things as God, if one may say so. In which way? Everything that God does, the righteous do. How [is this illustrated]? God remembers barren women; Elisha, too, remembered the Shunammite woman. . . . God quickens the dead; and Elisha, too, brought back to life the son of the Shunammite woman. God parts the seas; Elijah and Elisha, too, parted seas. . . . God heals without emollients, and Elisha healed Naaman without emollients. God sweetens the bitter waters, and Elisha sweetened the bitter waters. . . . God withholds the rain, and Elijah withheld the rain. . . . God causes rain to fall, and Samuel caused rain to fall. . . . God sends down fire, and Elijah brought down fire [from heaven]. . . . (*Deut. Rab.* 10.3; Soncino edition, 166–67)

The Jewish Christians were not innovating as much as extending a notion shared by their Jewish compatriots when they called themselves *Christoi*, the Anointed Ones. They did not mean to imply that they resembled the Messiah in every respect, but they believed that, in imitation of him, they were anointed with the Holy Spirit. The Spirit that descended on Jesus at his baptism has continued to fill initiates ever since (Gilles Quispel, *Gnostic Studies I* [Istanbul: Nederlands Historisch-Archaeologisch Instituut, 1974], 235).

23. The motif of mystical ascents to heaven is particularly widespread in that period. Such ascents were attributed to Enoch (*1 Enoch* 14; 37–71; *2 Enoch* 1–21; *3 Enoch* 3–16; 48C); Abraham (*T. Ab.* 10; *Apoc. Ab.* 15–31); Adam (*Life of Adam and Eve* 25–29); Levi (*T. Levi* 2:5); Baruch (*3 Baruch*); Isaiah (*Ascen. Isa.* 7); Elijah (2 Kings 2:11; Sir. 48:9-10; *1 Enoch* 90:31); Ezra (*4 Ezra* 14:9); and Abel (*T. Ab.* 11; *Ascen. Isa.* 9:8), to say nothing of the Merkabah mystics. Moses' ascent of Mount Sinai was taken by some as an ascent to heaven (Philo *Mos.* 1:158 and a host of others). See also James D. G. Dunn, "Let John Be John," in *Das Evangelium und die Evangelien*, ed. P. Stuhlmacher (Tübingen: Mohr/Siebeck, 1983), 309–39; Meeks, "Man from Heaven," 44–72; and Alan F. Segal, "Heavenly Ascent in Hellenistic Judaism, Early Christianity, and Their Environment," in *ANRW* 2.23.2 (1980).

It was against such heavenly journeys, and Jesus' ascension in particular, that Rabbi Abbahu polemicized: "If a man says to you, 'I am God,' he is lying; 'I am Son of man (*ben 'adam*),' he will repent it in the end; if he says, 'I am going up to heaven,' he has said it but he will not fulfill it" (*y. Ta'an.* 65b). In the face of twentieth-century false messiahs (Jim Jones, David Koresh, Herff Applewhite) who led their followers into mass suicide, the rabbi's warning is sobering indeed.

24. See chap. 3 of my *Engaging the Powers: Discernment and Resistance in a World of Domination* (Minneapolis: Fortress Press, 1992).

25. Burkett, *Son of Man in the Gospel of John*, 121–22.

26. Matthew Black, "The 'Son of Man' Passion Sayings in the Gospel Tradition," *ZNW* 60 (1969): 1–8; Dodd, *Interpretation of the Fourth Gospel*, 377.

27. E. A. Abbott, *The Son of Man, or Contributions to the Study of the Thoughts of Jesus* (Cambridge: Cambridge University Press, 1910), 561.

28. Carl Jung, "Answer to Job," *CW* 11:1, 457.

Chapter 14
The Human Being in Letters Ascribed to Paul

1. In this chapter I use "Paul" to represent not only Paul himself but his followers. I take Ephesians to be by his followers; Colossians is a toss-up. I do not include the Pastoral Epistles, which may have issued from the Paulinist school at a later time but no longer fully reflect Paul's spirit.

2. Kirsopp Lake and Foakes Jackson, *The Beginnings of Christianity*, 1:380; cited approvingly in T. W. Manson, *The Teaching of Jesus* (Cambridge: Cambridge University Press, 1959), 233.

3. John Pairman Brown, "The Son of Man: 'This Fellow,' " *Biblica* 58 (1977): 361–87.

4. E. A. Abbott, *The Son of Man, or Contributions to the Study of the Thoughts of Jesus* (Cambridge: Cambridge University Press, 1910), 142 n. 3154a.

5. Hans Dieter Betz attempts to account for Paul's language of "the inner *anthrōpos*" by tracing it back to Plato. His attempt to show Paul's dependency, however, is highly speculative. More significant, he fails to see the connection between the inner *anthrōpos* and the Gospels' son of the man ("The Concept of the 'Inner Human Being' [*ho eso anthrōpos*] in the Anthropology of Paul," *NTS* 46 [2000]: 315–41).

6. For bibliography, see Gosnell L. O. R. Yorke, *The Church as the Body of Christ in the Pauline Corpus: A Re-examination* (Lanham, Md.: University Press of America, 1991).

7. Donald W. Shriver Jr., review of *Bystanders: Conscience and Complicity during the Holocaust*, by Victoria J. Barnett, *Christian Century* 117 (2000): 813.

8. Eduard Schweizer, "The Son of Man," *JBL* 79 (1960): 124.

Chapter 15
The Human Being in Jewish Mysticism

1. I am grateful to Dan Merkur for his suggestions and corrections in this chapter (noted where his name appears in parentheses).

2. Nevertheless, to someone coming from the manicured lawns of New Testament study, Merkabah/*Hekhalot* lore seems a daunting wilderness, in which not even the beginning and ending of works can be established, nor a chief exemplar, nor a core document, nor even whether it *is* a document, nor whether it has been redacted, or is a hodgepodge of traditions thrown together. Nor is there an agreed way of referring to the texts, identifying verses, or transliterating terms into English (is it "merkavah" or "merkabah," "hekhalot" or "heikhalot," caps or lowercase, italics or roman?). One enters this field with great trepidation, just as the "merkabites" entered heaven. On the difficulties of this literature, see especially Peter Schäfer, "Tradition and Redaction in Hekhalot Literature," *JSJ* 14 (1983): 172–81.

To compound things further, sharp disagreement exists among scholars as to whether Merkabah mysticism was a literary movement, or whether it reflects actual mystical experiences, or both (but if so, in what measure?). See David Halperin, *The Faces of the Chariot: Early Jewish Responses to Ezekiel's Vision*, Texte und Studien zum antiken Judentum 16 (Tübingen: Mohr/Siebeck, 1988); and P. S. Alexander, "Comparing Merkavah Mysticism and Gnosticism: An Essay in Method," *JJS* (1984): 1–18.

3. Gershom Scholem, *Major Trends in Jewish Mysticism* (1941; New York: Schocken Books, 1965), 46–47. If the "descent" to the *merkabah* simply meant stepping down onto the throne chariot, as some have argued, how does one account for the fact that "descent" seems to have replaced "ascent" in referring to the entirety of the mystic's journey, or for the fact that "descent" was not used in this way earlier?

Paul's inability to decide whether his ecstatic visionary journey took place in the body or outside "is firm evidence of a mystical ascent and shows that the voyage has not been interiorized as a journey into the self, which becomes common in Kabbalah" (Alan F. Segal, *Paul the Convert: The Apostolate and Apostasy of Saul the Pharisee* [New Haven: Yale University Press, 1990], 58).

4. Scholem, *Major Trends in Jewish Mysticism*, 54.

5. "Visions of Ezekiel," trans. David J. Halperin, in *Faces of the Chariot*, 230.

6. David Bakan, *Sigmund Freud and the Jewish Mystical Tradition* (Princeton: D. Van Nostrand, 1958).

7. Gershom Scholem, *On the Mystical Shape of the Godhead: Basic Concepts in the Kabbalah* (New York: Schocken Books, 1991), 139.

8. On the emergence of unitive mysticism in Kabbalism, see Elliot R. Wolfson, "Forms of Visionary Ascent as Ecstatic Experience in the Zoharic Literature," in *Gershom Scholem's Major Trends in Jewish Mysticism Fifty Years After*, ed. P. Schäfer and J. Dan (Tübingen: Mohr/Siebeck, 1993), 209–35. Even in medieval Kabbalah, the emphasis was often on the union of human and divine *wills*.

9. *Shir ha-Shirim Rabba* on Song of Songs 1:4; cited in Gershom Scholem, *Jewish Gnosticism, Merkabah Mysticism, and Talmudic Tradition* (New York: Jewish Theological Seminary of America, 1960), 78. R. Levi countered the idea that one who sees God's face will die: "But they [the Israelites] had seen the face of the Holy One blessed be He [and therefore could not be destroyed] since anyone who sees the face of the Holy One blessed be He does not die, as it is said, 'In the light of a king's face there is life' " (Prov. 16:15) (*Pesiqta de Rab Kahana*, ed. Mandelbaum; cited in Ira Chernus, *Mysticism in Rabbinic Judaism*, Studia Judaica 11 [Berlin: Walter de Gruyter, 1982], 23).

10. *Hekhalot Rabbati, Synopse* 164, trans. Peter Schäfer, in *Hekhalot-Studien* (Tübingen: Mohr/Siebeck, 1988), 289.

11. Peter Schäfer, *The Hidden and Manifest God: Some Major Themes in Early Jewish Mysticism*, trans. A. Pomerance, SUNY Series in Judaica (Albany: State University of New York Press, 1992), 164.

12. *Pesiqta Rabbati*, Homily 20; text in Halperin, *Faces of the Chariot*, 306. Despite the prohibition against seeing God's face, the rabbis insisted that Israel had done that at Sinai. Rabbi Johanan (third century C.E.) said: "Just as with a statue, a thousand people look at it and each and every one says, 'It is looking at me,' so the Holy One blessed be He made each and every Israelite feel that He was looking at him." His pupil, Rabbi Levi, said: "The Holy One blessed be He appeared to them at Sinai with many faces: with an angry face, with a repelling face, with a defiant face, with a joyous face, with a laughing face, with a kind and friendly face" (*Pesiqta Rabbati* 21.6, 100ab; Chernus, *Mysticism in Rabbinic Judaism*, 69).

13. *Deuteronomy Rabbah*, ed. Lieberman, 65 [186]; Halperin, *Faces of the Chariot*, 313. *Deuteronomy Rabbah* also records that Moses spoke to God "face to face" (VII.8; XI.10, Soncino edition, pp. 140, 185).

14. Scholem, *Major Trends in Jewish Mysticism*, 278.

15. P. S. Alexander, "The Historical Setting of the Hebrew Book of Enoch," *JJS* 28 (1977): 156–80.

16. *Hekhalot Rabbati*, sec. 81; in Schäfer, *Hidden and Manifest God*, 155. A particularly fine example of the use of hymns to induce visions of the *merkabah* is the Qumran *Songs of the Sabbath Sacrifice* (4Q400 [4QShirShabb]).

17. P. Alexander, "3 (Hebrew Apocalypse of) Enoch," *OTP* 1:234.

18. Moshe Idel, *Kabbalah: New Perspectives* (New Haven: Yale University Press, 1988), 75–88. Ithamar Gruenwald is confident that these techniques resulted in actual visionary experiences (*From Apocalypticism to Gnosticism* [Frankfurt am Main: Peter Lang, 1988], 100–101; and *Apocalyptic and Merkavah Mysticism* [Leiden: E. J. Brill, 1980], 99–109). Some Merkabah mystics apparently fasted and recited their

hymns with their heads between their knees, in the manner of Elijah on Mount Carmel (1 Kings 18:42), thus constricting their breathing (Alexander, "3 [Hebrew Apocalypse of] Enoch," 1:233). Later, Hai Gaon (d. 1038) repeats the same advice and adds, "Then he will gaze inward and into the chambers [of his heart], like one who sees with his eyes the seven palaces. He contemplates as if he entered from palace to palace and sees what is in each one" ("Responsa to Tractate Hagigah," in *Otzar ha-Geonim*, vol. 4, p. 14; Eliot Wolfson, *Through a Speculum That Shines: Vision and Imagination in Medieval Jewish Mysticism* [Princeton: Princeton University Press, 1994], 145). Dan Merkur notes that the combination of rhythmic inattention with highly thoughtful or alert attention is consistent with the phenomenology of lucid hypnagogia (*Gnosis* [Albany: State University of New York Press, 1993], 168). David Halperin believes he has proven that Merkabah exposition had, in tannaitic times, no experiential element (*The Merkabah in Rabbinic Literature* [New Haven: American Oriental Society, 1980], 173); but that exposition had to have some purpose, and the natural inference is that it was expounded in order to induce ecstatic visions. Martha Himmelfarb, following Halperin, denies that apocalyptic (and, by extension, Merkabah) texts were used to induce experiences of heavenly ascent, because "rapture—being snatched up—does not require rites because it takes place not at the visionary's initiative but at God's," and thus cannot be induced (M. Himmelfarb, *Ascent to Heaven in Jewish and Christian Apocalypses* [New York: Oxford University Press, 1993], 110). This idea is not reflected in the texts. Nowhere do we find stress on God's initiative; the initiative is all the adept's. Himmelfarb concludes that this literature does not contain fictionalized accounts of personal experiences but works of fiction from start to finish. Surely the situation is more complex. No doubt "many expounded the Merkabah and never saw it" (*t. Meg.* 3[4].28). What began with actual experiences, and was nourished by new experiences as time went on, became the basis for induced experiences such as one finds in all religions, whether as a follower of Macumba or a kundalini yogi, or as a Jew or Christian meditating on Scripture. No doubt many, unable to replicate the experiences, simply told the stories, as Himmelfarb suggests (114). We see the latter in the children of Pentecostals who are unable to experience the "baptism of the Holy Spirit."

19. Schäfer, *Hidden and Manifest God*, 166.

20. *Hekhalot Rabbati* 1:2-6; Halperin, *Faces of the Chariot*, 407.

21. Luke 11:1-13 // Matt.6:9-13; Luke 18:1-8. See my *Engaging the Powers: Discernment and Resistance in a World of Domination* (Minneapolis: Fortress Press, 1992), chap. 16.

22. Dan Merkur, personal communication.

23. *Merkabah Rabbah*, sec. 675; Wink, *Engaging the Powers*, 150.

24. *Merkabah Rabbah*, sec. 680; quoted in Schäfer, *Hidden and Manifest God*, 114.

25. Merkur, *Gnosis*, 170.

26. *Hekhalot Rabbati* 3:4; cited in Scholem, *Jewish Gnosticism, Merkabah Mysticism, and Talmudic Tradition*, 60, italics added. This motif is elaborated in stunning detail in *3 Enoch* 15:1-2 (fifth to sixth century C.E.).

27. Scholem, *Jewish Gnosticism, Merkabah Mysticism, and Talmudic Tradition*, 60.

28. The Targums generally skirted or avoided the anthropomorphisms in the biblical text. In place of God appearing in human form, the Targum reads, "there was

like the appearance of Adam" (*bar Adam*, the first term Aramaic, the second a Hebrew proper name, so as to preclude this being a vision of God). See Samson H.
Levey, "The Targum to Ezekiel," *HUCA* 46 (1975): 139–58; and Alexander Altmann, "The Gnostic Background of the Rabbinic Adam Legends," *JQR* 35
(1944–45): 371–91. Halperin notes, however, that the bulk of rabbinic literature
does not share the Targum's horror of anthropomorphism (*Faces of the Chariot*,
251); the Hebrew Bible is full of references to God as human or possessing physical
or psychological attributes that we ascribe to humans.

29. *b. Sanh.* 1:1, XLII(93A), exegeting Zechariah, reads: " 'And behold a man riding' — 'man' refers only to the Holy One, blessed be he, as it is said, 'The Lord is a
man of war, the Lord is his name' " (Exod. 15:3).

Medieval Kabbalah mysticism carried further the revelation of God as Human. It
posited ten *sefirot* ("spheres") as divine potencies, archetypal energies, or potential
patterns of human existence. Together they represented the divine reality, and were
visualized in the shape of a human body. These *sefirot* thus form a kind of psychology of human spiritual development, in which the divine drives the integration of
the opposites.

30. *Midrash Mishle*, ed. Buber, f. 34a ff.; text in Scholem, *Major Trends in Jewish
Mysticism*, 71.

31. Scholem, *Major Trends in Jewish Mysticism*, 66.

32. Ibid., 64. The idea that the world is the body of the divine is Stoic; in Jewish
mysticism, the emphasis is on the body of God that fills the world. Both are ways of
asserting the omnipresence of God.

33. Joseph Dan, "The Concept of Knowledge in the *Shi'ur Qomah*," in *Studies
in Jewish Religious and Intellectual History: Presented to Alexander Altmann on the
Occasion of his Seventieth Birthday*, ed. S. Stein and R. Loewe (Tuscaloosa: University of Alabama Press, 1979), 68.

34. Scholem, *Major Trends in Jewish Mysticism*. So also Schäfer, *Hidden and
Manifest God*, 102.

35. Joseph Dan, *The Ancient Jewish Mysticism*, trans. S. Himelstein(Tel-Aviv:
MOD Books, 1993), 67.

36. The Pseudo-Clementine *Homilies* have a similar, if more subdued, picture of
God's beautiful bodily form, which contains all the limbs of a human body: "For He
who truly is, is He whose form the body of man bears" (3:7).

> For He has shape, and He has every limb primarily and solely for beauty's
> sake, and not for use. For He has not eyes that He may see with them; for He
> sees on every side, since He is incomparably more brilliant in His body than
> the visual spirit which is in us, and He is more splendid than everything, so
> that in comparison with Him the light of the sun may be reckoned as dark-
> ness. Nor has He ears that He may hear; for He hears, perceives, moves, ener-
> gizes, acts on every side. But he has the most beautiful shape on account of
> man, that the pure in heart may be able to see Him. . . . For He moulded man
> in His own shape as in the grandest seal, in order that he may be the ruler and
> lord of all, and that all may be subject to him. Wherefore, judging that He is
> the universe, and that man is His image (for He is Himself invisible, but His
> image man is visible), the man who wishes to worship Him honours His visi-

ble image, which is man. Whatsoever therefore any one does to man, be it good or bad, is regarded as being done to Him. . . . For He avenges His own shape. (Fourth century, Christian; ANF 8:240, 319–20)

In *Poimandres*, the first tractate of *Corpus Hermeticum*, it is said that Anthropos, the heavenly Man, "was exceedingly beautiful and wore his Father's image, and God really loved His own Form" (1:14) (Jarl Fossum, "Jewish-Christian Christology and Jewish Mysticism," *VC* 37 [1983]: 260–87).

37. Daniel C. Matt, *God and the Big Bang: Discovering Harmony Between Science and Spirituality* (Woodstock, Vt.: Jewish Lights, 1996), 73–76; and idem, *The Essential Kabbalah: The Heart of Jewish Mysticism* (San Francisco: HarperSanFrancisco, 1995), 72.

38. Michael Fishbane, "Arm of the Lord: Biblical Myth, Rabbinic Midrash, and the Mystery of History," in *Language, Theology, and the Bible: Essays in Honor of James Barr*, ed. S. E. Balentine and J. Barton (Oxford: Clarendon Press, 1994), 271–92.

39. Scholem, *Major Trends in Jewish Mysticism*, 269. Scholem is referring specifically to Lurianic Kabbalism, but his statement holds as well for the earlier *Shi'ur Qomah* speculations, or, for that matter, for any thoroughgoing anthropomorphic system.

40. MS Oxford 1531f. 40b; cited in Scholem, *Major Trends in Jewish Mysticism*, 66. In this light, Metatron prefigures the restored relationship of all humanity to God. This renders unnecessary the suggestion of Peter Schäfer, that 3 *Enoch* (which he dates at the end of the *Hekhalot* literature) represents the re-mything of the mystical tradition, in which the powers formerly vested in the human adept (even though this was a limited and elite number) have been absorbed by Metatron (*Hidden and Manifest God*, 134). More on the mark is Schäfer's statement that Enoch-Metatron is the prototype of the mystic, who shows that people can come very close to God — so close as to be almost similar to God, even mistaken for God — and whose name is only one letter short of God's (149).

41. Gruenwald, *Apocalyptic and Merkavah Mysticism*, 214.

42. Another text says, "When the youth [Metatron] enters beneath the throne of glory, God embraces him with a shining face. . . . The youth's stature fills the world, and God calls him 'youth' " (MS New York [Schäfer #385]; text in Halperin, *Faces of the Chariot*, 403). Later, in the same manuscript, God and the "youth" are said to "resemble each other from the loins downward, but do not resemble each other from the loins upward" (400). The *Hekhalot* writer is evidently not sure whether the humanlike being described as God in Ezek. 1:27 — or this lesser majesty, the "youth" — was seated on the throne of God. So he waffles and hints that the passage can apply more or less to both.

43. "The sharp distinction between heaven and earth that was characteristic of the Deuteronomic tradition and of much of the Hebrew Bible was not so strongly maintained in the Hellenistic age, even in the Hebrew- and Aramaic-speaking Judaism represented by the Dead Sea Scrolls" (John J. Collins, *The Scepter and the Star: Jewish Messianism in Light of the Dead Sea Scrolls* [New York: Doubleday, 1995], 149).

44. Himmelfarb, *Ascent to Heaven*, 61–62. See also Annalies Kuyt, *The "Descent to the Chariot: Towards a Description of the Terminology, Place, Function, and*

Nature of the Yeridah in Hekhalot Literature, Texte und Studien zum Autiken Judentum 45 (Tübingen: Mohr/Siebeck, 1995), whose systematic survey of the "descent" motif in *Hekhalot* literature stresses the heterogeneity of these texts without
accounting for their commonality.

45. The medieval Kabbalist Ibn Ezra identified Metatron as the one in whose
image the human was created (Wolfson, *Through a Speculum That Shines,* 259).

46. This language of the heavens "splitting open" as a symbol of revelation was
standard in Jewish mysticism. "At Sinai [God] *split open* the seven firmaments for
me . . . and He showed me there the chambers of the Merkabah" (*Midrash Hazita
on Song of Songs* 2:4, cited by R. Joshua ibn Shoeib in a version not found in the
standard text of *Song of Songs Rabbah,* 1574; cited in Scholem, *Jewish Gnosticism,
Merkabah Mysticism, and Talmudic Tradition,* 68 n. 12). Ira Chernus cites a similar
tradition in *Deuteronomy Rabbah,* ed. Lieberman, pp. 65–66, and comments that
the "splitting of the firmaments" played a role in Merkabah mysticism from one of
the earliest Merkabah texts, *Re'uyot Yehezkiel:* "While Ezekiel was gazing the Holy
One opened up the seven firmaments for him and he saw the glory" (Chernus, *Mysticism in Rabbinic Judaism,* 111). So also *Mek. Shirah Bahodesh* 3, p. 126; *Mek.
Rawest* 78. All of these texts based themselves on Ezek. 1:1 — "[And] the heavens
were opened and I saw visions of God" (Chernus, *Mysticism in Rabbinic Judaism,*
19). Revelation 4:1-2 belongs to this broad stream of Jewish mysticism.

Luke 10:22 // Matt. 11:27 also alludes to revelatory experiences that Jesus received through the Holy Spirit: "All things have been delivered to me by my Father;
and no one knows who the Son is except the Father, or who the Father is except the
Son and anyone to whom the Son chooses to reveal him."

47. For Levi, see *T. Levi* 2:5, 8; for Phinehas, see Palestinian Targum on Num.
25:12; for Moses, see, among others, "The Ascension of Moses," the twentieth homily of *Pesiqta Rabbati* (Halperin, *Faces of the Chariot,* 289–322). For background, see
Wayne A. Meeks, "Moses as God and King," in *Religions in Antiquity: Festschrift for
E. R. Goodenough,* ed. J. Neusner (Leiden: E. J. Brill, 1968), 354–71 — Moses was
seen as a god to Pharaoh (Exod. 7:1). The Targum altered that to "as God" (*elohim,*
not *YHWH*). Adam lost the divine image but Moses kept his (*Deut. Rab.* 1:3). At
Sinai, Moses received the status of an angel and the restoration of the glory lost by
Adam. Meeks comments, "Moses, crowned with both God's name and God's image,
became a sort of second Adam, a prototype of a new humanity." See also Alan F.
Segal, *Two Powers in Heaven: Early Rabbinic Reports about Christianity and Gnosti-
cism,* Studies in Judaism in Late Antiquity 25 (Leiden: E. J. Brill, 1977); and Joseph
P. Schultz, "Angelic Opposition to the Ascension of Moses and the Revelation of the
Law," *JQR* 61 (1971): 282–307.

48. *Pesiqta Rabbati,* Homily 20 (Halperin, *Faces of the Chariot,* 289–322). Levi
also ascended to the heavenly temple while still alive, where God invested him with
the priesthood (*T. Levi* 2–5; see Himmelfarb, *Ascent to Heaven,* 30–37). Himmelfarb
also cites the Mithras Liturgy (*PGM* 4.475–829), which offered initiates a ritual of ascent to heaven and divinization (47). In a fragment of text from Qumran, a human
speaker boasts of having been granted "a mighty throne in the congregation of the
gods ['*elim*]" and of having been "reckoned with the gods ['*elim*]." Himmelfarb comments, "The relevance of this extraordinary passage for the claims some early Christians made for Jesus should be apparent" (*Ascent to Heaven,* 49).

49. A. N. Whitehead, *Adventures in Ideas* (New York: Free Press, 1933), 167.

50. From the Ozhayah *Hekhalot* fragments from the Cairo Genizah text (cited in Halperin, *Faces of the Chariot*, 402). Some scholars have rejected the translation "youth," insisting that it means nothing more than "servant" (Gruenwald, *Apocalyptic and Merkavah Mysticism*, 238–39). But Halperin rightly points to 3 *Enoch* 4:10, in which Metatron tells R. Ishmael that he is called "youth" because he is the youngest of the angels.

51. See *b. Sanh.* 38b; *b. Hag.* 15a; and Segal, *Two Powers in Heaven*.

52. 3 *Enoch* 48D:1 (88).

53. Alexander, "3 (Hebrew Apocalypse of) Enoch," 1:235.

54. The Jewish Christian *Ascension of Isaiah* describes seven heavens; in the first five are thrones on which angels sit, surrounded by ministering angels. Each figure on the throne is greater than the figure before, and all are described in language used of God in scriptural theophanies such as Dan. 7:9. Christopher C. Rowland remarks how easy it would be to confuse these lower beings with God, or to attribute to them participation in the Godhead simply because they greatly resemble descriptions of God from biblical sources ("The Influence of the First Chapter of Ezekiel on Jewish and Early Christian Literature" [dissertation, Christ College, Cambridge University, 1974], 255). Again we are prompted to wonder why the writer endangers the centrality of Christ by introducing exalted beings that the untutored might falsely worship.

55. *Cairo Genizah Hekalot* A/2, 13–18 (ed. Gruenwald, pp. 362f.).

56. From a short text published by Jellinek under the title "Aggadath Shema Israel," cited in C. R. A. Morray Jones, "Transformational Mysticism in the Apocalyptic-Merkabah Tradition," *JJS* 43 (1992): 8.

57. Gruenwald, *Apocalyptic and Merkavah Mysticism*, 201. But, even then, these restless mystics were not content. Saul Lieberman mentions a rabbi who maintained that Moses was a *hemitheos*, a semi-god, his upper half a god, his lower half a man. According to other rabbis, he was sometimes a man and sometimes a god. Metatron was also called a minor god. As Lieberman points out, in pagan polytheism a human being who ascended to heaven could scarcely escape being called a god. But how does this happen in Jewish monotheism? Because it was always clear that Metatron, Moses, and other dignitaries in heaven were still mortals—still God's servants, attendants, and worshipers (Gruenwald, "Appendix 1: Metatron, the Meaning of His Name and His Functions," in idem, *Apocalyptic and Merkavah Mysticism*, 237).

58. See Peder Borgen, "God's Agent in the Fourth Gospel," in Neusner, *Religions in Antiquity*, 137–48. References in Philo include *Conf.* 41, 146; *Leg.* 1.43; *Somn.* 1.228-30.

59. Merkur believes that both the lesser YHWH and Christ are elaborations of the angel of Exod. 23:20-21.

60. Rachel Elior, "The Concept of God in Hekhalot Literature," in *Binah*, vol. 2: *Studies in Jewish Thought*, ed. J. Dan (New York: Praeger, 1989), 99.

61. Merkur, *Gnosis*, 170.

62. Ibid., 129–53.

63. See *Mystical Union in Judaism, Christianity, and Islam: An Ecumenical Dialogue*, ed. M. Idel and B. McGinn (New York: Continuum, 1996).

Chapter 16
The Human Being in Gnosticism

1. Henry Corbin, "The Eyes of the Flesh and Eyes of Fire: Science and Gnosis," *Material for Thought* 8 (1980): 7.

2. Michael A. Williams, *Rethinking "Gnosticism": An Argument for Dismantling a Dubious Category* (Princeton: Princeton University Press, 1996).

3. I have capitalized both nouns in the Nag Hammadi texts, since "the Son of the Man" has become the title of a specific heavenly being. *Eugnostos* is exceptional in that it lacks the definite articles.

4. The Coptic Nag Hammadi texts generally use "the son of the man" with both definite articles, suggesting their dependency on the four-Gospel tradition.

5. Irenaeus *Against Heresies* 1.12.4, trans. Foerster (Werner Foerster, *Gnosis* [Oxford: Clarendon Press, 1972], 1:197).

6. Simone Pétrement argues that the idea of a Gnostic redeemer myth comes no earlier than Mani in the third century, and cannot be used to understand earlier Gnostic thinking. "Thus the name Son of man is not explained by a Gnostic myth. Rather, the Gnostic myth of God called 'Man' is explained by the Evangelists' expression 'Son of the Man' " (*A Separate God: The Christian Origins of Gnosticism*, trans. C. Harrison [San Francisco: HarperSanFrancisco, 1990], 110).

7. Walter Wink, *Cracking the Gnostic Code: The Powers in Gnosticism*, SBL Monograph Series 46 (Atlanta: Scholars Press, 1993).

8. Quotations from Nag Hammadi texts are from the *Nag Hammadi Library in English*, 3d ed. (San Francisco: Harper & Row, 1988), henceforth *NHL*, unless the text varies from that volume, in which case quotations are generally from Foerster, *Gnosis*, or Bentley Layton, *The Gnostic Scriptures* (Garden City, N.Y.: Doubleday, 1987), or an earlier edition of *NHL*.

9. *Pistis Sophia* 106:13-14; 107–8; *NHL* 220–21.

10. *Origin of the World* 103:19; 104:2-3; 107:26; 108:8-9; 115:21-22. The redemption of humanity is called "the appearance of the true man" (123:24-25; 122:20).

11. *Melchizedek* 17:15. See *Nag Hammadi Codices IX and X*, ed. Birger A. Pearson, Nag Hammadi Studies 15 (Leiden: E. J. Brill, 1981), 37.

12. For example, the *Thought of Norea* refers to a Primal Man or Primal Father called Adamas, who is the supreme God and Perfect Man (27:25-26; 28:29-30). The fourth book of the Jung Codex says of Christ, "He alone is truly worthy, the Man of the Father, who is . . . the form of the formless, (the body) of the bodiless, the face of the invisible, the word of the unutterable, the thought of the unthinkable" (p. 66, 1:10-16; cited in Gilles Quispel, *Gnostic Studies I* [Istanbul: Nederlands Historisch-Archaeologisch Instituut, 1974], 210). The indescribable God is nevertheless described as a human being, a "man" with form, body, and face. So also the Gospel of John reproaches the religious authorities because they have not seen the form (*eidos*) of God (5:37; see Num. 12:8—Moses "beholds the form of the Lord"). In the *Second Treatise of the Great Seth*, the high God is called "the Father of Truth, the Man of the Greatness" (52:34-53:4), and Jesus is the Christ, the Son of the Man, who is exalted above the heavens (65:18-19; 69:21-22). Both Orthodox Christians and Jews are ignorant of the true redeemer (64:11-12). The *Apocalypse of Peter* also contains

the statement about the Son of the Man "who is exalted above the heavens" (71:12-13). Helmut Koester and Elaine H. Pagels believe that the heavenly figure that appears twice in *The Dialogue of the Savior* is not identified with Jesus or the risen Christ, but is an angelic figure (*NHL* 245). That is possible. But the Son of Man is identified with the divine Logos who descended and brought back the divine seed that had fallen into the world (135:16—136:6). So I see no reason to deny that the Son of the Man here is the exalted heavenly judge of all, who passes out heavenly garments to those who are saved (136:20-22; cf. Rev. 3:5), and who is identical with Christ. In *Zostrianos* 6:24-27, reference is made to "the first perfect man, and Seth Emmacha Seth, the son of Adamas, the father of the immovable race." This "Perfect Man" is identified in 13:11 as the Father God, and Seth is the son of Adam/son of the Man (30:10). In A *Valentinian Exposition*, and frequently in other Valentinian texts, Man and Church are paired within a tetrad of divine beings that have emanated from the Father (29:33-34). In *Trimorphic Protennoia* 49:18-20, the "sons of man" see the "Father of everyone" as simply a "son of man" (by capitalizing this expression the *NHL* misleadingly suggests that we are dealing with titles rather than the normal Jewish idiom for "human beings"). The meaning (contrary to the introduction by John D. Turner) is that the Father hid in a human body to escape detection by hostile Powers. In *The Prayer of the Apostle Paul* 17–18, the Son of the Man seems to be, not so much the Christ, but "the Spirit, the Paraclete of truth."

On the Origin of the World 115:21-22 speaks of God as Man: "I have come through the power of the man of light"—that is, the transcendent God, whose name is Man—"for the destruction of your [the archons'] work." In *The Untitled Text in the Bruce Codex* 17–18, and in *The Two Books of Jeu and the Untitled Text in the Bruce Codex*, trans. Violet Mackensie, NHS 13 (Leiden: Brill, 1978), 281–83, a gnostic text not found at Nag Hammadi, the Father of all is liturgically praised for having "begotten Man in thy self-originated mind, and in the thought and the perfect idea. . . . It is thou who hast given all things to Man. And he has worn them like garments, and he has put them on like clothing, and he has wrapped himself in the creation like a mantle. This is Man whom the All prays to know." This Man is the agent of salvation. It should be clear that this is no earthly being, but something akin to the divine Logos.

13. Frederick H. Borsch, *The Son of Man in Myth and History* (Philadelphia: Westminster Press, 1967), 55.

14. Werner Kelber, *The Oral and the Written Gospel: The Hermeneutics of Speaking and Writing in the Synoptic Tradition, Mark, Paul, and Q* (Philadelphia: Fortress Press, 1976), 67.

15. Stevan L. Davies, *Jesus the Healer: Possession, Trance, and the Origins of Christianity* (New York: Continuum, 1995), 125–31.

16. The distance between the Humanchild in the Gospels and in the Gnostics is vast. Jesus as lowly, homeless, a "nobody," or "Everyman," who identifies with others' suffering and goes to a wretched death, is in the Gnostics replaced with a divine being with virtually no contact with the earth or suffering.

17. *Testimony of Truth* 36:23-28. *Testimony of Truth* contains sixteen references to the Son of Man. It is by far the author's favorite christological expression—something one cannot say about a single "orthodox" theologian. The Son of the Man came forth from Imperishability and revealed a radical asceticism (30:18-19;

32:22-28; 38:4-5; 61:9). At times the Son of the Man is simply Jesus (37:10-11; 69:15-17); at others it is a heavenly revealer (31:6), judge (37:26-29; 40:24-25), or the inner *anthrōpos* (36:23-25). Three times Jesus' followers are called "the generation of the Son of the Man" (60:6; 67:7; 68:10-11), apparently alluding to something like the new "race" of Sethian Gnosticism, showing that, even here, the Son of the Man continues to have a corporate dimension. Two passages are too damaged to read (71:12-13; 72:25). For commentary, see Birger A. Pearson, "The Testimony of Truth," in Pearson, *Nag Hammadi Codices IX and X*, 104.

18. *The Book of Thomas the Contender* 138:16-18 makes a similar point. "For he who has not known himself has known nothing, but he who has known himself has at the same time already achieved knowledge about the depth of the all." But it is impossible for one who does not know herself to do so; hence the necessity of a Revealer. This is a universal insight. As the physicist Brian Swimme notes, a study of the universe is a study of the self (*The Universe Is a Green Dragon: A Cosmic Creation-Story* [Santa Fe, N.Mex.: Bear, 1985], 109).

Simone Pétrement criticizes the idea that knowledge of self is the heart of Gnosticism. She insists that the Gnostics' focus is on knowledge of *God*. The issue is not so much knowing oneself as knowing one's origin and destination in God. One comes upon this knowledge not by searching for it, but as a divine gift, through revelation. "*It is the Savior who has revealed us to ourselves*" (*Separate God*, 138, emphasis hers). This is surely overstated; "Does not Jesus say, 'Whoever finds himself is superior to the world'?" (*Gospel of Thomas* 111).

19. Others who see Christian influence in the *Apocalypse of Adam* include Jean Daniélou, review in *RSR* 54 (1966): 285–93; Hans-Martin Schenke, review in *OLZ* 61 (1966): 23–34; and Rodolphe Kasser, "Textes gnostiques: Remarques à propos des éditions récentes du Livre de Jean et des Apocalypses de Paul, Jacques et Adam," *Muséon* 78 (1965): 92 n. 49. Those opposed include George W. MacRae, "The Coptic Gnostic Apocalypse of Adam," in *Nag Hammadi Codices V,2–5 and VI with Pap. Ber. 8502,1 and 4*, ed. Douglas M. Parrott, NHS 11 (Leiden: E. J. Brill, 1979), 152; and Majella Franzmann, *Jesus in the Nag Hammadi Writings* (Edinburgh: T. & T. Clark, 1996), xvi–xvii.

20. Williams, *Rethinking "Gnosticism,"* 10.

21. John D. Turner, "Sethian Gnosticism: A Literary History," in *Nag Hammadi, Gnosticism, and Early Christianity*, ed. Charles W. Hedrick and Robert Hodgson Jr. (Peabody, Mass.: Hendrickson, 1986), 65.

22. Hans-Martin Schenke, *Der Gott "Mensch" in der Gnosis* (Göttingen: Vandenhoeck & Ruprecht, 1962), 38–43. Simone Pétrement counters that the Gnostics got the idea that God is "Man" by inference from Jesus' self-designation "the son of the Man" (*Separate God*, 101–26). Both ignore the generative impact of Ezekiel 1.

23. Hippolytus *Refutation* 8.12.

24. One set of occurrences is fragmentary but still valuable (76:1-2); another is a riddle that leaves me baffled (63:25-31). The remaining five references appear in 81:14-34.

25. William Blake, *Blake: Complete Writings*, ed. Geoffrey Keynes (London: Oxford University Press, 1966), 793.

26. Van A. Harvey, "The Historical Jesus, the Kerygma, and Christian Faith," *Religion in Life* 33 (1964): 450.

27. The *Gospel of Philip* contains one of the few real parables found outside the canonical Gospels. "The lord went into the dye works of Levi. He took seventy-two different colors and threw them into the vat. He took them out all white. And he said, 'Even so has the son of man come as a dyer' " (63:25-30). Whatever else he is, the Humanchild is a miraculous transformer of people. The reference to white suggests that they have been cleansed.

28. *Gospel of Philip* 71:35—72:4, Elaine Pagels's translation, in *Adam, Eve, and the Serpent* (New York: Random House, 1988), 65–66.

29. See Henry Corbin, "*Mundus Imaginalis* or the Imaginary and the Imaginal," *Spring* (1972): 12.

30. Thomas avoids reducing the divine encounter to inwardness. See sayings 77 ("split a piece of wood, and I am there. Lift up the stone, and you will find me there") and 113 ("the kingdom of the father is spread out upon the earth, and men do not see it") (Stevan Davies, "The Christology and Protology of the *Gospel of Thomas*," *JBL* 111 [1992]: 665).

31. Irenaeus *Against Heresy* 1.30.1-15 and Origen *Contra Celsus* 6.24-38.

32. Foerster's summary, *Gnosis I: Patristic Evidence*, 84–87, which I have severely abbreviated.

33. Irenaeus *Against Heresies* 1.12.4, Foerster's translation (*Gnosis*, 197), emphasis added.

34. Epiphanius *Panarion* 31.5.5, trans. Foerster.

35. Epiphanius *Panarion* 24.5.2; ed. Holl, GCS 1.262; cited in Quispel, "Gnostic Man: The Doctrine of Basilides," *Gnostic Studies I*, 119.

36. Hippolytus *Elenchos* 7.22.1; cited in Quispel, *Gnostic Studies I*, 119, 121.

37. Hippolytus *Refutation* 8.13.4, trans. Foerster.

38. Hippolytus *Refutation* 8.15.1, trans. Foerster.

39. Carl Jung, "The Archetypes of the Collective Unconscious," CW 7, 110.

40. Hippolytus *Refutation* 5.1-3, trans. Foerster. Hippolytus's presentation of Naassene thought "may represent a very excusable misunderstanding on his part" (Alastair H. B. Logan, *Gnostic Truth and Christian Heresy: A Study in the History of Gnosticism* [Edinburgh: T. & T. Clark, 1996], 173–83). I find this section of Hippolytus particularly incomprehensible. Perhaps that was his intention. One way to turn away potential gnostic converts was to render their beliefs irritatingly complex.

41. *Trimorphic Protennoia* 49:18-19; *Gospel of Thomas* 86.

42. *Poimandres*, in *Corpus Hermeticum* 1.1-32; 7.1-3; text in Foerster, *Gnosis*, 1.326-36.

43. Zosimus, "Omega," bk. 24 of *Chemeutika*, summarized in Kurt Rudolph, *Gnosis* (San Francisco: Harper & Row, 1985), 108–9; Schenke, *Der Gott "Mensch" in der Gnosis: The Nature and History of Gnosticism*, trans. R. M. Wilson, 52–56. On *Poimandres*, see Jens Holzhausen, *Der "Mythos vom Menschen" im hellenistischen Ägypten* (Bodenheim, Germany: Athenäum Hain Hanstein, 1994).

44. As early as 326 C.E., Constantine intervened to prohibit Valentinians (who considered themselves Christians) from holding further meetings. The edict could not be enforced since it specified no penalties for disobedience, but it did mark a momentous step in governmental intervention in church affairs (Layton, *Gnostic Scriptures*, 272).

Part 6
Results and Conclusions

1. Either Luke altered Mark 14:62 by omitting the second coming, or he drew on a special source (which Luke 22:67-68 seems to reflect). In any case, the movement is not toward earth, but heaven. Luke omits the reference to "seeing" the son of the man, apparently because he did not wish to impute visionary capacity to the authorities who opposed Jesus.

2. Edward F. Edinger, *Transformation of the God-Image: An Elucidation of Jung's Answer to Job*, Studies in Jungian Psychology (Toronto: Inner City Books, 1992), 64.

3. Gandhi: "And because the life of Jesus has the significance and the transcendency to which I have alluded, I believe that he belongs not solely to Christianity, but to the entire world" (*The Law of Love*, ed. Avand T. Hingorani [Bombay: Bharatiya Vidya Bhavan, 1962], 111).

4. Frederick Borsch, *The Son of Man in Myth and History* (Philadelphia: Westminster Press, 1967), 404. I disagree with Borsch only in his conviction that a universal myth of the Man informed Jesus. As we saw earlier, there was no such myth. But there was an archetypal stirring in the womb of history that demanded manifestation.

5. Ragnar Leivestad suggests that Jesus may have thought of himself as Ezekiel *redivivus* ("Der apokalyptische Menschensohn ein Phantom," *ASTI* 6 [1968]: 49–105), not a surprising possibility, since a notion, current with Jesus, that Israel's prophets would return seems to have existed (Mark 6:14-16; 8:27-28).

6. Delbert Burkett, *The Son of Man Debate: A History and Evaluation*, SNTSMS 107 (Cambridge: Cambridge University Press, 2000).

7. For "nobody," see Jer. 49:18, 32; 50:40; 51:12. According to Pss. 49:2 (49:3 Hebrew) and 4:3, the *bene ish* are children of *men*, that is, people of rank and distinction, whereas the *bene 'adam* are children of the common people, who are not distinctive. So also Ps. 62:9 (62:10 Hebrew); Prov. 8:4; Isa. 2:9; 5:15. See Georg Fohrer, "*Huios*," *TDNT* 8:345–47. Some of these verses may intend the distinction, but the distinction does not hold up elsewhere. The simple sense "nobody" is attested at Qumran in 1QapGen 21:13. E. A. Abbott suggests that Mark 2:10 read, "That you may know that a common or low-born man has power to forgive sins . . ." (*The Son of Man* [Cambridge: Cambridge University Press, 1910], 109 n. 3109b.

8. Kathlene Peterson Nicol, " 'Son of Man': Its Background and New Testament Usage" (B.D. thesis, Union Theological Seminary, New York, 1970), epilogue.

9. William L. Dols Jr., "Toward a Field Critical Hermeneutic of the Phrase *ho huios tou anthrōpou* in the Narrative World of Mark" (Ph.D. diss., Graduate Theological Union, Berkeley, California, 1987), iii.

10. Jung comments, "[A]s the historical Son of Man and anthropos he [Jesus] is the prototype of the individual inner man and at the same time the culmination, goal and totality of the empirical man" (*Civilization in Transition*, CW 10, 397).

11. Maurice Casey, "General, Generic, and Indefinite: The Use of the Term 'Son of Man' in Aramaic Sources and in the Teaching of Jesus," *JSNT* 29 (1987): 21–56.

12. Barnabas Lindars, *Jesus Son of Man* (London: SPCK, 1983), 24.

13. Richard Bauckham, "The Son of Man: 'A Man in My Position' or 'Someone'?" *JSNT* 23 (1985): 23–33.

14. John Pairman Brown also suggests a gesture ("The Son of Man: This Fellow," *Biblica* 58 [1977]: 361–87). "This fellow" also does not work well with the apocalyptic passages. It is conceivable that Jesus originally spoke about a heavenly son of the man and that, after his death and exaltation, some of his followers identified him in his exalted state with the son of the man, as Adela Yarbro Collins suggests ("The Origin of the Designation of Jesus as Son of Man," *HTR* 80 [1987]: 406).

15. Burkett, *Son of Man Debate*, 92–93. That the Targumim are themselves inconsistent in rendering the Hebrew *ben 'adam* makes the consistency of the Greek rendering *ho huios tou anthrōpou* in the Gospels all the more remarkable (Abbott, *Son of Man*, xxii n. 1).

16. "I" does *not* work in Luke 24:7; John 5:26-27; 12:34. "I" could be used in Mark 2:1-12; 2:28; Matt. 13:37, 41; 16:27-28; 24:30; but it would represent a false conclusion. Many of these texts are "apocalyptic"; if one believes that Jesus speaks of someone else in these passages, then "I" could not be substituted for the son of the man in any of them. Nor could "I" be used in Dan. 7:13.

17. Chrys C. Caragounis, *The Son of Man* (Tübingen: Mohr/Siebeck, 1986), 248. "If Son of Man does have a significance and overtones absent from 'I'—and this is abundantly clear in the Gospels—it cannot be a 'surrogate' for 'I'!" (26). Caragounis continues, "It is therefore quite probable that in some cases where no particular theological emphasis was recognized to lie in the expression Son of Man, the equivalent pronoun was felt sufficient to mark the grammatical subject or object of the sentence. But to use such an occasional practice as an argument for resolving the title Son of Man everywhere into the personal pronoun, as Vermes, Casey and Lindars have tried to do," is wrongheaded (166).

18. O. Cullmann, *Christology of the New Testament*, trans. S. C. Guthrie and C. A. M. Hall (Philadelphia: Westminster Press, 1959), 137.

19. Joseph A. Fitzmyer, S.J., *A Wandering Aramean*, SBLMS 25 (Missoula, Mont.: Scholars Press, 1978), 145. "Adam" in Aramaic does not mean "man," but is a proper name.

20. Mahlon Smith, "To Judge the Son of Man," *Foundations and Facets Forum* 7 (1991): 215. His is the best treatment of the linguistic difficulties of *ho huios tou anthrōpou*. In regard to the problem of the definite articles, C. F. D. Moule observes: "[O]nce the *huios* receives the article, it normally follows, by Greek idiom, that the dependent noun in the genitive will have the article also: *ho huios tou anthrōpou*, not *ho huios anthrōpou*; there is not necessarily, therefore, any special significance in the article before the genitive: the significant phenomenon is that the phrase as a whole is definite, not indefinite" ("Neglected Features in the Problem of the Son of Man," in *Essays in New Testament Interpretation* [Cambridge: Cambridge University Press, 1982], 82–83). Such linguistic solutions cannot explain why the initial definite article was added, the significance of that addition, and why Jesus alone employed it.

21. In a letter, Burkett hypothesizes an "earlier stage (now seen only in Acts 7:56), in which it was the church, not Jesus, that spoke about Jesus as the Son of Man. In this stage, third-person language about Jesus as the Son of Man would have been quite natural." For example, says Burkett, it is not hard to imagine an early Christian saying about Jesus, "The Son of Man came to seek and save the lost." But that is precisely what the Gospels do not say. Such a statement is made *about* Jesus, not *by* him, and it is the latter that is so puzzling.

22. Data in Bernard Spolsky and R. L. Cooper, *The Languages of Jerusalem* (Oxford: Clarendon Press, 1991).

23. Margaret Barker, *The Great Angel: A Study of Israel's Second God* (Louisville: Westminster Press, 1992), 219–21.

24. Randall Buth, "A More Complete Semitic Background for *bar-enasha* Son of Man," in *The Function of Scripture in Early Jewish and Christian Tradition*, ed. C. A. Evans and J. A. Sanders (Sheffield: Sheffield Academic Press, 1998), 176–89. According to George Howard, "The extant pre-Christian copies of the Septuagint that include passages incorporating the Divine Name preserve the Divine Name in the Greek text." "Yahweh" usually was written in Aramaic or paleo-Hebraic letters or was transliterated into Greek letters ("The Tetragram and the New Testament," *JBL* 96 [1977]: 63–83).

25. F. C. Burkitt, *The Four Gospels in Syriac* (London: C. J. Clay & Sons, 1894), 2:272.

26. Norman Perrin, *Christology and a Modern Pilgrimage: A Discussion with Norman Perrin*, ed. Hans Dieter Betz (Missoula, Mont.: Society of Biblical Literature, 1973), 22–23; idem, "Mark 14:62: The End Product of a Christian Pesher Tradition?" *NTS* 12 (1965–66): 150–55.

27. Burkett, *Son of Man Debate*, 56.

28. In postcanonical Hebrew there is only one instance of "*the* son of man," found at Qumran (1QS 11:20); there the *h* is an addition, written by a scribe over the line. As the synonymous parallelism with "one born of woman" indicates, "son of man" here simply means "human being." "Thus, with almost complete consistency, the New Testament, whenever the phrase is related to Jesus, adheres to a form which is otherwise virtually unexampled." The practically unprecedented use of a definite article with "son of man" in the sayings of Jesus is better explained as the result of Jesus' own sense of vocation and destiny than as a formula created by others (Moule, *Essays in New Testament Interpretation*, 82).

29. Seyoon Kim, *The "Son of Man" as the Son of God*, WUNT 30(Tübingen: Mohr/Siebeck, 1983), 1.

30. Rumi, *Unseen Rain: Quatrains of Rumi*, trans. J. Moyne and C. Barks (Putney, Vt.: Threshold Books, 1986), 31.

31. Rainer Maria Rilke, *Letters to a Young Poet*, rev. ed., trans. M. D. H. Norton (New York: Norton, 1962), 65.

32. Nicolas Berdyayev, *The Meaning of the Creative Act*, trans. D. A. Lowrie (New York: Harper & Brothers, 1954), 336–37. Berdyayev means by the coming Christ what I mean by the Human Being.

33. Ibid., 80–81.

34. Ibid., 94–101.

Appendix 1
Was There a Primal Man Myth?

1. Arthur Ferch, *The Son of Man in Daniel 7*, Andrews University Seminary Doctoral Dissertation Series 6 (Berrien Springs, Mich.: Andrews University Press, 1979), 37. The knockout blow was delivered by Carston Colpe in *Die religionsgeschichtliche Schule: Darstellung und Kritik ihres Bildes vom gnostischen Er-*

Iosermythus, FRLANT 87 (Göttingen: Vandenhoeck & Ruprecht, 1961. See also H.-M. Schenke, *Der Gott "Mensch" in der Gnosis: Ein religionsgeschichte licher Beitrag zur Diskussion über die paulinsche Anschauung von der Kirche als Leib Christi* (Göttingen: Vandenhoeck & Ruprecht, 1962).

2. Ferch, *The Son of Man in Daniel 7*, 47.

3. Carl H. Kraeling, *Anthropos and Son of Man* (New York: Columbia University Press, 1927), 91.

4. Sigmund Mowinckel, *He That Cometh* (Nashville: Abingdon Press, 1954), 346–450.

5. Oscar Cullmann, *The Christology of the New Testament*, trans. S. C. Guthrie and C. A. M. Hall (Philadelphia: Westminster Press, 1959), 150.

6. Ferch, *Son of Man in Daniel 7*, 51.

7. This observation undermines the case of Helge S. Kvanvig, *Roots of Apocalyptic: The Mesopotamian Background of the Enoch Figure and of the Son of Man*, Wissenschaftliche Monographien zum Alten und Neuen Testament 61 (Neukirchen-Vluyn: Neukirchener Verlag, 1988).

8. Alexander A. Di Lella, "The One in Human Likeness and the Holy Ones of the Most High in Daniel 7," *CBQ* 39 (1977): 1–19.

9. Ferch, *Son of Man in Daniel 7*, 76.

10. Thus the *Apocalypse of Abraham* 10 (first to second century C.E.) may have been inspired by the passage on the shield of Achilles in the *Iliad* 18.483ff., or the wondrous phoenix of classical antiquity adapted as a symbol of the resurrection of the Christ. But, significantly, this borrowing was illustrative and did not touch the mythic core (Mary Dean-Otting, *Heavenly Journeys: A Study of the Motif in Hellenistic Jewish Literature*, Judentum und Umwelt 8 [New York: Peter Lang, 1984], 130, 196–97).

11. Carl Jung, "Gnostic Symbols of the Self," *Aion* (*CW* 9.2 [1959]), 189.

Appendix 2
Philo on the Archetypes

1. *On the Creation* 16.

2. James Hillman and David Ray Griffin reject the distinction between archetype and archetypal image, a move that leaves them exposed to the charge of Lamarckism (David Ray Griffin, *Archetypal Process: Self and Divine in Whitehead, Jung, and Hillman* [Evanston, Ill.: Northwestern University Press, 1989]). I have dallied with this rejection as well, since it seems to conform to the notion in quantum mechanics that there are no realities behind reality, and that our functional image of God is the only god we get, and not some higher, unknowable God beyond the gods. Perhaps we have a genuine complementarity here, in which we are forced to say both that the God beyond the gods is, indeed, unknowable, and that God is like us, only more so, infinitely so, and therefore knowable to the degree that our puny brains can comprehend God.

3. *On the Creation* 31. This distinction between the archetype and its expression in archetypal images is underlined in *Who Is the Heir?* 280, in which Philo speaks of "the archetypal ideas which, invisible and intelligible *there*, are the patterns of things visible and sensible *here*. . . ."

4. *On Dreams I* 75. Philo had to face the same kinds of objections to his Platonism that Jungians face today: "Some aver that the Incorporeal Ideas or Forms are an empty name devoid of any real substance of fact, and thus they abolish in things the most essential element of their being, namely the archetypal patterns (*arxetupon paradeigma*) of all qualities in what exists, and on which the form and dimensions of each separate thing was modelled" (*The Special Laws I* 327).

5. *On the Creation* 69.

6. *Noah's Work as a Planter* 20.

7. *On the Creation* 134.

8. *Allegorical Interpretation I* 32.

9. *Migr. Abr.* 220; *Conf. Ling.* 41:62-63, 146-47.

10. *On Drunkenness* 133. This catalytic agency is alluded to when Philo explains why God appears in the form of angels, which does not alter God's own nature, for God (like a catalyst) "is unchangeable, but conveying to those which receive the impression of His presence [as an angel] a semblance in a different form, such that they take the image to be not a copy, but that original form itself" (*On Dreams I* 232). Thus archetypal images are able to communicate the actual archetype they image, without the actual archetype ever becoming visible, concrete, or substantial.

11. *The Confusion of Tongues* 63.

12. *Allegorical Interpretation II* 4.

13. *On Abraham* 4.

14. Andrew Newberg, Eugene d'Aquili, and Vince Rause, *Why God Won't Go Away: Brain Science and the Biology of Belief* (New York: Ballantine Books, 2001), 48.

Appendix 3
Ezekiel's Influence on Jesus

1. For example, H. E. Tödt begins his study of the Jewish background of the "son of man" phrase with Dan. 7:13-14, mentioning Ezekiel but once, and then only in passing. Having already decided that the apocalyptic "son of man" sayings are of most significance, Tödt could dismiss Ezekiel's ninety-three references as inconsequential because they were nonapocalyptic (*The Son of Man in the Synoptic Tradition*, trans. D. M. Barton [Philadelphia: Westminster Press, 1965], 304). So also A. J. B. Higgins, *Jesus and the Son of Man* (Philadelphia: Fortress Press, 1964), 195. In addition to the parallels I have noted, I have drawn on E. A. Abbott, *The Son of Man* (Cambridge: Cambridge University Press, 1910), 82–107.

2. Abbott, *Son of Man*, 101.

3. Ibid., 97.

Index of Ancient Sources

Hebrew Bible

GENESIS

1	28, 242, 265, 280
1:26-27	28, 237, 244, 265
3	244
5:1	28
5:24	225
9:4-6	28
16:13-14	46
17:12	22
18:2, 16, 22	279
18:7	22
28:10-17	199, 322
32:22-32	216, 279
40:13, 19	204

EXODUS

4:4	75
5:2-15	70
6:6	278
15:3	328
20:4	317
23:20-21	331
24:1-11	40, 217, 224, 279
33:20-22	217, 279

NUMBERS

12:8	332
15:32-36	71
23:19	281

DEUTERONOMY

5:4	280
5:21	217
18·15	307
21:20	87, 305
23:25	71
23:36	317

JUDGES

8:6	296

1 KINGS

18:42	327
20:35	276
22:19-23	24, 40, 226

2 KINGS

2:11	225, 324

JOB

16:21	281
25:6	281
35:8	281

PSALMS

4:3	331
8	33, 50, 61, 64, 82, 156, 255, 274, 276, 281, 301
49:2	336
80	50, 61, 78, 156, 209, 252, 291
80:14-18	51, 210, 281
82:6	203
82:9	336
89:20	308
110:1	255
132	307

PROVERBS

1:24	302
8:4	336

ISAIAH

2:9	336
5:15	336
6	24, 55, 215, 226
6:1	40
6:11	217
9:1-6	307, 308
11:1-9	308
35:10	109
40:12	222

49:3	199	10	24	7:7	306, 331
51:12	281	11	24	7:9-14	52, 56, 224,
53:2	32, 92, 93	16:48	268		279, 291, 296
53:4-6	267	17:2	268	7:13	21, 52, 53, 56, 59,
55:3-4	307	17:21	282		79, 156, 157, 169,
56:2	70, 281, 297	17:22-24	268		182, 253, 255, 261,
66:1	222	20:4	267		291, 292, 305, 315,
		21:17	282		337
JEREMIAH		21:32	282	7:13-14	340
17:19-25	307	22:2	178, 267	7:14	96, 292
18:7-11	163	22:26	269	7:16	291
23:1-3	307	23:34	282	7:18	52
23:5-6	308	23:36	267	7:21	52, 292, 306
30:9	307	24:2	282	7:22	52, 53
33:15	307, 308	24:3	268	7:23	306
49:18, 32	281, 336	26:14	282	7:25	53, 292, 306
50:40	336	28:10	282	7:27	53
51:12	336	30:12	282	8:15-17	280, 282
		31:14	33	9:21	280
LAMENTATIONS		33:12-13	268	10:9-11	281
3:13	22	33:22	280		
		33:25	28	**HOSEA**	
EZEKIEL		34:16	97, 268	3:5	307
1	9, 21, 24, 29,	34:17	268	5:14	42
	55, 205, 215, 226,	34:23-24	307, 308	12:10	41
	242, 267, 271, 330	34:24	282		
1:3	280	36:26	29	**JOEL**	
1:7, 27	224	36:36	282	2:28	57
1:9-25	29	37:1	280		
1:26	25, 224, 232,	37:5, 14	29	**AMOS**	
	280, 283	37:24	307, 308	9:11	307
1:27	34, 280, 329	39:5	282		
1:28	33	40:1	280	**MICAH**	
2:1—3:11	101, 267	43:11	282	4:8	307
2:3-5	32				
3:12, 14	280	**DANIEL**		**ZECHARIAH**	
3:22-24	24, 280, 281	1–6	51	4:14	22
3:27	268	7	9, 24, 51, 55, 93,	9:10	307
4:4	267		165, 209, 215, 226,	14:5	319
5:15, 17	282		252, 262, 291,		
8:1-4	24, 280, 282		293, 305, 315		

MALACHI

3:1-4	307
4:5-6	226

WISDOM OF SOLOMON

7	296
7:27	89, 302

SIRACH

48:9-10	324

BARUCH

3:16, 29-30	302

New Testament

MATTHEW

1:1-17	308
3:12	170
3:14-15	132, 302
4:1-11	220
5:6	16
5:11	274, 305
5:22	313, 316
5:43-48	178
5:45	161, 177
6:9-13	327
7:1-5	131, 180, 190
7:19	313, 316
7:21-27	190, 313, 317
8:2	310
8:10	134
8:11	274
8:12	313, 316
8:19-20	80, 157, 253, 274
8:27	30
9:1-8	74, 77, 78, 79, 156, 253, 274
9:8	156, 157, 209
9:27	308

10:10	300
10:15	313, 318
10:17-19	69, 304
10:19	69
10:23	171, 274, 275, 315
10:28	313
10:32-33	181, 313
10:42	184, 319
11:2-6	165
11:11	302
11:12	162
11:16-19	69, 86, 89, 193, 274, 302, 305
11:20-24	313
11:22-23	268, 314
11.27	330
12:1-8	67, 74, 274, 296
12:23	308
12:27	276, 313
12:28	85, 98, 162, 301, 315
12:31-32	83, 274, 313, 316, 318
12:36-37	313, 316
12:38-40	90, 133, 274, 303, 313
13:9	268
13:24-30	179, 182, 186
13:36-43	179, 182, 186, 187, 268, 274, 275, 311, 313, 315, 316, 319, 337
13:47	319
13:49-50	313, 319
14:30	138
15:13	313
15:21-28	134, 308

16:1-4	90
16:13	274
16:19	78
16:21	98, 304
16:27	170, 177, 274, 313, 316, 337
16:28	171, 274, 275, 314, 337
17:9	274
17:12	98, 274, 304
17:22	274, 304
18.8	316
18:11	97, 274, 275
18:6, 10, 14	184
18:18	78
18:21-22	180
18:33-35	313, 316, 319
19:17	132
19:20, 22	310
19:28	156, 171, 183, 267, 274, 315, 316, 319
19:29	319
19:30	303
20:16	303
20:18	274, 304
20:20-28	92-97, 274, 303
20:30-31	308
21:5	319
21:9, 15	308
19:29	319
21:32	89
22:2	319
22:7, 11	313, 319
22:13	294, 313, 316, 319
23:7-8	296
23:11	303
23:12	268
23:32	316

23:37-39	161, 168	5:37	134	12:18-27	313
24:3-45	170–72, 274,	6:1-6	134, 275, 297	12:35	308
	275, 303, 305,	6:6-13	78, 135,	13	162, 163,
	313, 314, 337		154, 299		168, 169
25:13, 30	313	6:14-16	336	13:8-19	169, 313
25:31-46	179, 182, 183,	6:34	268	13:24-27	257, 274,
	184, 186, 189,	6:39, 45	137		312–16
	240, 267, 268,	7:24-30	134	14:20	103
	274, 275, 312,	7:31-37	134	14:21	104, 274,
	313, 315, 316,	8:11-13	90, 92, 133		294, 319
	318–20	8:22-26	134	14:32-42	137, 274, 305
26:2	274, 275, 304	8:27-33	69, 99, 102,	14:62	166, 249,
26:24	274, 319		133, 274, 304,		274, 293,
26:45	274		305, 307,		311, 314, 336
26:64	274, 314		318, 336		
		8:38	181, 182, 274,	**LUKE**	
MARK			314–16, 318	1:27, 32, 69	308
1:9-11	81, 224, 267	8:34-35	79, 143	3:15	302
1:15	78	9:9	274	3:17	170
1:22	80	9:12	98, 101,	3:23-28	308
1:38	89		274, 304	4:1-13	220
2:1-12	74–81, 134,	9:14-29	136	5:17-26	74
	305, 337	9:18	134	5:22	97
2:10	157, 207, 274,	9:30-32	274, 304, 305	5:24	274
	276, 296,	9:35	303	6:1-5	67, 274, 297
	298, 336	9:38-41	193	6:20	162
2:15-17	190	9:42-48	313	6:22	101, 207,
2:18-20	69	10:17-18	85, 132		274, 305
2:23-28	67 – 74, 79,		133, 310	6:37-38	180, 190
	156, 175, 193,	10:28-30	69, 81	6:41-42	131, 180
	240, 274, 337	10:31	303	6:47-49	190, 313
3:5	133	10:32-34	98, 274,	7:9	134
3:6	74, 75		304, 305	7:28	79, 302
3:22	85	10:35-45	92–97, 183,	7:31-35	86–90, 97,
3:23-27	313		208, 267, 274,		193, 274,
3:28	274		303, 304		302, 305
3:35	213	10:47-48	308	7:38	306
4:1-9	101, 268	10:52	134	8:8	268
4:23	268	11:12-14	133	8:24	310
4:35-41	135	11:20	85	9:3	300
5:11	274	11:22-24	134	9:22	274, 304, 305
5:34	134	11:27	79	9:26	182, 274, 315

9:43-45	274, 305	17:20-21	162, 240, 313	**JOHN**
9:48	303	17:22	274, 275	1:1	321
9:49-50	193	17:24	172, 274	1:12-13	203
9:51-56	190, 274, 320	17:25	102, 304, 305	1:14	200, 236
9:56	97, 274	17:26-30	172, 274	1:18	226
9:57-58	69, 80–83, 98,	17:37	80	1:21	275
	156, 253, 274	18:1-8	313, 327	1:51	198, 274
9:62	191	18:8	173, 274,	2:21	210
10:4	300		275, 314	2:24-25	85
10:9, 17-20	78, 98,	18:9-14	78, 268	3:3	205
	136, 162	18:31	274, 304	3:13	155, 200, 203,
10:12-15	268, 313	18:38-39	308		206, 225, 274
10:22	330	19:10	97–98, 185,	3:14-15	202, 203,
11:1-20	301, 313		268, 274,		244, 305
11:29-32	90, 91, 133,		275, 320	3:16	107
	182, 274, 313	19:11-15, 27	303	3:17-21	203
12:4-5	313	19:27	313	3:17-19	177, 186, 320
12:8-9	64, 178, 182,	19:41-42	161	3:27-30	79
	207, 274, 313,	21:11	313	3:32	203
	317, 319	21:22-24	313	3:36	177
12:10	83–86, 274, 318	21:27	274	5:1-47	76–77, 177, 298
12:12	143	21:32-36	161, 274,	5:26-27	204, 276, 337
12:13-14	180, 190		275, 313	5:27	187, 198, 205,
12:40	172, 274, 314	22:3	104		267, 274
12:46-47	313	22:16-18	313	5:37	332
12:49	5	22:22	102, 274	6:5-6	136
12:57	74, 175, 195	22:24-27	92–97, 274,	6:27	274
13:26-29	313, 316		303, 304	6:28-29	203
13:30	303	22:28-30	183, 267,	6:35 53	201, 274
13:31-33	99, 274		274, 304, 315	6.62	155, 249, 274
13:32	80	22:48	104, 274, 275,	7:42	308
13:34-35	161, 168, 305		304, 305, 306	8:28, 29	204, 205, 274
14:11	268	22:67-68	336	8:31, 34	104
14:12-13	301	22:69	155, 170, 178,	8.59	305
14:14	313		256, 274	9:4	203
14:35	268	24:7	102, 274, 275,	9:13-41	203
15:3-7	268		305, 337	9:35-38	20, 201,
15:20	306	24:13-35	153		274, 321
16:16	302	24:21	141	10:30	205
16:23	313	27:3-10	104	10:31	305
17:3-4	180			10:34-35	203
17:5-6	134			10:39	305

11:50	307	6:6	208	3:16	208	
12:4-6	104	6:11	210	4:8-10	155	
12:17	203	6:23	210	4:12-13	208, 209	
12:23, 32	204, 274	7:4	210	4:22	246	
12:32	203	8:21	103	4:24	208	
12:34	20, 102, 201,	8:29	28, 252	5:2	208	
	204, 274,	10:6-7	155			
	305, 337	10:9	207	**Colossians**		
13:14	303	12:4-5	210	1:15-20	266	
13:31	204, 274			2:9	243	
14:2	203	**1 Corinthians**		2:18	146	
14:3	200, 203	1:4	211	3:9-10	208, 246	
14:6-7, 9	200, 203	1:23	141			
14:12	141, 203, 258	1:30	211	**1 Thessalonians**		
14:20	203	3:16	145, 211	5:3	294	
14:28	205	4:20	95			
15:1-11	200, 203, 210	5:9-13	87	**2 Thessalonians**		
15:15	145	6:9-11	87	1:7	294	
20:17	155	6:19	145, 211			
20:23	203	12:3	83	**1 Timothy**		
20:28	321	12:13	210	2:5-6	208	
		12:27-31	209, 210			
Acts		15:8	155	**2 Timothy**		
1:9-11	155	15:22	211	2:8	308	
1:16-20	104	15:47-49	209			
2:34-35	155			**Titus**		
3:1-10	141	**2 Corinthians**		2:13-14	208	
3:21	242	4:16	208			
7	14	5:14-21	107, 108, 132	**Hebrews**		
7:56	274, 308, 317	6:16	211	2:6	274	
9	100	12:1-10	24, 215, 225	2:10	132	
15:29	68	13:3, 5	211	4:14	155	
20:37	306			5:8	110	
		Galatians				
Romans		2:20	208	**1 Peter**		
1:3	308	3:27	246	3:4	208	
1:18-32	38			4:14	207	
3:23-24	108, 210	**Ephesians**				
3:25	106	1:7	207	**1 John**		
5:8	108	2:6	211	3:2	28, 48, 167,	
5:12-21	209	2:15-16	209		173 193, 209,	
6:3	210	3:6	210		224, 266	

REVELATION

1	24, 215
1:1	274
1:9-20	155, 224, 274, 317
2:17	1
2:21-22	312
3:5	317
4–5	24, 215
4:1-4	330
9:20-21	312
12:11	94
13:18	149
13:24-27	167
14:14	24, 274
16:9-14	312
18–20	163
19:11 15	189, 294
19:17-18	189
20:15	179
21–22	163, 312
21:1	294

Apocrypha and Pseudepigrapha

ACTS OF JOHN

89	309
96:25-32	309

APOCALYPSE OF ABRAHAM

	24, 224, 339
17-13	291
18:12-19	291

ASCENSION OF ISAIAH

7	324, 331
9:8	324

ASCENSION OF MOSES

	330

2 BARUCH

14:18	297

3 BARUCH

	324

1 ENOCH

14	24, 51, 281, 324
10:4	294
37–71	24, 55, 324
38:2	56, 294, 319
40:9	319
45:1	294
45:3-6	315
46:2-8	56, 315
48:2-7, 10	56
49:3-4	317
51:3	319
54:4-5	320
55:4	319
60:10	56, 61
61:8	319
61:10	294
62:1-14	56, 186, 294, 319, 320
63:1-11	320
69:27, 29	56, 319
70–71	226, 294
71:1	56
71:14, 17	56
90:31	324
93:8	302

2 ENOCH

	24, 324
20:3	291
22:1-7	291
39:1-6	291

3 ENOCH

	24, 324, 327, 329
9:2-5	224
10:1	227

12:5	226
15:12	327
16	226
48A:9	223
48D:1, 5	228, 331

EZEKIEL THE TRAGEDIAN

The Exodus	54

4 EZRA

7:33 35	318
13	59, 191, 252, 324

JUBILEES

50:11	296

LADDER OF JACOB

	322

LIFE OF ADAM AND EVE

25–29, 35	24

PSALMS OF SOLOMON

17-18	308

TESTAMENT OF ABRAHAM

10–13	317, 324

TESTAMENT OF ISSACHAR

5:7-8	307

TESTAMENT OF JOSEPH

18:1-11	307
19:4	307

TESTAMENT OF LEVI

2:5, 8	324, 330
18:1-12	307

Dead Sea Scrolls

1QAP GEN^AR
21:13   293, 336

1QH^A
4, 30   293

1QS
9, 11   307
11:20   291

4Q181
                     293

4Q386 (4QPSEZEK^A)
         24, 277, 282

**4Q400
(4QSHIRSHABB^A)**
         24, 277, 326

**4Q418 FRAG. 55
(FRAG.7, LINE 11)**
                     293

11Q13 (11QMELCH)
                     227

**11Q10
(11QTGJOB 9,9; 26,3)**
                     293

Philo

Allegorical Interpretation
I.32   340
II. 4   340

Migration of Abraham
220   340

Noah's Work as a Planter
20   340

On Abraham
4   340

*On the Confusion
of Tongues*
         283, 331, 340
63   340
146–147   283, 331, 340

On the Creation
16   339, 340

On Dreams
I.75   340
I.228-30   331

On Drunkenness
133   340

Who Is the Heir?   339

Rabbinic Texts

MISHNAH
'Abot
1:1-12   269

Baba Batra
6:7   68

'Erubin
4:7   68

Hagigah
2:1   277

Kerithot
2:1   297

Sabbat
10:6   296
7:2   296

Sotah
5:3   68

TOSEFTA
Beṣah
8a   297

Hagigah
2.1   277

Megillah
3 [4].28   327

MEKILTA
*Mekilta de-Rabbi
Ishmael Bahodesh*
2, 3   291, 330

MIDRASHIM
Deuteronomy Rabbah
1:3   330
7:8   280
10:1   297
10:3   323, 326

Genesis Rabbah
27:1   279, 322

*Midrash Hazita
on Song of Songs*
2:4   330

Midrash Mishle   328

TARGUMIM
Palestinian Targum
on Num. 25:12   330

Targum
to Ezekiel 1   280

HEKHALOT TEXTS

Cairo Genizah

Hekalot   331

The Chapter
of R. Nehniah
b. ha-Qanah   291

Hekhalot Rabbati   24

Hekhalot Zutreti   24

Ma'aseh Merkabah   24

Merhabah Rabbah   24

Ozhayah Hekhalot   331

Pesikta Rabbati   218

Re'uyot Jehezkiel   330

Shi'ur Qomah   24, 222,
                                   223

Visions of Ezekiel   24,
                                   325

BABYLONIAN TALMUD

'Abodah Zarah
42b   331

Hagigah
14b   277, 331

Yoma
83a   297

Mesi'a
87b   331

Sanhedrin
38b   328, 331

PALESTINIAN TALMUD

Berakot
1   298

Hagigah
77b   277

Ta'an
65b   324

OTHER

'Abot de Rabbi Nathan
38   297

Pesiqta de Rab
Kahana   326

Pesiqta Rabbati
20, 21.6, 100ab   326, 330

Zohar
19a   24, 283, 284

Gnostic Texts

I,2 THE APOCRYPHON
OF JAMES
2:28-33   235
3:11-25   234
4:4-16   234
6:19-20   235
7:14   235

II,2 GOSPEL OF THOMAS
3   240
8:4   268
21:10   268
24:2   268
63:4   268
65:8   268
77   335
86   253, 335
96:3   268

106   258
111   334
113   335

II,3 GOSPEL OF PHILIP
55:16-17   237
58:17-22   238
61:20-35   238
63:25-30   335
71:35—72:4   335
76:1-2   238
81:14-24   238

II,4 HYPOSTASIS
OF THE ARCHONS
96:31-97:7   239

III,2 GOSPEL
OF THE EGYPTIANS
59:3   237
64:1-3   237

III,5 DIALOGUE
OF THE SAVIOR
135:16-136:6   333
136:20-22   333

IV,1 APOCRYPHON
OF JOHN
14:13-18   236

V,5 APOCALYPSE
OF ADAM
65:7-9   236
77:4-10   236
77:16-17   236

VII,3 APOCALYPSE
OF PETER
71:12-13   332

IX,1 MELCHIZEDEK
17:15   332

IX,2 THOUGHT
OF NOREA

27:25-26	332
28:29-30	332

IX,3 TESTIMONY
OF TRUTH

30:18-19	333
31:6	334
32:22-28	334
36:23-25	334
36:23-28	333
37:10-11	334
37:26-29	334
38:4-5	334
40:6-7	235
40:24-25	334
60:6	334
61:9	334
67:7	334
68:10-11	334
69:15-17	334
71:12-13	334
72:25	334

XI,2 A VALENTINIAN
EXPOSITION

29:33-34	333

BG,1 GOSPEL OF MARY

8:15-9:12	240
10:17-23	240
18:16	241

THE BOOK OF THOMAS
THE CONTENDER

138:16-18	334

ON THE ORIGIN
OF THE WORLD

103:19	233, 332
104:2-3	332

107:26	332
108:8-9	332
115:21-22	332, 333
122:20	332
123:24-25	332

OXYRHYNCHUS
PAPYRI 654

4:2a	303

PISTIS SOPHIA

106:13-14	332
107–108	332

POIMANDRES

1:1-32	335
7:1-3	335

THE PRAYER
OF THE APOSTLE PAUL

17–18	333

SECOND TREATISE
OF THE GREAT SETH

52:34-53:4	332
64:11-12	332
65:18-19	332
69:21-22	332

TREATISE ON THE
RESURRECTION

44:21-34	235

TRIMORPHIC
PROTENNOIA

49:18-20	333
49:18-19	335

TRIPARTITE TRACTATE

51:14-15	233
73:2-3	233

THE UNTITLED TEXT
IN THE BRUCE CODEX

17–18	333

ZOSIMUS, "OMEGA"

24	
335	

ZOSTRIANOS

6:24-27	333
13:11	333
30:10	333

Early Christian Writings

BARNABAS

6.13a	303
12:10	275

CLEMENT
OF ALEXANDRIA
Paedogogus

3.1	287

CLEMENT OF JERUSALEM
Catechesis

10.4	275

CYRIL OF ALEXANDRIA
In Ioannem

9:1	281

EPIPHANIUS
Panarion

31.5.5	335

HEGESIPPUS,
IN EUSEBIUS
Ecclesiastical History

2.3.13	275

HIPPOLYTUS

Elenchos

7.22.1   335

Refutation

5.1-3   335
8.12   335
8.13.4   335
8.15.1   335

IGNATIUS

Ephesians 20:2   275
Romans 3:3   306

IRENAEUS

Against Heresy

1.12.4   332, 335
1.30.1-15   335
3.16.7   275
17.1   27

JUSTIN

Dialogue

31.1   275
76.1   275
128:2   283

Odes of Solomon

3:3   60
8:14, 16   60
11:2   60
14:1-2   60
17   34
19:2-4   60
35:5   60
36:3, 5   59

ORIGEN

*Commentary on the
Gospel of John*

2.31 on 1:6   311

Contra Celsus

6.24-38   335

PSEUDO-CLEMENTINE

Homilies

3.7   328

TERTULLIAN

De Spectaculis

1.30   318

Other Ancient Texts

DIOGENES LAERTIUS

6.34   301

**EGYPTIAN BOOK
OF THE DEAD**

125

HOMER

Iliad

22:209   178

MITHRAS LITURGY

                        330

PINDAR

Pithian Odes

II.72   279

PLATO

Laws

716C   285

VIRGIL

Fourth Decalog   57

Index of Names

Abbott, E. A., 204, 268, 275, 278, 300, 324, 336, 337, 340
Abelard, 106, 107, 306
Adorno, T., 273
Akers, K., 308
Akiba, R., 223
Albright, C. R., 43, 44, 287, 289
Alexander, P. S., 325, 326, 331
al-Hakim, 192
Altmann, A., 328
Anders, G., 159, 160, 313
Anselm, 33, 105, 106, 307
'Arabi, I., 27, 279, 287
Armstrong, K., 45, 289
Ashbrook, J., 43, 44, 287, 289
Auden, W. H., 159, 313
Augustine, 208

Baal Shem Tov, 131
Baer, M. D., 216, 223
Bakan, D., 326
Bammel, E., 72, 297
Barbotin, E., 34, 284

Barfield, O., 47, 290
Barker, M., 293, 338
Barrett, C. K., 322
Barrow, J. D., 287, 289
Barth, K., 36, 49, 285, 290
Basilides, 242
Basko, M., 310
Bauckham, R., 252, 336
Beach, B., xii
Becker, E., xii
Bedward, S., 192
Beker, J. C., 133
Belo, F., 303, 304
Bentzen, A., 262
Berdyayev, N., 47, 48, 173, 251, 257, 258, 287, 290, 297, 315, 316, 338
Berger, P., 287
Berkeley, G., 45
Betz, H. D., 301, 325
Beyschlag, W., 295
Bingen, H., 281
Black Elk, 112
Black, M., 324
Blake, W., 45, 184, 199, 238, 279, 281, 290, 314, 319, 322, 334

Bloch, E., 108, 110, 193, 286, 294, 306, 321
Bloom, H., 146, 311
Bonhoeffer, D., 36
Borg, M., 64, 296, 314
Borgen, P., 331
Borsch, F., 61, 250, 295, 333, 336
Bousset, W., 261
Branham, R. B., 300
Broek, R. van den, 278
Brown, J. P., 324, 337
Brückner, W., 295
Buber, M., 45, 290
Buddha, 15
Bultmann, R., 88, 202, 298, 302, 323
Burkett, D., xii, 202, 251, 252, 253, 255, 323, 324, 336–38
Burnier-Genton, J., 280
Buth, R., 254, 338

Calvin, J., 39
Caragounis, C. C., 291, 298, 299, 308, 315, 323, 337
Carpenter, E., 197, 321
Carroll, J. T., 307

Casey, P. M., 252, 253, 276, 293, 296, 302, 306, 336
Catchpole, D. R., 305
Celsus, 46
Ceroke, C. P., 298
Chamberlain, W. B., 285
Chancey, M., 301
Chardin, T. de, 15, 284, 287, 290
Charles, R. H., 55
Charlesworth, J. H., 295
Chernus, I., 280, 283, 326, 330
Chesterton, G. K., 146
Childs, H., xii, 7, 8, 12, 129, 188, 191, 273, 297, 309, 320
Chilton, B., 13, 274, 276, 277, 290, 301, 311, 316
Cobb, J. B. Jr., 176, 316
Cohen, R., 102, 103, 306
Collins, A. Y., 91, 303, 337
Collins, J. J., 293, 329
Colpe, C., 338
Cooper, R. L., 338
Corbin, H., 40, 46, 231, 279, 288, 320, 332, 335
Cox, D., 311
Crossan, J. D., 130, 309, 310, 314
Cullmann, O., 69, 253, 284, 296, 319, 337, 339

D'Aquili, E., 340
Dan, J., 222, 273, 328
Daniélou, J., 308, 334

Danker, F., 89, 302
Davaney, S., 194, 284, 321
Davies, S., 235, 333, 335
Davila, J. R., 284
Davis, E., 282
Dean-Otting, M., 312, 339
Deats, R., xii
Dewey, A., xii, 82, 275
Dibelius, M., 298
DiLella, A. A., 292, 339
Diogenes, 81
Dodd, C. H., 199, 200, 322–24
Dole, B., 20, 254
Dols, W. L. Jr., 251, 323, 336
Douglass, J., xii, 157, 168, 170, 204, 312, 314, 315
Downing, F. G., 300
Driver, T. F., 201, 289, 314, 323
Dunn, J. D. G., 83, 301, 324
Durkheim, É., 106, 107, 306

Echegaray, H., 304
Eckhart, M., 281, 287
Eddy, P. R., 300, 301
Edinger, E., 156, 249, 280, 281, 286, 293, 311, 312, 336
Edwards, J., 181
Eichrodt, W., 29, 279
Eisler, R., 306
Elior, R., 331
Emerton, J. A., 262
Engels, F., 285
Evans, C. A., 312

Ezra, Ibn, 330

Ferch, A. J., 261, 338
Feuerbach, L., 34, 35–40, 46, 47, 95, 239, 259, 284–88, 290, 294
Fishbane, M., 277, 329
Fitzmyer, J., 254, 337
Flowers, B. S., 13
Foerster, W., 332
Fohrer, G., 276, 336
Fortna, R., xii, 298
Fossum, J., 278, 283, 291
Francis of Assisi, 15
Franz, L. von, 286, 309
Franzmann, M., 309, 334
Freud, S., 15, 314
Frum, Jon, 192
Funk, R. W., 302, 314

Galluzo, G., 95
Gandhi, M., 15, 204, 260, 336
Gaon, Hai, 327
Geist, H., 299
Glasse, J., 285
Glaucon, 176
Godwin, J., 277
Goethe, J. W. von, 305
Goodhue, T., 302, 303
Goulet-Cazé, M.-O., 300
Gray, E., xii
Green, J. B., 307
Greenberg, M., 279
Grese, W. C., 323
Gressmann, H., 262
Griffin, D. R., 339
Gruenwald, I., 276, 277, 326, 329, 331

Hallenbeck, P., iv, xii
Halperin, D., 220, 276, 277, 279, 280, 291, 325–31
Hammarskjöld, D., 323
Hamza, 192
Hananel, 40
Handy, L. K., 291
Hardwick, C., 284
Hare, D. R. A., 21, 22, 84, 182, 275, 276, 302, 305, 319, 321
Harrington, A., 43, 289
Harrison, E., 43, 289
Hart, S., 304
Hartin, P. J., 88, 302
Harvey, V., 35, 238, 284–90, 294, 295, 334
Hatina, T. R., 313, 315
Heisenberg, W., 7, 38, 43
Herntrich, V., 276
Herzfeld, E., 262
Herzog, W., 298, 299
Hick, J., 33
Higgins, A. J. B., 91, 291, 303–5, 311, 315, 317, 319, 340
Hildegard of B., 38
Hill, C., 297
Hillman, J., 40, 288, 290, 339
Himmelfarb, M., 327, 329, 330
Hippolytus, 244, 261
Hitchcock, J., 173
Hoffmann, W., 295
Holzhausen, J., 335
Hooker, M., 20, 93, 96, 275, 293, 304–6, 312, 317
Horsley, R., 81, 94, 300, 302, 304

Howard, G., 338
Howes, E. B., v, xi, xii, 27, 67, 72, 73, 86, 95, 143, 153, 272, 293, 295, 297, 298, 301, 302, 308, 310, 311
Huebner, D., xii
Hultkrantz, Å., 284

Idel, M., 326

Jackson, B, 275
Jackson, F., 324
Jaeschke, W., 285
Jamblichus, 261
Jeremias, J., 88, 274–76, 302
Jewett, R., 181, 318
Joachim de Fiore, 258
Johnson, T. L., 310
Jung, C., 8, 15, 37, 83, 133, 146, 147, 151, 263, 270, 272, 276, 281, 282, 284, 286, 287, 289, 290, 292, 301, 309–11, 314, 321, 324, 335, 336, 339

Kafka, F., 131, 310
Kasper, W., 7, 273
Kasser, R., 334
Kelber, W., 235, 333
Kellermann, B. W., 279
Kerr, H. T., 287
Killen, J., 307
Kim, S., 338
Kittel, G., 289
Koester, H., 333
Kraeling, C., 261, 339
Krueger, D., 82, 300
Kutsko, J. F., 276, 279

Kuyt, A., 329
Kvanvig, H. S., 292, 339

Lake, K., 324
Lao-Tzu, 15
Lawrence, J. S., 181, 318
Layton, B., 332, 335
Leivestad, R., 336
Levey, S. H., 328
Levine, A.-J., xii, 26, 45,145, 163, 308
Liddell, H., 306
Liebermann, S., 331
Lieu, N. C., 310
Lightfoot, R. H., 322
Lindars, B., 182, 252, 253, 276, 319, 336
Logan, A. H. B., 335
Löwith, K., 285
Lust, J., 293
Luther, M., 306
Luz, U., 20, 275, 299, 314

MacKinnon, C. A., 273
MacRae, G. W., 334
Maimonides, 222
Malina, B., 10, 273
Manson, T. W., 78, 79, 299, 315, 324
Marcus, J., 308
Martínez, F. G., 282
Marx, K., 15, 287
Matt, D., 5, 149, 223, 273, 309, 329
McBrien, R., 105, 306
McClain, G., 304
Meeks, W. A., 323, 330
Megill-Cobbler, T., 106, 306
Meier, J. P., 162, 313, 314

Merkur, D., xii, 33, 218, 221, 225, 228, 278, 283, 293, 322, 325, 327, 331
Meyers, E. M., 301
Milik, J. T., 55
Milton, J., 297
Mithra, 192
Moloney, F. J., 323
Moltmann, J., 279, 285
Monoimus, 242, 243
Morgenstern, J., 262
Morray-Jones, C. R. A., 312, 331
Mottu, H., 286
Moule, C. F. D., 337, 338
Mowinckel, S., 261, 339
Muhammad, 15
Mullen, E. T., 291
Müller, U. B., 293
Müller-Fahrenholz, G., 280
Münzer, T., 311, 312
Murray, J. O. F., 323
Myers, C., 298

Neihardt, J. G., 307
Nelson-Pallmeyer, J., 110, 306, 307
Neumann, E., 310
Newberg, A., 340
Nicol, K. P., 251, 272, 336
Nietzsche, F., 309
Nineham, D. E., 296
Nixon, R., 275
Noth, M., 293

O'Brien, N., 304
O'Collins, G., 11, 273
O'Flaherty, D., 7, 274

Odell, M. S., 282
Oirot Khan, 192
Oliver, P., 303

Pagels, E. H., 333, 335
Pallares, J. C., 73, 297
Pamment, M., 202, 323
Parrott, D. M., 233, 334
Pascal, B., 279
Pearson, B., 334
Perrin, N., 63, 64, 255, 295, 317, 338
Pétrement, S., 310, 332, 334
Petroni, J., xii, 44, 46, 286
Pines, S., 307
Plevnik, J., 312
Poland, L., 7, 173, 274
Polkinghorne, J., 43, 289, 304
Presley, E., 192
Procksch, O., 304, 324, 332
Pugh, G. E., 174

Quispel, G., 242, 278, 283

Rad, G. von, 28, 279
Raël, 192
Rause, V., 340
Reizenstein, R., 261
Reuss, E., 295
Ricca, P., 377
Rice, C., 304
Ricoeur, P., 53, 139, 156, 235, 293, 310, 312, 314
Rilke, R. M., 257, 338
Rohr, R., 11, 273
Rosenstock-Huessy, E., 274

Roth, G., 310
Rowbotham, S., 273
Rowe, R. D., 54
Rowland, C. C., 277, 282, 331
Rudolph, K., 335
Rumi, 131, 256, 309, 338
Rupp, G., 307

Schäfer, P., 220, 273, 325–27, 329
Schenke, H.-M., 237, 310, 334, 335, 339
Schoenfeld, E., 285
Scholem, G., 5, 218, 219, 221, 222, 273, 277, 283, 309, 310, 317, 325–30
Schultz, J. P., 330
Schuon, F., 281
Schürmann, H., 299
Schweitzer, A., xvi, 9, 128, 309
Schweizer, E., 210, 276, 296, 305, 308, 325
Scott, R., 306
Seeley, D., 301
Segal, A. F., 275, 296, 324, 325, 330, 331
Shapiro, R. M., 301
Sharman, H. B., 297, 315
Shaw, G. B., 40, 288
Shim'on, R., 131
Shriver, D. W. Jr., 325
Sidebottom, E. M., 322, 323
Sierksma, F., 288
Sigal, P., 296, 302
Smith, M., xii, 81, 300, 337

Sobrino, J., 279, 310
Socrates, 176
Sophocles, 156
Spangler, D., 169
Spolsky, B., 338
Starkey, J., 140
Stevens, W., 7
Stevenson, T., 12, 274
Stock, B., 7, 273
Stringfellow, W., 30, 281
Stuhlmacher, P., 303
Swedenborg, E., 278
Swimme, B., 38, 287

Talbert, C. H., 323
Tamez, E., 290
Taylor, V., 298, 304, 322
Tertullian, 181
Theissen, G., 26, 179, 279, 296, 318
Thoho-ya-Ndou, 192
Tillich, P., 23, 44, 195, 321

Tipler, F. J., 287
Tödt, H. E., 92, 181, 193, 194, 276, 291, 298, 299, 305, 308, 313, 315–18, 320, 321, 340
Tuckett, C. M., 299
Turner, J. D., 333, 334
Twain, Mark, 297
Tyrrell, G., 129, 309

Uhlein, G., 287

Vaage, L. E., 299
Van Dyk, L., 307
Vermes, G., 20, 252, 253
Via, D. O. Jr., 279
Vielhauer, P., 21

Waetjen, J., 276, 300, 308
Wartofsky, M. W., 285
Weaver, D., 306
Westcott, B. F., 295

Wheeler, J., 287
Whitehead, A. N., 226, 331
Williams, D., 156, 312
Williams, M. A., 231, 332, 334
Wink, J. K., xii, 128
Wink, W., ii, 272, 274, 279, 288, 302, 308, 324, 327, 321
Witherington, B., 303
Wolfson, E. R., 278, 280, 288, 291, 326, 327, 330
Wyman, L. C., 289, 320

Yima, 192
Yoder, P., 307
Yorke, L. O. R., 325

Zahn, T., 295
Zimmerli, W., 276
Zoroaster, 15
Zosimus, 244, 245